WITNESS TO THE END

Cold War Revelations: 1959-1969

Bernard W. Poirier

University Press of America,® Inc.
Lanham · New York · Oxford

University Press of America,® Inc.
4720 Boston Way
Lanham, Maryland 20706

12 Hid's Copse Rd.
Cumnor Hill, Oxford OX2 9JJ

Printed in the United States of America
British Library Cataloging in Publication Information Available

Library of Congress Cataloging-in-Publication Data

Poirier, Bernard W.
Witness to the end : Cold War revelations, 1959-1969 / Bernard W. Poirier.
p. cm
Includes bibliographical references and index.
1. United States—Foreign relations—1945-1989. 2. United States—Politics and government—1945-1989. 3. United States—Military policy—20th century. 4. Cold War. 5. Nuclear nonproliferation. 6. Poirier, Bernard W. 7. United States. Navy. Special Projects Office—Biography. 8. United States. Navy—History—20th century. 9. World politics—1955-1965. 10. World politics—1965-1975. I. Title.
E840 .P57 2000 973.92—dc21 00-064821 CIP

ISBN 0-7618-1844-8 (cloth : alk. paper)
ISBN 0-7618-1845-6 (pbk.: alk. paper)

™ The paper used in this publication meets the minimum requirements of American National Standard for Information Sciences—Permanence of Paper for Printed Library Materials, ANSI Z39.48—1984

To: C. Normand Poirier
(1927–1988)

By whose craftsmanship the language of the *"Treaty to Ban Weapons of Mass Destruction from the Seabed"* found international agreement and acceptance.

It was signed on 2 February 1971.

Contents

List of Photographs

List of Abbreviations

ABC	American Broadcasting Company
AEC	Atomic Energy Commission
AMR	Atlantic missile range, included Cape Canaveral
APL	Applied Physics Laboratory
ASW	Anti-submarine warfare
AT&T	American Telephone and Telegraph Corporation
BND	*Bundesnachrichtendienst*, West German military intelligence organization during the Cold War
BuWeps	Bureau of Naval Weapons, US Navy
CEP	Circular error probability
CG	*Croix de Guerre*, France's highest military medal
CIA	Central Intelligence Agency
CNO	Chief of Naval Operations, US Navy
COD	Civilian on official duty, US Navy
COMSAT	Communications Satellite Corporation
DNA	Deoxyribonucleic acid; carries genetic information, useful to identify unique hereditary characteristics
DOD	US Department of Defense
ELDO	European Launcher Development Organization
ESRO	European Space Research Organization
FBI	Federal Bureau of Investigation

FBM	Fleet ballistic missile
GPS	Global positioning system
GTC	*Groupe Technique de Cannes*, Technical team in Cannes, France. Part of the Sud Aviation organization, an important defense contractor in France
HF/DF	High-frequency direction finder in World War II
HUFF DUFF	Nickname for the HF/DF ASW equipment
ICBM	Intercontinental ballistic missile
INTELSAT	International Telecommunications Satellite Corporation
IRBM	Intermediate range ballistic missile
ISA	International Security Affairs in OSD
IRS	Internal Revenue Service
ITT	International Telephone and Telegraph Corporation (New York City)
ITTE	ITT Europe, Inc. (Brussels, Belgium) European headquarters of ITT
ITTFL	ITT Federal Laboratories (Nutley, New Jersey)
ITU	International Telecommunications Union
ITV	Instructional television
KGB	*Komitet Gosudarstvennoi Bezopasnosti* (Committee of State Security), successor to NKVD, secret police and spy network of the Soviet Union
KT	Kiloton, thousand tons
LCT	*Laboratoire Centrale de Télécommunications* (ITT laboratory in Paris, France)
LTV	Launch test vehicle
MGM	Metro-Goldwyn-Mayer, Inc., an entertainment company
MIRV	Multiple independently targeted re-entry vehicle
MIT	Massachusetts Institute of Technology
MLF	Multilateral Nuclear Force
MMRBM	Mobile mid-range ballistic missile
MRBM	Mid-range ballistic missile. First meaning was a NATO IRBM. Later meaning was a Soviet IRBM in Cuba
MT	Megaton, a million tons

NASA	National Aeronautics and Space Administration
NATO	North Atlantic Treaty Organization
NCBC	National Center for Biomedical Communications
NDRC	National Defense Research Committee during World War II
NIH	National Institutes of Health
NKVD	Also N.K.V.D., *Narodny Kommissariat Vnutrennikh Del*, Soviet secret police and secret services from 1934 to 1954, replaced by the KGB until the end of the Cold War
NLM	National Library of Medicine
NSC	National Security Council (White House)
NO FORN	Not for foreigners. A US security classification
NSA	National Security Agency
ONI	Office of Naval Intelligence
OpNav	Formerly: a US Navy office attached to that of the Chief of Naval Operations; Example: OP 92 at the Pentagon was ONI
OSD	Office of the Secretary of Defense
PERT	Program evaluation and review technique
Ph.D.	Doctor of Philosophy
PIO	Public Information Officer
POW	Prisoner of war
RAF	Royal Air Force
R&D	Research and development
RFP	Request for a proposal
RFQ	Request for a quotation
RN	Royal Navy
RSO	Range Safety Officer at AMR. In the State Department, RSO means Regional Security Officer
SAC	USAF Strategic Air Command
SACEUR	NATO Supreme Allied Commander in Europe
SDAP	A submerged test launch of a *Polaris* missile
S.D.E.C.E.	French espionage and counter-espionage service until 1982, succeeded by D.G.S.E., *Direction générale de la sécurité extérieure*

S-D MICC	State-Defense Military Information Control Committee
SEL	Standard Electrik Lorenz (German affiliate of ITT)
SINS	Ship's inertial navigation system
SP	Special Projects Office, US Navy (until July 1968)
SPO	Special Projects Office, US Navy (until July 1968)
SSB(N)	US Navy nuclear-powered submarine that launches FBMs
SSN	US Navy nuclear-powered submarine, often an attack submarine
SSP	Strategic Systems Programs (after 23 December 1987)
SSPO	Strategic Systems Project Office (29 July 1968 to 23 December 1987)
START	Strategic Arms Reduction Treaty
STG	Steering task group
STL	Standard Telephone Laboratory (ITT laboratory in Harlow, England)
TCBM	Transcontinental ballistic missile
TNT	Trinitrotoluene, a powerful explosive
UK	United Kingdom
UNESCO	United Nations Educational, Scientific, and Cultural Organization
US	United States, United States of America
USA	United States of America, United States Army
USAF	United States Air Force
USIA	United States Information Agency
USN	United States Navy
USS	Also U.S.S., United States ship
USSR	Also U.S.R.R., Union of Soviet Socialist Republics, the Soviet Union
VCNO	Vice Chief of Naval Operations, US Navy

Preface

After many decades of silence, disclosures such as those in this work will help to complete the historical record of the Cold War. Not only did I witness many of the remarkable behind-the-scenes performances I've described, but they also wove the historical fabric of the western world between 1959 and 1969. At the time, however, we were simply doing our duty as we saw it. I watched many celebrated people first-hand, and sometimes contributed words and deeds to the actions of the key players on the world stage. My story starts with Soviet Chairman Nikita Khrushchev's spectacular visit to the United States in 1959 and ends with the American astronauts on the moon in 1969.

Of the intervening events that concerned me, I have discussed Sputnik's fallout as it influenced Eisenhower, our plans for recovering America's first astronauts, the development of long range missiles to be launched from submerged nuclear submarines, the sometimes bitter interservice rivalries at the Pentagon, the intraservice rivalries among the carrier navy, the diesel submarine navy and the nuclear navy, how the Central Intelligence Agency joined hands with the Office of Naval Intelligence to beat the best that the Soviet Union could throw at us, and how succeeding Secretaries of Defense and Secretaries of State never really got a grip on non-proliferation of nuclear arms—sometimes soberly, other times not so soberly.

As for Kennedy's famous meeting with British Prime Minister Macmillan at Nassau, I was one of the authors of the presidential position papers, and later I was on the US negotiating team for the US-

UK Polaris Sales Agreement, and was intimately involved in the unfortunate estrangement between the United States and France.

Readers will see how the momentum of World War II carried over into the Cold War in ways that have not always been obvious, and the anecdotes that flavor the text have in fact remained secret until now.

When I was graduated from Assumption Prep in Worcester, Massachusetts, in 1948, neither my classmates nor I ever suspected for a second that I would ever set foot in a submarine, let alone nuclear submarines that hadn't been invented yet. But no one in my graduating class was immune from events unfolding in Berlin and in Europe. There the United States started the Marshall Plan to rebuild Europe so it could care for itself.

I saw Europe rebuilding with Marshall Plan aid a few years later when cities like Le Havre and Cologne were still nothing but rubble that I tripped over. There were no such things as the best years of our lives because the Soviet Union, mainly Russia, dominated our future and we had to make the best of a bad deal. First it was the draft, then the Korean War, and being drafted or not. None of us knew from one semester to the other if we'd be drafted, because the Communist threats changed constantly and Congress regularly changed the rules for military conscription as a result. The American mindset was to make the most of it while the tune was called by Communists, and no one dared have private dreams to fulfill because Moscow invented one world crisis after another.

This is an eye-witness account, and the many people I have named performed memorable deeds under great stress. I am proud to be able to describe what they have done. Their behind-the-scenes performances permitted President John F. Kennedy to stand up to Soviet Chairman Khrushchev during the Cuban Crisis, and I have related details of the actual events that weren't reported accurately during or since.

As events have shown, President Dwight D. Eisenhower never received the credit he should have for building up the technological capabilities of the United States when so few officials in Washington were willing to face up to the progress of Soviet rocketry. Without Eisenhower's building blocks, Kennedy could not have resolved the Cuban Crisis as he did, nor could the United States have neutralized the Soviet Union in nuclear deterrence as early as we did.

Even in the waning days of Premier Mikhail Gorbachev's stewardship of the Soviet empire, the Communists were still boasting that they would force America to spend itself into destruction in its competition with them. But it was the Soviet Union that went bankrupt trying to catch up with the across-the-board technological advances of the United States. All President Ronald W. Reagan had to do was stick by his guns, and he did. And the bullets in his belt were molded between 1959 and 1969.

Even though it's not very fashionable today to cite beliefs and religion, any serious scholar studying the Cold War must recognize that the Cold War pitted the Soviet Union, a deliberately godless society, against the United States, an in-God-we-trust Democracy. On the world stage were bit players among whom some earned larger roles with time. But the only constant societal factor was the aggression of the Warsaw Pact countries, and calling their offensive plays was their quarterback Russia. Ranged against them was the North Atlantic Treaty Organization, and NATO's linebacker calling reactive defensive line-ups was the United States.

All this occurred in the wake of a sharp wake-up call provided by Sputnik. But during the international jockeying that followed, and while American promises were made to NATO and then withdrawn, the seeds of nuclear proliferation were sown.

Out of President Kennedy's assassination sprouted many histories that covered the Cuban Crisis, the Skybolt debacle with the United Kingdom, and Kennedy's afterthought following Nassau when he tried a desperate gamble to avoid an irreconcilable but predictable breakup with France's De Gaulle. Having been in the rocket business, I can attest to any serious reader that one need not be a rocket scientist to understand these chronicles. The reader will recognize where some historians have been more perfunctory than scholarly, or were simply politically self-serving in their literary production of that era.

Even in private life, Americans felt an obligation to beat the Soviet Union and to help their country. My old ties at the Pentagon stayed with me and events were ample in which I could help the CIA or the Navy, or like so many other Americans overseas, we stuck it to the Soviet Union whenever the opportunity presented itself. Those later events in Europe I've described carefully and as accurately as possible.

During this period the United States started giving up many of its deepest secrets to the United Kingdom, and I was one of the key witnesses and players to all the acts that initially produced this give-away. What Kennedy started has become far more than simple nuclear proliferation, and there has never been a national debate on the never-ending give-away that has continued and expanded without serious congressional debates during all the presidential terms that followed. Nor have the scholars of the nation risen to question this dilution of America's nuclear equity.

In the case of the irascible, but always predictable, Charles de Gaulle of France, the building blocks that led to his alienation have been set for the reader to follow. I was also one of the few eye witnesses to France's finally turning her back to her oldest ally in the matter of nuclear proliferation. The fact that France is now dependent, like the United Kingdom, on the give-away nuclear largess of the United States is left for others to explore, explain and expose.

Acknowledgments

On Saturday, 5 December 1998, my old friend Michael Getler and I met for an early dinner at the Italian restaurant Convivium on avenue Raymond Poincaré in Paris. The women in our lives were both in the United States, and Mike and I talked of old times, like when we wrote for the weekly magazine *Missiles and Rockets* in the early 1960s.

In 1998, Mike was the Executive Editor of the *International Herald Tribune* which has its worldwide headquarters in the Paris suburb of Neuilly-sur-Seine. During our dinner he convinced me to write about my experiences in the formerly secret development of the main US nuclear deterrent.

Mike and his wife Sandi returned to Washington, D.C. in August 2000 where he is now the *Washington Post*'s ombudsman. Thanks to his perseverance, *Witness to the End* will, I hope, help people to better understand the mindset of many Americans whose daily efforts were constantly in opposition to the Soviet Union during the Cold War. Michael Getler's urging made this book possible. Any shortcomings in it are mine alone to claim.

One person in particular patiently reviewed all my drafts and revisions, and made many helpful suggestions. Many thanks go to Captain Richard G. Shutt, US Navy (Ret.), an old mentor, an old friend, and a member of the 1941 graduating class of the US Naval Academy. As the readers will learn, Captain Shutt made his own surprising contribution to history on behalf of the class of '41.

Thanks go to Leah M. Marshall of Campbell River, British Columbia. Leah read all the early drafts and tolerated the chaos in my work area at home for the months it took to write this work. Her questions and observations contributed in many ways to whatever clarity a reader will find.

Also, I want to thank a young English woman from Dorset who was working in Paris at the time. Alexandra Thomas has since gone back to London. And like many of the younger generation, she barely knew the Cold War, and never had been exposed to rockets, jet fighters, long range missiles and nuclear warheads.

Like Leah, Alexandra patiently read through many early chapters, and asked for clarifications I dreaded to hear. Each question not only meant another rewrite, but also identified the historic background I needed to include for readers unfamiliar with the Cold War.

I have often written about the Holocaust for US and European publications, and during the research on that subject and for this book, I often relied on the US National Archives and Records Administration. I want to thank archivist John E. Taylor who has been a dedicated NARA researcher for over fifty-three years. Through John Taylor, I and many others have uncovered material important for the writing of history, including this work.

John is as important an American resource as are the boxes of old files that he manages to steer people like me to—dust and all.

A work of history is only as good as the archival record it incorporates. Luckily for this work, Gerald Luchansky is a key member of the aerial team at the National Archives. Based on his forty years of experience in aerial and space photo interpretation, his assistance was invaluable to help retrieve examples of what we, the so-called "Cold War warriors," had used and produced during the 1960s.

Because I write from Paris it proved indispensable for me to find a reliable US source of professionally produced manuscripts. I feel that I was fortunate to learn of Pat Kozma who heads up Manhattan Manuscripts in the Big Apple. Pat has collaborated with me on many projects during the last five years, including this work, and I am a better person for what she has accomplished on my behalf.

Pat Kozma's patience, thoroughness and unflappability in the face of my many rewrites and changes have reaped me a rich experience.

Special thanks go to Jacques Gauthier of Fort Lauderdale and Montréal, Canada, who helped to find persons I knew who played important roles in the Ottawa-Paris crisis during the De Gaulle era after his famous "Vive le Québec Libre" speech.

A warm expression of gratitude is extended to Paulette Brouwers née Fratacci for searching through old family archives to find the original documents related to her father's summary execution by German occupation troops in August 1944.

Antoine Fratacci was an unsung hero whose supreme sacrifice resulted in many allied soldiers returning home safely instead of resting in military cemeteries on the European continent.

I'm grateful to George Phélizon who dug through his own vast archives to find useful reference material and photographs related to LCT's history and to my assignment at the ITT laboratory in Paris.

Equal thanks go to all the veterans of the 83rd Infantry Division who fought veteran German troops hand-to-hand to liberate the French fortress at Saint-Malo at the very time Antoine Fratacci faced his executioners.

To Charlie and Evelyn McAuliff of Troy, Michigan, both members of the 83rd Infantry Division Association and of the Veterans of Foreign Wars, a hat tip for generously providing photos of the D-Day 50th anniversary ceremonies at Saint-Malo, France.

And to all the other allied veterans I met in Normandy whose scattered units broke out of the Falaise pocket three days after Fratacci's execution, a special thanks for their own sacrifices and stories; namely the US veterans of the 1st, 2nd, 4th, 8th, 9th, 28th, 29th, 30th, 35th, 79th, and 90th infantry divisions; the 82nd and 101st Airborne Divisions; and of the 3rd, 4th, 5th and 6th armored divisions, airmen, and others.

In particular, the former P-38 pilot from Texas who was shot down over Normandy and spent eleven months in a POW camp in Germany. I wish I still had the slip of paper with your name on it.

Some forty years ago I was privileged to work alongside some of the brightest scientists and naval officers that the United States had produced. Although time has claimed some, all deserve the tributes to their achievements about which this book testifies.

To the families and sweethearts of the victims of NASA's *Challenger* and of other early astronauts who have died, of the nuclear submarine *Thresher*, of *W.H.*, of all the workers who died in industrial accidents related to Cold War R&D, and of unsung heroes like Antoine Fratacci, their loved ones were heros just as much as military personnel who died in action.

I thank Major General Edward B. Atkeson, USA (Ret.) for his helpful suggestions and corrections when reviewing my manuscript.

I was very fortunate to have worked alongside many talented west Europeans between 1963 and 1969 during the very hot period of the

Cold War when many American companies firmly established footholds overseas.

Somewhat different from the majority of these companies, ITT had been in Europe for many years and employed nearly 130,000 people there, among whom were only a handful of Americans. Because of its prior experience, it was relatively easy for ITT to reintegrate its companies after the war.

The persons who most impressed and influenced me at ITT, New York, were Harold Geneen, Tim Dunleavy, Al Cookson and Bob Kirk, and I am grateful for the examples they set for me.

In Europe, I am indebted to many colleagues at ITT's affiliates in Stockholm, London, Harlow, Stuttgart, The Hague, Brussels, Antwerp, Zurich, Rome, Paris, and Madrid. Their contributions at our technical and marketing meetings added immeasurably to ITTE's many successes in Europe.

I am especially thankful to all my superiors, associates, and colleagues whose paths crossed mine during the events described in this work, and a "well done" to all those Polaris, Poseidon and Trident scientists and submariners who have followed.

Chapter 1

Fitting in at the Pentagon

When a person entered the Pentagon in 1959, it was a baffling experience in one of the world's largest office buildings. For me, I was the most insignificant statistic of the thirty thousand workers, military and civilian, assigned there. The building is like a bicycle wheel with five huge spokes extending from the core and linking five concentric pentagons with the smallest near the center and the largest the farthest away.

I expected my work to be mundane but it turned out exciting, and in little time fate dropped me into the vortex of the most stirring historical period of the twentieth century, during which I watched world characters at close hand and participated in some of their most daring moments of the Cold War.

During this most exciting period in modern history, my first civilian job with the United States Navy was as an analytical statistician. I analyzed complex weapons and reported their cost effectiveness and readiness to fight the Soviet Union, its Warsaw Pact allies, and Red China. It was 1959 and while the Cold War raged in the headlines, silent confrontations at sea were more like sailors with cutlasses in hand, ready to strike in a game of *who would flinch first.*

Yet, in apparent contradiction to my warlike mission, the United States and its President, Dwight D. Eisenhower, were preparing to receive blunt-speaking Premier Nikita Khrushchev of the Soviet Union—a truly historic first visit for a Soviet premier.

In a private meeting at Camp David, however, they would agree to a meeting that would have a terribly embarrassing outcome for President Eisenhower. Although I was far down the totem pole, the fallout from the president's public embarrassment would affect my job and those of many others in the defense establishment.

From the Office of the Navy Comptroller, I took a hard look at an aircraft carrier group and its air-to-air missile armament. Of the formidable combat weapons in our arsenal the *Sidewinder* missile was one of the most deadly, and our carrier-based fighters, as well as the Air Force fighters, always carried this heat-seeking missile and invariably gave our pilots a considerable advantage when facing enemy jet fighters. During the Quemoy crisis, Chinese Nationalist pilots used it dramatically against Chinese Communist jets.

Sometimes these Nationalist-fired *Sidewinders* failed to ignite and fell harmlessly to the ground where Chinese peasants or soldiers promptly handed them in to the Communist authorities. The Chinese sent them to Moscow for analysis. Khrushchev later joked, "In 1958 the Americans were sending us samples via China."

The missile's heat-seeking homing system meant it sought out the hottest temperature during jet combat which was the tail end of an opposing jet's exhaust. Once launched, the *Sidewinder* quite simply went straight toward the enemy's tail and up its gazoo.

In those days, no foreign air force had a counter-measure to the *Sidewinder*. But the United States did, and kept it *Top Secret* for years. I would later know one of the main brains behind this extraordinary missile and its counter-measure, and would participate in one of the most secret Cold War chapters alongside him. But it would take thirty years to play out, and President Reagan would pull the final plug.

Navy and Marine fighter jets also carried the *Sparrow* air-to-air missile which could be used to hit an enemy jet when the pilot's equipment couldn't detect the enemy's exhaust. It had a different homing system and could strike any solid part of a plane.

Before going to Washington I had studied every book on space and satellites I could get my hands on, and became quite a post-*Sputnik* expert on missiles, rockets, and the use of space satellites.

The analysis I was to perform at the Pentagon would determine the cost-effectiveness of a carrier group—which was comprised of an aircraft carrier and the ships to support and protect her in combat. This particular carrier group was in the Pacific, and I was to determine whether there was enough money left in the budget to keep the group steaming at sea until the end of the government's fiscal year. Because the carrier was home base to combat and anti-submarine squadrons, I started analyzing their combat-effectiveness and soon determined that the group only carried enough missiles and aircraft fuel for a very short naval engagement.

The Comptroller was Admiral Beardsley who had plenty of brass on his staff. After he indicated he'd probably sign my report and send it to the Chief of Naval Operations, his staff could look into my report, and they descended on me as if I were spreading the Black Plague. But in the end they agreed with my conclusions. My first report raised living hell for the people in charge of weapons procurement, logistics, and supply.

For whatever reason, my next assignment had nothing to do with combat readiness, and I was assigned a "special mission," as someone put it, "to fish some people out of the ocean in emergencies." To the best of my knowledge it wasn't exactly a mission everyone was competing for, although it was an exciting one.

The people to fish out of the drink turned out to be seven military test pilots recently assigned to be astronauts for a relatively new *re-organization*—the National Aeronautics and Space Administration. NASA wanted to launch these seven *Mercury* astronauts into space orbit. However, because the precise re-entry point of astronauts was somewhat unpredictable in those days, to say the least, the odds dictated they'd land in water. As every schoolchild knows, there still is over twice as much water surface than land surface on this planet.

However, all our ships, all the merchant marine freighters, and every fishing boat that could be leased in the world couldn't meet the Navy's *unwritten orders* to have a ship within "eyeball distance" of a returning space capsule carrying one of these astronauts. The idea was to make sure no autopsy report could possibly state that an astronaut *died of drowning*.

Certainly, NASA had come to the right place, and if there was anything the Navy Comptroller's Office had plenty of was innovative budgeteers, clever auditors, resourceful accountants, imaginative money planners and—especially important to get everyone's attention—all the purse strings to every Navy payroll.

Navy crews and ships were entitled to shakedown cruises, tests at sea, sea trials, and regular sea duty. Eventually, new schedules were prepared. When needed, we had so many ships and boats out in all three major oceans that if the Soviet Union had wanted to land an invasion force in the third world we would not have had a ship nearby to warn anyone. Also, as television news programs and newspapers everywhere have proven, there was always a ship and a television camera within "eyeball" distance of *Mercury* space capsules returning to earth.

Meanwhile I started writing a scientific paper about the use of satellites for spying and for decoding enemy messages by a special analysis of cryptography (writing in code), and I hoped to win a prize. Because I could read German, French, and Spanish, I used the Pentagon library at lunch and after-hours to read foreign language rocket manuals to determine new frequencies of letters in space or missile technology. I compared these to normal everyday language frequencies, and they were strikingly different in technical reports before *Sputnik* was launched on 4 October 1957, as opposed to those in the "post-*Sputnik*" technical literature of 1959.

For example, in pre-*Sputnik* American English the most frequently used letter was E, followed by T and then O, A, N and so on. But after *Sputnik*, the most frequently used letters in an English technical text were still E first, T second, but then followed by I, R, A and so on. Similar changes showed up in all the languages tested.

The paper was accepted by the 32nd Session of the International Statistical Institute to be held in Tokyo in May-June, 1959, and had the extraordinarily exciting and titillating title, "Measuring the Statistical Interrelationship of Rocket Technology and Cryptography." The originality of my proposed power supply for the satellite attracted the sole attention of one of the program chiefs at NASA, and the cryptography, a solitary visit by a counterespionage scientist from the super-secret National Security Agency. That was all. There was no prize, and also no time or money for the trip—known as a *boondoggle* —to Japan.

With additional emphasis on peaceful uses of outerspace, the paper was invited by Dr. Itokawa for the Second International Symposium on Rockets and Astronautics, 1960, whose conference was also in Tokyo. Professor Itokawa was widely regarded as the father-emeritus of Japanese rocket science and I was anxious to meet him. That didn't work out either, and I, now twenty-eight-years-old, didn't meet him, nor would I visit Tokyo until some ten years later.

What helped to shape my Pentagon career for the next four years developed from this paper's research which expanded to include Dutch, Italian, Portuguese, Serbo-Croatian (Yugoslavian) and Russian.

Unexpectedly for me the familiarity I gained about rocketry in foreign countries through current literature meant there were few missile or space programs that I didn't know something about.

One day my brother, Normand, who was an attorney in the Navy Counsel's office, called to ask, "Can you translate the specifications of a new French anti-tank missile that the Marine Corps wants to test at Quantico? It's got to be ready tomorrow." Quantico was a Marine base in Virginia, and the French invention was a wire-guided, anti-tank missile manufactured by Nord Aviation.

It was an easy assignment because I had just contributed a short item about that missile for a widely read page entitled *COUNTDOWN* in an influential technological and military trade magazine called *Missiles and Rockets*.

The fact that Norm was an attorney attached full-time to the most secret Navy program, and normally had no connection whatsoever to anti-tank missiles didn't cross my mind. In fact, my brother was working for Rear Admiral William F. "Red" Raborn who had a special *hunting license* from upper authority to hire, transfer or *kidnap* any employee or officer in the Department of the Navy whom "Red" thought fit to be part of his secret operations.

That famous letter had been signed by Admiral Arleigh Burke, Chief of Naval Operations on Friday, 2 December 1955. All I knew was that Normand worked in a place called the "Special Projects Office," and no one could visit those offices without a special security clearance. Rumor claimed that President Eisenhower had agreed with Secretary of Defense Charles E. Wilson to give Raborn this latitude to build up his team, and that Wilson bucked the presidential directive down to the Navy Secretary (p. 270).

After I performed that simple task and briefed some Marine officers before the French missile team arrived, I was asked to help prepare a secret document on rocketry in French for a military group inside the North Atlantic Treaty Organization.

The ink was barely dry when I received notice to report to a new job in the Special Projects Office. I was to be a budget analyst for the testing program of a new long range ballistic missile launched from submerged nuclear submarines. That meant I would be traveling to Cape Canaveral and would receive a grade raise in salary. But I would be obliged to work compulsory overtime—nights, weekends and holidays—and would do so for the next forty-two months. What I didn't know was that this missile program had the highest military priority in the United States. The missile was named *Polaris.*

During my time in the Office of the Navy Comptroller, I saw various budget proposals. Because of *Polaris*' popularity, some of the surface fleet officers had wanted to place more *Polaris* launching tubes in the 1959 budget, but their idea was to put eight of them into the Navy's first nuclear-powered cruiser *Long Beach* which was already under construction, and into other vessels. But the Defense Department torpedoed the idea.

Going to SP meant studying advanced statistics at night at an extension of George Washington University in a classroom located at the Department of Agriculture. All the students had a *secret* clearance or higher, and the professor, a Ph.D., was the Defense Department's expert for computing circular error probabilities. Known simply as *CEP* in the literature and the state of the art, it was the measure of the accuracy of at least one atomic warhead out of every two launched by long range ballistic missiles. Only God knew where the other one would go. Accuracy is still measured that way.

Such long range missiles were then called Intercontinental Ballistic Missiles (ICBMs), Transcontinental Ballistic Missiles (TCBMs), or Intermediate Range Ballistic Missiles (IRBMs). In 1959 the United States would have been happy to have a missile accurate enough to hit a suburb of Moscow, let alone Moscow itself. Although the United States didn't have an operational missile with that range in mid-1959, we knew that we'd need a CEP of one mile if one out of two missiles were to knock out everyone's favorite target—the Kremlin in the center of Moscow. For years most of us knew its longitude and latitude by heart.

As it turned out, I was to do much more than budget analysis. Everyone in SP would grieve over tragic and fatal incidents, and some of us would trade with spies—both ours and theirs. Together we'd suffer bitter disappointments and heartbreaking setbacks, or would enjoy spectacular scientific breakthroughs. And sometimes we'd sweat out stand-offs with Soviet ships beyond the international limits of territorial waters, or meet in top secret hideaways to participate in the selection of new nuclear warheads displayed by the Atomic Energy Commission to match up with targets, much like watching a fashion show put on by a department store to match clothing for children of different sizes. Also, we played roles in other life-and-death activities of the Cold War.

Of course, the first surprise was the small number of people in the Special Projects Office. But I was rapidly deflated when I learned that we had almost ten thousand industrial contractors throughout the country. Although SP had a lion's share of the research appropriations in the Defense Department, as compared to the Air Force, the Army and the carrier Navy, our Washington office had only about 250 persons in the ramshackle old Munitions building on Constitution Avenue across from the Federal Reserve. And Norm and I were the only brothers in it.

When I arrived, much of what SP was paid to invent wasn't working very well, and the Soviet Union was sticking our inferiority up our collective American noses at every opportunity. President Eisenhower jumped on everyone's case and insisted that salary increases be considered only if we earned at least B+ in compulsory graduate technical courses. His presidential instructions to the Pentagon were clear, if we were to overtake the Soviets we had to learn more about science, work harder and for longer hours than the Soviets did.

At that time Americans were still reeling from *Sputnik*'s fallout. Naturally, elected officials reflected the concern of the citizens, and all felt deceived that the country had not been aware of the Soviet progress. During the debates and finger-pointing, little public effort was made to explain the differences in scientific approaches. No one seemed to give a damn except the scientists and weapons analysts whose jobs consisted of defining and quantifying the precise differences.

The prevailing advantage of Soviet science rested on their huge rocket motors to carry extremely large nuclear warheads, clumsy electronics, and lots of mistakes. Such warheads weighed several tons, and published estimates suggested the warheads were equal to as much as five million tons of TNT. Privately, we pegged them at two million and growing. We referred to such a payload as having a two megaton warhead, and inserted it into our damage assessment equations as simply a *2MT*. The American atomic bomb at Hiroshima was reported to have been equal to 20,000 tons of TNT—20 kilotons—or *20KT*, and to have killed 64,000 and injured 70,000. Today, the Hiroshima bomb is estimated to have actually been equal to *only* 12,000 to 14,000 tons of TNT—a *baby* between *12KT* to *14KT*.

Luckily for our side, the Soviet authorities relied on a big club instead of the finesse of surgical precision, and developed large rockets to carry large warheads because their missiles were so inaccurate. While it was relatively easy for the Soviet Union to insert an 184-pound

Sputnik into a near-polar orbit—actually almost any orbit except synchronous—with such a large rocket, it would have been far more difficult to send a Soviet warhead to the intersection of Broadway and 42nd Street in New York City. In 1959 the Soviet Union probably would have aimed at Times Square but would have been lucky to hit Jersey City—which would have been no consolation to people in northern New Jersey or Manhattan.

Our goal was to have an *initial* CEP accuracy for *Polaris* equal to half a city block.

However, the 2MT nuclear warhead was very powerful—actually 165 times as powerful as the one dropped on Hiroshima, and could cause great damage to the entire region. And a 5MT warhead was over 400 times as powerful! If such a nuclear bomb is detonated at an altitude of only 7,000 feet, the damage would extend more than twenty miles from *point-zero*. Reinforced buildings would suffer high overpressures to damage them severely, and wooden buildings would be crushed or incinerated for twenty miles around. Casualties were estimated "to the closest five million."

Another excuse the impatient American public didn't want to hear was that the Soviets had made great strides in metallurgy, and obviously manufactured metals and coatings that could withstand the extremely high temperatures and the abrasive exhaust of a huge rocket. Without resistant metals and materials, the rocket casing would disintegrate in the area of the nozzle and cause a spectacular explosion like that of NASA's *Challenger* disaster on 28 January 1986. Seven American astronauts were killed in that American tragedy which was due to a fissure near an O ring and not a fissure near the exhaust, but the results would have been virtually identical. Many of us would witness many such failures.

Even as early as 1956, Soviet scientific advances were known but pooh-poohed by America's politicians. After the Anglo-French-Israeli invasion of the Suez Canal, the Soviet Union wanted to ingratiate itself to the third world by defending Egypt, and Khrushchev threatened to rain nuclear warheads delivered by missiles on London and Paris if the invaders didn't withdraw from Egypt. Even President Eisenhower called on the United Kingdom and France to back off.

By early December, the wake of each ship returning French and British troops etched out the painful truth that the UK and France had been humiliated, and were militarily naked without America's nuclear shield and without new weapons such as rockets.

As a result, the Cold War took on new dimensions. Less than a year later *Sputnik* soared into earth orbit, and America's NATO allies really started to get nervous.

Despite the setbacks over technology in the United States, the whole issue of huge nuclear weapons set the stage for the most important military debates of the Cold War—Counterforce versus Nuclear Deterrence.

Basically, counterforce would match the Soviets, megaton for megaton, and would inflict such damage on the Soviet Union that it would not recover for years, even if the Soviets first inflicted great damage on America. Only the U.S. Strategic Air Command had the planes capable of carrying such heavy nuclear weapons to Moscow, Leningrad and Stalingrad. Furthermore, SAC commanders believed they had the capability to penetrate Soviet air defenses, and would have Atlas ICBMs in late 1959. This doctrine always left open the *first strike* option which meant hitting the other side first, like the Japanese did at Pearl Harbor on 7 December 1941.

Actually, the bombers and the land-based missiles were so vulnerable to a missile attack that they presented attractive targets. They were nothing less than lightning rods to attract an all-out Soviet first strike on our American turf.

Nuclear Deterrence would deliver unrecoverable damage as well, but the Soviets could not defend themselves from the American retaliatory strike. If the Soviets couldn't find the American weapons, then the Americans could strike back no matter what the Soviets did first. At least the United States didn't have to strike first, but suffice that it could if need be.

It was a great argument for nuclear submarines that hid in the ocean depths, and could fire nuclear missiles from undetectable launch-platforms that the Soviets couldn't target. The only problem in 1959 was that the system didn't exist yet, the inertial guidance for such missiles hadn't passed its tests, the inertial navigational system needed for the submarines still didn't work accurately enough, the computers for the submerged fire control system didn't even fit, the crews weren't ready, no nuclear submarine had ever launched a missile, and our first empty missile-launching submarine wouldn't be commissioned until the end of 1959.

The president and the congressional leaders told Admiral William F. Raborn, Jr. and his people to deliver the Fleet Ballistic Missile, now called *Polaris*, operational within one year!

Senator John F. Kennedy was again running for the Democratic presidential nomination, and the country was in an uproar over disclosures during recent testimony before congress. Secretary Of Defense Neil McElroy had testified it was probably true that the Soviet Union would have three times more ICBMs than the United States in a few years!

"The Missile Gap" was born, and John F. Kennedy had the issue he needed to run for president in 1960.

Billions were riding on *Polaris*, and the players faced table stakes. It was all or nothing.

Chapter 2

A legend molds his team's spirit

On the side streets off Constitution Avenue parking was limited, and as the early days went by, I learned that the employees of the State Department, George Washington University, and the Federal Reserve Board would employ any form of subterfuge to prevent the early-arriving Navy people from taking available parking places in the morning.

Phony initiatives included leaving signs at night, like *No Parking*, *No Waiting*, and *Police Take Notice*, but which were offset by *No They Don't* and *Mental Patients Only*-paper slip-overs from our own graphics branch. This was a first lesson in understanding *measures and counter-measures* in downtown Washington. But this was child's play compared to the intensifying interservice rivalry that would manifest itself in congressional hearings, newspapers, and in Washington's fierce rumor mills.

Tourists wanting to visit the nearby Lincoln Memorial would have to find paying parking lots a half-mile away because no parking spaces were ever left unused by Navy personnel after 7 a.m.

Although most people said that our Munitions building and its twin neighbor, the Main Navy Building, were constructed during World War I, anyone entering them in 1960 could have supposed that they had been built during the 1898 Spanish-American War. After working in the cavernous and modern Pentagon building across the Potomac River, the Munitions building seemed to be more like the outdated textile factories

I knew so well in the Blackstone River Valley of my native Rhode Island.

But the new neighborhood was nice. A few blocks away, in the area known as Foggy Bottom, was the State Department, and directly across the street was the Federal Reserve Board building where a former fraternity brother, Harry Felix, worked. He arranged for me to eat in their cafeteria from time to time where thick T-bone steaks with two vegetables cost as little as thirty cents. "All the banks in America help subsidize these benefits," my former classmate at Georgetown University's School of Foreign Service explained only half-jokingly.

For several years Harry has been the only classmate I ran into. While at Georgetown, Harry, Pete Polimeni, and I had formed a trio of guitar, piano and accordion during Kappa Alpha Phi songfests.

Although the cafeterias in our buildings were never quite as inexpensive as the exclusive FRB cafeteria, the Navy always ate well, which is also why the Navy has always operated the cafeteria at the White House. About the only "benefit" we had at SP, however frequent, was the visit of Navy trolleys pushed by spic-and-span sailors who offered free coffee, tea, lemon and sometimes cookies. I guess it's because there's no alcohol on Navy ships that so much coffee is consumed by Navy people, and the coffee habit I developed at SP required a dozen mugs a day to quench.

The Special Projects Offices were on the third floor of the Munitions Building, and I remember that I often ran the stairs several times every day. (Just about every president wanted to get rid of these buildings, but the one who succeeded was Richard M. Nixon who threatened "to reduce some admiral to scrubbing decks if those buildings aren't demolished—soon.")

Other *temporary* structures were behind us where part of the Vietnam Memorial grounds are today. Notably present in our corner of Washington were the highly-guarded offices of Admiral Hyman G. Rickover, the father of the nuclear Navy. He was a thin man and appeared frail just like the oceanographer Jacques-Yves Cousteau appeared to me when we collaborated years later. On the opposite end of impressions was Admiral Raborn who appeared husky, had distinctive red hair and a contagious grin.

Eventually, Admiral "Red" Raborn had a *Polaris* mock-up set up at the base of the stairs after its shape became common knowledge through news photographs in magazines and newspapers as far away as Moscow!

I can't remember whether the mock-up had the distinctive black calibrated and graduated markings at the base of the first stage. Still, this was a copy of a Launch Test Vehicle (LTV) seen in so many news clips and photos. Visitors often asked why such markings were on so many boosters in the first place.

Whenever a test vehicle blasted off, scientists wanted to know exactly how the missile behaved, whether the launch was considered successful or not. Because of the markings, all of which were black on white and of a different lengths, the developed film from high speed cameras could tell us if the LTV performed a quarter-roll, or a half-roll, or no roll, as it sought the correct path to follow into the sky. Actually, we even had one LTV perform loop-the-loops—unintentionally on our part, but something the missile thought up on its own.

Had the missile been all white, it would have been very difficult to determine what went wrong (or right) at launch. We had occasions when a test missile completely misbehaved right after blast-off, but recovered higher up and went on to complete a so-called *successful* test flight. This was just as baffling to figure out as one that blew apart five hundred feet above the launch pad. Unfortunately, many early tests blew up. Like all the other services and agencies involved in rocket development, we relied on slow motion film and telemetry recordings to perform a diagnostic analysis.

Telemetry was a wonderful communications technique with an adventurous "Far West" American legend. It consisted of sensors detecting a value and transmitting this value through radio waves or by a wire to a recording device that could be monitored and studied. It was a technique exploited under harsh environmental conditions by two French brothers from the Schlumberger family. The fact that drilling through rock was as difficult on electronics as the buffeting a rocket suffers in the boost phase explains why the Schlumberger equipment adapted itself so readily to the space age.

One day the Schlumbergers met an oil prospector at a chance meeting in a west Texas bar. They explained to the oil driller that their telemetry could be placed near the tip of his oil drill and record the geological features of the earth's layers as it dug deeper during the drilling. The driller's name was Howard Hughes, and both family names later became synonymous with fabulous wealth, adventure, actresses, space programs, satellite communications, binary mathematics and digital science.

Facing page. In this sequence of photos from 1990, a test launch of a *Trident 2* (D-5) from a submerged nuclear submarine went haywire. After 89 successful launches in a row, this *Trident* imitated one of its predecessors, a *Polaris* test missile in 1959, by performing acrobatic loops. Note that the *Trident* LTV had no calibration markings.

Government photo

No missile, satellite or nose cone could be launched without telemetry produced by Schlumberger. One of their main factories (EMR) was in Orlando, and we passed it whenever we drove from Orlando to Cape Canaveral when we didn't fly into Patrick Air Force Base. Defense officials really became goosey about America's dependence on a vital and key product owned and controlled by non-Americans. In very quiet moves, pressure was put on the French family with such strong ties to the United States, and finally one of the key Schlumberger family officers took the oath as a citizen of the United States. A few other family members soon followed, and everyone was happy.

After a missile blasted off from a launch pad, telemetry and film recorded how the missile followed its designated launch *path*, called its azimuth—one of the key elements in a ballistic computer program, or for the insertion of a satellite into orbit, or for the path to follow for a landing on the moon. In the 1980s and 1990s people often saw the NASA space shuttle roll over on its back during the boost phase. That maneuver was a safety feature of long-standing in case the crew had to abandon ship during that phase, but it also served as an early indicator for the launch phase engineers that at least some things were going as they should.

At SP in Washington, Admiral Raborn's office had corner windows facing Constitution Avenue. To the right of Raborn's office was that of his principal military assistant, the Deputy Director, and the next one was the Public Affairs Office. To the left of Admiral Raborn's office was the suite attached to the Chief Scientist. And just down the first corridor was one of the most talked about meeting rooms in the Defense Department.

For years, writers praised Raborn's Management Center, partly because it was a highly secured meeting place. To first-time visitors it appeared like a steel box constructed inside another steel box, so to speak, to prevent unauthorized access. Inside, nearly one hundred people could be seated facing a sixteen-square-foot plate glass on which we projected vu-graphs, slides and movies from a small room behind the glass.

Around the walls were bar charts, line of balance charts and milestone charts, but the ones that impressed all the writers and the management experts worldwide were our PERT charts. Even if the meaning of PERT evolved over time, the original acronym stood for *Program Evaluation and Review Technique*, and had been developed by SP, and its management techniques, as much as SP's scientific breakthroughs, helped to tip the power balance of world powers upside down. PERT performed well for research and development when almost limitless money and manpower could be poured into a problem in order for it to be solved no later than key dates engraved indelibly on a PERT chart. Invariably, that date was one that had to be met for the nation's highest priority military program.

Important newsmen, congressmen, and high ranking foreign allies always wanted to visit the Management Center. Before they arrived, we had a group of quick-change artists remove *top secret* charts and deftly switch benign ones into their place. Labels reading *Confidential* and *Secret* were strategically placed to impress the visitors. And most of the time those visitors reacted as if they had just entered the Sistine Chapel.

SP also put together a great movie, a sort of old-time selected short subjects that really excited viewers who had never seen rockets in action. Most of our carefully narrated documentaries were often classified as Confidential, and American viewers immediately recognized the voice but couldn't always put a name to it. Often they winked knowingly to one another, and occasionally one declared aloud, "Hey, that's the fellow on the Groucho Marx Show, you know, what's his name—yeah, that's right, it's Groucho's announcer—George Fenneman!"

And it was. Raborn's team left no stone unturned to impress people on the value of the Fleet Ballistic Missile for America's survival. And our defense effort needed all the help it could get in Washington, in our factories and shipyards, at Cape Canaveral, and in Hollywood!

What no visitor ever saw at SP was the top secret planning and operations room in SP where little magnetic submarines were stuck to a metal world map, a room with a very sensitive radar device that set off alarms if a mouse ran across the room or if a paper fell from the table. Whenever the alarm sounded, Marines with submachine guns would rush in with a finger on the trigger. Even though there was a hidden safety switch, emergencies like a fire, as I learned the hard way, triggered a reaction that made me feel as if I were in the path of a Marine division landing on Iwo Jima. One of America's most sacred secrets was where nuclear submarines deployed, and very few individuals ever saw where our nuclear-powered subs really operated.

Along the Atlantic Missile Range, which was managed by the Air Force, we saw many early Titans, Atlases and Minutemen launched from Cape Canaveral go *crazy*, as well as those of the Navy. On one occasion a nose cone apparently landed in a Cuban pasture, and Cuba's Communist dictator howled and railed for hours on Havana Radio.

"The Americans intentionally practiced a sneak attack on Cuba," Fidel Castro ranted, and he even claimed to possess the innocent dead cow done in by the sneaky American missile.

No American service was anxious to admit that one of its missiles might have gone awry, and no one in the Polaris program was authorized (1) to admit anything, (2) to deny anything or (3) to know anything about (a) Cuban agriculture, (b) rocket testing in the 20th century or (c) about any country south of Key West.

One of my colleagues said dryly, "Hell, better Cuba than Bermuda." But we didn't have a choice and it was an unfortunate incident.

I no longer can remember if it was one of ours (a Navy *Polaris*) or one of theirs (an Air Force *Titan* or *Atlas*), but deep down I think the Air Force might have been innocent this once.

Considerable competition and interservice rivalry festered under the surface about the Range Safety Officer who was always an Air Force officer or a civilian employee of the USAF, and privately we always felt the RSO was, unjustifiably or not, just plain trigger-happy. Nonetheless, the Air Force insisted he was "fair and square." Yet, those of us meeting in our *secret Club R* were convinced that Navy missiles were blown up faster than necessary, and that Air Force missiles could be "half way to Georgia and hell's half-acre" before the RSO woke up and gave their missile the *juice*.

A few hotels or motels existed south of the Cape in Cocoa Beach, Florida, but only the *Sea Missile Motel* had rooms distinctively designated by letters. It was on Merritt Island on the road to Patrick Air Force Base. We felt like real *zeros* down there and had to communicate through the Air Force. When we had time to think of such things, we admitted that the USAF did allot us office space, OK, but always too small, sure they provided communications with never enough lines, office supplies without erasers on the pencils, and a great photocopier—a quarter-mile away. Not that we were whiners, but "what do you expect us to think when the eager beaver RSO blows up our missiles faster than circumstances justify," observed our most accomplished complainer.

Ever since the Navy first needed a launch pad at the Cape, the rumor was spread that the Air Force performed a swampland wildlife survey first, and our assigned spot, Pad 25A, was known forever thereafter as having more poisonous snakes, mosquitoes and alligators than any comparable acreage or swamp at the range. Coincidence? Not as far as we were concerned. I'm sure the famous SP dictum was coined there, "I only meant to drain the swamp, so how come I'm up to my ass in alligators."

Room R at the *Sea Missile* should be on the *National Register of Historic Places* because of all the valuable meetings held by Navy scientists there. USAF officers always wondered where we hung out before a submarine launch, and it would have been treason to tell them. Our TWX cable traffic (through the USAF) often referred to Club R but, cleverly, never where, when or what day. We just knew.

Every third time someone attended an *important* Club R meeting he was expected to bring along his entry ticket—normally some soft drinks and chips, maybe even some hamburgers or hot-dogs. Carrying on the same arguments about technical trade-offs as we had left behind in Washington; Pittsfield, Massachusetts; or Sunnyvale, California; we'd stay up well after midnight before heading to the submarine.

Anything we left behind was stored by the owner who kept the liquid containers safely away from Air Force officers, Soviet spies, and other undesirables, but he was welcome to eat any remaining food. Many was the time when we considered awarding him some sort of prestigious medal for keeping such national secrets safe.

When someone received verbal official orders to board a submarine for a submerged launch he was expected aboard by four o'clock in the morning. This gave us time to get the submarine off safely, away from our man-dredged Port Canaveral, and out to sea under the cover of darkness. We always hoped to reach our launch zone when the sun was highest and brightest, because our high speed cameras, including those bolted to the deck of the submarine, needed as much light as possible to photograph the launches.

At dockside where the submarine was berthed, a cordon of security greeted us. Floodlights illuminated the sail and upper sixth of the submarine's black hulk and the dock area as brightly as a theater stage. As if the high drama of the moment needed accentuation, heavily armed Marine and Navy Military Police were everywhere. Seamen ran up and down the dock preparing to cast off, and armed Navy frogmen swarmed like water beetles in the water around the submarine looking for mines, Soviet saboteurs and, for all I knew, Air Force missilemen. But once you climbed down through the hatch, it was quiet and all business-like inside. All these nuclear submarines capable of launching the *Polaris* IRBMs were designated SSB(N)s. Our first, the SSB(N) 598, was the U.S.S. *George Washington.*

Until the United States had several submarines to train from, Blue and Gold crews trained together and members of both crews were already aboard and busy. So once we boarded we were allowed to find an empty bunk to get some sleep. But there was much to do before the submarine was far enough out to sea to start the launch countdown while the sun was approaching its zenith. Unfortunately, I never saw anyone smart enough to get some sleep in a bunk. Most of the time we gained a few winks by resting on folded arms in one of the mess halls.

Even though I never saw any alcohol on board a Navy vessel, we all knew that our enemies at the Cape maliciously spread the rumor with straight faces that not only officers but even Navy civilians were "*literally* piped aboard *Polaris* submarines." Of course, everyone knew that such a calumny was slanderous and a downright bald-faced lie. We were tempted to retaliate but remained gentlemen to the end.

When the white gloves did come off, it was of no little wonder that interservice rivalry extended later into congressional hearings and into the national press in an interservice battle-royal for a bigger slice of the military budget pie.

But this is not what I first ran into at SP, and I'm getting ahead of my story.

The head of budget was a civilian balance sheet impresario and workaholic called Tom Aiken, a slave merchant, who made sure all the analysts wore their noses down against the budgetary grinding wheel. His boss was an expenditure-control wizard named Bernard Kahn, who in turn reported to George W. Bergquist, Director of the Plans and Programs Division.

Money appropriated by Congress and approved by the Department of Defense and the Department of the Navy was the life blood of SP, and the number one Defense Department priority needed a lot of it, and we used it all. We spent millions of dollars per hour and my job was to see to it that the missile testing branch had enough before its engineers ordered more test missiles than we had money for, or to find the money if their procurement orders had already exceeded what money balance we had on hand.

In four years at SP I doubt if I ever saw anyone walk. Everyone ran, and no one ever seemed to take sick leave. I heard that SP had the lowest sick leave ratio per capita of any unit in the entire government. Morale and mutual reliance were such that a day away from work gave the absent party a massive dose of the guilts.

One day, George Bergquist went to an important meeting at the Pentagon, and when his car door was closed, it slammed on his hand and broke several fingers. Without a word he wrapped his bloody hand in a handkerchief and attended the meeting anyway. We all had a little more respect for the Mormon religion after that incident because George was a Mormon.

As time went on, SP was often at the center of political debates involving NATO and I was increasingly sought out by the submariners and the technical managers to keep them up to date. Because of my nighttime-writing for newspapers and magazines on foreign subjects they assumed I was *up to snuff* on all international developments. Editors of publications in Washington, Philadelphia and Chicago used many of my articles, and even Admiral Rickover asked me to collaborate on one involving foreign school education techniques. Rickover was famous for his perceived fear that America was raising idiots instead of children.

Wanting me to continue my outside writing, the Navy decided to give me formal written permission to protect me from any accusations of having a conflict of interest, and because it was in their best interest. Signing the special authorization was SP's Deputy Director Captain Tom Rudden who eventually made admiral. The extra income was welcome because I had four children at home ranging from eight years old to the one born the previous Easter, and all rarely saw me during daylight hours. Whenever the two oldest, André and Geneviève, eight and five respectively, saw a *Polaris* launching on television news they thought I was in it. They would cheer and scream, "There goes Daddy!"

And the two youngest, Greg, two, and Céleste, four months, joined in because it was politically correct.

Senior planners in SP decided to move me next door to Admiral Raborn's office. In fact, Chief Scientist John P. Craven and Navy Captain Richard G. Shutt, the military head of the Plans and Programs Branch, jointly arranged to transfer me to Dr. Craven's office as his assistant, but much of my time would be spent with Captain Shutt, a Naval Academy graduate in 1941 who went straight from Annapolis to submarine warfare against the Japanese in the Pacific.

However, on my first official day in the Office of the Chief Scientist only an elderly man whom I didn't know was there, and I walked into his office to introduce myself. He looked at me and recited, "*Notre Père qui êtes aux cieux, que Votre nom soit sanctifié, que Votre règne arrive, que Votre volonté soit faite sur la terre comme au ciel*...how do you like my accent? I'm Tommy Thompson."

He looked at my bewildered expression and explained, "I learned the *Our Father* in French class fifty years ago—pretty good, huh? I know it all. Well, what do you think of my accent?"

"Er...yes, sir... Dr. Thompson, your accent's great."

Dr. L.T.E. Thompson was a legend around SP. Even though his official title was Consulting Senior Scientist, he was revered like a scientist-emeritus. As a young man in the 1930s Tommy had assisted the rocket pioneer Dr. Robert H. Goddard at Clark University in Worcester, Massachusetts. After Raborn hand-picked Tommy as a scientific advisor, the elder scientist set up a selection board that eventually hired SP's young Chief Scientist, John P. Craven.

"You're going to share this office with me, and I promise not to bother you because I only come in from time to time," he said modestly. He tried to put me at ease, but I knew too much about his reputation, like when NASA dedicated the famed Goddard Space Flight Center, it had been Dr. Thompson who escorted Goddard's widow to the podium.

He offset my nervousness with stories of the good old days. As time went on Dr. Thompson took me under his wing, and had me attend scientific meetings with some of the greatest scientific brains in the United States. Although John Craven and Dick Shutt were paying the bills from their budgets, they gave Tommy, who became my guardian angel, complete liberty to manage my learning curve. That's how I caught on that SP exploited the intellectual findings of these minds at laboratories and universities by funding most if not all of their research.

On *Boeing 707* transcontinental flights, Tommy and I often sat side by side, and out of the blue he'd recite loudly enough to be heard a few rows away, "*...Donnez-nous aujourd'hui notre pain quotidien...*Give us today our daily bread—get it?" And invariably, I'd answer, "Keep going, Doctor, you're getting better all the time."

It was easy to determine which poor soul nearby understood French, because invariably that innocent character who heard Tommy praying was as white as a sheet!

I never did learn his religion, but I was convinced that when Tommy would arrive at the pearly gates, all he'd have to do is recite his *Our Father* just once in French, and the gates would fly open to let in this gray-haired gentleman—or else.

Whenever I helped to write parts of a Navy *position paper* and would refer to Communism, he'd correct me to qualify it as "*godless* Communism." To him, Communism was a curse on the world's societies, and an anathema to condemn at every opportunity.

Among my wake-up calls at SP was my first exposure to political opinion polls wherein Ph.D.s at Harvard, MIT, Stanford and elsewhere would suggest "key" questions for our review and funding, and would then go to Europe or Asia to perform statistically valid polls. When they returned and wrote up their analyses, we would have before us foreign public opinions on American strategies, deterrence, internal political figures including opposition personalities, NATO, foreign issues—even those distasteful to Americans or allies, or our nation's enemies! Some information was selectively and self-servingly spoon-fed to some of the most widely-read columnists in America—including Walter Lipmann and Joe Alsop. Their exclusive reports and columns would influence other national writers, radio and television reporters, and in turn they influenced congressional leaders.

One day, Tommy invited me to lunch with him at the Cosmos Club, a very prestigious scientific and non-political organization on Massachusetts Avenue, and definitely not frequented by the hoi polloi. Posted on the walls between two dining rooms were the names of important people nominated for membership and who could be blackballed by an existing member. Next to the name were two or three words to remind people who the nominees were.

I think the occasion was in December 1960 after the national elections, but before the New Year. Under the letter M was the entry "Robert S. McNamara—industrialist." Of course, this was a good inside joke because everyone knew he had already been nominated to be the

Secretary of Defense, but politicians weren't considered to have lofty enough achievements for membership in the Cosmos Club.

As if to prove that no over-achievement was sufficient to automatically entitle anyone to the club's prestigious membership, another nominee had been the author of the Pulitzer Prize winning *Profiles in Courage* in 1957. So under the Ks was the entry "John F. Kennedy—author!"

Eventually, President Kennedy used many of the results of our academic *polls* to convince the Soviets about deterrence, and in a few surprisingly bold moves during the next few years, after the president developed confidence in SP and the Fleet Ballistic Missile, he did just that. Meanwhile, his own ideas often influenced SP's thinking to innovate new uses from research for ourselves, other services and the Central Intelligence Agency. As time went on, I'd see that planners from the CIA were quick to exploit some of our secret developments to undermine Red China's rigid and godless hold over its own citizens and those of its neighbors in southeast Asia.

Many of these new tools and strategies were born out of the skull sessions organized by Dr. Craven, and these thought-provoking sessions were intentionally free wheeling to encourage a free exchange of ideas. Some of the most intelligent Naval officers often participated with the civilian scientists, and were usually encouraged to do so by Captain Levering Smith, SP's Technical Director, a genius and everyone's role model as a gentlemen. Like Raborn he had red hair, but he always spoke so quietly that his nick-name was that of a notorious Wild West gunman—*Whispering Smith.*

Smith had one historic characteristic in common with Hyman Rickover, they were both elevated to the rank of admiral by a Presidential Directive rather than through a military selection board. These promotions helped protect them because their new rank permitted them to overcome red tape and bureaucratic delays.

Technical coordination meetings required so many managers to be on hand that they all assembled in the Management Center. A decision could involve thousands of people in the factories and shipyards, cost or save millions of dollars, and could save that most important commodity—time. But when the hammer came down in whispers many people a few rows back didn't have a clue what Smith decided.

Soon, whenever Levering Smith presided, we placed several tape recorders and microphones on the table in front of him, with the volumes on full. As soon as he left, people scrambled to hear the playbacks. Many of America's most significant technical breakthroughs arose from these comic innovations.

Some comic interludes, however, had near-tragic consequences and never were made known in those days. For example, by the end of 1999 everyone had heard about the GPS—Global Positioning Satellites—that advise the driver of a taxi, an ambulance, or a disabled car where she or he is within thirty yards. This is a NASA offshoot of a satellite known as *Transit* which was developed by the Applied Physics Laboratory under contract to the Bureau of Naval Weapons . Actually, BuWeps did it for SP with SP's money because we didn't want anyone to suspect that SP didn't know where the hell our submarines were. Unlike many other satellites then in orbit, *Transit* didn't spin to maintain operational stability. Based on the doppler principle, like the sound of a train's whistle increasing as it gets closer and diminishing as it goes farther from the listener, it had to avoid spinning in order to work right.

The trick, then, was to stop the very spin which permitted it to be inserted into orbit. Our scientists thought of using a yo-yo. By releasing the yo-yo, the force of the spin would force the device to absorb all the spin's energy as it went into its own orbit somewhere in a distant constellation. No matter how clever it sounded, no one wanted to spend a few million to find out. So a test was arranged in a secret location in Maryland—a cow pasture behind one of the laboratories at Johns Hopkins University. On a solid metal post that resembled a normal fence post, the satellite was spun-up, and then the yo-yo was released. It left the satellite like a shell shot from a 16-inch cannon on a battleship. It hit a cow, a different non-Cuban cow, thank you, in one of its nipples.

No longer interested in the grass in the John Hopkins pasture, that cow headed for points unknown, jumping anything in its path until it reached a highway and a car innocently traveling the other way. Unfortunately the cow was killed, and fortunately the driver was only shaken up, but he screamed for an explanation.

Because no one could or would tell him, my brother Normand was dispatched to settle the driver's claims against (1) the university, (2) the farmer who owned the *aggressive* cow, (3) the fence installer who negligently built a poor fence, and (4, 5...) so on. Normand could represent anyone except the Navy or SP or APL—all of whom would have nothing to do with the accident, and whose identities had to remain secret.

SP successfully developed the *Transit* satellite system for our *Polaris* submarines, and in recent years the civilian GPS applications for thousands of uses from yachts to bushplanes in Alaska have become routine history. Yes, our yo-yo worked and continues to do so.

In the name of national security, this was one of those in-house secrets that have sometimes disappeared with time and have been lost to history.

Needless to say, my brother Norm settled for the Navy. In fact, even the farmer received a new cow.

Chapter 3

Espionage, shortcomings, and fatalities

In late December 1959, there was still a glow in the Soviet press as a result of Premier Nikita Khrushchev's precedent-setting coast-to-coast visit to the United States the previous September. In Moscow, an assistant attaché of the United States embassy was preparing gift baskets to bring to the apartments of Soviet couples and families of Soviet individuals who belonged to a Soviet-Amerika Friendship Group. The new year presented the rare occasion to offer modest gifts to Soviet citizens and, especially, the rare opportunity to enter private Soviet households.

The embassy employee, Rose Marie, was a cheery and vivacious native of Minnesota who was very popular at the parties organized by the Marine guards at the embassy, and she always volunteered to sell tickets and raffle coupons. Even the Soviets couldn't avoid noticing her genuine popularity and interest in Soviet culture and lifestyle. A plus for Rose Marie was the fact that the Russian winter was a sweet reminder of her own home in Saint Paul.

Celebrating Christmas in the Soviet Union was very definitely politically incorrect, but tipping a little vodka at New Year's was not only OK, but Americans with a clean record of political correctness by Soviet standards could expect a lot of vodka and private invitations in early 1960.

For the last seven months, Rose Marie had taken up a hobby in curtains, shades and window decorations, and no one associated with the foreign colony in Moscow remained unaware of her enthusiastic interest in Soviet handicrafts.

When the invitations to private homes arrived, Rose Marie accepted as many as she could for herself and her husband Bob. In every apartment the scenario was the same, and after a few minutes she would go to the curtains facing a street to fuss over the design, quality and texture. Eventually, the hostess would tell her where the cloth tissue had been purchased, and Rose Marie would carefully note the information and would coax the hostess for a small sample from the upper seam area of the curtain. This was an area on most curtains where seamstresses often would leave extra tissue, out of sight on the window side, to better anchor the seam.

"No one will ever notice," Rose Marie would say, "and I won't pick the wrong fabric when I buy some for myself!"

After the season for calling on Soviet friends dried up for at least a year, Rose Marie carefully inserted each sample in its own individual envelope with all the information she had gathered about it. In particular, she followed the verbal instructions to "make sure we know the direction the window faces." Lastly, she added the notation, "Two hundred yards from the closest corner." Before attending the next Marine potluck Mardi Gras party at the embassy annex, she first went to a locker in which she placed a shopping bag full of these envelopes.

The envelope and its contents went with all the others by diplomatic pouch to a private laboratory near Washington under contract with a think tank owned 100% by the CIA, and the results of the analyses were shared with a restricted number of offices in the Atomic Energy Commission, and in the intelligence offices of the Army, Navy, and Air Force.

Governmental photographic laboratories with highly sophisticated enlargement cameras would be asked by intelligence analysts to enlarge small segments of aerial negatives exposed by a specially designed new camera aboard a screwy looking airplane with droopy wings called a U-2.

One such segment at an oblique edge of an aerial negative was of a Moscow street, and on that street, the fourth building from the top on the west side was two hundred yards from *point zero*. Laboratory technicians at the CIA had already determined that the tissue sample from the second floor window curtain was inflammable.

After enlarging the area on the infrared negative to an eight inch by ten inch, black-and-white print, from a negative area no bigger than the end of a normal pencil eraser, a spectrum analyzer was placed over the curtain to read photo-electronically the gray infrared signature of the texture of the curtain. In techniques similar to photogrammetric interpretation of the 1970s, the scientists started the meticulous task of comparing Rose Marie's window curtain to those in about twenty windows in that print. Secondly, they compared it to all the other windows in the entire Moscow neighborhood where the slant angle of the photo revealed a curtain behind a window.

During the U-2's overflight, the complete set of photos had taken only two minutes to expose, but the U-2 spy plane had taken over half a day to reach Moscow. It had taken off at dawn from an airfield near an ancient Roman military outpost in remote, southern Turkey. On board the U-2, the pilot still had a long way to go to finish his 2,500 mile overflight to Norway. Both Turkey and Norway were NATO allies of the United States.

The U-2 had been designed and constructed by Lockheed Aircraft Company, the same company that served as the prime contractor for the development of the Navy's *Polaris* missile system. The U-2 had been the brainchild of aeronautical engineers at a secret Lockheed laboratory affectionately called the *Skunk Works*.

That single series of a few photos revealed that half of the windows in that area of Moscow had curtains manufactured with similar inflammable textile tissue as the one analyzed earlier that Rose Marie had collected. In fact, the samples that she collected filled-in important confirming data through a simple scientific technique known as *ground-truthing*. Fortunately, Rose Marie had collected enough textures that produced similar spectrum analyses to reliably certify the photogrammetric definition of the gray shade attributed to that particular textile type of inflammability. Spying had developed into a very complicated business since the days in Paris of Indonesian-dancing Mata Hari, and all comparable modern data proved important to assess potential damage if ever a nuclear war erupted.

In order to quantify and formulate nuclear damage assessments, the US intelligence community, and presumably the Soviet intelligence services, had already determined by 1959 and 1960 that New York City had about 600,000 buildings of which 250,000 were made of wood; 300,000 brick; 42,000 stucco and the last 8,000 just weren't a factor to worry about, unless you were the tax collector. Detroit had an even higher ratio of wooden structures with about 160,000 out of 270,000. Of

105,000 buildings, San Francisco had 61,000 of wood, 41,000 of stucco, and only 2,300 of brick.

Such real estate tax assessments were considered public information in a free democracy like the United States, but were generally unattainable in the Soviet Union. The US resorted to great expense to develop the U-2, and to organize the necessary spy operations to acquire the type of information about Russia and the other Soviet republics that the Soviet agents were acquiring about the United States for only a few dollars.

Separately from the U-2, scientists had combined the Navy's experience in recovering astronauts at sea with the experience gained by the Air Force research efforts in launching satellites and intercontinental ballistic missiles. Extrapolating from the earlier research they produced the design of a secret satellite system known as WS 117. They added the new optical techniques discovered by the Eastman Kodak company to develop a USAF reconnaissance satellite called *Samos*.

By gerrymandering a stack of several rockets like the *Atlas, Agena* and *Thor*, the USAF put almost four tons into a polar orbit. Unlike Sputnik that barely sent out a single radio single, the *Samos* conglomeration of hardware could take thousands of high precision photographs at appropriate times while its polar orbit permitted the satellite to wind its way around the earth much like everyone's grandmother used to wind a ball of yarn.

Effectively, the Air Force made sure every house, munitions factory, naval base, and concrete launching pad on earth could be photographed. To make sure the photos were completely exploited of all their data, the Air Force devised an adventurous method for snatching the 20-day old film canisters from each *Samos* satellite that made it into the earth's atmosphere and slowed-down by braking-parachutes in order to be snared in flight by USAF pilots.

Americans were madmen when it came to the acquisition of sufficient data, the accuracy of the classification of that data, and their careful analyses. In fact, the analyses of tests of thermonuclear weapons, another term for H-bombs, had earlier added a startling dimension to the concept of destructiveness. Nuclear damage assessors knew that a 10 megaton (MT) dropped from a USAF bomber could make a crater over a half-mile across and six hundred feet deep, and the new findings on air blasts were especially telling.

Although the US services were ready to debate the chances of a SAC bomber arriving safely over Moscow, we in the Navy couldn't even locate our submarines within its own length, let alone launch a missile with a CEP of a half a mile. But the new H-bomb data had given the Navy new hope until such time as the FBM improved its accuracy.

An air blast would permit us to cause unacceptable damage anyway. If, for example, a warhead went off about five thousand feet over *ground zero*, the damage would be felt for ten miles, and if the wooden structures near Moscow didn't collapse, they would be incinerated, and *we knew that half the apartments in stone buildings would catch fire virtually simultaneously because the curtains facing the streets would immediately burst into flames.*

Because of the intelligence data made possible by the achievements of the USAF and the CIA, not only did we know more about Soviet cities than did their own tax assessors, but we could quantify risks of fire better than could any insurance adjusters from one end of the Soviet Union to the other.

Of course, I must admit that the second floor apartment and the fourth building on the west side from the corner never existed like they've been described above. And no apocryphal woman named Rose Marie from St. Paul, Minnesota, worked in Moscow in late 1959 and early 1960. It would be too contrived to suggest in this work that the coordinates of the Moscow street corner were 55° 45' 05"N, 37° 37' 30"E. The point here is that maybe they were.

Even though the Soviet cars on the street might only be dented, all their windows would be blown in, for miles in every direction. Until we acquired the accuracy needed for the *Polaris*, we had to devise the ways to inflict heavy damage on the Soviet Union if it attacked our mainland first. In 1959 the United States didn't even have the luxury of planning a first strike without committing national suicide. No one who knew that was about to admit it publicly.

The team members at Special Projects had to solve all the factors that comprise accuracy and reliability. Day after day the words *accuracy* and *reliability* haunted them. These goals had to be achieved, but as hard as the SP members tried, accuracy and reliability always *just slipped* out of reach. Congress had given SP all the money needed to get the job done. But missiles and men's bodies kept blowing up in SP's faces, and the most sophisticated equipment wouldn't even fit into the new nuclear submarines, and when the missile's solid-fueled boosters worked real well, SP engineers still hadn't proven their solution operationally on how to stop the rocket motors' acceleration.

00809 6 15 5 7 56 A2014 TOP SECRET TALENT
A-2014
0 8 1 3
R-6

Facing page. On May 7, 1956 this Soviet military airfield near Moscow was photographed by a U-2 contract pilot whose family name was Vito. This rare CIA photo is almost contact size and represents about one-third of the original 18 inch-long aerial negative.

In 1956, an average spool of film from a U-2 contained 165 negatives and totalled an average of 250 feet long. Clouds often obscured visibility as can be seen on the left of this photo, and most of the earlier frames on this roll had little intelligence value because of the cloud cover.

Nonetheless, camera and photographic technology improved rapidly after these early U-2 flights, enabling photo-interpreters to greatly enlarge small segments of the negatives from the U-2*s* operated by the CIA and from the secret USAF military satellites.

Photographic intelligence was as valuable to nuclear deterrence as were the improvements in the yields of nuclear warheads. The first removed many uncertainties about potential enemy targets and provided precision, while the second permitted America's submarine-launched *Polaris* missiles to increase their range.

Photo courtesy of National Archives and Records Administration.

Facing page. This heavily manipulated photo taken from a USAF "spy" satellite in 1970 shows the dramatic improvement in the U.S. photographic state of the art. The small-fingernail-sized square in the upper right segment of the original contact print shows how it was enlarged to what dominates this page.

The lower center square, the size of a small postage stamp, shows the Kremlin distinctly, Lenin's mausoleum, and above the word "tomb" is St. Basil's church in Red Square. The faint line, one-quarter inch long, leading from the mausoleum is about 250 tourists patiently waiting their turn to visit the monument on Thursday afternoon, 28 May 1970.

The heavy black line that weaves through Moscow is the Moscow River, and the narrower line that parallels the river near the Kremlin is the Moscow Canal.

The USAF/CIA program was part of the top secret "Corona" program that produced 800,000 similar images between August 1960 and May 1972. Although Soviet Premier Khrushchev pushed President Eisenhower to cancel the U-2 missions over Russia after CIA contract-pilot Powers was shot down on 1 May 1960, the U.S. president still had an ace up his sleeve—the *Samos* "spy-satellite" that he had secretly authorized in 1958, and that led to such photos.

In some ways the U-2 photos provided more interpretable "target" data for the *Polaris* FBM system during the time the U-2 operated over the Soviet Union and other "problem areas.

Photo courtesy of the National Archives and Records Administration. Original cooperation of the USAF, CIA, National Reconnaissance Office and Central Imagery Office.

MOSCOW, USSR: 28 MAY 1970
his graphic illustrates some of the best resolution imagery acquired by the KH-4B system, about 6 feet. In the enlargement of the Kremlin, individual vehicles can be identified as trucks or cars, and the line of people waiting to enter Lenin's Tomb in Red Square is apparent.
Kremlin

Much time had been lost earlier because the Defense Department had initially wanted the Navy to place liquid-fueled *Jupiter* missiles on surface ships and in submarines. The *Jupiter* was a 65-foot missile, eight feet in diameter, and as far as the Navy was concerned, early tests proved that the slightest mishap with a liquid fuel or an oxidizer on a surface ship could sink it, and in a submarine such an accident would probably be fatal to everyone on board.

Almost all liquid-fueled rocket motors used liquid-oxygen, a few drops of which could blow a man in two. And no one wanted to waste money on naval blueprints for a submarine with eight working decks inside a pressure hull with time bombs aboard. The Navy was convinced that a liquid-fueled rocket was nothing less than a booby trap sure to go off some day.

Each major *subsystem* of the missile and the submarine had a group of highly skilled engineers and scientists working on the problems unique to that subsystem. The first stage of the missile included more than a rocket motor. There was the *steering* mechanism to make it go where you wanted it to go, and that steering was directed by little motors that received their instructions through signals from the guidance system. In the *Polaris* missile the guidance package was located above the second stage rocket motor, between the latter and the payload—in this case, the nuclear warhead.

As solid rocket fuel burned hotter, more corrosively, and ever so violently, the early rudders or steering vanes in the rocket's exhaust deteriorated very quickly. Like the names on a headstone being inscribed by the use of a sandblaster, as each letter turns from rock to stone-dust, the steering devices in the rocket's exhaust simply dissolved before the fuel inside the rocket motor stopped burning. As materials and new designs were invented to resist the exhaust's corrosion, the Army popped up with the innovation for swiveling the nozzles, and industrial engineers tried having a ring around the open end of a nozzle, a ring shaped like a cigar band, and to angle it in and out of the exhaust, much like steering a canoe by angling the rear paddle against the water. Soon the ring became a *jetavator*, and the swiveling nozzles simply became *swozzles*.

Often the public would question news stories reporting that the first stage had 90% reliability, but were puzzled when they read that the steering-servos were only 85% reliable. The *servos* were the servo-mechanisms that had sturdy, hydraulically-driven metal arms that moved the swozzles, and the signals from the guidance system told the servos which arm to push or pull, and how far to push or pull.

One of the most brilliant discoveries or innovations came about in order to terminate the thrust of the solid-fuel rocket motors. A comparison that's useful is the one about the cannon that shoots a man over a Ferris wheel at a carnival.

When the cannon's power is constant, the man doing the flying should not gain weight. If he gains fifty pounds, he's liable to go through a seat near the top of the Ferris wheel. Or if he loses weight, he might land on a pile of rocks beyond the net he was supposed to land in. And when a new spring or an explosive charge is used and is stronger than the one formerly used, the flyer will end up in the rocks if he's the same weight. One way carnival performers adjusted to this was by using iron weights, much like jockeys do in horse races to keep their weight corresponding to the rules. Of course, the carnival manager could change the strength of the spring or the explosive charge. Whenever one factor changed, it affected all the others.

Whether a rocket motor is used to carry a nuclear warhead to a target or to carry a space capsule to the moon, similarities between the carnival and rocket fuel become apparent.

When a liquid-fueled rocket has gone far enough and is traveling fast enough, the valves can be closed to cut off the fuel and the oxidizer. The solution is as simple as turning off a faucet in a bathroom. But if the motor burns two seconds too long, the warhead may miss the intended target by ten miles, and if it burns ten seconds too long, the business end may miss by fifty miles!

One of the great drawbacks of solid fuel was the fact in 1956 no one knew how to stop the thrust in a solid-fueled rocket, nor how to stop its fuel from burning. Inside the motor, the propellant and the oxidizer were mixed in a material that looked like hard rubber, and once lit, the damn thing stayed lit until burn-out. Had SP not discovered the technique to terminate the solid-fueled rocket's thrust, the fleet ballistic missile (and the *Pershing* and the *Minuteman*) would never have worked. By applying Newton's third law of motion, SP scientists devised a thrust terminator by proving once again that for every force there is an equal and opposite force or reaction. In this case, ports ahead of the motor were blown out, letting the rocket motor brake its own motion.

All the first stage subsystems were functioning in 1960. But we didn't have 100% reliability of the first stage subsystem. For example, the motor nozzles were 99%, and the solid engine 95%, and guidance, servos, and swozzles were all near perfect. But if five major subsystems were each 99%, then the first stage's statistical reliability was actually only 95.099%.

Launching from a solid concrete pad was one thing, but the notion of launching a missile from a moving platform was challenging to say the least. When a missile sat on a pad, we knew where it was because the best geometrists and surveyors had studied its location to the closest tenth of an inch. And the elevation of the base of the missile was known to a fraction of an inch above mean sea level. Moreover, the pad was perfectly level, thereby ensuring that an imaginary vertical line drawn straight through the missile all the way to the center of the earth remained absolutely straight. This factor was called the *local vertical.* Later on, deep inside a nuclear submarine, a deadman's switch was the only way to keep this important factor under control.

The *local vertical* was vital and important to all missilemen, and it permitted them to plot the path the missile must follow through the earth's atmosphere and through space. During a theoretical re-entry into the earth's atmosphere, a warhead would bull its way through fiery heat and flames, and would have to survive those adverse elements with its heat shield (the same type developed to protect all our early astronauts), and then it would follow its predetermined ballistic path straight to *ground zero*—say, exactly 4,231.78114 statute miles from a key launch pad in the middle of the United States. That path, azimuth and distance to *ground zero* wouldn't change for a thousand years, nor would the flight of a pre-emptive nuclear strike from a launch pad in the Soviet Union to the American launch pad.

To a sailor, it was a nightmare. Admittedly the Navy had a bellyful of problems with the missile. As for a submerged submarine, there were plenty of problems—heck, we didn't even know where the submarine was in terms of precision in 1959. We only thought it ought to be within 300 feet of ... of ... what? The periscope? The engine room 250 feet thataway? The torpedo room, 90 feet the other way? From the SINS?

For a thousand years, sailors have fought the fickle ocean that causes a vessel to roll, pitch, yaw, heave, accelerate, and decelerate in various and unpredictable combinations thereof. But those were naval problems for all naval ships. They've always had to cope with drift that affects precise knowledge of location. But when a missile was launched, the heading of the ship introduced a crucial element for the launch tubes, independent of location. In submarines, all these motions combined with additional complications like undercurrents and thermal layers. In addition, the submarine would be expected to launch from underwater, day or night, where a 300-foot error in the launch location could translate into a miss of *ground zero* by many miles.

Engineers love to explain that the gyroscope phenomena is what permits kids to boldly defy Sir Isaac Newton, their parents and gravity by riding a bike and yelling, "Look, Mom, no hands!"

It took a great deal of money and brains for America to master the gyros in inertial systems and to keep them floating in an electromagnetic field regardless of whether the equipment room was doing a heave, yaw, roll, pitch and so on. It was such a mystery that all the materials used in their construction had to be the purest possible. When ordering the early research gyros through research and development contracts, my Navy-attorney brother always marveled over the technical specifications. The scientists and engineers insisted the gyro units be made of *pure gold*!

On the submarine, a rather large installation was set aside for the Ship's Inertial Navigation System, commonly called SINS. In our missile, a rather small compartment was set aside for the Inertial Guidance system between the second stage rocket motor and the payload above. Everything depended on gyros for both systems, and they offered great promise of technological advances heretofore unknown and unimaginable. The unavoidable realization was that neither of them had been tested in a submerged launch, nor could the SINS mock-ups fit into their assigned spaces inside the first *Polaris* submarine.

Visiting the laboratories and production plants performing under SP contracts was always informative, if not exciting. Before designing the final sleek equipment and vital subsystems, the guts were often spread out on floors and lab tables, with wires dangling every which way in a Rube-Goldberg paradise. These contraptions were often subterfuged from reality by calling them laboratory breadboards which impressed technical writers and editors immensely. The breadboard served to illustrate that the *whatchamacallit* really did work, and the head scientist only needed six more months and six million dollars to make it fit into something the size of a breadbox. In legalese, such undefinable breadboxes were called black boxes because no engineer, contracting officer or lawyer could define what would go inside. Nobody knew. Only the input and hoped-for output could be defined—more or less.

Since it took as long to train a crew of a *Polaris* submarine as it did to construct the nuclear submarine the crewmen would serve in, it took literary wizardry to define the training equipment with all the lights, switches, bells, buzzers and buttons that did what the real equipment might do in the submarine four years later. Hence the black box also set new engineering standards for subsequent production. Coupled to the black box standards were all the improbabilities incumbent to the design, especially the printing, years ahead of time, of the training and the repair manuals for the equipment to be used by the crews. One of the techniques adopted was the use of dated substitute pages in the manuals.

Without exaggeration it is impossible to overstate the difficulties that my colleagues faced. When we realized early on that we could not develop a missile-launching nuclear submarine in time to meet one of our early schedules, the Bureau of Ships stepped in and cut in two a nuclear submarine already under construction, and inserted an entire new section between the two halves. Thus, the old hull of the *Scorpion* became the new longer hull of the future *SSB(N)598 U.S.S. George Washington.* That earlier *Scorpion* was unrelated to its successor, the *SSN 589 U.S.S. Scorpion* that sadly sank with all hands in 1968.

All our major subsystems had to improve overall odds—guidance, launch and ignition, SINS, communications, stage separation, second stage, warhead, submarine silence, fire control, and the pressure hull for increased depth. To achieve better odds the United States declared all out war on every technological barrier.

In the case of the warhead, it was the Atomic Energy Commission laboratories that started offering a better, lighter and smaller warhead in 1956, one with more bang per pound, as opposed to the often-repeated phrase "more bang per buck."

This AEC development was an extremely important breakthrough, one that dramatically changed the dynamics and interrelationships of all SP's designs, and greatly affected the calculations of CEP and total system reliability.

A few years later, I accompanied some of the Navy scientists to a secluded, heavily guarded location for a meeting during which various new models of nuclear weapons were paraded in front of the users—those who might find use for them. All the military services attended, as well as representatives of each major weapons system, eager to learn what additional options were available to fight an enemy that had delivery advantages plus a growing nuclear stockpile.

Each nuclear device presented by the AEC scientists was accompanied by a recital of its predictable damage assessment against different target profiles such as a hardened missile launch site or a city area with high-risers of modern construction, military bases and ports, cities with older architecture and so on.

It was a dizzying challenge to moral sensibilities, and at the first coffee break I had to go outside for fresh air because I felt nauseous. But as the succeeding sessions progressed so did my enthusiasm, particularly when I recognized new *Polaris* applications for the new nuclear models coming out of AEC laboratories.

(Years later I saw the stage play *Sheep on the Runway* by Art Buchwald, a hilarious story about Pentagon salesmen selling weapons out of a huge shopping catalog to third world despots. I thought how much Buchwald would have loved writing about AEC's *annual fashion show*.)

Our atomic scientists taught us a great deal about density and cross sections of nuclear warheads. Consequently we always tried to avoid releasing photographs of a *Polaris* missile with something in the photograph that might provide a scale of measurement against which someone could figure out the length and circumference of the nose cone. In fact, the Soviets were always tracking our ships whenever they could during the years when we tested our launching tubes and the launch systems because the Soviets wanted to snare one of our launch-*dummies*. Whether these were made from Redwood logs or other floatable design, the measurements were accurate.

In order to avoid the press and news cameras we often conducted test launches beyond the three-mile limit, but we constantly changed locations. I remember one incident in Long Island Sound when a Soviet trawler almost beat one of our escort ships to a *Polaris dummy*. But the threat of being rammed forced the trawler to veer.

Due to the fact that we changed our MO on a regular basis to avoid the *pirates at sea*, we once lost a *dummy* and despite all our searches, we couldn't find it. About a month later, the Pentagon received a message from the United States embassy in Brazil which forwarded a complaint from a Brazilian fisherman who found SP's *dummy* in his fishing net. Clearly painted on the missile-*dummy* was "Property of the US Navy," accompanied by serial numbers. Needless to say, the fisherman was damned mad because his net was torn, and if the Navy didn't pay up for a new net he—and now he said the magic words—would write a nasty letter to a newspaper.

Once again, by brother Norm was elected to negotiate this deal as quietly as possible to avoid a bidding war with some strawman from the U.S.S.R.

Norm settled. The fisherman ended up a happy camper with a new net. No Soviets ever measured one of our *dummies*.

Such distractions aside, no part of any major subsystem at that time exceeded 95%, which really put the FBM *Polaris* system below the 48% percentile of total system reliability for solid-fueled missiles. Secretly everyone knew, despite that, it was the best the United States had.

Despite the breakthroughs, technical difficulties could be multiplied ten times over, each day. Although we had the money, talent, manpower and the top national priority, there was more sand ominously at the bottom of the hourglass than on top. And the Monday morning reports showed increasing weekly casualties.

Often these reports were about multiple fatalities during our solid propellant stability tests at Indian Head, Maryland. I don't ever recall a news story revealing that *Polaris* propellant was the cause of the explosions.

Chapter 4

Eisenhower's last watch

In the early years of research to develop nuclear weapons, Americans scientists had welcomed their British counterparts. But after the Americans realized that they could go faster alone, they dropped cooperation with London soon after the United States dropped atomic bombs on Hiroshima and Nagasaki in August 1945.

Later, Americans learned that the British spy Klaus Fuchs had been one of the British scientists who had worked at the super secret American installation at Los Alamos, New Mexico, where the two bombs had been produced. Fuchs' treason had helped the Soviet Union to develop its own atomic bomb at a double-time rate.

Meanwhile, in the back rooms of British politics, the strategic importance of nuclear power was a paramount concern. The Chancellor of the Exchequer Sir John Anderson wrote, "We cannot afford, after the war, to face the future without this weapon and rely entirely on America should Russia or some other power develop it."

Several countries rushed to break down technological barriers while volatile political crosswinds swept across the world stage. Soviet Marshal Bulganin probably stated the politico-military problem as well as anyone in 1955 when he said, "Atomic weapons cannot be used without a means of delivery to their target." Later, in 1956, Soviet Premier Khrushchev added bluntly, "Bombers are obsolete."

At the end of that same year, The U. S. Secretary of State John Foster Dulles went to Paris for the December ministerial meeting of NATO countries, where the fifteen allies were to meet in NATO's temporary headquarters at the *Palais de Chaillot*. Some acrimony was expected because Britain and France had been embarrassed earlier when the United States had forced them to abandon their attack on Suez.

Arriving with Dulles the day before, were George M. Humphrey, Secretary of the Treasury, and Charles E. Wilson, Secretary of Defense.

Wilson arrived in an upbeat mood because he had settled a bitter interservice rivalry on 8 December by assigning the responsibility of all ballistic missiles with a range over 250 miles to the Air Force, except for a Navy missile. He had ordered the Navy to drop the *Jupiter* and to begin the development of a new Navy missile.

On Tuesday, 11 December, spirited squabbling over Suez highlighted the first session of the ministers. French Foreign Minister Christian Pineau and British Foreign Secretary Selwyn Lloyd had fully expected a bellyful of criticism and were not unhappy to see the session close. The only happy note of the session had been the report submitted by Lester B. Pearson, Gaetano Martino and Halvard M. Lange, the Foreign Ministers of Canada, Italy and Norway respectively. Their report covered the need for non-military cooperation as well as closer political consultation within the alliance. Everyone appeared quite ready to agree on the last point, particularly Pineau and Lloyd.

However, at the second session, Dulles jolted his allies by reminding them of all the American commitments that extended around the world, and that under certain circumstances, when a crisis demanded prompt American action, they could not expect the United States to have time to consult with its European allies. Dulles cited the example of the troubled waters of the 115-mile-wide Formosa Strait between the Chinese Nationalist forces on Taiwan and the Chinese Communists in Fukien province on the mainland of China.

Without meaning to, Dulles set the stage for the freedom of action exercised by President John F. Kennedy during the explosive Cuban crisis seven years later.

During NATO's third session, the Defense Minister of the Netherlands Cornelis Staf struck the core of new business: the Europeans understood that the law of the United States prevented disclosure of nuclear information, but was convinced that nuclear weapons were needed for the defense of Europe. "If need be," Staf conceded, "the control of these weapons could remain totally in the hands of the United States."

Agreeing with Staf were Defense Ministers Anthony Head of Britain, Maurice Bourges-Manoury of France, Franz Josef Strauss of West Germany, and Nuri Birgi of the Turkish Foreign Ministry.

The next day, Secretary Wilson of the United States replied and recognized Europe's eagerness to have nuclear weapons and modern weapons like rockets. He offered to plan with them the manner of introducing nuclear weapons. As for rockets, the "technical data to produce them" would be provided by the United States. He made it clear that the design of nuclear warheads for missiles would not be shared with other nations.

From the very first days of nuclear development the greatest scientific minds had been recruited, and many advocated action that only became true long after the ideas were expressed. At the Naval Research Laboratory in 1939, Dr. Ross Gunn advised his superiors of the possibilities of atomic propulsion for submarines. He pointed out the "tremendous military advantage" in possessing a submarine with enormous increases in "range and military effectiveness."

Two other scientists important for recognizing issues ahead of their time were Harvard University president James B. Conant, Chairman of the US National Defense Research Committee, and Vannevar Bush who organized American science under the NDRC. They warned the Secretary of War Henry L. Stimson that the development of the hydrogen bomb, quite possible after the atomic bomb, could place every population center in the world at the mercy of any nation which struck first.

Thanks to the treason of Julius and Ethel Rosenberg, it's certain today that Soviet Premier Stalin knew about America's atomic bomb long before President Harry S. Truman learned of it after Roosevelt's death. In fact, Khrushchev himself was told by Stalin of the Rosenbergs' "very significant help." Nonetheless, Truman used the bomb to quickly end the war, and slammed the door shut on exchanging nuclear information with anyone, including the British, when he signed the United States Atomic Energy Act of 1946, often called the McMahon Act.

On 3 October 1952, Britain detonated its first atomic bomb off the coast of Australia. Churchill had once again been elected UK Prime Minister, and as soon as Dwight D. Eisenhower replaced Truman as U. S. president, Churchill started pressing for renewal of the nuclear information exchanges. In a December meeting between President Eisenhower and Churchill in Bermuda, the Prime Minister argued that

Britain needed up-to-date atomic information to ensure that the bomb bay doors of Royal Air Force bombers were large enough and that bomb-release equipment was compatible with the latest, modern weapons which surely all would use in a war against a common enemy.

Churchill went on, "We will have to spend millions we poor Britons can ill afford to learn what you chaps already know and could tell us if you would. We will learn it, of course, but at what an unnecessary cost. It makes no sense whatever to go at it like that. The enemy will be a common one. The means to stop him should be common means."

In 1954, the Atomic Energy Act was amended. And another "security" stamp was born for classifying national defense secrets. The new one read, *RESTRICTED DATA* under the terms of the McMahon Act, as amended. Such information could not be made available to anyone. A second new US stamp read *NO FORN*, which simply meant that a classified document was not meant to be read by any foreigners, even NATO allies with the appropriate security clearance. The British might have access to some *CONFIDENTIAL*, *SECRET* or *TOP SECRET* nuclear documents, but not those additionally classified as *NO FORN* or *RESTRICTED DATA*.

In the Special Projects office, we used every restrictive tool at hand to safeguard information about our nuclear submarines and our new *Polaris* missile. But we could not work in a vacuum, as if we were unaware of the developments affecting us. In particular, we were very sensitive to repeated British and French spy scandals that seemed to pour US secrets into Moscow.

When Prime Minister Harold Macmillan later met with President Eisenhower at Camp David in 1959, he steered away from the *Polaris* Fleet Ballistic Missile program because the Royal Navy only wanted to expand its conventional surface fleet. The prime minister simply focused on his Royal Air Force bombers as his nuclear strike force.

Toward the end of President Eisenhower's second term, Secretary of State John Foster Dulles died from cancer on 24 May 1959, and was succeeded by former Massachusetts governor Christian A. Herter. Secretary of the Navy Thomas S. Gates, Jr. moved up to replace Donald A. Quarles as Deputy Secretary of Defense.

Herter and Gates were both surprised by the intensity of NATO's preoccupation over the east-west nuclear imbalance, weapons technology and their doubts about the credibility of the American nuclear deterrent to protect western Europe.

Significantly, a special fact-finding committee established by President Eisenhower to study military aid recommended that the *Polaris* missile be distributed to NATO countries. The committee chairman, Brig. General William Draper, said the missile would meet the military requirements laid down by NATO planners. Such a recommendation simply complicated an already confused subject because the Europeans were still smarting from the stalling which followed the late Secretary Wilson's offer of "technical data to produce them" and of the late Secretary Dulles' offer of "cooperation in production of modern weapons."

In mid-August, 1959, the Special Projects Office tested a *Polaris* test missile from a gyrating tube from a ship-motion simulator at Cape Canaveral. The tube was a replica of the ones being built for our nuclear submarines, and the simulator, developed by Westinghouse, was called by their engineers "the cocktail shaker." It imitated the various motions of a ship at sea. The test was the first successful launch from a moving tube, or any other kind of tube.

On the 27th, a *Polaris* was successfully launched from the EAG 154 *Observation Island* which had been outfitted with two launch tubes. Inside SP, the ship was affectionately called the "Obs Island," and was a converted Mariner-class merchant vessel. Considerable political pressure was on the Navy. Everyone kept his fingers crossed, and the launch was a momentous occasion for SP and was hailed by the Navy. What no one admitted was that the rocket motors used had defects, and our dumb luck prevented the missile from exploding early in its flight. The Navy couldn't wait for new motors and used what was available in SP's assembly building at the Cape. Anyway, SP reasoned it was the launch test that was important. If the flight was successful, all the better.

The Eisenhower administration needed good news, and Congress was hammering Defense Secretary Neil H. McElroy who finally admitted to the now-famous "missile gap" that was exploited during the later presidential campaign.

For Herter and Gates, 1959 revealed a widening split in the NATO alliance where serious doubts persisted about the United States intervening with nuclear weapons to save Europe when American cities were not directly threatened. The American pledge to defend Europe "at all costs" appeared a little too good to be true. The Europeans doubted the Soviet Union would even believe it. Many believed the only good nuclear defense was one's own. That was British policy. It was also the policy of French President Charles de Gaulle. Germany's hands were tied by treaty and post-war military occupation. Although she had the resources, Germany contented herself to join the other smaller have-nots, and they clamored for a hand on the American nuclear stockpile, for a finger on the trigger.

Europeans started insisting that nuclear weapons be stockpiled on the continent, and the United States insisted on outright custody of nuclear bombs or warheads, or no less than a double-key system in which the United States had one of the keys. The Supreme NATO Commander, General Lauris Norstad, had already asked for these weapons. To distinguish between a NATO missile and an American Intermediate Range Ballistic Missile, he wanted any such missile intended to be stationed in Europe to be called a Mid-Range Ballistic Missile. From this definition arose a new acronym, the MRBM.

With little else to fall back on, Herter and Gates prepared an offer for NATO which would permit European allies to purchase *Polaris* missiles and to deploy them on canal barges, highway eighteen-wheelers and railroad cars. The selection of *Polaris* thoroughly upset flag-ranked Army and Air Force missilemen and their defense contractors who instigated an intensive interservice rivalry in the rings and corridors of the Pentagon, in the committee rooms of the Senate and the House of Representatives, and on the front pages of every major newspaper in America and in Europe.

With the largest military procurement contracts potentially hanging in the historic balance, the competition was dragged into the cloakrooms of foreign defense ministries and into the antichambers of the new NATO headquarters at Porte Dauphine, Paris. As a result of the official move to offer *Polaris* to America's NATO allies, the major politico-military issue before NATO became entangled in a web of industrial-military intrigue, the likes of which the western world had never seen.

As if the world needed another crisis in 1959, Soviet Premier Khrushchev wasted no time after visiting the United States, and fabricated more unrest in West Berlin to which 2,203,109 East German refugees had already escaped since 1950. To meet the crisis, the Supreme Allied Commander in Europe, SACEUR, General Lauris Norstad appealed for no less than thirty divisions with one hundred battalions armed with tactical nuclear missiles.

Although President Eisenhower's personal visit to Paris during the ministerial meeting reaped a strong, mutual stand by France, Britain, West Germany and the United States on Berlin's defense, there was clearly some unraveling of NATO when de Gaulle withdrew his Mediterranean forces from NATO's integrated naval command.

In December, McElroy resigned and President Eisenhower named Gates to replace him as Secretary of Defense. By the end of 1959, Herter and Gates knew the NATO ministerial meeting the following May would be a tail-twister. Nonetheless, for the first time, the Navy had a former service secretary at the helm of the Defense Department. And SP had the same man who had endorsed giving Admiral Raborn his famous "hunting license" to attract the best personnel for the nation's highest priority.

Meanwhile, American U-2s carrying sophisticated photographic equipment had been overflying the Soviet Union for three years with complete immunity from anti-aircraft weapons, because the Soviets had no missile capable of reaching the spy plane. The Soviets gritted their teeth and said nothing, not wanting to admit their impotence to the world. The Americans held their breath and said nothing, not wanting to crow about the aerial photos.

On 13 February, near a lonely road southward in the Algerian Sahara—the only road, often only a Jeep trail, leading to Mali—French nuclear scientists detonated France's first atomic bomb. The 100 kiloton blast was near Reggane, the town used as a staging point for France's nuclear development, and exceeded the blast at Hiroshima by more than eight times. De Gaulle had pushed his scientists because he wanted the test to occur before the official visit to Paris by British Prime Minister Harold Macmillan in mid-March. By the time the British leader arrived, de Gaulle was in high spirits. The two men discussed a wide range of topics, among which were the Common Market established by the Treaty of Rome, and the British-led rival group, the European Free Trade Area. In the Rome treaty was the traditional favored-nations-clause which allows preferential tariffs by one member for all the others.

However, Britain wanted to retain her favored-nations-clause within the Commonwealth. To adopt the clause in the Common Market would force her to stop receiving lucrative tariff reductions through her traditional ties within the British Commonwealth. Macmillan wanted special treatment for entering the Common Market. But this type of argument rubbed raw a sensitive nerve in de Gaulle because of Britain's special relationship in political and nuclear matters with the United States—thus outside the Common Market.

Because they found no middle ground on most issues, the British and French leaders ended by discussing the upcoming summit meeting in Paris with Khrushchev and Eisenhower.

After leaving de Gaulle, Macmillan went to Camp David in Maryland to meet with Eisenhower. Because the president idolized his grandson David, Eisenhower changed the name of "Shangri La," as Franklin D. Roosevelt called it, to Camp David. There, Macmillan and Eisenhower discussed Britain's impending cancellation of its IRBM *Blue Streak*, a virtual copy of the US Air Force's *Thor* missile, and the fact that Britain wanted to replace their IRBM with an advanced nuclear delivery system.

Although Eisenhower reminded his visitor of the general *Polaris* offer to NATO, Macmillan wanted the strategic role to stay with the Royal Air Force. The USAF had thoroughly briefed the RAF on a new USAF missile on the drawing boards—what the USAF sold as the "*Polaris* in the sky" was the *Skybolt* air-to-surface missile. Some British claim that *Polaris* missiles were offered as back-up, but I never saw any records to substantiate those claims.

The two leaders agreed to let their defense ministers work out the details. On 13 April, the UK announced it had canceled its IRBM *Blue Streak*, and would continue to use her air force as its principal nuclear strike force.

Going into the next NATO meeting in a few weeks, the USAF was one up on the US Navy. At least one NATO country wanted no part of the US Navy's *Polaris*.

Without much fanfare, the United States was preparing English and French language documents on the implementation of a NATO nuclear force utilizing *Polaris* missiles. In April, Gates sent aloft the first trial balloon by declaring that there had been progress in the program for equipping NATO with mobile, solid-fuel *Polaris* missiles during the next phase of the weapons development plan for the alliance. This raised considerable speculation as eyes turned toward Turkey where the next ministerial meeting would be held. With the meeting only two weeks away, last minute touches were made on the new municipal building in Istanbul where the NATO ministers would meet on Monday, 2 May 1960.

Shortly after Gates' trial balloon, a civilian U-2 contract pilot for the CIA, Francis Gary Powers, flew a spy mission from Turkey over Iraq to photograph government installations including the presidential palace in Baghdad. Ever since Iraq's new government started leaning toward the Soviet Union, the CIA had developed a keener interest in Iraq. As for Powers, his next scheduled mission was an overflight of Russia for which he'd rest up after his trek over Iraq.

On Sunday, May 1st, radar at Yesilköy airport outside Istanbul picked up each plane arriving with NATO ministers. Further south, at an airfield at Inarlik, a jet with odd-shaped wings took off, and as it rose, two pegleg-type wheels dropped from each wing tip. The airport controllers at Yesilköy did not bother to track the U-2 as it slowly gained enough altitude to appear faintly on their screens before heading east.

Later that day, radar operators at Tashkent tracked a spot on their radar as the high flying U-2 crossed into the Soviet Union. Batteries of new missiles were armed and launched. The spy plane came down near Sverdlovsk on the east slope of the Ural Mountains. Its CIA-contract pilot, Powers, and his U-2 reconnaissance jet were photographed and carted off to Moscow. Russia waited five days before announcing the U-2 affair, and quickly followed with threats from Soviet Marshall Rodion Malinovsky to launch missiles at Turkey, Pakistan and Norway whose bases were involved in the overflights of Russia. This Soviet tactic replicated the threats of missile reprisals at the time of the Suez crisis. Khrushchev turned the screw because the US had no credible nuclear deterrent.

The sequel of events: Khrushchev's temper tantrum in Paris, Eisenhower's embarrassment, the abortive 16 May Summit Conference—all are now history.

At the end of May, British Defense Minister Harold Watkinson arrived in Washington to firm up the *Skybolt* agreement with Secretary Gates. According to Watkinson, his quest was to procure "second-generation" missiles, an obvious *Polaris* put-down. Quickly repeated, however, was General Norstad's warning about bilateral agreements which, like the IRBMs in Italy, Turkey and England had done, undermine his authority. Despite Norstad's military logic, collective security crumbled in the face of the special political relationship between Britain and the United States, and the *Skybolt* Agreement became official. The United States would pay for all its development, and the British would pay only the conversion costs to modify their bombers to carry the missile.

The other principal NATO countries preferred to study the *Polaris* which existed in reality and not only on drawing boards. To the

Germans, *Polaris* was hailed as *verteidigungswaffe*, the defense weapon, and to the French, it was *l'arme idéale*, the perfect weapon. But the Soviet press accused it of being a "sneaky" weapon, nothing but a "revanchist tool."

At the Pentagon, the Army smarted from Gate's refusal to permit a sales campaign for the *Pershing* missile, despite an Army spokesman's assertion that a bigger *Pershing* could be ready for mobile land deployment before the *Polaris* could be converted from sea-use to land-use. Moreover, claimed the Army, *Polaris* could not withstand the rigors of land travel, unlike its Army rival.

However, this argument had been anticipated. In the early morning hours when the fog had not yet lifted in San Francisco Harbor, an eighteen wheeler pulled up to the edge of a wharf, and a huge hydraulic-operated tube rose from the interior of the van. Suddenly, in a roar of smoke, a huge bottle-shaped object shot from the tube. One of the Navy engineers observing the launch test and aware of the Army's statement, told another, "Let's drive it to Washington."

In July, the *Observation Island* and other escort ships took rendezvous about thirty miles east of Cape Canaveral, and waited for the nuclear submarine *George Washington* to take a submerged position nearby. Both Blue and Gold crews were on board the submarine, and so were Admiral Raborn and two Polaris missiles. It was a culminating occasion, the first occasion to fire IRBMs from beneath the sea. Although both firings were successful, the second launch was the picture-perfect launch seen in most photographs of the "first" submerged launching. On 20 July 1960, President Eisenhower, who was vacationing in Newport, Rhode Island, received the cryptic message: "*Polaris*—from out of the deep to target. Perfect."

Soon thereafter, Admiral Raborn gave all of us in SP a signed certificate in appreciation for all the work that went into that occasion.

The *George Washington* went to collect its full complement of sixteen blue-ribbon birds, each with a nuclear warhead, and Commander Osborn, skipper of the Blue crew will be remembered for his last press conference before going on patrol for a few months. A technical writer asked him whether the ballast system could compensate if all sixteen missiles were fired in rapid succession, and 450 tons of water rushed into the empty launch tubes.

Not wanting to divulge military secrets, he rolled a cigar while he thought. Then Osborn replied, "If we ever receive that order from

Washington, the boat would soon be so full of pee, the damned thing will ballast itself." In those days, writers politely rephrased and reworded such declarations to make them fit to read in family newspapers.

Soviet trawler traffic increased along the Atlantic coast, and more than the usual number of Soviet vessels were between Iceland and Ireland, and east of Scotland and England, all waiting to detect the first nuclear *Polaris* submarine. We knew that the supreme test was to have the submarine return in a few months time. Osborn's orders were clear. He would not transmit any messages while on patrol as an extra precaution to prevent the Soviets from tracing his location. Our own intelligence suggested that the Soviets would like nothing better than to fabricate a seagoing accident to sink this "perfect" deterrent. But the Soviets had to find this silently running submarine that left no trail, no signals, no wake...

Some people complained that the Navy would not announce the exact date when she slipped into the sea on that first patrol. Well, if you'd think about it, the valid reasons then are still good ones. Now it's almost forty-one years later, and whenever I'm at a roulette table, I still bet 15 for the November day when she submerged. Before the end of the year, the SSB(N) 599 *Patrick Henry* would join her sister sub on patrol somewhere in the black underwater sea.

However, despite Osborn's enthusiasm, things were not "perfect," and SP had monumental problems it could not admit. Whatever the anomaly was in our missile Levering Smith was determined to solve the problem. Statistically, it would take thirteen flight test vehicles to prove a design change, so long as there was only one variable to check out to the exclusion of all others.

Levering went to his favorite attorney and said, "Norm, find me a legal way to contract for a boat-load of blue ribbon birds. I'll find the money, you write the contract."

One night near Charlston, South Carolina, a *Polaris* submarine loaded its launch tubes and headed for a secret rendezvous with the *Observation Island* and other support ships "beyond" Bermuda. With its own range safety officer on the *Obs Island*, the Navy conducted a virtual free-for-all with almost a full load of missiles. Neither before or since has the Navy launched so many test missiles to solve a serious technical problem.

Students of history will note the record that the Soviets were never again as contemptuous of the American deterrent, nor as boisterous about attacking the United States after the SSB(N) *USS George Washington* returned safely to America's shores early in 1961 with a broom stuck proudly upright from its mast. She had performed a clean sweep.

During the 1960 presidential campaign between Republican Richard M. Nixon and Democrat John F. Kennedy, two important reports were issued that affected the United States and NATO for the next four years. One was the Bowie Report, named after Robert R. Bowie, Director of the Center for International Affairs at Harvard University, and previously a top planning official at the State Department. Among other things the report advocated an independent *Polaris* submarine force under the Supreme Allied Commander of NATO. The second report by John N. Irwin, Assistant Secretary of Defense, was notable in that it didn't disagree with any military findings in the Bowie report.

In November, 1960, the British agreed to allow the United States Navy to use a small anchorage called Holy Loch in a Scottish inlet, the Firth of Clyde, for *Polaris* submarines. This forward anchorage would permit these missile-carrying submarines to spend more time within range of Soviet targets instead of being in transit to distant American ports. British critics immediately seized the Holy Loch announcement to complain bitterly about placing this nuclear-lightning rod, this tantalizing military target, on British soil.

In fact, the Defense Minister Harold Watkinson defended the issue in a Commons' debate on November 4th by side-stepping the issue by asserting that the nuclear warheads aboard the US submarines would be under British control while in British waters. No one challenged his statement, although it was clearly contrary to US law for any American to relinquish such control to any foreign national. Since the American national election campaign was in its last torrid week, no American paid much attention to this slip-up during a debate in the House of Commons.

Shortly after the November elections, I met President Charles de Gaulle for the first time while attending a reception in his honor at the elegant French embassy in Washington. Notably, I recall that Admiral Raborn attended, as did Lt. General Bernard Schriever, the highly respected Air Force director of the development of the *Atlas, Titan* and *Minuteman* ICBM programs. The President-elect was resting at his father's Palm Beach estate, but his wife Jacqueline Bouvier Kennedy was at the French reception.

Not many people realized at that time that President de Gaulle was almost blind, and that he learned all his speeches by heart. When the towering 6'4" French president was introduced to me, he extended his hand straight out and slightly upward. It was only by my quick reflexes that I ducked in time to avoid a "French" poke in the eye.

By far, the star of the reception was Mrs. Kennedy. The Soviet ambassador fluttered like a moth around her, much like the East European who hovered around Elisa Doolittle to decipher her accent in the musical *My Fair Lady*. It was then that I realized the truth about the old saying: "A woman is never as lovely as when she is carrying a child."

Young Mrs. Kennedy was almost nine months pregnant.

Overleaf. On 8 May 1962, at the Electric Boat division of General Dynamics in Groton, Connecticut, Mrs. John F. Kennedy christened the SSB(N) 616, the *U.S.S. Lafayette*. At that time, the 425-foot-long *Lafayette* was the largest nuclear submarine ever built. The civilian in the photo who shared the champagne spray with the 33-year-old first lady is Roger Lewis, president of General Dynamics.

By Contrast, in 2001, *Trident* FBM nuclear submarines are 560 feet long and carry 24 *Trident* missiles. The *Lafayette* carried 16 *Polaris* missiles for several years before her conversion to longer range *Poseidon* missiles.

Official U.S. Navy photo

Chapter 5

Kennedy relies on Polaris

An irony of history, destiny or coincidence occurs when an incongruously unimportant personal detail in one man's life leaps back into the forefront some thirty or forty years later. For example, the U-2 photos taken by Gary Powers can serve as a baseline to determine what military facilities Iraqi leaders like Saddam Hussein have constructed since 1960, by simply comparing aerial photos taken in 2000 to the 1960 photos. Another such coincidence was the case in January 1961 for George H.R. Ross of Highland Park, Illinois, whose mother was born at Largs on the Firth of Clyde, Scotland.

As a youth, Ross often spent his summers sailing in those Scottish waters, including across Holy Loch, and later in lakes of Wisconsin and Michigan. His background was similar to President-elect Kennedy who sailed as a youth in the waters between Cape Cod, Massachusetts, and Narragansett Bay in Rhode Island. It was this similarity that brought both young men into the swift patrol torpedo boats of the United States Navy in World War II.

Both men went through torpedo boat training at Melville, Rhode Island, and met again at Lumberi, a small coral and palm tree base for Patrol Torpedo boats, in the Solomon Islands near Guadalcanal. In the early morning of 2 August 1943, Lt. John F. Kennedy's boat, PT 109, of which he was the skipper, was sliced in two by the Japanese destroyer *Amagiri* in Blackett Strait that led to the famous "slot" used by Japanese warships. The US Navy used the term to denote New Georgia Sound between Guadalcanal Island and Bougainville Island.

This is the same "slot" that figured so prominently in James Michener's *Tales of the South Pacific*, first as a novel, then as a stage musical, and later as an award-winning Hollywood musical.

Two crewmen of Kennedy's PT 109 were killed. Subsequently, the courage of Lt. Kennedy in rescuing his 10 surviving crewmen, with the help of Australian coastwatchers and the local Natives of the South Pacific islands, gave birth to the type of naval legends that endures in history. An early injury to Kennedy's back worsened from that wartime action, and plagued him for the rest of his life. At the inauguration of President Kennedy, former-Ensign Ross already knew he'd be appointed to a presidential commission by his former shipmate.

By the time Kennedy was inaugurated on 20 January 1961, the Soviet Union had already derided Britain's decision to provide the US resupply ship *Proteus* an anchorage at Holy Loch in the Firth of Clyde. But the derision only masked the anxiety of the Soviet Union over its own inability to locate either the *George Washington* or the *Patrick Henry* while both were on patrol beyond the North Atlantic. Each submarine carried sixteen *Polaris* IRBMs, and each warhead was twenty times more powerful than the nuclear bomb dropped on Hiroshima.

Because these missiles were of value only when they were within the limited 1,200-mile range of our first *Polaris A-1s* from Soviet targets, the Holy Loch anchorage permitted the United States to exchange crews in Scotland rather than in the United States. This saved the Navy the cross-Atlantic transit time—thus time lost, and the Navy rotated the gold and blue crews—named for the colors of the Naval Academy in Annapolis, Maryland—of each submarine more quickly in Scotland than in New London, Connecticut. Nonetheless, each crew of ten officers and ninety enlisted men would be away from home for 110 days of which about ninety days would be spent submerged and on station. In Captain Shutt's highly classified operational planning center, the little magnetic submarines on our world map took on more ominous significance.

When Kennedy delivered his inaugural address, the American deterrent was very much on his mind, as were the Soviet threats that Premier Nikita Khrushchev regularly leveled at the United States and its allies. The Navy's boss was Admiral Arleigh "31 knots" Burke whose small destroyer flotilla was patrolling the "slot" in the Solomons the night Kennedy's torpedo boat was sunk. For several years, it had been Burke who put his reputation on the line to protect Special Projects and Admiral Raborn at the Pentagon and before Congress.

Another guardian angel of SP was the Deputy Chief of Naval Operations, Vice Admiral John T. Hayward. Although Captain Tom Rudden was SP's deputy director, it was really Dick Shutt who was Raborn's key daily liaison to CNO through Hayward's staff, and those officers spread a protective wing over Shutt's branch, SP-11. In the waning days of the Eisenhower administration, the president approved an increase in the number of *Polaris* submarines to fourteen. In less than a week after Kennedy was inaugurated we knew that he was planning to add even more submarines. In a surprising and spectacular move, Kennedy started placing calls to middle-ranked civilian employees of the government to obtain fast and uncensored information. This unheard-of-initiative alarmed the service secretaries, assistant service secretaries, admirals and generals—to say the least.

But even before the press and the public were aware of this presidential propensity to cut through bureaucratic red tape, I started meeting secretly with Jeff Kitchen, a new administration official in the military-political office at the State Department. It's not that we were doing anything wrong, but we always met in the fresh air on a side street between the State Department building and Constitution Avenue. Often we'd simply sit on a low wall to discuss our business or exchange documents. Walt W. Rostow became a key State official who developed policy planning papers for Dean Rusk, Secretary of State, and Kitchen developed much of the pivotal documentation important to Rostow and to the doctrine of seaborne nuclear deterrence. Suddenly, the Pentagon found itself pleasantly amazed that the State Department started articulating nuclear deterrence in such accurate detail.

Meanwhile Robert R. "Bob" Bowie of Harvard was given more responsibility in this area and liaised directly with McGeorge Bundy, the powerful science advisor to President Kennedy. Bowie started relying on my input for many background papers intended for the oval office. While I performed this toe-dance for SP, Dick Shutt and John Craven often held their breath when Kennedy started to make a speech using words that exactly matched SP's internal doctrine. Of course, Shutt had a direct pipeline to the VCNO and CNO, and I maintained the link with the State Department and the White House. Although the Navy was happy, the USAF and the Army were outraged.

In a sandbox like Washington, the sides started throwing sand at each other, and even the State Department officials got nervous at the flood of different position papers generated by the other services. To give my contacts comfort, I arranged for some hands-on experience for them, and discussed with Dick Shutt the possibility of Admiral Raborn giving a special briefing for Bob Bowie. One night, about 10 p.m., I went to meet Bob Bowie on Constitution Avenue. On the third floor of the Munitions Building, I left him with Captain Shutt who escorted him into Raborn's private office.

Meanwhile, the USAF and the Army started offering visits to their missile bases and test missile launches. Although we knew that a "ride" on a nuclear sub during a submerged launch was a "sexy" invitation, it was one I opposed because there really was no thrill in an underwater launch. "You can lean on the launch tube selected, and feel nothing, hear nothing, see nothing, it's as thrilling as listening to a toilet flush," I'd say.

Shutt finally convinced SP's military brain trust to let me bring key officials on the *Observation Island* when a *Polaris* submarine happened to be nearby to launch a test vehicle. Because the movements of a nuclear submarine were highly classified, this was tricky. I had to make sure the "invitee" would not disclose something highly classified when cutting his own travel orders.

As for us in the Navy, we had been lying for years while making out such orders. As unlawful as it was to file false travel orders, it was also unlawful to state that we were going out on a nuclear submarine or escorting one. We stated that we were going to a meeting at Patrick Air Force Base or going to inspect guidance units in the assembly building near our alligator-infested test pad, or check out some equipment on the *Observation Island.* All this appeared very innocent at the time, but when we lost the *Thresher* "with all hands" the situation became both dramatic and, for a time, tragic to the families of those we lost in the *Thresher*.

My first invited guest was an official of the National Security Advisor's office whose name I no longer remember. Nor, can I remember which submarine was to conduct a submerged launch. I do recall it was "SDAPs" for a *Polaris A-1*. An SDAP was an in-house term for a submerged launch, but I no longer remember what the letters stood for. We pronounced it, "S-dap." Forty years later, an SDAP is now called a DASO.

There were new ground rules for the escort ships that arose following an event that the Navy kept very quiet for a long time. After some successful submerged launches the Navy decided to invite a "lot of brass" like members of the House and Senate military appropriations committees, and civilian top brass at the Pentagon. A friend told me that there was "so much brass in white shirts lining the rails of one of the escort ships," a destroyer I think, that the damn thing listed. Sure as the devil, there were a million cameras whirling when the countdown on the sub went, "minus three, minus two, minus one..."

It was a spectacular launch except for one problem, the first stage erupted free of the surface WITHOUT THE SECOND STAGE! The second stage, the guidance package, and the instrumented nose cone bounced a couple of times on the hull of the submarine, scared the living hell out of the crew, and disappeared into the Atlantic. Meanwhile, the first stage, without guidance, roared along the top of the waves, imagining itself a torpedo rather than a missile, and headed straight amidships of the escort ship with all those white shirts. As if an angel was guiding the first stage, it went underwater about 400 yards from the ship.

During this brief time, the little white dots on the viewing decks started moving quickly in the same order and with as much discipline as Red Army Ants in Africa. While not exactly crawling over each other, those little white dots were mixing their courses every which way, because everybody on the ship suspected this was not part of the act, but also had no idea where the safest direction was without running over a few congressmen and senators, none of whom were track stars. Thank God for the Navy and SP, the first stage stayed underwater, and for all I know it ran up on a beach five hundred miles away. We ducked the bullet that day.

Already warned about the effect of the noise of an IRBM, my White House guest joined me for a coffee or two in the mess of the *Observation Island* until we heard the count get to minus twenty minutes. I led my visitor to a good viewing spot on the port side of the ship where the submarine was. Along the way, I pointed out the launch tube area where we launched *Polarises* from this seaborne launch pad. A Navy helicopter from the Cape flew overhead, conducting its last lane count, a technique we used to count the wave lengths from a Loran C navigational aid, and we used it to triple-check the distance of the submarine from the old but useful Loran C station. Luckily we had no "snoopers" that day, those Soviet trawlers with more electronics than fishing nets that often *just* happened by...

After his eyes adjusted to the expanse of the sea, he located the tall telemetry mast of the submarine which left a thin white wake. This mast was only used in tests.

I said, "This is the last *head* call until the launch."

"I'm OK," he replied.

I didn't bother to explain that just before the launch, all the doors and hatches would be bolted shut, making the ship watertight in case the *Polaris* headed straight toward us, somewhat like a bazooka or a torpedo. In such an explanation, I'd probably have to admit what once *almost happened.* While the embarrassing earlier incident had too many witnesses to be classified, it was still one of the Navy's best kept secrets. We always had our priorities in order.

Of course, my invited guest was also my personal guinea pig whose reactions would determine whether we'd try this routine again.

"Looks pretty far away," said my guest.

"Distance is tough to judge at sea, it's closer than you think," I replied about the mast. I knew he wanted to be as close as possible. "Don't forget, the noise is like an explosion that just won't quit, it'll be plenty impressive," I added.

Because of the heat, we wore no suit jacket, and I stationed myself just behind him. Not only did this give him an unobstructed view, but I could also grab his belt in case the noise would startle him so much he might lose his balance, and fall over the side.

Without realizing it, I had picked a spot near the ship's blast horn, which let a volley go to alert everyone on board that the *Obs Island* was going on watertight battle status. That blast made us both jump out of our shoes. After we calmed down, we laughed like schoolboys and bonded in friendship.

When the count got down to minus nine, minus eight...we went quiet. About ten seconds later, a white and black *Polaris* broached the surface of the sea, splashing water, fire and smoke all over hell and gone. It took only a half-second or so for the roar of the rocket motor to smother our senses. Instinctively, he extended his arms to balance himself. Between us and the thundering missile, a crackling boom clapped across the waves. There was no sound barrier, no vegetation, no barbed wire fence, nothing to soften the onslaught of the intrusive vibration of noise, of a steady crackly explosion without end. He stood transfixed as the plume of smoke followed the missile that soon broke the sound barrier without stopping for an encore. He watched it as it arched gracefully toward outer space. The splashdown a thousand miles downrange into our underwater hydrophone net would tell us in fifteen or twenty minutes whether it landed in our proverbial pickle barrel.

By the time we returned to Cape Canaveral, I knew that SP and the Navy had another trueblue hands-on believer in nuclear deterrence based on our seaborne weapons system. Thereafter, he always picked up his White House telephone when I called.

Meanwhile in Washington, the Kennedy administration had progressed from the snow blizzard of his inauguration to the spring when cherry blossoms blanketed the Tidal Basin and the Jefferson Memorial with pink lace.

Secretary Rusk was expected by our NATO allies to explain the American offer last given by Secretary Herter about nuclear participation. However, at the Oslo meeting in May, Rusk only renewed the commitment of five *Polaris*-carrying submarines to the defense of NATO-Europe. One State Department desk officer told me, "Rusk is giving them the idiot treatment." This contemptuous statement struck me like an admission of mutiny, and surprised me.

Another State Department official told me, "When you don't know what to do or say, you just throw in another idea, just to keep the pot boiling."

Long before the President and Mrs. Kennedy left Washington on their 30 May visit to Paris, as a stop on the way to Vienna, Austria, the President had already heard the grumbling from the European NATO allies about Rusk's statements at Oslo. Even the *Christian Science Monitor* headlined its editorial with the words, "Crisis, Thy Name is NATO!" Kennedy used the occasion of his visit to Canada to try to improve what Rusk had started at the Oslo ministerial meeting.

In his speech before a joint session of the Canadian parliament, Kennedy reinforced the pledge of five submarines, and went on to proclaim, "Beyond this, we look to the possibility of eventually establishing a NATO seaborne missile force, which would be truly multilateral in ownership and control, if this should be desired and found feasible by our allies once NATO's non-nuclear goals have been achieved."

The situation in the world had degraded since the inauguration. Portugal disagreed with everyone on how to give freedom to Angola, Belgium had similar pains over the Congo, and the Netherlands had troubles disengaging itself from its former colonies in Indonesia. Fidel Castro threatened to send Cuban *volunteers* anywhere to help throw out Imperialism. After the Bay of Pigs incident, Castro had literally jumped into the arms of the Soviet Union. Even worst was the crisis in Berlin, where Khrushchev threatened to throw out the allies and unilaterally abolish any western rights in West Berlin "by the end of the year."

When the President and Mrs. Kennedy arrived in Paris on 31 May the French gave them, especially *Jacqueline Bouvier* Kennedy, a tumultuous reception. The French press oozed, aahed and oohed over her, and always emphasized her *French* origins. Presidents de Gaulle and Kennedy hit it off but settled no issues. De Gaulle didn't rub Kennedy's nose into it over the Bay of Pigs fiasco in Cuba, but both leaders knew that the Berlin crisis was the darkest cloud threatening stability in Europe.

Thereafter, the 44-year-old Kennedy flew to Vienna for his momentous meeting with Nikita Khrushchev. The two antagonists could not have been more different in character and in social background. Kennedy came from an extremely wealthy Boston family, and spent his summers sailing, and the rest of his time studying in the best private schools or at Harvard University. By the time he was 23-years-old he was the published book author of *Why England Slept*. His sailing experience prepared him for his World War II military service in motor torpedo boats where he distinguished himself with courage and valor.

Khrushchev, at 67-years-old, was eager for a confrontation with the new American president. When Khrushchev was born, it was into a household gripped by poverty. His father was a miner, who sent Nikita to a Russian Orthodox parochial school. But he rarely could stay in school and had to work. By the time he was 29, he only had four years of grammar school in education. He said himself, "I could add, subtract, multiply and divide." In fact, when the teacher had to go into town, Nikita "taught numbers" to his classmates.

He rose through the bureaucratic ranks of the Communist party, and survived the rough and tumble years under the cruel dictates of Stalin. Hundreds of his comrades were exterminated by Stalin. It had been Stalin's wife who brought Khrushchev, a former schoolmate, to the attention on the Communist leader. Later, while Stalin cheated on her, she killed herself. When the Soviet Union helped Hitler partition Poland, Khrushchev was assigned to the eastern part of occupied Poland. After Hitler double-crossed Stalin and invaded Russia without warning, Khrushchev was sent to Kiev in the Ukraine as a political commissar and as a member of the Soviet military committee to defend that city from Germany's armored divisions.

After the Ukraine fell to the Germans, Khrushchev was sent to Stalingrad where he was again a commissar with the rank of Lieutenant-General. Anyone who survived that terrible military campaign deserved to be a Soviet hero, but Khrushchev was the genuine article, and had suffered the starvation, the freezing days and nights when there wasn't fuel enough to melt the snow to drink. He dug in under the German bombardments, and tried to find saws to cut frozen horse carcasses. He barely survived a strafing attack by German fighter planes. There was so little food that the Soviet wounded and sick were permitted to starve, and only men and women still fit to fight shared what little food was available. The others were left to die because only the fighters could receive medicine or blankets.

Before the Vienna meeting, Kennedy's intelligence reports had already prepared him for Khrushchev's blunt talk and boasts that the Soviet Union produced missiles "like sausages." Everyone knew that Khrushchev called anyone who protected Stalin "ass-kissers," that Berlin represented the "testicles of the West," and "that he would squeeze its western balls to make it scream over Berlin." At their meeting, Khrushchev hyperbolized that he would "lance the boil of Berlin, cut out the cancer, pull the rotten tooth..."

Still, all intelligence sources in the United States knew about Khrushchev's outrageously opinionated statements. Many an eyebrow had been raised twenty years earlier when Churchill was in Teheran, Iran, for the three-power summit between 28 November and 1 December 1943. After Churchill presented Joseph Stalin the "Sword of Stalingrad" gift from King George VI, Soviet Marshal Kliment Voroshilov let the sword fall loudly to the floor. Khrushchev disliked Voroshilov and had credited him with sending Soviet troops to the Finnish front without rifles.

As far as Khrushchev was concerned, "Klim was the biggest bag of shit in the army!"

When Kennedy used Washington inner beltway buzz words like *miscalculation* and *misjudgment* during the Vienna conference the Soviet leader went ballistic, and threatened dire circumstances if those words were shoved in his face again. A week later, the Soviet leader went on television dressed in his military uniform to announce that if the West didn't establish separate peace treaties with East and West Berlin, and agree that West Berlin would be a "free city," he would sign unilaterally with East Germany. He gave the West "until the end of the year."

Back in the United States, Kennedy rested in Middleburg, Virginia, where he was fitted with a back brace and crutches. Having surprised the public with his ailment, the presidential press secretary, Pierre Salinger, admitted that the President had strained his weak back during a tree-planting ceremony in Ottawa on 16 May—before his trip to Paris and Vienna.

Two months later, Khrushchev went good on his warnings, and during the early morning hours of 13 August, the East German government started building the Berlin Wall.

It's not the purpose of this book to dwell on geopolitical trends and curves, but to state the political background that gave the *Polaris* weapons system the impetus that overrode all technical and operational difficulties. Kennedy's call in Ottawa for a seaborne multilateral nuclear force was tied to a build-up of conventional forces. In some areas of NATO, the European reply to Kennedy's call adopted more physical proportions.

In a protected inlet of one of the calmest harbors of the Mediterranean Sea, where the entrances since medieval times have been guarded by fortifications, Italian engineers finished working on a thirty-foot steel tube about five feet in diameter. Here, on 10 October 1961, occurred the test launch of a thirty-ton missile-dummy with a cut of solid fuel, mysteriously shaped like a *Polaris*! It shot out of the tube, had a brief flight and plopped into the harbor. I don't remember how I learned of this, but we was incredulous. I leaned on my sources for proof, for a photograph, for film footage if available. Meanwhile, the Italian missile cruiser, CLG 551 *Giuseppe Garibaldi*, meant to carry US Navy *Terrier* ship-to-air missiles, was being secretly outfitted with four thirty-foot tubes, each about five feet in diameter, hidden under canvas on the afterdeck. The tubes were set in pairs, canted to either side of the ship. Between the tubes was a large gyroscope installation.

Insofar as Kennedy had made an offer, *la Marina Italiana* would be ready. But the whole design appeared so contrived that I was afraid that the US Navy would be blamed, especially SP, of having "gone too far this time." I was confident that none of the intelligence services were on top of this yet, and I continued to twist a few arms until I had the color photographs.

"I want these back, as is," demanded my source.

As soon as I could, I brought the prints to SP, and had exact copies printed from photographs of the prints my source provided. It was decided that I couldn't just sit on these photographs, so I had prints hand-carried to friends in OP-92, the Office of Naval Intelligence, and in the Central Intelligence Agency, and I time-and-date-stamped three other sets to go by regular internal mail to the offices of the Army, Air Force and Defense Intelligence Agencies. My question to ONI and the

CIA was "where were the photos taken," because the landscape and background were very clear. I already knew the date, but I wanted independent confirmation of the place.

A few days later, my CIA contact came to see me and complained, "Those damn photos are pictures of pictures!"

"Well I'll be damned, is that important?"

"You should have informed me. Our lab wasted a lot of time trying to determine whether the photo was duped on a false background."

"Well?"

"It was at La Spezia in Italy. No one knew that you guys were screwing around with the Eye-ties."

"We're not. This is a surprise to us," I answered.

"Kennedy's going to shit when he finds out...," he predicted.

"It's not your job to tell him, it's our discovery..."

"It'll be in our newsletter footnotes next week," he replied, talking about the classified publication that the CIA promulgated to a restricted list of readers.

As soon as we split, I hurried to protect my pipelines to the White House and to State. So I rushed to the Pentagon and asked ONI to pull together a little intelligence report on the Italian Navy and the probable unauthorized encouragement or design assistance given by unknown Navy contractors. We kept it low key and ran a photo of a photo and classified it Secret so that we could keep the lid on. While the ink was *still drying* I hand-carried copies of the ONI report to my contacts at State and the NSC, and told them, "Luckily we learned of this before the papers because we didn't want the administration to be accused of favoritism by other NATO countries." I knew that it was in their interest to keep it quiet.

Meanwhile, Dick Shutt, "Mac" McCallum and other naval officers were sending stern warnings to Navy contractors to get their act together, and to cease and desist whatever was going on with the Italian Navy. It worked, and no one found out publicly about the incidents for almost two years. The news only broke in late 1963 in an Italian publication entitled *Le Ore*. SP and the Navy had ducked the bullet again.

Also about this time in late 1961, a 46-year-old electronic whiz named Herman Cohn visited President Kennedy in the Oval Office. Cohn's only daughter had worked for Kennedy ever since he had been a senator. Kennedy autographed a copy of the book Cohn brought with him, *PT 109, John F. Kennedy in World War II*. With an eye toward history, Kennedy asked Cohn to install some discrete microphones and tape recorders in the Oval Office. Cohn, whose daughter later died from a brain tumor, had worked on the top secret Norden bombsight during World War II. He told me, "I looked around his desk and the drapes. It was no big deal." He added, "I sold lots of this equipment at my electronics store to the FBI and the CIA."

Over time, Cohn installed the private recording system. Whenever Herman spoke of this, he'd grin. He once explained to me, "I was the first to do it." (A reference to President Nixon's famous tape recordings.)

During the same time that our A-1 went operational in new submarines, we were busy developing new rocket motors for the longer range A-2 which would go 300 miles farther, and for the A-3 which would have a range of 2,500 miles. And we already were developing the components for the bigger diameter B-3 which would go farther and carry a more powerful payload. Our submarine launchers were being improved, and in the ship's area, we were designing submarine features to go deeper than ever before in history, to run ever more silently, and to have more speed when needed.

Admiral Hayward supported John Craven's plans to plow extra SP money into the SSN 593 attack submarine *Thresher* to incorporate new design improvements. In turn, these would serve us in the construction of a completely new class of *Polaris* submarines, starting with the SSB(N) 616 *Lafayette*.

Chapter 6

Mixed manning, NATO, and the MLF

Without any doubt, we all took for granted that 1962 would be a watershed year for Special Projects, but none of us expected 1962 to be the year of the fiercest inter and intra-service rivalry, and upside-down international developments. Luckily much of the ugly truth would remain hidden, for the most part, below the surface where the nuclear and non-*Polaris* submariners engaged in an in-house "civil war," in which the players were for or against SP with an intensity that the public never learned about. Ironically, the Royal Navy hated Admiral Hyman Rickover because nuclear propulsion threatened the traditional *surface* navy, and the RN ignored Admiral Raborn.

Yet, by 1962 everyone else's idol was *Polaris*. Its admirers included the Soviet Union's Khrushchev, France's de Gaulle, Belgium's Paul-Henri Spaak, and batting in the clean-up spot was President John F. Kennedy.

Khrushchev's navy wanted to steal or make a carbon copy of our Navy's Fleet Ballistic Missile, and De Gaulle was already developing his own submerged clone as fast as French industry and laboratories could produce it. Spaak, the Secretary-General of NATO said, "The nuclear issue was NATO's most important dilemma to solve." And as far as the Italian Navy was concerned, it put its money where its heart was.

Just about everyone on earth knew that Kennedy's seaborne *Multilateral Nuclear Force* had two options for NATO: surface ships—like the *Observation Island*, or nuclear submarines—like the *George*

Washington. For the next few years, we called Kennedy's NATO initiative the "MLF," and eventually so did everyone else in the press and in the Departments of Defense and State.

Within the US Navy, the battlelines had formerly been limited between the surface ship fleet and the submarines, but now the battle was more refined; it was the combination of the surface ship fleet and all the diesel or nuclear non-*Polaris* submarines, along with the Air Force and the Army aligned against Special Projects...only because we in SP seemed to be appropriated all the fresh money and public attention. The truth, however, was that the USAF received the lion's share. Believing that SP "got it all" brought jealousy and envy from all the have-nots of whom there was a barrelful. Suddenly disgruntled grumbling at the Pentagon threatened to transform popularity into notoriety for SP. In any event, we still had to make the *Polaris* A-2, A-3 and B-3 operational, and now we also had the MLF on our plate.

Notoriety manifested itself in various, unexpected ways—sometimes even humorously. I remember the next time I went to the Cape when I sailed on the *Observation Island* to accompany one of our subs whose blue and gold crews were making their first SDAP launch. It seemed to me that every tramp freighter within a hundred miles steamed our way to watch the show. Already on station were two Soviet trawlers loaded down with electronic gear and photographic equipment. Ships in the Atlantic had learned to eavesdrop by monitoring our frequencies at Cape Canaveral. Because we exploited the three mile and the twelve mile territoriality limits ourselves, near the shores of the Soviet Union, we never quibbled with the Soviet Union's right to be about thirty miles offshore the American coast.

Nearby were a couple of tramp steamers standing by in a calm sea, one was from Liberia, and the other from Panama. Obviously, the longer we took to launch the missile, the greater number of ships could arrive for a ringside seat. The one from Liberia actually tried to maneuver around in order to move closer to where its skipper thought the submarine would launch. The trampers were threatening to royally screw things up, and refused to move when requested.

On the *Obs Island* and in the sub no one wanted to stop and recycle the countdown. We had already performed a helicopter lane count and were in no mood to repeat another. Contrary to the trampers, the Soviet trawlers moved over when requested, especially when we advised them by Morse code in what direction to aim their high speed cameras. Under a very hot sun, the heat broiled everyone exposed to it on the surface

Soviet monitoring ships became a common sight when U.S. Navy nuclear submarines test-launched *Polaris* missiles in the Atlantic Ocean about 30 miles east of Cape Canaveral. Like this one, probably from Cuba, the vessels monitored radio traffic that warned ships to stay away from launch zones. Setting his watch by the warnings, the trawler's captain moved into the zone at high noon to wait for the launch.

Most Soviet "fishing" trawlers that recorded intelligence during *Polaris* launches carried more photographic equipment than the "monitor" shown here.

Government Photo

ships, and we could have fried eggs and heated tea on any metal part of the hot decks.

But the maverick skipper of the Liberian tramper turned out to be a real pain, and the sub's CO reserved some choice and descriptive adjectives for that moron. With reluctance the CO accepted the situation and said tersely, "We'll move just enough."

Dressed only in soiled skivvies, the very overweight maverick skipper installed himself on the freighter's fantail in a lounge chair that he unfolded. Over his head a crewman installed a parasol and gave the skipper a can of beverage. Dumbfounded, we watched him light a cigar, and separate his fat legs so that his feet would not spoil his view. However, it was obvious to us that he could never have seen his feet over his ample beer belly.

Because the freighter had little cargo it rode high in the water, placing the fantail high over the water. Consequently, the skipper didn't see the sub's masts and aerials move in below him, behind the freighter. While we held our breath, a *Polaris* broached the surface with all four swozzles roaring. The thundering wave swept over the freighter's stern before the skipper ever saw the missile, and its hell-on-earth explosive rumble toppled the skipper ass-over-teakettle from his lounge comfort. Keeping one eye on the missile and one on the skipper, we were amazed by the speed with which his heavy belly and his bare feet skipped over the hot deck. He flew up the searing steps of a metal ladder that led to his wheelhouse.

Even before the missile arched toward Africa, thicker smoke rose from the tramper's stack as its boilers built up steam. Within a few minutes, the tramp freighter adopted the same heading as the missile. As for the trawlers, they sat too low to have seen the sideshow on the freighter's stern, but the humor of the missile blasting out of the ocean and the ship's quick getaway couldn't have been lost on the Soviet officers and crews. I'm sure that the only good information they collected were great photographs, which was good for our deterrent that had to be believed to be valuable. But we spread so much electronic gaff underwater that they never were able to make any recording of a noise profile or underwater signature of the submarine. In those days, such a signature was the DNA of anti-submarine warfare. The *Obs Island*, however, was a typical ocean cargo vessel when viewed from a distance.

Other than the normal one-fingered Hungarian salutes, occasionally punctuated by an energetic fore-armed Italian-styled lifted fist, the

American and Soviet sailors exchanged the usual cordial pleasantries and international niceties they always performed in those enlightening encounters at sea where no press was present.

As for a surface MLF, its vulnerability was studied carefully. From an airplane or a satellite, ships like the *Observation Island* could easily pass for any ocean or coastal freighters. Obviously, if nuclear-tipped IRBM's were hidden below their decks the ships would sail in sea lanes frequented by freighters, container ships and other commercial vessels. However, a cruiser like the *Garibaldi* would stand out like a swollen thumb, an observation those of us in SP had gamed-out for months.

But because of the internal incivilities, we started hearing young Naval officers in the Pentagon speak disparagingly instead of jokingly about "polyglot crews." Young officers repeated politically-correct dictums expressed by superior officers exactly as children repeat kitchen-slurs of their parents. This was one of the first open signals of naval disharmony as far as it concerned the NATO MLF.

Also, as the old year ended, we knew that we would soon lose our guardian angels. Even if "Red" Raborn had been promoted to Vice Admiral, he was tired. He had fought his fights and had succeeded. The Chief of Naval Operations Arleigh Burke was just as tired. Burke was a surface ship officer, and Raborn was a Navy pilot, an aircraft carrier officer. Yet both saw beyond those fraternities.

Reaping the benefit of Burke's experience and protection, Raborn had been given a direct pipeline into the office of CNO via the Fleet Ballistic Missiles Division which was under Captain J.L.P. McCallum. "Mac" maintained very close coordination with Captain Dick Shutt in SP-11. Both of these officers were submariners and very loyal to Raborn. Ever since October, 1959, Shutt had been Raborn's first line of defense to protect SP, *Polaris* and our growing fleet of nuclear submarines. I always felt that when the War College would offer a course in *Machiavellian Naval Politics*, Shutt would be the professor to teach it.

In addition, Raborn had a special coordinating office at SP with the Bureau of Ships in our Technical Division under Captain Levering Smith who would soon be an admiral himself. SP maintained a very close and daily relationship with the Bureau of Naval Personnel and the Bureau of Naval Weapons. All these liaisons had been crafted by Admiral Arleigh Burke. These links constituted Burke's protective shield that never failed to protect Raborn and SP.

In SP we felt right made might, and had little time for infighting while we concentrated on solving problems, such as that presented by the MLF's polyglot crews—crews comprising sailors who spoke different languages.

Having armies or navies with crewmen or soldiers speaking different languages was not new, what was new in Kennedy's proposal was that the *mixed-manning* was intentional and not incidental. A brief overlook at the history of mixed-manning will explain the naval military judgments that eventually evolved on the MLF.

To begin with, multinational armies and navies had colored the pageantry of empires, dynasties and races throughout history. Three of the most recent examples were during the Soviet drive on Berlin in 1945. In the First Belorussian Army commanded by Soviet Marshal Georgi K. Zhukov, and in the First Ukrainian Army under Soviet Marshal Ivan Stepanovich Koniev, were Tartars, Cossacks, Russians, Belorussians, Mongols, Poles, Ukrainians, Karelians, Georgians, Armenians, Azebaijanis, Bashkirs, Mordovinians, Itkutsks, Uzbeks, Bulgarians, Romanians, Czechoslovakians, Tibetans and even Germans. Nonetheless, these armies were well disciplined. Marshal Rodio Y. Malinovsky's army, on the other hand, also had a similar mix of *nationalities*, but had a great number of criminals forced into service. German civilians lodged many more complaints against Malinovsky's troops for robbery, rape, torture and murder than against Zhukov's and Koniev's troops.

If a sergeant-major from the Ukraine in the two first-named armies belittled and vilified an infantryman from Armenia by way of his Armenian ancestors and all their saints, it's doubtful that such verbal exchanges would have been tolerated by a Soviet officer. Soldiers, not malcontents, were needed to fight an enemy.

As proposed to NATO by the United States, the MLF would be an extension of armies manned by mixed nationalities. As the expression of the early 1960s labeled it, the seaborne ships would be "mixed-manned." The Americans intended that the mixed-manning of the MLF be by volunteers, and not by conscripts or mercenaries. Based on the stellar performances of its volunteer services, such as the submarine service and the Marine Corps, the Navy was convinced that the best results would be obtained from volunteers for such an elite service as the MLF was meant to be. Although the vehicle language would be English, volunteers would be the easiest to train in complex weaponry, even in a language foreign to the majority of the crews.

However, this was the first time in history that mixed-manning became a primary form of a military organization.

Although the famed French Foreign Legion permitted anyone to join, it was not a requirement that all Legion units be manned by different nationalities. The latter was incidental. Thus, the French Foreign Legion has always been composed of volunteers, usually escapees of local politics, political refugees, adventurers or even convicted criminals on the run. Yet, French Legionnaires have ranked among the elite combat troops of the world.

Except for a brief period during World War II when the Legion accepted volunteers for the duration of the war, its troops have always been accepted for a specified and extended tour of duty. The 165-year-old Legion still requires an initial enlistment term of ten years. Its officers normally have remained French, and a few top-ranked graduates from France's St. Cyr military academy have traditionally served their first tours with the Legion.

One of the rare official Legion documents appeared *semi-publicly* in a 1950 recruiting brochure entitled "The Truth about the Foreign Legion." In it was the statement, "As many as 52 nationalities have been counted in the Legion, but the most astonishing fact remains that despite the most profound differences a perfect amalgamation of all these men has been realized...if the French language is the vehicle language of the command it serves as a means of unification between everybody...however each is free to use his own native language outside of service..."

Sponsors of the MLF proposed English as the only vehicle language. This was a logical choice since modern languages incorporating words of current technology had been absorbing Americanisms for years, and the common language at technical conferences was broken-English, as it still is in 2000. That fact, plus the proposed location of their training in the United States, made the choice a logical one. In preceding years, the US Navy had trained 13,000 foreigners: 7,000 in 1960 and 6,000 in 1961 for complex applications like ship's operations, missile firing and maintenance. All those US courses had been taught in English.

For over 250 years in every Crusade to the Holy Land, there wasn't even a single vehicle language. In fact, during the First Crusade between 1096 and 1099, Fulcher, a French priest from Chartres, wrote in his diary, "Who had ever heard so many languages in one army before? Here were Franks, Flemings, Lotharginians, Bavarians,

Normans, Angles, Scots, Italians, Britons, Greeks and Armenians all together."

History shows that when Saladin, a Kurd whose family immigrated to Syria, faced the troops of Friedrich Red Beard, emperor of Bavaria and Lombardy, Philippe Auguste, king of France, and Richard the Lion Heart, king of England, in the Third Crusade between 1189 and 1192, he had as many languages under his own command as did his opponents. Eventually, the Anglo-Saxon Richard and the Kurd Saladin fought to a three-year truce in 1192.

When the 13th Demi-Brigade of the French Foreign Legion lost 1,850 Legionnaires out of the 2,000 who attacked the German stronghold at Narvik, Norway, in April, 1940, one of the survivors observed, "Whether on maneuvers or in combat, national differences disappeared. There was no trace of it."

In our studies of the proposed MLF, it soon became apparent to us that national differences entailed far more than language, which had been overcome so often in the past. In varying degrees of importance, individuals attached subjective values to eating habits, religion, discipline, cleanliness, recreation habits and standards of living. Such questions kept bubbling up to challenge us. In addition to these factors, other questions arose related to command and control, two buzz words of the period, and even to segregation by nationalities.

The possibility that the MLF might be a submarine force sent chills down the spines of submarine officers. They faced the possibility of a momentary hesitation due to language in tense submerged situations where hair-trigger reaction might determine whether a submarine could be saved.

The submariners argued that there was no room for hesitation, and there could not be a second's delay in mentally translating an order. Everyone was convinced that split-second reactions in closing a salt-water valve or the emptying of a ballast tank could be the difference in saving a submarine. On the question of mixed-manning of submarines for NATO, the US Navy was united in its opposition. Also, we felt that harnessing nuclear propulsion was more difficult than making a nuclear bomb, and we didn't want to share our advanced state of the art in nuclear submarines with anyone. Period. Congress agreed. The Kennedy administration quietly backed away from any submerged MLF option.

All the voices that counted, the President, McGeorge Bundy, Bob Bowie, Paul Nitze, Assistant Secretary of Defense for International Security Affairs, Dean Rusk, Walt Rostow, and Robert McNamara still preferred the seaborne MLF to any landborne alternative being touted by the Air Force and the Army.

The surface fleets, on the other hand, had overcome mixed-manning for hundreds of years. In 1872, Commodore Stephen B. Luce reported to the Secretary of the Navy, George M. Robeson, that American naval vessels had crews "representing nearly every country on the face of the globe."

Of the five sailing ships in the Mediterranean, Luce added, "over fifty percent are non-Americans representing thirty-five nations."

The pressing question for those of us studying the question went beyond what the great naval strategist Admiral A.T. Mahan wrote, "It will matter little whether the crews of such ships are native or foreign born, provided they are attached to the flag."

The flag-question was just another problem.

Whose flag?

NATO's?

During World War II, many foreigners from countries overrun by Nazi Germany made their way to England and volunteered to fight under England's flag, the Union Jack. It represented a country, and any serviceman made prisoner could fall back on the Geneva Convention, and declare himself a British prisoner-of-war. For example, Royal Air Force Squadron 317, Group II, was made up of Spitfire fighters piloted by Polish volunteers. This was much like the Eagle Squadron made up of American pilots who volunteered before the United States entered the war. The only difference in their RAF uniform was a small shoulder patch inscribed with "Poland," and so on.

In screaming dog fights, these fighters often became separated from their own groups, and joined any other group returning to England, with no discrimination over whether the stragglers were Polish, American, Czech, French, or British. In fact, during the entire war the only oft-repeated discriminatory remark occurred when over a million American military personnel were in England waiting for D-Day. Englishmen often complained that the only thing wrong with Americans was the fact that they were "overbearing, over-sexed, over-paid and over here."

However, back in SP our time and attention were severely affected by the MLF and by all the renewed interest in what we were doing. Invariably, every foreign military and politico-military delegation visiting Washington from a NATO country asked for a briefing on *Polaris*. Suddenly, every Assistant Secretary of Defense started calling on us for these briefings. Even though our numbers had almost doubled because our authorized submarines had tripled, the number of requests strained our relatively small staff. For the first time we were given well-educated interns to ease the workload. Two who crossed my path of 1962 were both extremely attuned to nuclear deterrence, and they were very helpful to Tommy Thompson, John Craven and myself. One, Burton Wides, went on to Capitol Hill and a career as a worldly-wise attorney, and I encouraged the other, Robert E. Hunter, to continue his education at the London School of Economics. He did. Thirty years later, Bob became the US Ambassador to NATO under President Clinton.

One of the most interesting highly classified briefings SP made was to a large NATO delegation on behalf of the NATO Military Committee at the Pentagon. The delegation included senior officers from every branch of service from almost every NATO country. It was standing room only in SP's Management Center as we alternated Navy and key contractor-speakers in and out to make space for our visitors. Some of our industrial scientists had once been scientists who worked on Hitler's secret weapons in World War II. The V-1 rockets had been launched from the secret base at Peenemünde on a small German island in the Baltic Sea, close to today's Polish border. The visiting West German military officers knew that several former German scientists worked for us and were anxious to meet some of them once the briefing ended.

One of our important contractors, Aerojet General, produced our rocket motors, and its key speaker was Werner Kirchner who, incidentally, had never lost what sounded to me like a thick, old-fashioned Prussian accent. Not lost on the visiting German brass was that same Kirchner accent, and as soon as they could during the post-briefing socializing, they approached him. A Luftwaffe officer asked him, "Did you vly in the vor?"

"*Ja*, more than vour years," answered Vern.

"Ah, zo. Vas it a Messerschmitt? I vas a fighter pilot, too."

"*Nein*. I vlew Spitfires." (Vern pronounced it: *schpitfires*.)

Kirchner had escaped from his native Poland when it was overrun by Germany in 1939, and made his way to the Middle East and then back to France. Despite the fact that he learned to fly in the French Air Force, he ended up in the French army because there were no planes for him. After France capitulated in 1940, he made his way to England and flew in a Spitfire fighter squadron. His shoulder patch had spelled out *Poland*. I watched Vern and the German officer examine each other, and wondered (as I'm sure they did, too) if they had ever met in aerial combat.

Then Vern broke the ice, "Let me tell you about our rocket engines. Did you know that jetavators steered our early versions of *Polaris*, they were invented by Willie Fiedler. Willie was at Peenemünde—he even test flew a V-1. I used to shoot those down—over London or over the Channel if I could catch them there."

Guiding the Luftwaffe officer by the elbow, he added, "Come on. Let me introduce you to the Lockheed people. Willie works for them."

All the time I was at SP our team always included a few German scientific refugees from Peenemünde, for whom we had arranged citizenship. Dr. Wernher von Braun was probably the most important, at least the most famous ex-German scientist in the United States, and the Army placed him at the Redstone Arsenal where von Braun helped to develop all of America's biggest rockets. As a teenager he had experimented with rockets at the *Raketenplatz* in Berlin, and worshipped Professor Hermann Oberth, one of the giant figures in rocket history.

Because SP had been thrown into bed with the *Jupiter* missile in the early days, von Braun was well known to us. One day I studied some captured wartime German photos in Maryland, and one was unmistakingly of von Braun in his early twenties standing next to his idol, Oberth. I called von Braun to ask him if he already had this photograph from the 1930s.

"No. I remember when it was taken and I've looked for it for almost twenty-five years," answered von Braun, "How did you find it?" he asked with growing excitement in his voice.

After he heard all the details, he asked eagerly, "Can you get me a print?"

I arranged to send him a few.

Von Braun was a very proud man. I recall that in the early 1960s there was a popular watering hole in Washington called Ebbet's Bar and Grill. On one full wall was a Rogue's gallery with hundreds of framed photographs, some autographed, of famous people. For a short while the only one in color was the one of von Braun.

Command and control are normal functions when a crew is an all-American one, with a single loyalty. The MLF presented a singular problem because it went beyond an American missile in a foreign country, where the host country, even if an ally, might demand equal authority with launching a nuclear-tipped missile from its territory. In such a case, the solution was a dual key system, wherein each country's representative had a key. In a submarine under the sea, or in a ICBM silo in the midwest, an American officer would receive an order, and the commander would order his troops to prepare for a launch. He would have strict controls over the missile and over the codes for arming the warhead. However, the application of this simple concept of command and control became clouded and convoluted when four of five nationalities became involved in the launching of a nuclear weapon.

Questions were raised about situations when the United States might want to launch, and of the four remaining officers, were two of nationalities of countries opposing the order, and two others in favor; or whether the four foreigners might want to, but the American did not. The most frequently asked question for the next year from every country in NATO was, "Whose finger is on the trigger?"

Furious about the idea of a NATO nuclear force, the Soviets both harangued the west about the idea and ridiculed it. Soviet First Deputy Foreign Minister Vasily V. Kuznetsov attended a 17-nation disarmament conference in Geneva where he accused the United States of plotting to proliferate nuclear arms by giving non-nuclear nations, in particular West Germany, "a finger on the nuclear trigger."

Snickered Kuznetsov, "The United States insists that sailors from non-nuclear powers only scrub decks and polish the anchor, and have nothing to do with the ship's rockets."

The Navy, including SP, wrestled with MLF command and control and its many unacceptable solutions, and struggled with solutions whose definitions defied easy articulation. The *Polaris* weapons system had many key positions at many levels of the submarine, and in different centers on the same deck. Several officers had to perform precise functions as well as many crewmen in order to launch a missile. The warhead required arming and targeting. At the time we faced all the MLF riddles, we already had controls that required key "veto" actions, especially in the last actions to accurately launch a missile. One of the key actions related to the alignment of the missile, to establish its *local vertical*, whose importance was discussed earlier and was so critical that the man who performed it was given a "dead man's switch."

A dead man's switch was similar in application to a common exercise device to strengthen a person's grip by squeezing the device repeatedly. The device I have in mind is the one with two short wooden handles about five inches long. One end of each handle is connected to the other by a single hinge and a strong metal spring. When unused, the spring keeps the handles apart. It only works when the user applies enough strength to draw the two handles close to each other. Another dead man's switch resembled a trigger of a revolver.

If the submariner died before completing his action, his death would cut the power from the dead man's switch, and that would interrupt the countdown and stop the launch. If not, only God would know where that missile might go, regardless of the targeting instructions. This is only one example of the controls incorporated in our *Polaris*-launching nuclear submarines. In any event, one major problem to solve was how to make sure the MLF missile would be fired under appropriate authority. The second problem was to make sure there would be no unauthorized launch.

These busy problems closed the curtain on 1961, and our new director, Admiral I.J. Galantin, and my colleagues in SP geared up all their grit to be responsive in 1962 to President Kennedy's initiative with NATO.

Chapter 7

The evolution of new weapons

Admittedly, spying on our nation's enemies took many different forms, and vice versa. Rather than take chances, we always assumed the enemy was more intelligent than we thought we were, and the most prudent souls assumed the enemy was a lot more. Consequently all measures to protect our advantages were employed to prevent unauthorized disclosures to anyone.

I recall when a CIA newsletter with restricted distribution reproduced good photographs taken inside a Soviet missile-launching submarine. I don't think it was a nuclear submarine because other intelligence suggested the Soviet Union had yet to perfect that type of propulsion.

In one photograph were a couple of equipment racks, and many of us instinctively examined the racks with a magnifying glass to determine whether the Soviets had purchased some "Made in the USA" equipment. Nonetheless, almost all racks in the world were about the same size, and we compared the racks to other consoles and computers in the photograph to try determining the room size and the Soviets' ability to miniaturize, depending on what we thought their consoles were used for. Even the position of toggle switches, buttons and dials, and their height from the deck *told* us a great deal about Soviet submarines and crews. But publishing the photo's date might point an accusing finger at our source, and virtually guarantee a death sentence to that source. It was not unusual for the Soviets to accuse one of their own of treason or sabotage, and to torture to death the accused in front of his peers as a good lesson in Soviet citizenship.

More than once a valuable agent inside Soviet intelligence was executed by sliding him *live* into an incinerator in front of his work colleagues. Thus was lost a valuable resource to the United States, and often the denunciation was made to the Soviet espionage organization, KGB, by British, French, German, and even American traitors in exchange for cash. For these reasons we were often reluctant to share such photographs with our allies or anyone without a need to know because if the information or copies were leaked to Communist agents, the arrangement of equipment in the racks could narrow the time-line enough to identify who had been in the Soviet submarine at the time the photograph had been taken.

Periodically in SP we had meetings called the "Polaris/SSBN Steering Task Group or STG" which had been instituted by Admiral Raborn, and I think by Captain (later Admiral) Levering Smith. The "Advanced Sea-Based Deterrent" component of the STG was very much the domain of out Chief Scientist, Dr. John Craven. Whenever we discussed or wrote about where our research was leading, it reflected the state of the art of the United States. Nothing was more highly classified than that type of information, and the distribution list was restricted to individuals with a strict need to know.

I had been talking to Dr. "Tommy" Thompson and Captain Dick Shutt about a long range guided missile to be launched from a submerged submarine's torpedo tube. Our idea was to use a guidance system similar to the one proposed by the USAF for their *Skybolt* air-to-surface missile, the same missile that the RAF wanted for its V bombers. We wrestled with a type of guidance using terrain recognition of land features, instead of inertial or radar-guidance. However, the dark cloud over our idea was the fact that the Air Force had so much trouble with *Skybolt*'s guidance. "If they can't solve an airborne problem," asked Tommy, "how do you think we will?"

In fact, both President Kennedy and Secretary McNamara had dropped hints to British officials about these same guidance problems that troubled us about *Skybolt* during our study of a new missile in SP.

For reasons I never knew, Dick Shutt had already christened the missile *Venus*, another celestial body like the North Star *Polaris*. But the idea was limited by factors like the size of conventional torpedo tubes, the specific impulse (like octane in gasoline) of the solid propellants of the 1962's state of the art, and the size of nuclear warheads. We wanted *Venus* to have the right diameter and length to fit in the torpedo racks that all our submarines would have for years-to-come, and a warhead small enough to fit and light enough to give the missile a range of 500 to 1000 nautical miles, and for it to fly low enough to avoid radar-detection—unlike a ballistic missile. True, a conventional warhead could be fitted on *Venus*, just as on any missile or in any bomb, but the trick was to be able to use one or the other. In any case, *Venus* was an extremely attractive idea and we pursued it.

In particular, I wanted to catch some time with John Craven whose back-office Tommy and I shared, and go through a matrix of possibilities with him. Most of the state of the art for *Venus* existed on a potential basis yet our matrix discussion centered on (1) why, when and where it was needed and (2) our nuclear options. I was very much hung up on small nuclear yields, and very opposed to the use of biggies like 1 MT or even 100 KT. This was in line with President Kennedy's flexible response doctrine.

Some of our scientists had run mathematical problems involving several small nuclear devices delivered to enemy targets in clusters, and they theorized that three "small" devices properly placed could generate more destruction than a single warhead five times larger in capacity than the combined capacity of the three "small" ones. It appeared to us that the progress made by the AEC could easily fit *Venus* with one of these "small" ones for a nuclear warhead. It was out of discussions like this one that the idea for clustering small warheads for Navy and Air Force missiles was born. Insofar as targets susceptible to a cluster treatment, there were a group of officers in Dick Shutt's branch who were experts at identifying proper targets. In fact, they were headed by a fighter pilot, Commander Pat Burnham, one of the brightest individuals the Navy had in operations research.

We didn't limit our knowledge to *Venus* because we had modified versions of *Polaris* to worry about. From these meetings in preparation for the STG of 17 to 19 January 1962 came the adaptation of findings from a top secret project called *Project Winston*.

In those days, there were radio and television advertisements that claimed, "It's what's up front that counts," and had to do with cigarettes and their filters.

Ironically, *Winston* had nothing to do with nuclear devices nor cigarettes, but the extrapolations of its findings permitted the United States to experiment with maneuverable re-entry bodies. Later, these were called MIRVs, the acronym for Multiple Independently Targeted Re-Entry Vehicles. For the United States, MIRVs constituted an important element for the deterrence value of the *Polaris A-3* and its succeeding versions. Upon these building blocks the United States took a commanding lead in the scientific state of the art in the world, and reversed the short-lived lead that *Sputnik* had indisputably given the Soviet Union in 1957.

Because of Kennedy's flexible response criterion, and Robert McNamara's complete support for it, "More bang per buck" meant just that. Weapons had to be reliable and worth the cost, or else. This caused evolution in the design of all major missile systems. For example, Norstad's call for a MRBM soon became a USAF MMRBM—a Mobile Mid-Range Ballistic Missile.

Actually the Air Force and the Army did everyone a favor by pushing their versions of a MMRBM and a modified surface-to-surface *Pershing* for so-called *tactical nuclear interdiction*. That was the new doctrine of using *small* nuclear bombs, shells or warheads to slow down any Soviet ground invasion in Europe. However, ever since 1945 everyone had been betting on *bigger and better nukes*, but the new notions of tactical interdiction revealed the sorry fact that we really didn't have any *small* nuclear weapons. The need for *small* nuclear weapons opened another option, one that fit *Venus* quite nicely.

As if we weren't already busy enough, the Defense Department and the Chief of Naval Operations booted a European NATO MLF proposal to SP for study and comment. At the same time, Thomas D. Morris, Assistant Secretary of Defense for Installations and Logistics, asked me to prepare a special SP briefing for French General Lavaud and his staff. All I can recall is that the Lavaud delegation was involved with France's own IRBM program which President de Gaulle called the *force de frappe*, a strike force for France's independent nuclear deterrent. Morris sent Admiral Galantin, SP's new director, and me a commendation for arranging that Lavaud briefing on short notice.

I can't deny that there was considerable hostility to De Gaulle's policy at the State Department and elsewhere in Washington, which reflected itself at the working level at State and at the United States Embassy in Paris. Whenever De Gaulle made a speech and statement on nuclear matters I would ask for the official translation as soon as possible. However, State took so long that I started getting the French language copy almost immediately from the French Embassy in

Washington, as well as the relevant news item from *Agence France Presse* which was the French equivalent to the Associated Press and other English language news services. Because I was bi-lingual, I could immediately ascertain whether anything De Gaulle said impacted on our activities at SP, and usually it did. I'd so advise Navy authorities if and when it did. Later, I would receive the State Department's official translation, read it over and file it.

As time went on, I started noticing that these translations from State or from the US Embassy in Paris often exhibited an unnecessarily hostile spin in the choice of verbs or adjectives in the English translations of De Gaulle's comments. These same translations went to the White House and were promulgated throughout Washington and went to any news bureaus that requested copies. There was no question in my mind that someone was performing a disservice to the United States by intentionally misleading higher authority about a foreign leader's statements. After several such instances I prepared an "observation paper" for my contacts at the State Department and the White House. In it I simply showed the examples in French and in the translations, and pointed out the bias in what our agencies were producing.

The practice stopped. I suspected that the White House had put its foot down, and State eventually transferred a few individuals out of Paris. Someone later told me that one of the most hostile individuals to De Gaulle had been a former military intelligence operative during World War II who performed translations at the embassy. I never did learn how much harm someone's personal agenda could have done to undermine United States policy planning or our relations with France. I guess we'll never know.

President Kennedy was very alert to the problem of nuclear proliferation, whether it was via the MLF or via America's help to the United Kingdom with *Skybolt*. Russia, of course, had the H-bomb, and both England and France had demonstrated their own atomic weapons, and Communist China was busy developing one that would be detonated in 1964. Because of the McMahon Act as amended, Kennedy inherited both the incoherent UK problem and France's jealous fits from the Eisenhower administration. In addition, the UK and France experienced sorry examples of losing secrets to Soviet spies, and Congress was very alert to the loss of US secrets via one country or the other. But the French were languid, inept and less outraged in explaining theirs, convincing Congress that losing secrets was somehow a little dirtier in a foreign language. According to presidential biographer Theodore C. Sorensen, President Kennedy "saw no point in a small independent British deterrent anyway."

Kennedy opposed these small independent deterrents, like France's was intended to be, and had written, "If we are to be caught up in a nuclear war, should we not have a voice in the decision that launches it?" Everyone close to the issue knew that London and Paris would have forces potent enough to unleash nuclear war, maybe one the United States might oppose, but inevitably America would be sucked in and would pay the consequences.

Kennedy had pulled in some of the best minds in the country to sort out the contradictions in the nuclear deterrence and the nuclear proliferation issues. In the Department of Defense was Paul H. Nitze, Assistant Secretary of Defense for International Security Affairs. Within Defense, he was the closest thing to a Secretary of State that the Pentagon had. Immediately after World War II, Nitze had been involved in the American assessment of strategic aerial bombardment. That study revealed weaknesses and strengths of these bombardments, whether by day or by night. These studies, like those related to Hitler's buzz bomb and rocket attacks on England and Belgium, often startled readers, like the fact that only 40% of the V-2 rockets launched against London actually reached England!

In one week in 1943, 43,000 Germans died from allied air raids on Hamburg, and later, 135,000 Germans died from raids on Dresden. An employee of mine had been a war prisoner who had been a part of the French "slave labor corps" working in a German armaments factory outside the city limits of Dresden. He told me later, "Usually the German guards marched us out of our barracks, and made us sit on a high hill during the air raids. We looked down on the city and watched a blanket of fire from one end of Dresden to the other. It was terrible for the Germans in Dresden."

In a single incendiary raid over Tokyo in March, 1945, over 80,000 Japanese were killed and over 100,000 injured, and sixteen square miles of Tokyo were destroyed.

President Harry S. Truman permitted witnesses and journalists to monitor the *Able* nuclear explosion at Bikini Atoll in the Pacific on 30 June 1946, hoping that it would help to convince nations to enact nuclear arms control. However, the opposite proved true and it reinforced the opinion of an already convinced Soviet Union that she needed nuclear weapons of her own. The American monopoly had lasted four years, from the Alamogordo blast on 16 July 1945 to 29 August 1949 when the first Soviet nuclear detonation occurred in the atmosphere. Shortly thereafter the United States detonated its first hydrogen (thermonuclear) bomb at Eniwetok on 31 October 1952 with a force equivalent to 10 megatons. The American H-bomb monopoly lasted less than ten months because Soviet scientists were as efficient as their spies. But the H-bomb at Eniwetok added a startling dimension to the concept of destructiveness.

A 10 MT blast can produce a crater six hundred feet deep and a half-mile across. Millions of tons of dirt, rock and buildings would be piled into a lip around the crater in a three-mile circle. Thousand of tons near the center would simply vaporize and become part of a fireball attaining the temperature of the sun. By the time John Kennedy had been elected president, some people claimed that the USSR and the USA had stockpiled enough nuclear weapons to represent 40,000 pounds of TNT for each man, woman and child in the world!

Despite Khrushchev's rancorous exhibition of desk-pounding with his shoe and fists at the United Nations, there was as much serious consideration in Moscow as in Washington about a ban on nuclear testing. Often the sides transposed their own positions over time, as each proposed one set of rules for disarmament and inspection, only to reverse positions when it was discovered that the state of the art didn't support the proposals, or that more tests were needed. The disarmament talks were a three-ring propaganda circus which resulted in each side going full circle in its own position. Often, this was directly influenced by detection problems.

An underground explosion reacts according to the type of substance the nearby terrain is composed of; such as tuff, alluvial deposits, salt, granite and so forth. A 90-kiloton underground explosion coupled in tuff is equal to an earthquake of a magnitude of 5 1/4. Any earthquake of a Richter value of 6 or below was not considered a major event. Out of the estimated 10,000 annual earthquakes on earth, only some 50 (a half of 1%) were equal to a magnitude of 6 or higher. Because the Richter scale is logarithmic, a 7 is ten times as powerful as a 6.

One of the greatest earthquakes in history occurred on Good Friday, 27 March 1964, near Alaska's Kodiak Island when the ocean floor rose fifty feet and hit the Richter scale at 8.3. Had the earthquake occurred in a densely populated area, the death toll would have been disastrous. In 1920, 180,000 were killed by a quake in China, and in 1923, a Japanese quake killed 143,000. In the case of an earthquake equivalent to a 90-kiloton blast, such as the one in central Asia on 7 January 1958, which had a magnitude of 5 1/4, most of the world's seismographs didn't even record it!

After 1958, great strides had been perfected, but were still limited, in the art of detecting earthquakes or underground atomic tests. But during Kennedy's presidency, it was not always possible to identify which of the two events had occurred, even with the best instrumentation and techniques. Once a suspicious event happened, the only way to really be sure what happened was to send an inspection team quickly into the area before the evidence disappeared, and that was the key factor behind the arguments about "on-site inspections."

In one small 3KT test, 1,200 feet below the ground surface, an infrared investigation revealed vegetation reflectance. This disappeared after nine days. Had it been necessary for an inspection team to go to the site, the delays associated with mobilization, movement of scientific equipment and just plain travel time to a remote area would probably have precluded finding any evidence on site. Remote mountainous areas up the Asian Pacific coast and up the western coast of the United States are active seismic areas and near the very areas where most underground nuclear tests were apt to be conducted. Consequently, the issue of site inspection was compounded by normal travel and border-crossing problems, and having the right equipment at the right place.

Aerial inspection could help but could not perform the complete verification by itself. While an underground test sometimes produced cracks in the earth's surface, that was not always the case, and could be extremely difficult to find without some reliable seismic data. Among the difficulties that the United States and the Soviet Union faced was aerial inspection for underground nuclear tests and for arms control verification for a finite number of rockets in an arms control situation.

In the latter case, one must explore the potential of the weapons and the military or political consequences of deception or cheating.

Militarily, two hundred nuclear armed intercontinental ballistic missiles might appear sufficient to destroy all the major population areas of any country or of any block of countries. Even an imbalance of nuclear forces, such as 235 to 200, hardly gives an important advantage to one country. Perhaps 275 to 200 is an important difference, although doubtful to some people, and a country disposed to cheating would want to hide at least seventy-five missiles (37%) more than its quota. Politically, a nation caught cheating would, after relaxing tensions in an overwrought world, face serious damage to its reputation.

This so-called damage to some people might appear tenuous and unrealistic enough to warrant a gamble on a treaty. Many books have been written to expose all these problems, and the discussion here is simply to remind the reader of the many unanswered questions and problems that existed during the Kennedy administration.

In 1994 I spoke with an American inspector who oversaw the destruction of Russian missiles under the Strategic Arms Reduction Treaty (START I). His job was to visually observe compliance. How he proceeded was enlightening. He would actually walk and inspect a ex-Soviet long range missile whose warhead and guidance capsule had been removed. He'd inspect the solid-fueled rocket motors while they were separated to safe distances from one another. Then, with another American observer never diverting his eyes from those rocket motors by looking out a rear window, he'd drive to an observation site well away from and above the rocket motors. With the use of binoculars they'd watch the static testing of each rocket motor until the solid fuel burned out. Such an inspection was unthinkable during the 1960s.

Secrecy in both the Soviet Union and in the United States was valued so highly that in the minds of militarists in both camps it was the most highly prized and shielded asset. To lose a missile or a warhead to the other side would at the same time reveal all one country's strength and its weakness. The American nuclear weapons lost at sea in 1966 near Palomares, Spain, showed to what extent and extremes the US would undertake the means to recover all parts of a nuclear weapons system.

The truth within NATO in 1962 was that France and Britain just didn't believe that the United States would risk losing New York or Kansas City to save Manchester or Strasbourg or even Hamburg. Because the Soviet forces in East Europe had such an overwhelming advantage over NATO's ground forces in West Europe, our allies wanted an immediate nuclear response or a pre-emptive strike, using American nuclear weapons in a first strike. Such an exchange would automatically signal the start of an all-out nuclear exchange against targets in the United States, something that President Kennedy wanted to avoid. Hence, his call for a build-up of conventional forces to hold off any aggression from the east. He wanted options for a flexible response.

However, the Germans who were on the first line of any invasion route insisted on the first strike option, and wanted an automatic US nuclear response if the Warsaw Pact invaded first or threatened to do so. As far as the Germans were concerned, they wanted the United States in a guaranteed response straight jacket, with no wiggle room.

However, if each European NATO ally could get a finger on the MLF trigger, then that might offer additional guarantees. Meanwhile, Kennedy was forcing NATO allies to build up their conventional forces for the precise reason that he wanted options to slow up any Soviet aggression in Europe. He wanted time to think—exactly what the West Germans didn't want.

Everyone involved with the MLF knew, however, that if a nuclear missile landed on Moscow, no one in Russia could be sure where it came from. From England? From France? From an American nuclear submarine in the Mediterranean? From an ICBM silo in Wyoming or Colorado? No one I knew in Washington had any doubt where the Soviet Union would unload to get even. Our role as we saw it in SP was to make that latter option so painful to the Soviet Union that the godless Communists would hesitate, think twice and hopefully back off such a decision.

Meanwhile *Venus* made its way to Chief of Naval Operations and to the Office of the Secretary of Defense. I've often wondered since then whether *Venus* had been the precursor of both the USAF *Cruise Missile* and the Navy *Tomahawk* used in the Middle East during and after the Gulf War—thirty-six years later.

Chapter 8

Political pressure on military developments

Much to President Eisenhower's credit was his willingness to shine the spotlight on the dangers to the public from the "military-industrial complex" and its influence in American politics. Just before Eisenhower turned over the executive reins to John F. Kennedy, he used the occasion of his farewell address to highlight this *problem* to the American public.

Eisenhower's point was not about corruption or buying political influence, but the want and need of public recognition for what the danger was. No industry had to out-and-out bribe a congressman or a senator when all the pressures needed to mobilize a favorable vote on appropriations were those applied by local communities needing employment for their citizens, local unions needing jobs for their members, and retail trade boards and chambers of commerce lobbying on behalf of the added payrolls of their local defense industries. But Eisenhower had seen unscrupulous defense contractors use congressional hearings to embarrass and intimidate civilian officials inside the Defense Department in an effort to receive unjustified approval for weapons systems or to receive unrequested extra funds through supplemental appropriations.

To understand the economics of the Cold War independently from expenditures for great naval ships, highly performing aircraft and sophisticated missile systems is like trying to explain scurvy, the centuries-old curse of sailing crews, without any reference to some vegetables, certain citrus fruits, fresh tea leaves or Vitamin C.

Although small rockets had been around for centuries, the first meaningful application was by the Germans in World War II and was the successor to the V-1 buzz bomb, a sort of unmanned flying bomb with wings, that could be shot down by fighter planes. The *real* missile was the V-2 rocket. Weighing about 28,000 pounds, it was a liquid-fueled rocket with minimum guidance that used alcohol as its fuel and liquid oxygen as its oxidizer. Because its range was limited to about 180 miles, the Germans used trailers as mobile launchers and moved them close to the English Channel in occupied Netherlands, France and elsewhere. The rocket climbed about 100 miles in a programmed flight and dove toward its target at a speed between 3,000 and 4,000 miles per hour. Used only late in the war, the V-2s inflicted several thousand deaths on the English, mostly in or around London. Out of the 3,300 V-2s launched by the Germans, only 1,300 actually arrived anywhere near their intended targets. It was a cumbersome weapon—sixty-four feet tall—and its oxidizer was difficult and very dangerous to handle.

Because airplanes represented the most efficient means to deliver conventional bombs as well as the huge, heavy atomic bombs, there was no great rush to develop military missiles after the war, and it was only when the new H-bomb permitted the design of smaller nuclear warheads that the military took second looks at missiles.

Even without Khrushchev's threats at the time of the Suez invasion in October 1956 and the Soviet's scientific triumph twelve months later with *Sputnik*, America's scientists and military leaders were already embarked in an arms race with the Soviet Union. Although at times it seemed that only Eisenhower wouldn't fan the flames of this competition for what it was, or that his was the sole patient voice in the public din that followed.

On center stage the first interservice antagonists were the Army and the Air Force. Arguing that missiles were an extension of artillery and ballistics, the principles of which hadn't changed since the manuals were published in the seventeenth century, the Army developed the sixty-nine-foot *Redstone* and the equally tall *Jupiter*. Both were liquid-fueled and developed by the Wernher von Braun team in Huntsville, Alabama. Although the *Redstone* had a tactical range of only 200 miles, *Jupiter* had a 1,500-mile-range which put it in the strategic IRBM category, and it would eventually be deployed by the US Army in Italy and Turkey, both NATO allies.

On the other hand, the Air Force argued that missiles were a logical extension of strategic bombing, but with additional speed to boot. The

USAF was working on an *Atlas* missile with a range of 5,500 miles to carry a warhead equivalent to several megatons, and was also working on a *Thor* missile with a limited range of 1,500 miles. Although everyone cited the ranges of missiles in miles, these ranges were actually nautical miles—about 15% longer than the statute or land mile. In any event, the *Thor* would eventually be deployed in England. In effect, these *Thors* and *Jupiters* encircled the Soviet Union, but lacked accuracy and large payloads.

A ballistic path of an IRBM usually carried it a few hundred miles above the earth and its reentry body approached an enemy target at around 7000 to 8000 mph, but an ICBM might attain a height of about 750 to 900 miles (three times higher than the Soviet *Mir* space station in the 1990s) and approach a target at 15,000 mph. Because of the differences in the distances traveled, an IRBM took about 15 to 20 minutes to reach a target, while an ICBM reentry body took about a half hour. Consequently, the reaction time for an enemy to launch a counterattack or an anti-missile missile varied between 15 and 30 minutes. This was sometimes called response time, and the military services went to great efforts to shorten the elapsed time between an authorization to launch and the actual blast off.

The challenge to the Air Force particularly was to survive the difference in the amount of time that a missile crew had to launch a retaliatory strike after radar defenses alerted Washington that an enemy missile was approaching the United States. Claims of response times ranged in exaggerations from ridiculous assertions of 15 seconds to technically achievable twenty minutes with certain missiles. The trouble with these claims then was the fact that no president would relinquish or delegate to others his right to decide if and when to launch nuclear weapons. Both Eisenhower and Kennedy kept tight reins on these presidential prerogatives. Nonetheless, the military services had to address the readiness problems, and their solutions cost far more than ever admitted to the US taxpayers.

Most inertial guidance systems in missiles used advanced gyros, and the devices had to be *spun up* to be useful. To keep them spun up and in a state of immediate readiness was technically possible but very expensive because of their short life span in maintaining the accuracy needed for long range missiles. Not only were initial procurement costs high, but so were maintenance and replacement costs. The basic budgetary reality of the time-delay to receive presidential authorization actually mitigated in favor of letting the gyros *sit* until being spun up before a launch. In interservice meetings it was not unusual to hear a senior commander of ICBM squadrons bemoan the fact that ICBMs wouldn't be given a *technical threshold-trigger* to launch without waiting for a presidential decision.

As frightening as that thought was then, and certainly still is today, a lengthy treatise could define what-if situations wherein such a trigger might be the only solution to save the United States. Some scary cases in point would be some versions of *Star Wars* and of anti-missile missiles with nuclear warheads. Without presidential derogations the very reasons justifying such weapons would be null and void. Yet, another nation's ability to launch a first strike against the United States will remain justification for research and development even though society's ability to govern hasn't caught up with technological innovation any more in 2000 than it had in 1962.

Because the nuclear response business was, and is, so demanding, secretive and frightening, it was normal for the top brass in each service to want thinkers and doers around them who could be relied upon.

The Army tended to use contractors who were a known-value, like Chrysler Corporation, Martin Orlando, Bendix's Eclipse-Pioneer Division, FMC Corporation, Collins Radio, Rocketdyne, Thiokol, Sperry Farragut, Philco Aeronutronic, General Motors-Cadillac Division, Western Electric, and Firestone Tire. Many of these corporations have since merged, been bought out by others or have taken on new names. But in 1962 they were household names of the Cold War. However, even if occasional industrial contracting overlapped between the services, some missile contractors stayed identified with one particular service, especially the think tanks.

The Air Force was strongly identified with Martin Denver, AMF, North American Aviation, General Electric and Burroughs, General Dynamics, Martin, Aerojet, Boeing, Hughes Aircraft, Sperry Rand, Thiokol, Hercules, Goodyear, AC Sparkplug, Fairchild and General Precision.

By the time *Polaris* came along, we picked Lockheed as our prime contractor; Aerojet General and Hercules and others for propulsion; General Electric, MIT, and Hughes for inertial guidance; Westinghouse for our launching system, Sperry for the inertial navigation system in the submarine, and others. As for think tanks, I had always wanted to visit Rand but was persona non grata because Rand was usually reserved for Air Force problem-solving. In SP we used Stanford Research Institute, MIT, and Harvard quite often, and generally gave research funds to our Navy laboratories and to other universities around the country. Likewise, the Army and the Air Force spread their own research money because we all strove to pick the best minds available. When it came to buying and cultivating brain power, no service was bashful.

As for *Skybolt*, Douglas Aircraft was the prime contractor, but in England, the Royal Air Force concentrated its budget on the V-bombers to carry the USAF missile. The older Valiant bombers were being replaced by the newer Vulcan and Victor bombers, all designed to carry the 500-mile-range British *Blue Steel* air-to-surface missile until the *Skybolt* became operational. The major contractors for the 35-foot *Blue Steel* with its four-foot-diameter body were Hawker Siddeley Dynamics, part of A. V. Roe; Elliott Brothers for guidance, and Bristol Siddeley Engines for propulsion.

The British *Blue Streak*, earmarked for space applications after its military cancellation, was produced by de Havilland, a subsidiary of Hawker Siddeley Dynamics. For the most part, the aerospace defense industry in Great Britain was always concentrated in the same companies, most of which were partially owned by the government. In France, however, almost every single defense contractor was 100% owned, controlled and managed by the government—almost the exact opposite of the defense industry in the United States. Exceptions in France like the private company Dassault Aircraft were few.

Carrying De Gaulle's program for an independent nuclear strike force was the private company Dassault for the French airborne deterrent by building advanced *Mirage* fighter-bombers. But the naval shipyards and the defense contractors included many governmental organizations that had been absorbed, expanded or taken over. The notable ones at that time included Société pour l'Étude et la Réalisation d'Engins Balistiques (SEREB), the Groupe Technique de Cannes a subsidiary of Sud Aviation. Inside the SEREB agency, often considered the IRBM agency for France, were Sud Aviation, Nord Aviation, the engine company SNECMA, the electronics and propulsion organization MATRA and the propulsion agency SEPR. All the major French electronics and telecommunications companies were also involved. The major difference between the efforts of Britain and France was the fact that France was doing the development and achievement by its own bootstraps.

For testing its rockets, France used the missile test facilities at Colomb-Béchar in nearby Algeria, and Britain used the Woomera

Missile Range in distant Australia. While Britain developed its *blue* series: *Blue Streak, Blue Steel* and the tactical *Blue Water*, France developed its *precious stones series*: Diamond, Emerald, Sapphire, Ruby and Topaze (*Diamant, Emeraude, Saphir, Rubis* and *Topaze*). The amalgamation of these and their end product for the French program looked remarkably like our *Polaris*.

Several British defense contractors, like Elliott Brothers (London), A.V. Roe, English Electric and Ferranti, transferred technical personnel to Woomera at the edge of the great Australian deserts, and to the Salisbury Missile Depot, about seven miles north of Adelaide, and 285 miles south of Woomera. To accommodate the overland testing, Australia set aside a 275-mile-wide shooting corridor extending 1,250 miles over its aboriginal territories to Talgarno on the shore of the Indian Ocean. Once nothing more than a shacktown, Woomera grew to a scientific boomtown of over 4,500, and water was piped in 107 miles to support the town's new population.

In a similar move, France transferred over 5,000 technical and scientific personnel to its former French Foreign Legion post at Colomb-Béchar. The entire area was converted to serve as the staging point for all long range, surface-launched or air-launched missile tests. Missiles with a range under a thousand miles would land in Algeria, but thereafter those with a greater range would overfly or land in the Republic of Niger, or the Republic of Chad. Like the Woomera range, the Algerian shooting corridor was largely over deserts and mountainous plateaus, sparsely used by nomads and caravans.

Probably no modern era was as complex in weaponry as was 1962. Usually a mission was defined and a system was designed to fulfill it. After the subsystems were developed and tested, a new weapons system took its place in the armed forces. Sometimes, a new weapon was conceived and the responsible service and its *intended* contractors hit the hustings and beat the bushes to find a mission for it.

The major missile systems that captured most of the attention included the US Army's operational 34.5-foot *Sergeant*, a tactical weapon with a range of 25 to 75 miles, and the 35-foot *Pershing* with a tactical range between 100 and 400 miles. The first nuclear-tipped *Pershings* started to arrive in Germany for the US troops stationed there in late 1962. The only NATO competition to the *Sergeant* was the British *Blue Water*. Both missiles had been developed to meet NATO's military requirement to make available "battlefield-type atomic weapons" for brigade-sized units of 4,000 men. This pitted the manufacturers, English Electric and its parent British Aircraft Corporation, against Sperry Utah Engineering Laboratories, manufacturers of the *Sergeant*.

The US Air Force really had no competition for its big missiles: the 53.7-foot *Minuteman*, the 98-foot *Titan I*, the 103-foot *Titan II* and the 82.5-foot *Atlas*. All except *Minuteman* used liquid fuel, had huge base diameters of ten feet or more and demanded the greatest precautions and discipline to fuel up while in a mandatory vertical position. The nuclear warheads they could deliver ranged into the twin digits—15, 20MT. The newer and smaller *Minuteman* had a diameter of six feet, a 1MT warhead, far more precision, and its solid fuel permitted it to have a technical response or reaction time of 32 seconds (once its gyro was spun). Only by overcoming problems of long lead-time real estate acquisition, breaking many technological barriers, setting new metallurgical standards and training crews long before the overall designs were completed was the Air Force able to deploy so many missiles in so short a time as it did.

Complete new terminology was invented, and squadrons could now contain six *Atlas* missiles instead of twelve or more fighter planes. Also in the Air Force's hip pocket was a competitor for the British *Blue Steel*, the air-launched *Hound Dog*. It was a 42.5-foot cruise-type inertially guided missile manufactured by North American Aviation. In order not to have this missile compete with *Skybolt*, the Air Force maintained publicly that *Hound Dog*, despite the fact it was operational, had a lower priority than *Skybolt*, and would be used as a stand-off weapon to destroy enemy defenses. Once these defenses were neutralized, the Air Force's B-52 bombers could penetrate enemy territory to reach their targets.

At the end of 1962, the staunchest supporter of counterforce and of overwhelming retaliation, General Curtis LeMay, was scheduled to become the Air Force Chief of Staff. If ever there were a person willing to use his finger to draw a line in the sand it was LeMay. He was a tough-talking, cigar-smoking military officer who thought nothing of baiting a Soviet officer at Washington receptions, and was eager to gather all long range American missiles under the aegis of the Air Force. I had always considered LeMay as a reincarnation of General George Patton, but with wings on his chest instead of pearlhandled six shooters at his sides, and I learned first hand that LeMay had aligned his gunsights on *Polaris*.

On that occasion I had gone to Port Canaveral to set out on our submarine SSB(N) 608 *Ethan Allen* to monitor key launch steps that might have an important bearing on the issue of command and control for a MLF surface ship. Although we were scheduled to launch an advanced 30.5-foot *Polaris A-2*, that hadn't influenced my choice to board her, other than the fact that she was there for an SDAP and my own problem-solving needed solutions quickly. The only differences in the new version of the missile was its additional two-and-a-half feet in length and an increase of 300 miles to an effective range of 1,500 nautical miles. It also weighed a ton more.

As compared to all other missiles with an extended range, *Polaris* was a small missile. What made her size possible had been the electronic miniaturization of her guidance and controls, and the high specific impulse of her solid fuel. As a matter of fact, it had been the breakthroughs in inertial guidance miniaturization for *Polaris* by our contractor, the MIT Instrumentation Laboratory, that had permitted the *Apollo* lunar landing spacecraft to keep its manned rendezvous with the moon seven years later.

When I arrived at the pier around 4:00 a.m., everything appeared normal: blazing floodlights, armed security, frog men, and the usual checks before descending into the submarine. Suddenly, I heard the whirling thump-thump of helicopters. As soon as one landed and took off at the land end of the pier, another came down. Out stepped Robert McNamara followed by several of his assistant secretaries of Defense, the Secretary of the Navy and his assistants, the Chief of Naval Operations, and several Army and Air Force officers, including the unmistakable Curtis LeMay. I felt it couldn't be the new version of the missile that attracted so much attention. Although the SSB(N) 608 was a new class of nuclear submarine, it wasn't so different from our earlier 598-class subs as would be the SSB(N) 616 *Lafayette* which was a year away from its first SDAPs.

It was only after we were underway that I learned the reason. For the first time we were expected to demonstrate that we could launch two missiles from a submerged position in less than one minute. Such a feat had never been done officially. I felt this was unfair to the crews who would be launching missiles for the first time, and SDAPs often had technical or training *holds* during the countdown.

The fact that we had launched many more than two during the still secret series of launches *east of Bermuda* was nothing we wanted to crow about. Even though that *secret* series had used A-1s, that didn't ease my mental reservations. If there had been extra tension on board, I think it was only in my own mind because the count went without a hitch. I was standing next to the tube selected for launch #1 and not only did I fail to hear a flush, I didn't even feel a shudder. By the time the loud speaker picked up the second count, it was already at "T minus 30 (seconds) and counting." That count also went without a hold. I can still recall one of the junior officers with a stop watch proclaiming a bit proudly, "The second launch followed by fifty-two seconds, Sir."

Just about everyone on the submarine grew an extra two inches at that news. When the downrange instrumentation field reported that missile #1 was in the "pickle barrel," it took a great deal of discipline not to strut about or act cocky. Still, we all held our breath, waiting for the results of the second launch. Finally, after an eternity of waiting, the announcement came for all to hear, "Number two in the same barrel, Sir."

No, we didn't jump and dance, but there were many smiles and *thumbs-up* gestures between the crewmen and many handshakes among the officers and scientists. And above all, more than one "Well done, gentlemen" from the brass.

Following an SDAP, it always took several hours to return to Port Canaveral. Because I was a *rider*, I didn't have a clue what was going on above us on the surface, or whether the VIPs would stay with us all the way back until late afternoon. I went to a ward room for coffee while I wrote my report and read correspondence I brought with me.

One of the documents from NATO riveted my attention because it was a rehash of German objections to Kennedy's graduated response policy. Germany still objected to anything short of a hair-trigger response. German General Adolf Heusinger who would take over the chairmanship of the NATO Military Committee was outspoken in his support for a doctrine closer to the thinking of Curtis Lemay than to Robert McNamara's. We were living in a Pandora's box, and the irony of the moment didn't escape me.

Here we were in a *Polaris* submarine, one the taxpayers had spent as much on to make it quiet as it cost to send the first men to the moon. No magic wand made these submarines quiet. Hard work, long hours of studies and tests with models, new materials, new designs, all very expensive—that's what it took. And, many lives were lost as well.

It had been a bitterly learned lesson in World War II that almost every instance of a US submarine lost to enemy action occurred during or as a consequence of offensive action by the submarine lost. Chance encounters were rare and when they did occur, it was due to the diesel submarine's need to surface often for long enough periods of time to recharge batteries and replenish fresh air. A nuclear submarine, ours in particular, submerged for months, avoided contact and reduced its vulnerability to almost zero.

Moreover, the earth's oceans offered each *Polaris* submarine an area in which to hide the size of France and Germany combined, and it would still be within range of major targets in the Communist Soviet Union or Communist China. In addition, the nuclear submarine could travel at top speed near-indefinitely if need be. The *Ethan Allen*, like all her sister boats, could travel out of a launch area as many as twenty miles before an enemy radar picked up the reentry body coming in. Our submarines were not fixed targets like a silo or an airfield. We knew how difficult it was to find one of our subs. The Air Force and the Navy had experimented with every form of anti-submarine warfare including infrared signatures in cold oceans, and failed to locate us. What consoled us was the belief that our Air Force had better equipment than the Soviets.

During World War II, an average submarine cruised at nine knots for only a half hour, or at five knots for six hours, or at three knots for eighteen hours. Then the skipper kept enough juice in the batteries for lighting, to blow ballast, and to rise to the surface. Once on the surface, he'd run the engines to recharge the spent batteries. The nuclear submarine with unlimited range and revolutionary, submerged speed was a dramatic new dimension in modern warfare. In 1962, to destroy another's military nuclear forces, an aggressor would attack the enemy's hardened missile silos and bomber airfields. These targets served as *lightning rods* to attract nuclear attacks. In comparison, however, the outlook for attacking an ocean to hit a submarine was forlorn to say the least.

When we arrived at Canaveral, I was one of the first to climb through the main hatch. With any luck, I might catch the last flight from Orlando to Washington. As I sorted out my belongings on the pier, General Lemay and his aide walked past me.

I heard Lemay say, "Pretty damn impressive."

"Yes, Sir, I agree," replied the aide.

"We'll just have to get these things..."

Chapter 9

Changing of the guard

It was around this time when Paul H. Nitze, the Assistant Secretary of Defense for International Security Affairs, sent to the Chief of Naval Operations and to SP the MLF proposal from NATO. Many such proposals had been contrived because the Navy or the Air Force liaison officers in Paris were voluntarily willing to *suggest* language, and this one definitely had a Navy *lean* to it, hence OSD bucked it as noted.

Because I was a civilian armed with a broad and special "highly political" charter (p. 287), I went straight to the Pentagon to see Paul Nitze whom I had already met. After he informed me that there was need for fast action, Dick Shutt, Mac McCallum and I authored the final draft that someone in Nitze's shop handcarried to Paris the same afternoon.

Within a few days, a US Navy captain in Paris sounded me out by phone about SP giving NATO headquarters a briefing on *Polaris*. According to him, the Air Force was giving briefings on MMRBMs, *Midgetman, Missile X*, and if I'd wait a week, "they'll pull another missile out of the hat."

I hated to say "no," but in light of all the flak trying to shoot down the MLF and *Polaris*, no one at SP wanted to raise his head too high for fear "of having the damn thing shot off." After he gave me his direct tie-line telephone number in Paris, I told him I'd find a way to introduce *Polaris* to the people at NATO without too many middlemen. "We'll make it happen. I'll get back to you soon," I promised.

Dick Shutt and Mac McCallum had to find the correct routing for any invitation to go through channels, yet without going astray. Knowing the devious ways of Naval officers, we all knew that any senior flag officer along the way whose staff might want a spring trip to Paris could easily waylay *our* precious NATO invitation. It was too easy for anyone at the Pentagon to say, "Everyone in SP is too busy." Such an assertion would be disastrous to our plans. Also, since intramural skirmishes or ambushes had to be avoided at all costs, the solution was strict secrecy, absolute surprise, a surgical first strike. Admittedly, great cunning was needed because our problem was not only with the Department of Defense, the Department of State, or the Air Force. Our collective foe in Washington was far more clever, it was everyone else in the Navy!

Consequently, Shutt and McCallum would grease the Navy skids, and I would have to convince my Navy contact in Paris that he was to tell no one until I gave him the "favorable word." Anyway, if he wanted the real McCoy, he should definitely keep the State Department out of it, and we'd keep it "just among us Navy folks." Meanwhile, he should scout the spring schedule and let me know the best dates to be ready to respond to.

Until we got this NATO briefing under control, we regarded everyone as our foe, not only the Air Force missilemen who were rampaging through Europe with all sorts of wild exaggerations about their missiles and overstating every shortcoming about our dear *Polaris*, but anyone else who even dared to use a French word in a routine conversation. Paris! That beat alligator-infested Pad 25A, sweating on the deck of the *Obs Island*, or briefings, invigorating as they may be, at Westinghouse.

We had decided that the NATO letter would have to go to the CNO, but that we'd add Mac's interoffice code—OpNav 023 or whatever the number was. A Navy-to-Navy letter would work so it was imperative to avoid the diplomats—no telling what side they were on, and to avoid Defense which had been infiltrated by too many Air Force and Army types. I thought we'd go schizophrenic protecting our hind quarters. Nothing sacred was safe from the spies and highwaymen who lurked everywhere in Washington.

Dick Shutt had to make sure that all the bases were covered in SP. There we had Admirals, Captains-striking-for-admiral, senior captains of earlier graduation classes at Annapolis—nothing but problems. And what if the original letter went astray? Mac would have to know when it was coming to assure its routing to none other than himself. As luck would have it, the Navy had no pouch service in Paris but shared one with the Defense Department. Of course, State had one and so did the CIA. No way would we let State near it because we knew they'd run with the ball, and there were neurotic reasons aplenty to imagine that the CIA could probably exchange it with the Soviet KGB secret service as some kind of "chicken feed" just to earn brownie points at our expense. So we bit the bullet and *arranged* to have the letter come to Washington in the Defense pouch. Our invitation would be for the last half of May which, in light of national security prioritization and extremely demanding submarine schedules, was—plainly speaking—a nice time to do our sacred duty by briefing our country's NATO allies in Paris.

Meanwhile, the Air Force lobbying effort manifested itself at a critical moment. NATO Secretary-General Dirk U. Stikker came to Washington, and his appointment at the Pentagon with Secretary of Defense Robert McNamara was high on the NATO leader's agenda. All the wizards on McNamara's staff prepared their boss to be responsive to Stikker's main item of discussion—the MLF. These whiz-kids obviously went to the Air Force to get all the latest IRBM information, and by the time Stikker arrived, McNamara was well-stuffed with facts.

However, McNamara became so confused by the technical alphabet soup of General Norstad's MRBM, the Air Force's land-based MMRBM, *Midgetman, Missile X*, and other alphabetic derivatives that he elaborated the accuracy, the performance, range and effectiveness of a missile that was no more than an artist's impression on some defense contractor's drawing boards. He completely forgot about the American IRBM called *Polaris* and the MLF. By the time Stikker returned to Paris, he was completely mystified and confused.

Meanwhile, Navy supporters heard about the Air Force salesmen and their contractors on the prowl of NATO capitals in Europe, selling their own brand of MLF. Not to be outdone, mysterious forces came together during dark pre-dawn hours on a weekday, when a moving van and an accompanying rig parked easily in front of the Tidal Basin in Washington. Nearby was a elaborate set up with projector-lights and movie cameras aimed toward where the sun would rise. The field of view dramatically included the Thomas Jefferson Memorial at the right edge of the field of view.

With enterprising ardor the cameraman angled the lens so that President Jefferson's imposing profile could be dramatically discerned between the massive marble pillars of the elegant memorial. After the roof of the van separated and the two *doors* fell to the side, a cylinder-shaped object angled upwards and canted toward the water. Suddenly, a bottle-shaped missile shot out of the cylinder and splashed heavily into the basin, one of the premier tourist attractions in the nation's capital. With that background in this historic document, no cut line was needed to say "Washington, DC".

"Cut," yelled the director. The rig fished the dummy-missile out of the water, and the film was rushed to a lab for development. By the time Washington's office workers reported for work, all the evidence of the *test launching* was gone. For us, that wasn't necessarily *new* or welcome news. The worst news was that President Kennedy found out about it before SP did. Not only did the President rocket through the overhead of the oval office but, as he often did when blindsided, enriched everyone's vocabulary with Naval epithets that he obviously learned the night a Japanese destroyer cut his PT boat in two. Maybe it was because he was a former Naval officer, but Kennedy often reserved his richest embellishments to the English language when in his sole judgment the Navy had somehow screwed up.

Although we knew damn well that some of our own contractors had been in a jealous fit because the Air Force's MMRBM study managers were having all the fun briefing any European ally who cared to listen, we were just as mad as Kennedy. After laying the law down to our inspired supporters about rendering film copies scarce, and generally knocking off the comedy, SP settled back into its protective cocoon. Only a few believed we weren't behind it. But we weren't. The storm passed and SP had ducked the bullet again.

Despite fate and everyone's obvious attempts to divert our attention from our rendezvous with destiny in Paris, we held true to the course and settled for the dates of 15 May to 18 May 1962. While we celebrated in Shutt's office, and congratulated ourselves by the clever scheduling just before a weekend, heavy artillery shells landed. The news came from our Deputy Director, Tom Rudden, who was striking for admiral and wasn't going to let anything go wrong on his watch. "Admiral Galantin was going to lead the SP delegation," Rudden declared, and somehow Rudden had been designated in a self-proclamation as "a one-man advance team to check everything out in Paris!"

Our carefully laid plans had not included Rudden and now we wondered if we had left any stone unturned that could somehow be disarranged by his going to Paris first and alone. But our fears proved unfounded upon his return, and the Polaris Management Team named to put on the NATO Seminar comprised Admiral Ignatius J. "Pete" Galantin, George W. Bergquist, Captain Richard G. Shutt, Captain J.L.P. McCallum, Bernard W. Poirier, Commander John J.S. Daniel, Commander H.D. Butler, and Thomas H. Enzor. For the first time, an all-SP team would brief NATO allies outside the United States, and the news caused quite a stir.

Just before we left, Galantin called us in. Naval Intelligence had briefed him on the special problems we'd be expected to encounter, and the Policy Planning officers in OpNav wanted SP to toe the line as to what we could disclose. Of course, we were experts on disclosure parameters because we helped write many of them, but we were surprised about the *problems*.

ONI believed that we would face *bugging* of our phones in hotels, microphones buried in the walls or microrecorders in the mattresses of our rooms by the French as well as by enemy agents. If we had to discuss anything classified, we should go for a walk in a park. Any classified documents would be handcarried and always within reach, under our legs or an elbow or on our laps, and never left unattended in our hotel rooms. Because of security concerns and the political nature of the MLF debate, we could discuss PERT management techniques and very little about our missile or our submarines.

By the time we arrived in Paris, I was so concerned about security that when a diplomat from the US Embassy asked for me to be interviewed about *Polaris* or the MLF in French on Radio Free Europe and another local USIA station, I refused. "No," I answered, "and I won't in English, either."

As it turned out, our own Navy people stationed in Paris only knew what the diplomatic party line was about the MLF and what they learned from defense contractors. Frankly it wasn't much, not even from our own contractors. In Europe *Polaris* was a mystery, or maybe a legend, so effective had been the Navy's security barriers.

Our prime contractor had a large office in Paris to cover western Europe. We tended to forget that Lockheed had other interests besides *Polaris* and the U-2. Although their Paris office was headed up by a retired US admiral, Lockheed concentrated on selling airplanes. Admiral Vosseler and his wife invited Shutt, Mac and me to their home for drinks one evening. It was a high-ceilinged and expensively appointed apartment in a swanky Paris neighborhood near *La Madeleine*, the enormous Pantheon-shaped church popular with tourists. While we walked to the admiral's apartment building in the evening, we noticed many rather attractive women on the sidewalk that encircles the *Madeleine*, and it was obvious to us that each of these streetwalkers "owned" her own square of the sidewalk. And across the street were their male *enforcers*.

After being greeted by the admiral and his lovely wife, we asked him why so many *fresh air* prostitutes were permitted to hang around one of the architectural gems of Paris. Without blinking an eye he answered, "Just lucky, I guess."

But the elegant Mrs. Vosseler objected to the connotations of her husband's reply, and she set the evening's course in a lively fashion, much to our enjoyment. What I noticed about that evening was the fact that the mention of *Polaris* never came up—for which we were grateful.

Even though I hadn't been in Paris in over ten years, everyone relied on me to recommend places to visit or see at the end of each day. We arranged to store our classified material under lock and key in the offices of the American delegation to NATO, and at least didn't have to cart this material around with us. Most of the time two or three of us would go one way, and a few the other.

On Saturday, the last night, most of us went as a group to Montmartre where all the buildings were, and still are, very old, and dined in a restaurant whose interior decoration was that of a stable for cows and goats. Very careful to avoid shop talk, we were able to enjoy the French folk songs and provincial food from the menu. So long as Shutt had his snails he stayed a happy camper, and I always wondered where a life-long sailor had acquired such an insatiable taste for snails prepared French style.

Two things I noticed had changed in Paris in slightly less than ten years. In 1962 most of the cancan cabarets that existed in 1951 were sadly gone. Back then, you could find one in almost every Paris neighborhood, and it only cost a bit to have some wine and see the dancers in ruffles kick exuberantly and soar to Offenbach's rich music. On the other hand, one major improvement was the cleaning of Paris buildings that had accumulated dirt and grime and that were still so dirty after World War II.

One noticeable constant of the Parisian landscape remained, the inimitable and screechy F-sharp-G and G-sharp-A taxi horns memorialized by Jerome Kern for Oscar Hammerstein 2nd who fled Paris in 1940 with the invading German army at his heels, and then wrote *The Last Time I Saw Paris*. The next day we enplaned at Orly airport for the return trip, and at Shannon airport in Ireland we shopped while the plane was refueled. We never suspected that this routine refueling stop in Shannon, no less than Parisian taxi horns, would soon be a faded experience of the past. Jet engines became more efficient as modern technology that we helped to develop would permit planes to fly non-stop between the United States and continental Europe, and the charm of discordant horns would progress to authoritative blast horns.

Paris had been a welcome break for us, and NATO had profited by hearing a few unvarnished facts from the experts. Favorable repercussions later would follow us to Washington. The next morning we were all in SP by 6:30 to prepare for the 7 a.m. weekly management meeting. Luckily nothing adverse had happened since last Monday's status meeting.

Chapter 10

State department's inconsistent foreign policy

It was only after we returned from NATO headquarters in Paris did a fresh wave of anti-French sentiment spilling over publicly from the State Department make its full impact on me. Frequent news reports would cite a State Department source who had ridiculed the French nuclear program, or poked fun at the amateurish French accomplishments with rocketry. Just where State received its information was beyond me, because all the intelligence agencies and I knew just the opposite.

I knew that Roger Hilsman, Director of the Bureau of Intelligence and Research in the State Department, knew better and so did his people.

Misleading the American public was one thing, but it was stupid in light of what our allies and our enemies already knew. The Europeans had just authorized an initial $300 million (over $2 billion in 2000 values) to set up the European Space Research Organization in the same Paris building that housed the French national space agency. Also located there was the new European Launcher Development Agency sponsored by seven countries.

Both the CIA and the French agency SEREB—the IRBM developer—had promulgated photographs of a huge new steel-girded tower for static testing of large rocket motors, such as those of the three-staged Emerald test vehicle. On one hand the third stage was rumored to be intended for the Diamond satellite launcher, but the solid-fueled second stage was intended to be the first stage of an IRBM military missile.

Out of secret negotiations with the Algerians, France could plug a big financial drain through a final settlement, and the De Gaulle government was scrapping antiquated bureaucracies and streamlining agencies like SEREB. In effect, France was enjoying a technological boom that would have staggered anyone who saw France after the war, or simply ten years ago. I realized that I should have noted more changes while we were in Paris, like finding strawberry jam and blackberry jam at breakfast, and remembering that ten years earlier the only choices were a small jar of marmalade or two small jars of marmalade.

Also, we had seen many overpasses and highway exchanges under construction, something I never saw at the start of the Marshall Plan. Even the Colomb-Béchar rocket range in Algeria was to be phased out, and the French were studying new options for a major range. Everyone knew this, I thought, except for some unnamed talebearers at the State Department.

At Special Projects, we had such a steady growth of authorized submarines and missiles to manufacture that for a brief respite during Admiral Galantin's first six months it would have been easy for a visitor to think we had a tedious existence. Much of the early pressure was off, and wives started to see their SP husbands, and children their fathers, during daylight hours.

Long-gone were the occasional classified morale-boosting briefings for wives by Admiral Raborn in the Management Center on Saturday mornings. During such briefings our spouses had been shown the many missile failures never seen by the press, or heard explanations about the heartache of equipment failures when successes were critical for our nuclear submarines. All were detailed by the admiral. "That," he would explain, "is why your husbands leave before sun-up and arrive home long past sundown." It always amazed me that Raborn's management practice to keep families together was keep secret for a half-century. We never had a security leak or any problem result from Raborn's innovation.

For that short period of time, both the technical division and the plans and programs division took on a feeling of routine, the repetition of production, of "what else is new?" Dick Shutt received word that he would soon have formal orders to command a ship, and that his replacement would be another submarine officer.

Meanwhile, not only was the posturing of the Air Force on the MMRBM running out of gas, but so was the Kennedy administration over the MLF. In its independence, France had renounced taking part in it, a fact that probably explained the cranky loose cannon at the State Department.

Interestingly enough, the British also renounced the MLF, and the State Department couldn't have been sweeter and more syrupy to London, making it difficult for others to keep fairness in NATO on an even keel. But in its refusal London simply glowed in superiority because of its "special nuclear relationship" with America, something no other ally enjoyed.

The rest of NATO was plainly second-class, and unlike Kilroy, the World War II GI symbol, they couldn't even peak over the wall but cowered behind it, completely at the mercy of US nuclear policy to deter Soviet aggression against distant NATO borders. At Whitehall, the Macmillan government simply strutted proud as a peacock while continental Europe looked on enviously.

Through its commitment of troops and money, the United States proved its willingness to protect Europe by convincing our NATO allies that we certainly would use nuclear weapons to prevent a million of our soldiers and their dependents in Europe from being overrun by Warsaw Pact armies. Nonetheless, every ally except France and the United States had fallen behind in the number of combat troops they were supposed to have on line, and in the quality of weapons available to their troops. "NATO," insisted the United States, "must increase the levels of its conventional troops and weapons." Despite the best arguments floated by Germany and others, Kennedy had no intention of being without military options in NATO Europe.

On one hand, Kennedy wanted it costly for the Soviet Union and its own allies to venture toward West Germany or toward Greece and Turkey, and on the other hand, the president wanted to make the consequences of Soviet aggression against the US mainland too terrible for Moscow to seriously contemplate.

Because of the impasse over the MLF, Dr. Thompson encouraged me to write a monograph, a "think piece," on the MLF that would have a chance to pass the Navy and Defense Department censors. It would be the only time that I would write publicly about *Polaris*. Tommy appointed himself my chief editor in charge of sanitizing what I wrote—keeping the text politically acceptable and technically sound without revealing secrets. John Craven took one look at an early draft and contributed the working title that made it all the way to publication, "Lightning Rod in the Sea (p. 318)."

One of Dick Shutt's last two acts at SP was to recruit Walt Seedlock, a Naval Academy classmate who was at Lockheed, to help find the right publisher. Both men had been in the class of '41, and Dick had dated Walt's sister for some academy functions. It was one of the ironies of destiny that when it came to justify the total number of *Polaris*-launching submarines that the United States needed, the final number was at least forty, but no one could agree on what President Kennedy would finally accept. Dick Shutt articulated the justification, scheduling and targeting to have the Navy accept forty-one missile-launching submarines. Later Shutt admitted that it was "in memory of the Class of '41 that went straight to war after graduation." McNamara, Kennedy and Congress bought Shutt's logic, and authorized a *Polaris* fleet comprising forty-one nuclear submarines!

Facing page. A *Polaris A-2* LTV launched from the EAG 154, *U.S.S. Observation Island*, in early 1962. The first test launches at sea of any new FBM models were always performed by the *Obs Island* in the Atlantic Ocean. The EAG's crew received special training in missile guidance, launching and handling, propulsion, and ordnance. She accompanied SSB(N)s whenever the subs launched their own LTVs. This photo was taken from a helicopter over thirty miles east of Cape Canaveral, Florida.

Every incremental increase in the range of a new *Polaris* missile added important credibility to the nuclear deterrence policy of the United States.

Government Photo

Because the thrust of my article was the surface ship MLF, the Navy released a dramatic photograph of a *Polaris A-2* launch from the *Observation Island.* I wanted to finish the article and get it cleared for publication in time to appear as soon after the next NATO Ministerial meeting as possible. In May, 1962, the meeting was scheduled to be held in Athens where we knew the administration was going to repeat its MLF offer.

The trouble with such an article was the fact it had to be on such a lofty plane that it lulled both reviewers and readers to sleep, except maybe those decision makers in NATO countries who could use the article's guidance. As best as I could, I articulated the choices of mobility—restricted on land or random at sea; on survivability—escaping an enemy's detection at sea and avoiding espionage surveillance on land; on costs, on command and control, and even on the tough issue of political derogation. While I was at it I criticized a recent analysis that appeared in *Foreign Affairs*, a distinguished publication dominated by existing or former State Department officials, but applauded a second one in the same issue.

My article finally appeared in the June-July 1962 issue of *NATO'S FIFTEEN NATIONS* which was published in Amsterdam. The magazine was one of the most read publications in NATO's Atlantic Council and in the offices of the Chiefs of Staffs of all the allied capitals. Shortly thereafter, the White House sources told me that the administration would organize an official Multilateral Nuclear Force study group at the State Department, comprised of Naval and State Department personnel.

Increasingly, the different offices of naval operations started sharing some of SP's activities, including some I had with the State Department. Of course, the Navy had an officer as liaison at the White House who was very effective for all Navy matters, but was not as influential for SP as my own civilian trapline was. After Dick Shutt went to sea, there were a few weak attempts to reel in my far ranging activities. This prospect of change caused me apprehension at first, but that feeling soon dissipated because of the quality of officers assigned and the amount of work that piled up.

Initially, many fresh officers arriving in SP had never run into a civilian responsible for *Polaris* Foreign Programs, and who had the authority to speak for the Navy in this narrow field. The fact that international affairs and SP's achievements widened the field to enormous dimensions was beside the point, because my authority had also been widened in writing, with two Secretarial exceptions to permit quicker pay raises and promotions. Such was the influence of Raborn's "hunting license." By and large, civilian employees were often considered just one rank removed from prisoners-of-war. Depending on the speaker, it could be one rank below a POW, or one rank above. What protected me during the transition was the fact that John Craven, Levering Smith and respected old-timers vouched for me.

Meanwhile, a surprise event shook up the entire military establishment in Washington, and that was the unilateral decision by the Soviet Union on 25 April 1962 to resume atmospheric testing of nuclear weapons.

From what my sources in the White House told me, President Kennedy had no warning politically that Khrushchev might do that. However, the CIA had been circulating information that the Soviet atomic scientists had made progress in weapons' design, probably revolutionary enough to require testing to prove them. Likewise our own scientists at the Atomic Energy Commission had also made great progress, and like the other services, the Navy wanted to test its new warheads and not let the Soviets surge ahead in the state of the art.

After Kennedy agreed to start testing, the Navy received authorization to test a live nuclear warhead delivered to the test zone by a *Polaris* missile launched from a submarine. That would be a first.

Following Kennedy's green light, the services competed for a "blast slot" just as airlines compete for landing slots at major airports around the world. To avoid redundant testing of nuclear devices, our referee was the Atomic Energy Commission, and the scheduling comptrollers were the British whose Christmas Island Test Site in the Pacific was available. This was the only time that the entire *Polaris* weapons system was ever tested at one time: the launch, the arming of the nuclear device, and the where and how the detonation would occur.

The Navy selected the *Ethan Allen* to fire an A-2, and she sailed through the Panama Canal with its missile and live warhead. However, it was more than a test missile, it was what we called a *blue ribbon bird*, one that had undergone vigorous check-outs and more than once. Levering Smith led a small group of SP officers and scientists on board the submarine, and he was responsible for launching the live missile. The Soviet Navy was advised of where we would launch and where the warhead was aimed. This was by Kennedy's personal decision (and gamble) for the Soviet Union to appreciate America's confidence in her top deterrents, and for them to witness ours. In a bizarre twist, however, no one could talk about it or report it ahead of time or even after to the

American public, and we in SP simply treated the test, code-named *Frigate Bird*, it as *top secret*.

This entire sequence established such a new chapter in U.S.-U.S.S.R. relations that it behooves me to stress it again. Kennedy believed that deterrence must be believed to be effective. The Soviet Union was advised about our submarine test, and was told the where and when about the launching, and exactly where the warhead would be headed. This was a major-time pressure cooker for us. But the American public, under Kennedy's domestic muzzle on the A-tests, was kept in the dark about why, what, where and when.

Kennedy's domestic concerns were strictly political because some of his advisors were afraid of a backlash from groups of voters who opposed nuclear testing.

Because of the secrecy, this event like so many others, prevented us from making private notes. In any event, everyone worked that Sunday, 6 May 1962, and the on-board conversations in the weapons control compartment of the *Ethan Allen* and the countdown were transmitted over a secure communications link so that SP could follow the progress of the test.

Absolutely no one in SP wanted to miss that historical event. Never had so many of us tried to squeeze into the Management Center. We also had a lot of Navy visitors from the Pentagon. In order to accommodate the high demand, the inner security door was left open and many were obliged to stand in the standing room *bleachers*. Out in the main corridor we had armed Marine guards stationed. Although the secure telecommunications link was clear enough, there were times when we could barely hear the commentary. Of course, at those times we knew that "Whispering Smith" was speaking, and know-it-all-smiles and private winks were exchanged. There were two to three voices alternating including the "official" voice of a crewman or officer reciting the countdown, and the others could have been anyone, whoever was responsible for throwing a toggle switch, or pushing a button, or calmly reading off a value from an analog or digital dial.

What might have passed as idle, almost sleepy, chatter to an outsider meant a great deal to us. Slowly and imperceptibly a sense of tension built up, and listeners started to grit their teeth as the count approached launch. Although it was "our" test, fleet command controlled the operation, and for the first time, we in SP were in the dark about the final number of support ships, and whether someone would let us know whether the launch was successful. Everyone knew several of the men on the *Ethan Allen* and just about everyone of us had been on a submarine when an earlier launch hadn't worked right. One voice repeated a report from the launch officer, and when one reported from the guidance-level deck of "Sherwood Forest," the so-called main missile compartment where the tubes were lined up like trees in a park, we knew the launch was imminent.

"Launch!" exclaimed a voice.

Not a word was said or whispered as we waited for information. "*Did it broach?*" "*Did it clear?*" we wondered silently.

"*Was ignition normal?*" Most of us had been in SP long enough to remember that our missile had been known to revisit its launcher.

"*Is she on vector?*"

I heard someone mumble impatiently, between clinched teeth, "Damn it!" The tension was deafening, as we were sure it was on the submarine.

A few minutes felt like an eternity until a new voice, probably someone on an escort ship, announced, "Separation." Over a hundred men exhaled their breath at the same time.

The same calm voice added, "Second stage ignition." Some laughter, nervous but happy. Then silence. A long silence.

We knew deep down that at least six hundred enemy Soviet officers and crewmen had an exclusive bird's eye view of what we had worked for years to accomplish, and we only had the knowledge of flight sequences and the memory of many *Polaris* launchings to fall back on as the few words came back over the speaker.

"*Damn it,*" I thought jealously, "*Moscow will have the results before we do.*"

When another new voice announced, "Telemetry," it took us a few seconds to fathom the meaning which circumvented security—the nuclear warhead had armed! Smiles broke out, and few amicable shoves or shoulder-squeezes replaced any spoken words. The very fact that the weapon had armed was a *suggestion* that the "shot" might be a good one. As tightly as our tension was wound, we could only imagine the sweat that our friends on the *Ethan Allen* were exposed to. Like us, they were now completely dependent on a British or AEC voice to speak up, about fifteen hundred miles west of the submarine.

For the next twenty minutes or so, only occasional high pitched Morse encryptions and the scratchy background of the squawk box punctuated the background. Breaking the monotony was the nervous shuffling of impatient feet. When the word finally came, cheering erupted and must have been heard as far away as the Lincoln Memorial.

If so, it would have been fitting. It had been a long, often lonely road for SP.

Facing page. Code named *Frigate Bird*, the live nuclear test of the Navy's FBM authorized by President Kennedy took place on Sunday, 6 May 1962. Only the Soviets, in addition to authorized U.S. and U.K. personnel, had witnessed this 600 kiloton blast of the *Polaris A-2* missile. The above-surface detonation occurred between 1.8 miles and 2.8 miles above the Pacific Ocean at the U.K.'s Christmas Island Test Range.

The diesel-powered submarine SS-337 *U.S.S. Carbanaro* was running on the surface about 30 miles from ground zero when this photograph of the nuclear blast was taken through her periscope. Like this photo, other photos taken from the navigation deck of her conning tower, remained classified for 38 years.

The blast was over 40 times as powerful as the nuclear bomb that devastated Hiroshima, Japan, and that helped to quickly end World War II in August 1945.

Government Photo

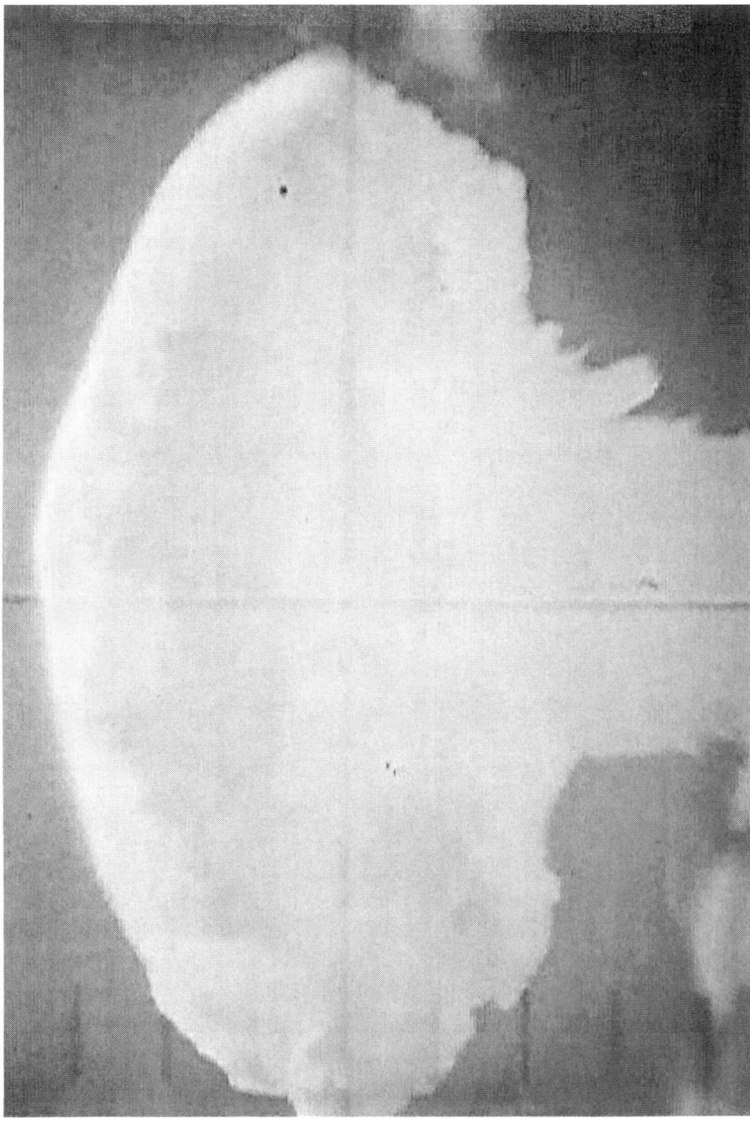

Chapter 11

Vietnam, CIA, and naval intelligence

Just because the times were confused, we coped as well as we could with the ebb and flow of events, and refused to be distracted. Accomplishing our mission was anchored to the research and development of a wholly new weapons system and to deliver the operational product to the fleet as fast as safely possible. But there were reasons why so many people came to us, and it was our duty to pay attention to their needs. Earlier I mentioned that SP had a great deal of research money to get the mysteries and problems out of the way, and the resources at our disposal provided the key reason why others often came by.

No one had ever imposed blinders on us like those worn by horses that couldn't be trusted to see what's going on to the side of them because of the their propensity to freak out. Admiral Raborn had imposed a sense of responsibility on everyone to pass on worthwhile findings to whatever other service needed the data, without waiting for a formal request.

It stands to reason that with a great deal of research going on very unexpected results did pop up. Future cases in point included attitude control for communications satellites, the global positioning system-GPS, Teflon and other non-stick metals, maneuverable re-entry bodies, hand-held electronic computers (I was still using a slide rule in 1962), cavitation spoilers on the wings of jet airliners, miniaturized controls for kitchen ovens and coffee pots, and many others.

Unsettling events were unfolding in former French Indochina whose last convoluted vestiges of colonialism had been given up by France after signing the Geneva Accords in July 1954, a treaty the United States had not signed. Although SP wasn't directly involved, when President Kennedy took interest, so did everyone else in the Defense Department. After the French suffered disastrous losses at Diên-Biên-Phû in North Vietnam near the Laos border, France was forced into negotiations to give the Communist North Vietnamese full independence, and recognized the independence of Cambodia, Laos and South Vietnam as well.

Soon thereafter, from Hanoi in North Vietnam, Communist President Hô Chi Minh started sending agents to infiltrate into South Vietnam to support the Communist opposition, the Vietcong. Actually, the infiltrators at the time were political-military advisors called the Vietminh, who were later militarized into the regular army of North Vietnam.

At first the Vietminh traveled southward through the jungle on rural trains or by simply hiking or bicycling down the "Hô-Chi-Minh trail" and hiding out in the jungle at night.

In a game of copy cat, Kennedy and his advisors decided to send in "military advisors" of our own to counter-balance the situation, and expanded the US Army Special Forces who became popularly known as the elite "Green Berets." One of the main forces behind the Green Berets' counterinsurgency mission was Air Force Colonel Ed Lansdale who wrote several treatises and monographs about the art of fighting guerrilla warfare in southeast Asia. Because I had met several French soldiers who ended up at Diên-Biên-Phû, I followed the events closely. In fact, my first job out of college had been exporting tank tracks to the French Army in Indochina from the B.F. Goodrich Company in Akron, Ohio, as part of Eisenhower's assistance to France in her war against the Communist insurgents.

The fact that Lansdale had been a CIA agent in the Philippines and later in South Vietnam was well known. Much of his writings and secret reports came to us while he was Deputy Director of Special Operations in the Defense Department. Even though he made the rank of general I always remembered him as Colonel Lansdale.

To help the Green Berets, the CIA and the various intelligence agencies published reports on R&D projects that might be responsive to the need of guerrilla warfare.

One that arose from the development of rubbery solid fuel for rockets was a material similar to the terrorist plastic explosive developed in Czechoslovakia during the Cold War. The product came about as surprisingly as did the desperately needed synthetic rubber during World War II. A simple laboratory spill at a B. F. Goodrich lab north of Akron provided the United States with a tremendous military advantage after the Japanese Army had captured all the rubber plantations in Southeast Asia. Because of all the military efforts put into stabilizing solid fuel for *Polaris, Pershing*, and *Minuteman*, it was possible to offer the Green Berets a good sabotage weapon for Vietnam.

Samples of rock used in Vietnamese railbeds were studied in order to classify them by color, and their shapes, color, and sizes were copied identically with stable explosives produced for these advisors sent by Kennedy to Vietnam. By placing the "new" rocks on the railbed, the explosives would detonate when the vibrations of trains passing set them off.

Other ingenious equipment had been developed by the French during their Algerian War which had just terminated. It was a clever adaptation of our own *Transit* satellite of yo-yo fame. But the French applied our Doppler principles for surveillance of remote trails, paths and dirt roads. Even at several miles it could pinpoint people walking, running, bicycling, even opening and shutting doors of jeeps and a lot more. Obviously, this equipment offered enticing applications for the Hô-Chi-Minh Trail.

One of the field units had been captured in Algeria and started a circuitous route to the Syrians who wanted to sell it to the Soviet Union, but was captured beforehand by Israel during one of the lightning wars in the Mideast. This is how US Army Intelligence learned of the equipment's capabilities. But the United States never obtained the French equipment until after the Kennedy Administration, and is a story to be continued later.

One of the studies that SP had partially funded concerned the use of radio broadcasting to help destabilize the Communist Chinese mainland. In large measure the study's principal investigator had relied on the reputation of the British Broadcasting Corporation for honest and uncolored news reports. Our study had incorporated local radio news broadcasts in the Philippines, and surveys were conducted locally before and after.

In some cases, the broadcasts contained a regular diet of misleading or untruthful news items. In other broadcasts, the news items were always truthful, until one major item was falsified. The study concluded that the one major "lie" influenced the listeners more than did all the other "white lies." We recommended that the United States find a radio transmitting situation to beam strictly truthful Chinese language broadcasts into Red China, until such time when a destabilizing "big lie" was needed in the interest of the United States. In those days, no truthful reports entered Red China, and truthful reports as being suggested by us was a capital crime there.

One of the reasons our hours were so long at SP was because the required daily reading for the top people in SP-11 and the Office of the Chief Scientist included the *Chicago Tribune*, *New York* or *Los Angeles Times*, the *Washington Star* and the *Washington Post*. These we all scanned. We split the chores on others; such as, The (Paris) *Le Monde* or the (Brussels) *Le Soir*, a major London daily—whichever arrived first—and several English-language Hong Kong newspapers and the major news weeklies. Although we received CIA summaries regularly, we read enough of the foreign press to make up our own minds, but we read and trusted the regular CIA radio digests. As for the foreign technology news, it soon became apparent that the CIA, and in a few cases Congress, relied a great deal on my own writing in the *Washington Star* and in the weekly magazine *Missiles and Rockets*.

When defense contractors wanted to sell know-how or equipment to NATO allies, the requests were scrutinized to prevent unauthorized disclosures of vital, secret information. Admittedly, the defense contractors wanted to pursue every legitimate lead or sale, but were known to stretch the innocence of their export license application. Invariably, such requests ended up in the Office of Naval Intelligence. As more and more export requests came in for review, increased numbers of the packages of documents, justifications and blueprints landed on my desk.

After a while I asked that they stay in ONI, and I offered to go there once a week to plow through the paper. But soon I had to go twice a week. We had a paradox on our hands because we wanted our industry to get the sales when appropriate, but we were concerned about the state of the art falling in the wrong hands.

In addition to the classified reports we received from our Navy attachés overseas, we relied on what the CIA reported on the company to whom the documents were intended, particularly how strictly that foreign company protected defense secrets. We were sensitive to the shortcomings of our own contractors with offices overseas, and generally refused an export license of any critical data useful to the Soviet Union, and we forced the foreign governments to buy from the United States production lines. But after NATO adopted infrastructure production as local content for multilaterally financed procurements, we started getting political pressure for a favorable export decision.

Nonetheless, as long as there was the slightest question of a compromise on security, I refused my approval. A personal veto was a "black ball." If one member said, "No," the issue was closed and the package returned to the Defense, Commerce and State Departments with a "refused" stamp on it. The type of export requests that we disapproved generally included the critical components and the unique manufacturing equipment or machine tools needed for the production of missiles, weapons control, navigation, computers, propellants, inertial guidance and especially alignment techniques and attitude control. Rolling stock for aircraft stairways, airport navigational equipment and luggage handling equipment were normally approved readily.

Industry in France, Britain, Germany, Italy, Belgium, Denmark and the Netherlands was eager to participate in the latest production techniques such as promised to them by the US Secretaries of State and of Defense, but there was no way at the expert level that unauthorized disclosure would be exported until there was a political agreement or a direct authorization from the highest levels of the US government.

Soon I was named an ad hoc member of the State-Defense Military Information Control Committee, an assignment that took up a great amount of my time. Pronounced "S-D-Micc" in three syllables, one of its jobs was to either pass, approve, modify or refuse the exchange of highly classified information, usually with hard copies, to be used by the CIA with Soviet double agents, or with American double-double agents for information that our side wanted. Because we trusted the CIA to keep the allegiances straight, we usually focused on the secret materials, and on what our side would gain in exchange. However, there was so much room for disappointment or for losing an agent (for whatever side) it was like a chess game with thousands of moves.

On occasion, I'd ask that a scale be changed, requiring that the print go back and be copied enough times to look like it had been done surreptitiously. The object being to force the other side to lose time—and maybe never be sure our information was true. Truthfully, the dodge was like spreading chicken feed to make the chickens come closer, and that's exactly what we called it: "chicken feed."

In addition to the chicken feed, there were other ways to "sex" up drawings and prints besides simple scale changes, and we had a whole list of actions we could use to "sex-up"—yes, that was the expression used—the exchange, to make the object more attractive to the Soviets, knowing full well that they might be doing the same thing for whatever was destined to come our way. This was very much like the "big lie" and the "white lies," wherein it was important for us to build up the quality of information produced by the Soviet traitor who was being handled by a CIA agent. The last thing we wanted was to have a worthless traitor taking up our time.

When the CIA had small cameras installed in photocopy machines inside key Moscow ministries, it only worked because a Soviet citizen accepted money for his treason. On a regular basis, he'd do routine maintenance during which he'd replace the film canister and returned the exposed film to a CIA intermediary. The first picture of any photocopy run about Soviet military capabilities would be worth its weight in gold for our side. Looking back on the events of that time, the CIA even had the brain power to apply microprinting techniques in glossy American magazines, such as the *National Geographic*, to send secret messages to their Soviet double agents. And to the degree that any of our chicken feed helped to bring down Communism, there was enough credit to spread around.

Once I was through at Op-92 (ONI), I'd take a shuttle from the Pentagon to Munitions. Most of my messages were taken by Dr. Craven's secretary but because they were increasing in number, his second secretary had started collecting them for me. At this point, I must confess that Craven and our personnel director in SP, Vic Domenick, were geniuses. Our second secretary, Joy, was the sweetest, hardest working, and most bashful young woman I had ever met. But she was probably the most beautiful young woman that SP had ever hired, and our young bachelor officers (and not as young) suddenly beat a path to Craven's offices, a phenomena we had never seen before because our end of the building had been exciting, scientifically speaking, but this wasn't exactly what most young officers were looking for.

One morning at 6 a.m. on WMAL radio, I was rushing down George Washington Memorial Highway, trying to keep up with the sunrise Virginia traffic, when I heard that Joy had been selected "Miss Navy" in an important contest "before a huge crowd," so said the news report, leading to I-don't-know-what, maybe Miss World! No need for any stirring Sousa march to wake me up after that announcement, and it didn't surprise me to find Joy at her desk, first as always, when I arrived. Obviously we were all very proud of her, her victory and ourselves for having possessed the keen foresight and probing intelligence needed to have picked her for our office.

My messages were always arranged by Joy with the Navy ones on top, and I'd automatically look for the names important to me, Craven, Thompson, Captain Jerry Clarke who had replaced Dick Shutt, and then those from the outside—State and the White House, and so on. On this occasion was one from Admiral Rickover's office which I answered right away because the only thing shorter than Rickover's stature was his temper. His aide had been waiting for my call. My first thought was, "*Now what?*"

"The Admiral really liked your article, can you send him a copy of the material you used?" asked the admiral's aide.

"The piece in *NATO'S FIFTEEN NATIONS*?"

"Sorry, Mr. Poirier, the one with the headline "U.S. Schools Trail in Survey," in Sunday's *Washington Star*—you know what interests the admiral..."

"Oh, sure, I'll send the stuff over," I replied with disappointment.

As I went through the messages, I learned that State would only organize the MLF study group in September, and that I would be the only Navy civilian on it. The others included three Navy captains, C. Jackson, J.E. Clarke from SP, and F.H. Michaelis who went on to become admiral. Also named were Commanders F.F. Clifford and J.L. Jackson, and Lt. Commander R.R. Jefferson. Judging by the uniformed talent, this assignment promised to be a barn-burner, to say the least.

From my sources at State I also learned that Britain had a new Minister of Defense. In a general house cleaning of his cabinet, Prime Minister Harold Macmillan replaced Watkinson with Peter Thorneycroft, a former Chancellor of the Exchequer. Macmillan's slashing of heads earned him the nickname of "Mac the Knife." One of Thorneycroft's first acts was to curry favor with the British aerospace industry by preparing a procurement for more long-range jet aircraft, and extending the production life of *Blue Steel* for the Royal Air Force, a move consistent with the guidance problems that we heard the US Air Force continued to have with *Skybolt*.

Two of the reasons why McNamara was losing confidence in *Skybolt* were its escalating development costs and the rapid progress of *Minuteman* whose production exceeded all expectations. Normally we would not follow this issue closely but we were in a budget battle again with the Air Force, and the *Skybolt* threatened to gobble up another $2.5 billion on top of everything already spent on its R&D. Once before *Skybolt* had been taken out of the Defense Budget, by the Eisenhower administration during the last month before Kennedy's inauguration. However, McNamara put it back in because he didn't know where Kennedy's "missile gap" was. We were always conscious of costs because there never were enough appropriations-dollars around for everyone.

When I met "Mike" Michaelis, the senior Navy captain who would head up our MLF contingent at State, dollars again showed their dominant role. When we ran out our numbers for NATO, we realized that the seaborne MLF would cost less than four times what the submarine MLF would cost. The Navy was still unconvinced that the submarine option wouldn't again be raised, even if some people we dealt with at State didn't favor giving *Polaris* to anyone. The NATO MLF cost factor favored the surface ship option. But we had to do something because the President wanted to find an acceptable alternative to stop Europeans from pursuing independent nuclear deterrents, and the Navy absolutely didn't want State proposing some half-baked scheme that no Navy could live with. Although we had a much better idea of French progress with their rockets than with their nuclear submarines, the UK's program was so dependent on us that it probably would have taken very little to get them out of the race. The entire UK deterrent was based on outmoded Vulcan and Victor bombers, but so was the British aerospace industry.

For the moment, we were married to Eisenhower's *Skybolt* commitment, subsequently endorsed by the Kennedy administration, and to Kennedy's seaborne Multilateral Nuclear Force.

Chapter 12

Naval contributions to foreign affairs

The strong man of the Multilateral Nuclear Force team at the State Department was Walt W. Rostow, Counselor and Chairman of the Policy Planning Council. His counterpart on the Defense side was Henry S. Rowen, Deputy Assistant Secretary to Paul H. Nitze who continued to be my informal contact in International Security Affairs at the Pentagon. Our top military man assisting Rowen was Navy Captain F. H. "Mike" Michaelis who came out of naval operations in CNO. Only Captain Clarke and I were from the Special Projects Office.

I was accustomed to walking people through the technicalities of launching a *Polaris* missile from a seaborne platform, submerged or not. The State Department people on the joint team, however, often couldn't follow and required more step-by-step explanations than we were used to providing. In view of the fact that diplomats would be explaining the military side of the MLF to foreign diplomats, we realized that the common denominator was simplicity.

When we expressed some concern over a uniform code of military discipline and of military justice, State tended to dismiss the notion as if it were a distasteful wine to go with a main course. But for anyone facing a command situation with a mixed-manned crew on a ship of war, it was the main course. Just about everyone in the Defense Department had heard about the lax military discipline in the Dutch services, the extreme example in NATO at the time, and that served as the worst case scenario for potential onboard disciplinary problems. When a naval officer ordered the hatch of number three launch tube opened, he would also expect to hear, "Aye, aye, Sir," and not a debate about the afternoon watch maybe staying past duty into the dogwatch.

Private discussions would include a comparison of submarines to surface ships when the group split into pairs or small groups. Invariably we would explain the differences between diesel and nuclear propulsion, or the fact that an entire submarine may perish when all power goes out, and that a surface ship can still float after it loses all power. But discussion of a nuclear submarine MLF just plain scared us, and we learned that the best argument against it was: "a submerged MLF costs four times more than a surface ship MLF."

Toward the end of September we learned that the US Ambassador to NATO Thomas K. Finletter had obtained agreement from the other NATO ambassadors to hear the American MLF proposal on Monday, 22 October 1962. Realizing that we had less than four weeks to develop a "final" MLF position struck terror into our lives. Although our State colleagues never admitted their fears, if any, to us, we feared that a definition of a workable naval concept acceptable to State might elude the Navy members.

In addition, a considerable number of news stories on the MLF were being generated in Europe and published in the United States, and others were obviously being generated by people in the State Department, some of which we thought were argumentative and out of place. So wrapped up were we in the day-to-day wrestling matches over the MLF that we didn't bother even once discussing the debate sparked in the Senate about the Soviet military presence in Cuba and some Soviet anti-aircraft missile batteries under construction there, nor did we give much serious credence to the reports that Roswell Gilpatric, the Deputy Secretary of Defense, was in France to offer De Gaulle a Nautilus-type nuclear submarine for $63 million.

In late September it was my assignment to conceptualize some onboard scenarios during a missile launch from a surface ship, something that we could transform into color vugraphs and explain to the NATO Council in Paris. Invariably my ideas provoked arguments: I showed too much, or I showed too little. One scene showed the lower area of launch tubes, and an argument broke out over whether the launcher should be the compressed air system with its tanks and pipes or the one using a small solid rocket blasting into a pool of water, creating steam under pressure. One person objected, "It looks like a damn brewery."

It wasn't always so much the display of classified information, as much as it was too political! For example, all crewmen were shown in different NATO uniforms, and on some caps or berets was a distinctive pompom. All hell broke out over that one, so we decided to put everyone into work fatigues, but on second or third thought that was shot down by State because NATO members might feel that all the weapons and launch crewmen were American after all! Every change took my artists three or four days to recycle, and time was running out. By now it was early October and we had no unified position on what the NATO Multilateral Nuclear Force might look like!

I was very concerned about a leak to the press about our internal debates over the MLF which would be very embarrassing to the United States, and about any of the various drawings getting into the hands of reporters from newspapers or magazines like *The New York Times*, the *Washington Post* or *U.S. News and World Report*. I had resorted to an outside graphics firm with a high security clearance because our own graphics department in Special Projects was too busy to take on such a labor intensive package. I got together with ONI and the CIA to salt or place on each shift in the graphics firm some intelligence agents under the cover that they were my approved language experts for the texts on the vugraphs. Their primary job, however, was to make sure all copies of rejected sketches, drawings or colored renderings were accounted for, and then shredded, burned and flushed down a toilet.

For reasons I no longer remember, during this period I had to go to Cape Canaveral and back the same day, and the only way to do so would be by a military plane from one of the airports around Washington to Patrick Air Force Base just south of Cocoa Beach, Florida. After alighting from the plane, I walked toward a hangar but stopped to watch a U-2 circling for a landing, something I had never seen. Like a giant albatross with eighty-foot wings and a forty-nine-foot body, it glided slowly toward a landing. To my surprise the modified glider had no landing gear and only what looked like double wheels tucked under the fuselage. To my greater surprise, its markings seemed part of an Air Force operation, and not one operated by the CIA. I peered carefully in case I was missing something while its turboprop-jet engine pushed it along.

In any event, the U-2 landed on the double-wheel assembly and careened down the runway with the two wings staying horizontal by the pilot's efforts and skills. I watched while two Jeeps chased the U-2 at breakneck speed, and when the plane decelerated to about 50 mph or so, a second man in each Jeep held what looked like a long stick or pole, about four feet long with a wheel at one end, in his outstretched hand. Then the driver practically drove the Jeep's hood under the tip of the wing closest to him.

With an upward jerk, almost like an uppercut, the pole was inserted by the second man into a lock-socket under the wingtip. Then each jeep turned away, letting the U-2 wobble to a stop in the same fashion as the old float transatlantic Clippers and Navy PBY's landed on water. I didn't continue to the hangar until I saw it park near other U-2s at the far side of the field. I had always heard Lockheed engineers boast about how the U-2 was made lighter to climb so high and fly all day, and the absence of a landing gear was just one of the clever ways they did it.

When I returned to a joint meeting in Washington the following day, we enjoyed one of our last arguments about showing equipment in the visuals, arguing either for the 1962 state of the art, or the one that we knew would be operational in 1968. We assumed it would take NATO at least two years to agree politically, and four years to train a crew and construct a surface ship. The arguments even went to whether we should show the latest *Polaris A-2* which was operational, or the A-3 which had already been tested in August. If for any reason NATO decided on a submerged MLF, then we'd just add two more years to the lead time— all the way into 1970.

Like students cramming for exams, we were often in our offices until midnight because out of every briefing at a higher level, other changes crept into the presentation. By mid-month, the United States position on the MLF was as clear as it would ever get because of the many political caveats and waffles the State Department imposed, and the team started forming for the Paris trip. I learned a good lesson in international negotiations one Saturday when my wife and children picked me up, and we gave Mike Michaelis a ride home from State.

I asked, "Do you think they'll include me on the Paris team?"

"I haven't heard your name mentioned," Mike answered diplomatically.

He could sense my disappointment.

I added, "What does it take?"

Finally he observed, "You know, sometimes you can know too much..."

Over time, I've often remembered that lesson Mike taught me, and how right his observation was, and how often I had to do the same to some expert during early negotiation sessions. Anyway, we rushed through the final week, and just before they left for Paris, I was one of three selected to brief the generals and admirals of the full NATO Military Committee at the Pentagon on Monday morning, the same day and at almost the same time that the rest of the group would be briefing the NATO diplomats at the Atlantic Council's headquarters in Paris.

Our briefing at the Pentagon turned into one of the most memorable events in my life. I easily recognized the German, French and British uniforms and soon the entire room was packed for a briefing for which they had been waiting very patiently—for over a year and a half. Just after we started, three or four Air Force officers and some civilians literally raced down the aisle to stop us.

The subsequent conversation in whispers went something like this:

"We're sorry but in the name of national security we've been ordered to go first!"

"By whose order?"

"The President's..."

The three of us looked for seats, and I settled for an empty seat behind some German officers near the front, and watched two officers of the new briefing team put up enlarged aerial photographs while the others reviewed notes and photos.

The first speaker said, "As I stand here before you, I can assure you that Prime Minister Macmillan, President De Gaulle and Chancellor Adenauer and all the NATO heads of state have been briefed this morning, but without the technical information that you will receive from us... I don't know when your ambassadors in Washington will receive this information..."

With a pointer, he indicated a construction site on the first enlargement. "This is an almost completed launch complex with four medium-range missile launch pads under construction by the Soviet army troops commanded by General Issa A. Pliyev... the site is about sixty miles east of Havana, Cuba..."

Afraid that I would have a heart attack, I didn't breathe. But my inaction was out of fear that I'd miss one word. No one else was breathing and for precisely the same reason. No one understood why some Soviet missile was being called a MRBM by the CIA, but everyone in this military audience knew that the Soviet surface-to-surface missile with the range described was a rather recent Soviet Army missile with a nuclear warhead and whose range was sufficient to reach Washington from Cuba.

Although we remembered that NATO's General Norstad had coined the acronym MRBM to differentiate between an American IRBM and a NATO IRBM, for some reason the analysts used the term to indicate a missile with a range of about 1,000 nautical miles, and an IRBM for one with a range of two thousand nautical miles. It confused military men who knew better. Up until that Monday morning I had always considered the accuracy of the shorter range missile as maybe being able to hit the proverbial barn door—the red one, but having less range than indicated by the speakers.

Although the speakers didn't bother to explain everything in the photos, I recognized the tanker trailers—tankers that could carry liquid oxidizers and others designed for the liquid fuel of the rocket motors. To me this represented missiles limited in mobility and in response capability. This was good for our side.

Everyone was reminded that the information being provided was top secret, that as many prints as possible of the photos would be handed out, and that the members should take notes but were warned to use all secure systems for communicating with their capitols or their local Washington embassies.

The last speaker announced, "President Kennedy will discuss this issue publicly on television tonight at seven."

I remember the photographs and the rush by NATO officers to return to their offices, but I don't remember any conversations or the return trip on the Navy shuttle bus to the Munitions Building. I went straight to my brother's office where he took one look at me and asked with concern, "What happened to you?"

"The Soviets are installing dozens of IRBM's in Cuba, and some of their launch pads will be ready in about a week."

I described the briefing by the Air Force and the CIA. Because Norm and I had lived and breathed nuclear weapons for several years, we both knew how deadly the situation was for Washington and its suburbs. I said, "Only a few of them can reach New England and Montreal, but the speakers claimed all of them could hit here, Texas, Atlanta, the Cape, anything within a thousand miles of Cuba."

"They'll cream this area," Norm observed.

"If they have as many zeroed in on the Pentagon as we have on the Kremlin..." I started but left the sentence unfinished.

"I'm going home early to make sure we catch Kennedy."

"Me, too," my brother agreed.

"You can't tell Frances ahead of time. Security," I reminded him.

"Call me after the speech," said Norm.

As dramatic as the occasion was for me, my family and my country, the truth is that some details are difficult to remember because of the anxieties at the time, but the overall impression and other reactions and actions are still quite clear. Kennedy spoke of the underhanded way the Soviets acted and lied to him, of his declaration of a quarantine against any offensive Soviet weapons being transported on ships going to Cuba, and especially the warning that any missile fired from Cuba would be considered as a Soviet attack on the United States and as sufficient reason for us to retaliate.

After what I had seen and learned at the Pentagon that morning, to me, President Kennedy's words rang true, and I was convinced that he would launch a nuclear strike if the Cubans or Soviets got careless. Unconvinced as I was that the so-called MRBM was accurate, the more convinced I became that of a half dozen of them launched against the Pentagon, three would land in the Mantua area of Fairfax County where Normand's family lived, and three would land in McLean, Virginia where my family lived. After Kennedy's speech, Norm and I talked.

"We only have two options," he said, "and one is to get our families to Rhode Island, using roads as far away as possible from any prime targets. That'll take a couple of days to organize...you, know... plan the right route, buy groceries for the trip, get some cash, prepare some sort of shelter in case something breaks beforehand..."

I added other practical concerns, "But we don't get paid for ten more days—I've got to buy aluminum foil, some plywood, enough canned food and bottled water for six mouths for two weeks, batteries, candles—Jesus, Mary and Joseph, what a stinking mess!"

Normand was thinking and sometimes out loud, because he often lowered his voice when he did, "Frances and the kids could stay with her folks in North Smithfield..."

I agreed, "Yes, maybe Anne Hope and the kids could stay with George (our brother and former World War II fighter pilot) or with the folks at Spring Lake (near the village post office of Glendale in the township of Burrillville, Rhode Island)...but she's eight months pregnant."

"You study the map and the different safe routes, and I'll study the list of provisions the fall-out people recommend. I'll see you for lunch," he concluded.

I calculated how much gas our 1962 Mercury Comet station wagon consumed. Staying up late, I circled targets that the Soviets might select—obvious ones like New York City, Philadelphia and maybe Boston. I figured that they'd certainly target Chicago and Detroit. *"If I were the Soviet targeter, I'd target Denver or Houston before Boston."* Now I alarmed myself, because I couldn't remember whether the CIA analysts had said how many 2,000-mile-range missiles, whatever type or name they had, were in the Cuban mix. Heck, I couldn't even remember whether the president had quantified the number of Soviet missiles in his telecast only a few hours earlier. (Actually, Kennedy hadn't. The official records are still unclear how many of the longer range IRBMs were in Cuba.)

The following morning everyone in Special Projects discussed the Cuban events, and a considerable effort was mounted to put out to sea our *Polaris* submarines capable of safely going with or without test missiles. All the operational SSBNs would retake to the sea if they were in Holy Loch or in a US port like the SSB(N) 610 *USS Thomas A. Edison*. The main objective was to safeguard what we could from any first or retaliatory strike from Cuba. The command of the Atlantic Fleet out of Norfolk was mobilizing a picket line of warships about five hundred miles in a circle around Cuba, and particularly across the usual shipping lanes from the Soviet Union.

Without a doubt, the quarantine picket line—many of us called it a sanitary belt—dominated our attention, and the classified communications between the Fleet headquarters, the Pentagon and the ships at sea dominated most of the military links. In addition, the Navy and Air Force coordinated patrols over the ocean to spot, track and, if possible, photograph any Soviet vessels traveling toward Cuba from any direction. Invasion units from the Army and Marines were alerted. It was obvious that all the naval officers in SP would have wanted to be in on the Quarantine action.

Norm and I had lunch in the packed Navy mess downstairs, but unexpectedly it was not as noisy as usual.

The various Navy counsels had met first thing in the morning to discuss the legality and precedence for a naval quarantine, and Norm reported on the amount of legal work the Navy Counsel's office had done for the White House. Many of the words used by the President had significant legal meaning. Legality was very important in the event there were marine commercial losses and loss of life, insurance claims and the like.

While the military could take care of its own, there were always the problems of liability for civilians and private shipping. Otherwise the results could be chaos for our Latin American neighbors and our own American citizens, as is the case whenever there are losses due to riots and insurrections after which insurance companies refuse to kick-in any compensation on their policies.

Playing around with his mashed potatoes with his fork, he lowered his voice, "How many IRBMs did the CIA report yesterday?" asked Norm about the meeting of the NATO Military Committee at the Pentagon.

"They really didn't say—didn't even guesstimate...the CIA doesn't even know what an IRBM is."

"Well, what do you think? You saw the photos—were they the same that were in the papers this morning?"

Here goes the lawyer's cross examination again, I thought. "Some were of anti-aircraft missiles—like the battery of *Nike-Hercules* missiles outside many US cities—storage bunkers, ramps, work hangar, radar, perimeter clearing—the same thing. I doubt that they could even reach Florida on the slant. They were guessing about the IRBMs."

"Some of the lawyers said that those anti-aircraft missiles had a short range and only could attain about 70,000 feet."

"Well, that's more than I know," I admitted, "But I'm sure the Air Force has all that kind of information—their necks will be on the line to take them out."

"You said all the IRBMs could reach Washington, right?"

"They said, *all of them*—I'm guessing that all the site photos we saw probably accounted for a couple dozen missile pads. One CIA analyst claimed that one missile could reach Hudson Bay."

"Of course, we don't know if you were shown all the photos..." he opined.

"A friend of mine in ONI was in SP this morning, he told me that the U-2s are returning with miles of film—everyday."

"If you were doing the Soviet targeting, how would you do it?"

"Reliability is better when you don't select targets at the limit of the missile's range, statistically it's better to select targets between 60% and 85% of the range for two-stage missiles launched from a fixed land site...less things to go wrong...less lateral and downrange errors. The problems are different with a sea launch. I figure they'll pulverize the southeast—Huntsville, Charleston, Cape Canaveral, New Orleans. Certainly Miami because so many who left Cuba live there—Castro won't lose this chance to get even."

Norm looked around and said, "I called the Navy Credit Union, they're going to arrange emergency hardship loans for people sending their families out of town. I guess we weren't very original."

"Good idea, Norm. I wonder if my friends in the Navy Comptroller's office can push to cut our monthly checks a few days early. I'll call them later."

"What about the route to Rhode Island?" he asked.

"I'm amazed that so few bridges cross the Hudson. Anne Hope thinks the bridge near Tarrytown is OK, the Tappan Zee. But that's still close to New York City. I'd rather find some inland route farther from coastal prime targets...go to the Finger Lakes (upper New York state), then head east toward Mohegan country..."

"It might be easier if Frances and Anne Hope followed each other, give each other a hand with the kids..." added Norm. Then he added a second thought, "But to hear your thoughts, Washington would only have a few missiles aimed at it."

"You only need one to incinerate Fairfax County and irradiate any survivor of the blast who sticks his stupid nose above ground the first couple of weeks."

Chapter 13

Double crisis: Cuba and Nassau

Despite the chilling events swirling around us and the demands of our own jobs, my brother and I met at least once a day, and when one of us gleaned a new bit of information which seemed decisive, we spoke by telephone. Radio reports were the most sought-after media for homemakers, drivers and people outdoors who had access to portable radios, although the most powerful medium was still the daily newspaper. Only the latter gave sweeping descriptions of what American citizens in range of Soviet military rockets were doing to protect themselves during this Cuban missile crisis. Our wives, too, spoke daily and felt the pressure that their husbands were applying to make good an escape from highly targetable Washington to the benign havens in Rhode Island.

In addition to practicing hiding under desks and sitting along corridor walls, my two oldest, André and Geneviève, returned home to repeat what the teachers related about other schools having their windows sandbagged from the outside to prevent shards of glass showering classrooms in the event of a nuclear blast within five miles. There was a run on aluminum foil in supermarkets and eventually we found some in a hardware store. That foil was vital to reflect radiation. Arguments flared up between customers when people noticed that others were hoarding canned goods, bottled water, and batteries for flashlights and portable radios. Civil Defense authorities applied their own form of stress on local households by testing sirens with more frequency and purpose, and radio commentators repeatedly announced the emergency frequencies to listen to—just in case. Listeners were reminded to write down these emergency radio frequencies, and to keep their bathtubs full of water—just in case the water mains ruptured.

By the time that Normand and I arrived home at night we found that our spouses knew more than we did! Having access to secret information often brought us into conflict with the floodgates of public information pouring out of press rooms, radio and television studios, and with hard fact and white lies from the White House, the State Department and Defense. What McNamara, Rusk and Kennedy were saying publicly didn't always square with the content of messages, reports and cables Normand and I could read at work. It was easy to become dizzy over what we could admit and discuss outside the office.

After a few days I was able to learn that the so-called IRBMs were apparently at a single base a few miles west of Havana, and in fact the *aggressive* missile sites—the others being the mysterious MRBMs concocted by the CIA—were on the western half of the island, on the side closest to the Gulf of Mexico. Luckily, as the number of IRBMs decreased, the safer did New England seem to Norm and me. But for the 50,000,000+ Americans in key target areas within a great arc from Miami, New Orleans, Houston, and Memphis to Washington, it was definitely sandbag time, and public hysteria was poured on.

Although magazines like *Newsweek* and *Time* didn't feature the crisis right away, others like *U.S. News and World Report* whose format and schedule permitted breaking news had a field day by printing photos and maps showing the cities within range of each "deadly" type of missile. I even called my friend Marvin L. Stone who was on the national staff of *USN&WR* to seek information from him! (Marvin eventually became Executive Editor, and years later became Deputy Director of the United States Information Agency when Normand was named acting-General Counsel there.)

In the upside-down Washington world of contradictions, newshounds had become news sources. In fact, when writing this memoir some thirty-eight years later I had to resist the temptation to straighten out "insider" histories written of that era and accepted for many years as the "gospel truth." However, a few were often self-servingly truthful, somewhat shy of historically truthful and, alas, missing the mark of "nothing but the truth." In some cases the authors seemed to have been denied access to official records by succeeding administrations, or they elected not to use them.

After five days, we felt frazzled. Our Navy vessels were reporting plenty of encounters and some contradictory descriptions of what Soviet freighters were doing. A couple of Soviet subs had been forced to the surface and we royally screwed up their ability to communicate with Moscow. But we didn't know what, which kind or how many long range missiles were already in Cuba. We knew that as high drama unfolded at sea, one mishap, one pistol fired in anger, anything ignited by a nervous crewman or skipper could unleash a manure-load of worldwide problems.

We had a younger brother who often left Spring Lake, Rhode Island, in the fall to take on off-season work in Washington. We speculated that he might be willing to accompany our wives on the trek to Rhode Island.

"I'm sure Richard would do it if we asked," said Normand.

"Sure," I agreed. Having served with the US Army in Germany, Richard was still a happy-go-lucky bachelor.

There was some irony is what was occurring. Exactly one year earlier to the day when the Cuban missile crisis broke, Soviet tanks and US Army tanks had faced off on 22 October 1961, "muzzle-to-muzzle" at US Checkpoint Charlie in Berlin, as aptly described by Alexandra Richie in her "*Faust's Metropolis*." American soldiers who manned checkpoints between the US sectors and the Soviet sectors were the cream of the military, and they were normally very difficult to pass without one's papers being in order. Many times had I passed a similar checkpoint at Linz in Austria, and I was always proud of the soldiers' appearances and their sticking to all the rules. If I ever had trouble with Soviet soldiers after the Linz checkpoint, as I'll describe in Chapter Twenty, it was because of Soviet perfidy and not American laxity. In Berlin, the crisis was due to a spoiled American diplomat who insisted on attending the opera in East Berlin despite the challenging events that followed the construction of the Berlin Wall.

A year later, however, the crisis was now at home!

By the end of the week, it was crunch time because the US Navy Task Force 136 had now gone gunwale-to-gunwale with Soviet ships loaded with contraband to the Quarantine, and while politicians hesitated, my brother and I absolutely had to fish or cut bait. By Friday night, my own wife had been warned by her doctor not to travel that far by car, and Norm's wife didn't want to leave with her two toddlers without him. (The oldest, Michel, went on to become a US naval officer in nuclear submarines, including Trident launching SSBNs.) So Norm and I concentrated on stocking the cellar or back rooms we had been working on with sleeping bags or mattresses, pillows, blankets, everything that a child might remember—like a rainy night in a tent with grandma. Spare cash was placed in metal cookie cans, and water filled every spare receptacle including the children's' playpool which was brought inside.

After cutting plywood to fit cellar windows, the exterior faces were covered with aluminum foil. There was no SP for us that Friday night and all day Saturday, and like many parents we always kept one ear glued to the radio, except for the evening TV news, until Sunday night when Kennedy announced that Khrushchev had agreed to withdraw the Soviet missiles from Cuba.

Nonetheless, the crisis had lasted over three more weeks, until 20 November, six days after my son Jean-Marc was born, when Khrushchev also agreed to pull out his IL-18 bombers. Each one of them could have carried several megatons of nuclear weapons as far as New Orleans, Atlanta and Jacksonville and return again their airfield near Havana. It is beyond reasonable interpretation for a sane person to comprehend the Soviet belief that the Air Force would have permitted any IL-28 to penetrate US air space. To me, Khrushchev and Castro were hallucinating to believe those bombers would ever have returned to Cuba or would have reached Florida.

It was easy to laugh and look back on hell week and make light of the agony that millions of Americans went through. Norm and I had a good chuckle when the news leaked out that the television commentator John Scali had been a conduit of information from the Soviet embassy to Attorney General Robert F. Kennedy. Scali had married Denise St. Germain whose family we knew well in Woonsocket, Rhode Island.

Inside SP and the Navy, things slowly regained normality. A tremendous budget battle quickly resurfaced after the Cuban missile crisis, especially over the TFX military aircraft and, over the objections of the Defense Comptroller Charles Hitch, more money was earmarked for *Skybolt*'s continuing research and development. Following the Congressional elections, we prepared additional MLF documentation for NATO's December ministerial meeting in Paris that Rusk and McNamara would be attending. December promised to be a momentous month for us, one that could double SP's contribution to western defense, and everyone was so sure of it that we helped CNO run cost numbers of MLF surface fleets with ten, twenty or thirty ships.

The push to eliminate nuclear proliferation was on, and although this issue was worded to address the whole world, the message was actually aimed between De Gaulle's eyes. Even the UK had to take a shot when former Secretary of State Dean Acheson gave a speech on 5 December that more-or-less ridiculed Britain's pretense at being a nuclear power. With the NATO meeting only a week off, it started to appear as if they'd be some lively discussions for three days in Paris. The ministerial meeting would start on Wednesday, 12 December, and run through Friday afternoon. Well, there sure were a lot of fireworks, but not the ones we expected, and not in Paris!

On Tuesday, 11 December I received a call to go to the State Department to pick up a copy of an important cable from London. In the afternoon I was given a copy of a message to McGeorge Bundy which described that day's meeting between the British Defense Minister Thorneycroft and Defense Secretary McNamara. When I was given the copy I was told, "Most of the blood on the floor was McNamara's." Of course, I couldn't wait to read the cable. Obviously written by an onlooker to the meeting between the two, it described a shouting match between two deaf people, speaking loudly and hearing nothing from the other side. Tempers flared. It was so bad that they had to agree to meet again later after they cooled down.

Basically, Thorneycroft accused McNamara of the grossest bad manners for canceling the air-to-surface *Skybolt* upon which the entire British deterrent program was based, upon which the entire British government rested, upon which the world depended, and for having crudely announced the cancellation to the British press at the London airport even before extending Thorneycroft the elementary courtesy of an advanced warning. Guilt and more guilt battered down on McNamara's culpable head at the hands of the righteous Thorneycroft.

Of course, the British press had a field day peeling away McNamara's skin one thin layer at a time. "Macmillan's government may fall," screamed some opposition writers gleefully. Other papers explained, "It's all McNamara's fault."

I could not figure out why the devil all this was so important for SP and why I had been made privy to this politically sensitive cable. After calling some sources at State and at the NSC, finally one person said, "The Brits claim Eisenhower had offered *Polaris* as a backup if *Skybolt* failed."

"You don't expect me to believe that do you?"

"What the hell do I know, I wasn't at Camp David."

"The Brits also claim that McNamara has no manners," I reminded him.

"They also claim he's a fat head, and they're just warming up," he added.

"So what does Rusk say?" I asked.

"He's on the way to Paris. He took his lumps last month from the President for not having taken those *Jupiter* missiles out of Turkey like the President asked him in July or whenever. Khrushchev blindsided Kennedy who thought the missiles were already gone when the Soviets offered to trade *Jupiters* in Turkey in exchange for the Soviet missiles in Cuba."

"Hell, I didn't know that!"

"A few weeks ago, McNamara told the President that he'd take care of any *Skybolt* problems with the Brits, and Rusk joined McNamara to assure Kennedy that it'd be no big deal."

"You guys really have your act put together over there," I chided.

"Spare me any fancy Navy BS, my friend. Macmillan is demanding to discuss this in the face-to-face meeting before Christmas with Kennedy who is once again upset over something. If McNamara has any skin left when he returns, Kennedy will make Rusk eat it raw!"

"So," I asked, "what about *Polaris*?"

"Nothing."

"Nothing? You said..."

"Trust me. The Brits are just fuming over the public embarrassment," he explained.

After rereading the cable I brought it to Captain Jerry Clarke, and filled him in on what I'd been told. We had never, we agreed, never heard of *Polaris* as a backup to anything with the British. I left the cable with him and returned to my office to bring John Craven up to speed.

The next few mornings we looked for any available British newspaper, but the US papers were ahead of their overseas rivals, and removed much of the partisan ranting that creeps into British news columns. We started to pay more attention when the British openly claimed that our *Polaris* anchorage at Holy Loch had been a *quid pro quo* for our guaranteeing a deterrent to the UK, which came as a surprise to us. Their veiled threat was groundless because our deterrent was the west's guarantee for liberty.

Nonetheless, the *Skybolt* crisis overshadowed the NATO meeting and the MLF. Kennedy agreed to discuss this at the meeting with

Macmillan at Nassau on Tuesday, 18 December, after the British leader would have had his private meeting with De Gaulle at Château Rambouillet south of Paris on Saturday the 15th. After repeated assurances from the State Department to ignore British claims about *Polaris*, we did just that and ignored the rumors.

However, once again State was behind the curve. It seemed that the President had just arrived in Nassau when the Navy was ordered to prepare some *Polaris* options for the President to discuss with Macmillan. Five of us were thrown into a boiling cauldron and ordered to produce before being let out. Captain Jim Calvert was one of the four officers I was tossed in with to start writing *something*, whatever the hell it was supposed to be. I liked Jim right off and it didn't surprise me to hear he had made admiral sometime later.

There were only so many options we could develop regarding *Polaris* and by now we were experts. "A little Tidal Basin launch, anyone?" we joked, as we worked late into the night.

"The Royal Navy doesn't even want a deterrent, and they loathe nuclear submarines!" reminded another, as he stressed the word "loathe."

Well, orders were orders, and we cranked out our proposals and their options, and damn near worked twenty-four straight hours by the time it was done. I think it was on the 19th when someone from the Pentagon flew to Nassau so that Kennedy could present a "talking paper on *Polaris*" that night to Macmillan. We caught up on our rest without knowing whether other missile options were in Kennedy's grab bag of assorted gifts and trinkets. In all my time at SP this had been the first time that we had been caught with our pants at half mast, but it was also the first time we were so well experienced in fire drills of this kind.

On Friday, 21 December 1962, Kennedy and Macmillan announced their *Polaris* Agreement by which Britain would furnish its own nuclear submarines and nuclear warheads, and the US would furnish everything else. By the time it all sank in after Christmas, I was notified that I was a member of the Defense Department team named to negotiate with the British to come up with the formal "working" agreement. During the second week of January, Admiral Galantin forwarded me a laudatory letter of appreciation from Henry S. Rowen in Paul H. Nitze's office for my "notably competent and productive effort...in preparing the presentation of the Multilateral MRBM Force concept given the North Atlantic Council on 22 October 1962."

Facing page. Holy Loch, Scotland. The American submarine FBM tender AS 33 *U.S.S. Simon Lake* at anchorage with two U.S. Navy SSB(N)s alongside in 1987. By this time, only *Trident C4* and *Poseidon C3* missiles were in the fleet. In 1982, *Polaris* had become history after 22 years as a useful deterrent weapon.

Government Photo

Attached to Rowen's letter was a particularly warm letter from Walt Rostow the Policy Planning Chairman at State to Paul Nitze about me in which Rostow described the "delicate and demanding nature" of our work at State for the MLF and that "Mr. Poirier performed most valuable services (p. 298)." As an indication of how much the Cuban affair and Nassau had interrupted the Pentagon, Rostow's letter was dated 5 November 1962, Rowen's 21 November, and Galantin's 10 January 1963. Such laudatory letters were dangerous and simply made the praised person a target. It therefore came as no surprise when President Kennedy in the person of McGeorge Bundy dropped another bombshell in SP's lap, or more accurately, in mine.

By this time Kennedy learned that Rusk had failed to keep De Gaulle in the loop about Nassau, and that the French President was already furious. Not only had Macmillan double-crossed the French president at Rambouillet, but De Gaulle felt that both Kennedy and Macmillan had also joined up to triple-cross him at Nassau. Kennedy once again was livid at Rusk's oversight. Many of us had heard that Rusk often took to the bottle, and now I was wondering whether that was why he was making my own life so miserable. The White House solution was to organize one of the most elaborate classified briefings for the French, and I was going to give it in French.

It was my turn to go through the overhead. "That type of briefing is illegal!" I claimed.

"Balls," came one answer.

"The McMahon Act makes it illegal," I insisted.

"Only in the United States," came the retort.

"What the devil's that supposed to mean?"

"The US territory stops 200 nautical miles offshore..."

"So what...? The law doesn't." I replied.

"You're going to fly out to a carrier, the *USS Franklin D. Roosevelt* where you'll brief the French delegation."

"How'll they get to the ship?" I asked in surprise.

"We're still working on it, but I imagine we'll fly them in from Martinique or Guadeloupe."

As dumbfounded as I was, I could understand Kennedy's desperate move. De Gaulle had been royally "shafted," as simply stated in one of Kennedy's favorite expressions pronounced with a long *Boston A*. Proliferation was on the line, but De Gaulle had been the first to rally to Kennedy in the Cuban crisis, and while Macmillan waffled, De Gaulle was the first to pledge any, all and unqualified support to the United States against the Soviet Union's threat in Cuba.

But I immediately recognized the many problems because for years I had lived and breathed the limitations imposed by the United States Atomic Energy Act of 1946, usually called the "McMahon Act as amended in 1954." Even my own senator, John O. Pastore of Rhode Island, was a rock of Gibraltar against sharing nuclear information with other countries, and so was Representative Chet Holifield of California, both powerhouses on the Joint Committee for Atomic Energy in Congress. In fact, a few months earlier Chet Holifield's simple comment about it being unwise to transfer classified information "to nations whose political structure is unstable and whose security capability is questionable" was enough to nip in the bud the idea for the Nautilus-type submarine sale to France. The strength of the French Communist party had poisoned Franco-American relations for many years, much to France's disadvantage.

My SP and Navy colleagues often relied on my personal recommendations and decisions on the release of classified information, and they knew me to be very conservative and prudent. In addition, I felt that the decision to brief the French under these circumstances was reckless and desperate in the face of obvious Congressional outrage if the Hill ever found out. Although I knew that State was in on the planning, I was too cautious to dare take my apprehensions outside the Navy. An order was an order, except, *"How to change the orders?"*

"You can't," said Commander Ken Wade, one of SP's two Public Information Officers.

"That's right," agreed Commander Tom Rhees, the other PIO in SP.

One of the stickiest points was the fact that Kennedy wanted a classified briefing, and under the circumstances he wanted a briefing that would please De Gaulle because we in SP knew the level of briefings we had given the French over the last three years. The truth was that only rarely had we given briefings to the French outside of NATO briefings. I had been involved in one for the French Navy Minister in 1960 or 1961 in California, but he had been more interested in the Napa Valley grape crop than in *Polaris*. He had been a comical sight whenever he jumped from his chauffeur-driven limousine, provided by Lockheed and Westinghouse, to pace off the distance between grape plants in California's famed vineyards. Then, of course, there had been the General Lavaud briefing in May 1962 for which I received written honors and couldn't even remember. What I could remember was what we could tell NATO or the French or the British, and what we couldn't.

For ten weeks our feet had been held to the fire without letup by Kennedy's Multilateral Nuclear Force for NATO and by the Cuban Missile Crisis. Now the Kennedy-Macmillan Nassau Agreement had unexpectedly turned my immediate mission into a political salvage job of unknown dimensions. A big part of the problem was that I had no idea how attendance at the briefing was being sold to De Gaulle in Paris. And by whom? To be polite he could simply send a bunch of technicians, or if he were really interested he could send his Navy Minister again, the one who liked raising grapes.

To my mind, De Gaulle had been insulted by Gilpatric's leak to the press in October that he'd make an offer to the French of an American nuclear submarine before he knew he had the right to make it. The only way De Gaulle could save face in the light of a sure withdrawal of the offer would be to refuse it if it were made in the first place. Only a handful of fools in the world were ignorant of De Gaulle's pride.

Suddenly the United States was offering classified information that France had never received before. And down in my gut I felt we didn't have the legal right to do it.

Chapter 14

Kennedy and nuclear proliferation

In no manner, shape or form was I ready to split hairs over what constituted classified material that was releasable or not, and I was not about to present the material in a foreign language when no US participant could attest whether it was in fact releasable. And as I argued, additional Navy opinions shared mine. Even though both the White House and State wanted to make amends to France, and I just couldn't see how the devil we could pull the rabbit out of the hat for the diplomats or the President. On one hand the quality of the French delegation was unknown to us—politically savvy or technically competent. Usually it was one or the other. And on the other hand we knew that the information they'd like on our IRBM would be impossible to get into during the type of meeting being proposed to us.

We were really clueless as to which foot to start dancing on, and I expected that on such short notice we had no right to expect a very high powered French delegation. While we waited for the French to identify their delegation, and to move them from France to the Caribbean, the aircraft carrier *CVA 42 Franklin D. Roosevelt* performed its duties on the high seas, far beyond 200 nautical miles from the US mainland. It was my intention to fly to Mayport, Florida, and catch a Navy COD flight to the carrier. COD was simply an acronym for civilian-on-official-duty. While waiting for final instructions we agreed that Commander Rhees would lead off the presentation as a Naval officer in uniform. So the two of us stayed close by in SP until we received the date and green light to leave Washington.

Once the details arrived, we flew directly to the Mayport Naval Base some fifteen miles east of and downstream from Jacksonville, Florida on the St. Johns River. The newly re-commissioned deep water naval base was a frequent port of call for the largest aircraft carriers seeking supplies or repairs. Carriers would have their aircraft fly in the last few hundred miles to the air station, and would leave Mayport without its planes. After the carrier was well out to sea, the aircraft would fly out to the carrier.

After boarding the twin-engine Navy plane, Tom took the co-pilot's seat and I took the one immediately behind the pilot. Because the plane was configured for landing on carriers, my seat faced backward. It was a long flight and I no longer remember how long it took. I often stood between the two pilots to chat and break up the boredom. Finally we spotted the carrier below, no bigger than a postage stamp, and many miles away. The carrier's control tower had picked us up by radar to help guide us in, and we had the advantage of visual contact on a clear day. It was routine for the carrier to be headed into the wind when we approached for a landing.

After strapping myself into my seat with the belt and harness, I watched over my shoulder as best as I could while the pilot aligned the plane with the flight deck. When I could see the deck cable that our tailhook would snatch, I leaned back, preparing for the sudden deceleration when the cable would arrest our forward progression. It did bring us to a complete stop, and then the plane bounced backward. Otherwise, the plane would have gone over the side into the ocean.

Now seventeen-years-old, the *Roosevelt* had originally been christened the *Coral Sea* on 29 April 1945. President Roosevelt had died earlier on the 12th, and later it was decided, with President Truman's approval, to rename the new attack carrier. While I was in the Navy Comptroller's office at the Pentagon I had costed-out the *Roosevelt*'s "steaming" hours with its full crew and full complement of fighter aircraft, but I couldn't recall the exact dollars and cents. I knew, however, that this briefing for the French would normally have cost many millions of dollars, but in the records it would be absorbed into training, take off-and-landing practice and sea trials. For purposes of comparison, a 1963 dollar was worth about five 2000 dollars.

The small room I was given onboard was comfortable enough, and with all the sea air it was easy to fall soundly asleep. At dawn an explosion woke me, and I thought we had been torpedoed. In a startled state, I sat at the edge of my bunk-sized bed, waiting for sirens and an abandon-ship order. Silence, all around. No running feet. I started to doubt my ears, and wondered if I had dreamt the noise. Just as I laid my head to the pillow again, a second explosion shot me straight up. This was no imaginary noise, but I couldn't understand why no one among the thousands on board was running around. I decided to wash and shave and go find food and conversational comfort. While shaving I noticed for the first time the roar of an engine and then a third explosion.

It finally dawned on me that the noise was the report of the catapult hurling jet fighters off the deck. Acting much like a slingshot pulled back, the catapult operation waited for the fighter's engine to be revved up before the catapulting mechanism was released. I had noticed the F4 *Phantom* jet fighters parked on deck the previous day. My room, I thought, was immediately below the catapult, and that assuredly I had not been given the visiting admiral's quarters.

When I finally was in the corridor the humdrum of carrier activity was in full swing, a routine I found different from submarines. I concluded that no one on a carrier ever whispered on purpose, and that no one on a submarine ever raised his voice intentionally. Of course the background noise on a nuclear submarine usually is not nearly as noisy as that on an aircraft carrier. By the time I entered the mess for breakfast, I assumed that some *Phantoms* had been launched to escort the French delegation. It had been planned to brief them in a rather large room where a screen and a small buffet had been set up by the crew.

Later, the ship's captain and other officers escorted the French, a US Navy escort-attaché with all the gold braid and a similarly bedecked French military attaché. We welcomed the French in a cordial naval style that was limited only by the businesslike procedures of an aircraft carrier at sea. Although I hadn't seen them arrive, there were some seven or eight dignitaries and I guessed that they had arrived in two Navy planes the size of mine. The head of the French delegation was none other than Pierre Messmer, the Minister of Defense. I hadn't expected someone that high up or as close to De Gaulle. Also with him was a Colonel Hoffman whose reputation I knew because he was one of the top point men in the French IRBM development. Another was Pierre Aigrain, the head of the *Centre National de la Recherche Scientifique*, the National Center for Scientific Research, which was the French working equivalent combining the National Academy of Sciences and the Bureau of Standards in Washington.

I guess their flight had been as long as mine, but from a different direction, and as a sort of comic relief everyone who had just arrived asked directions to the head. I thought that was a good idea because I had several cups of coffee in me. In the washroom about a dozen men headed straight for the urinals except for Dr. Aigrain who first went to wash his hands. While he was drying them, some of his colleagues joined him at the wash basins and kidded Aigrain's reversal of tradition.

One said to the other, "Pierre's a little mixed up, isn't he? Was it the lack of oxygen in the American plane?"

The other rose to the bait, and asked Aigrain, "What's the matter, Pierre, don't you wash AFTER instead of BEFORE like everyone else."

With blinking an eye, the chief of French research answered, "It depends on which is the dirtier."

Some of his colleagues pretended being deeply hurt and protested the insinuation about the lack of private cleanliness. Obviously well at ease, the French bantered good-naturedly among themselves before rejoining the others in the wardroom.

I learned that most, and maybe all, understood English. Pierre Aigrain had received his Ph.D. at the Massachusetts Institute of Technology. His command of English might have been the best of the group. I sat next to Pierre Messmer for the entire time, but he only spoke to me in French and I did likewise. I never did find out how well he understood the briefings in English, although I knew he had spent some time in London after he joined the Free French and De Gaulle there in 1940. The others certainly understood because they asked sharp but polite questions and good follow-up questions.

Some of the films we showed were classified secret and I doubt that any other Frenchmen had ever seen them. One was even new to me. Whenever we had a dialogue interchange Messmer struck me as warmer than what I expected after reading the briefing paper prepared about him that a US naval officer handed me. In one scene of a *Polaris* launch, the missile and spray were joined by what looked like flotsam and sections of a life vest used in marine rescues. Mr. Messmer leaned to me and asked, "What are those things?"

I explained, "The missile model is smaller than the launch tube which will accommodate a bigger model someday. So we stuff the space between the missile and the tube with mattress-type or stiff cushion liners...somewhat like corking used in life vests. They help to keep the launching force concentrated under the missile to expel it far enough from the submarine. Privately, we call those liners *garbage.*" (I used the word *cochonneries* which brought a smile to his face.)

"*Ah oui, je vois*," he answered in French. "Oh yes, I see."

Later he spoke to the whole group in French, and one of his delegation translated very well into English. He spoke about the French program, and the fact that France would continue to go alone. When he returned to his seat, I whispered in French, "Does that mean we're wasting our time with the Multilateral Nuclear Force?"

Before answering he looked at me, and then simply shrugged as if he didn't know or care, or maybe that it was none of my business what he thought, or maybe it was none of his business what the United States was doing with the MLF.

I would have liked talking with him more, because he had served with distinction during the Second World War with the mixed-manned French Foreign Legion in North Africa and in Italy. After the Allies invaded Normandy, they were boxed in by the German Army for two months in western France. Following the Normandy breakthrough at Caen by the Canadian Third Division, Messmer joined General Leclerc's 3rd Armored Division in the desperate Franco-US drive of August 1944 to liberate Paris.

But for him the war didn't end in 1945, and he parachuted into North Vietnam during the war in Indochina, the one that the Eisenhower and Kennedy administrations had funded up to 80% to help the French. Messmer was captured and held prisoner by the North Vietnamese. Following his release, most of his subsequent bureaucratic career was in the Colonial service in Africa. Picked to be the Minister of Defense on 5 February 1960. Messmer was known to have unwavering allegiance to President Charles de Gaulle, and had spearheaded France's policy to develop its own independent nuclear deterrent. Everyone in that wardroom knew that the only higher French authority on defense matters was De Gaulle himself.

It was clear that once our briefing was finished, the rest of the formalities didn't include SP, so Tom and I waited for the right moment to politely present our adieux to the French visitors before heading for the flight deck to arrange our return trip to the mainland. The catapult was unneeded for our plane, and I had the best reverse view of our take off from the carrier, particularly as we dipped below the deck level and sunk toward sea level before leveling off and gaining altitude. I couldn't help but notice how unattractive wave tops were from that viewing position.

On the return trip I reflected on the day: *"Could we have done better? Had we done what Kennedy wanted?"* So went my thoughts. As far as the technical quality of the Frenchmen there, we could not have been honored with better. Politically, we could not have expected more clout-power, short of de Gaulle himself. Yet, the secret background paper on Messmer made it clear that he was not considered to be a politician, and was uncharitably described by the State Department author as a colorless bureaucrat. I'm sure that in 1962 Messmer never expected to be France's longest serving defense minister since the days of the French kings nor that he would be the prime minister of France ten years later.

Had any State Department officials overheard my impertinent remark about the MLF I'm sure they would have lodged a formal protest to the Navy because I was too forward by their standards. But I and the Navy interpreted Messmer's shrug as more eloquent than a speech, and could save us a lot of time and energy. For all I knew he probably appreciated my question and the chance to shrug. The French had passed through an extremely important election in the fall, just as the United States did a week or so after the Cuban crisis. De Gaulle and his wife had miraculously escaped a second assassination attempt the previous August when 14 bullets entered the car he and his wife were in, and for the first time in years he had taken a lot of gaff and personal criticism from the press and the opposition for dissolving parliament, but his party had still won a healthy majority in new parliamentary elections to everyone's surprise including his own.

It would have been foolhardy for me to believe that Tom and I had somehow removed the insult to De Gaulle occasioned by Rusk's inaction during Nassau and its aftermath. Had Kennedy really wanted to appease De Gaulle, all he had to do was to certify that France was a friendly nation which had made substantial progress on its own in nuclear development.

Without such a declaration, our hands were tied and no information prohibited by the McMahon Act could be released or exchanged. Nonetheless, Kennedy had expressed several times that France and England were small but that their nuclear capability could drag the US into a nuclear war. But on the other hand, De Gaulle felt that the US would never sacrifice Kansas City or Boston to save Lyon or Bordeaux. He believed in "proportional deterrence," whereby his small force would be able to inflict such damage on Soviet cities that the cost would be too much for Moscow to bear for whatever advantages it could possibly gain by defeating France.

"Had the United States pushed the cork too far into the bottle with De Gaulle?" I wondered. On the subject of nuclear knowledge, even Kennedy had said that it was difficult to put the *jinni* back into the bottle once it was out. To insult the seventy-two-year-old French president was one thing, but to repeatedly force his country, America's oldest ally, to publicly play second fiddle was stupid, even if it was unintentional—something that was getting harder to believe. When I had noticed the incorrect translations of De Gaulle's words, the Kennedy people had stopped it quickly. Yet the anglophiles at the State Department constituted a strong clique. Some of them imitated the English diplomats with London-tailored pin-striped suits, long umbrellas and the thin mustache so stylish in the British foreign service, and even feigned the very correct English accent. London-tailoring, I had to admit, was hard to beat, but pushing the accent was a bit much and definitely showed a latent bias—I started to believe. I saw none of this affectation at the White House or at the Pentagon but often, unfortunately, at the State Department.

Preventing nuclear war through deterrence was one of our priorities, and another was non-proliferation of nuclear weapons. But, when the United States had a chance to ease the UK out of the nuclear deterrent business, Eisenhower was out-negotiated by Macmillan at Camp David. Eisenhower let the British off the hook very cheaply when they abandoned the *Blue Streak* IRBM and he offered them the *Skybolt* air-to-surface missile in March 1960 without obligating the UK to pay one red cent in research and development costs.

As a consequence the United States swallowed the almost-billion-dollar-loss on its own. And a month ago, America once again had the opportunity to ease the British out of the nuclear weapons market. But it seemed as if President Kennedy felt obliged to save Macmillan from a temporary political death of a thousand paper cuts from the British press, and simply put up America's most exclusive weapon to save the Prime Minister's political hide. Militarily, the west didn't need a *Polaris* with a Union Jack painted on its side. Certainly the American delegation that went to Nassau hadn't thought about it, otherwise *why were five of us forced to work around the clock to produce talking papers on Polaris after the President left for Nassau?* These thoughts and questions haunted my flight back to Washington.

At the time of the Nassau meeting, we had no intelligence on what deals Macmillan had cut or discussed with De Gaulle at Rambouillet after the December NATO ministerial meeting, and thereafter Macmillan had made a short overnight stop before flying straight to Nassau on 17 December. As far as I could tell, the only UK contribution the White House or the State Department achieved in the Nassau Agreement, was for the British to give lip service and some undefined political support for the MLF. In exchange, the British received the queen bee of the American missile arsenal, and there would be no double key on the warheads. The Royal Navy would have its own and sole finger on the trigger. *Hell, the Royal Navy had never even liked Polaris and had wanted the RAF to have the deterrent!*

Thinking back on our grudging briefing on the aircraft carrier, I felt we had done nothing to halt nuclear proliferation, and maybe we simply helped to convince the French that they were on the right track—that an independent nuclear deterrent was the only honorable solution. Years earlier, De Gaulle had refused to permit American IRBMs on French soil because he wouldn't accept a dual key system like Italy had done for the *Jupiters* stationed on their territory. De Gaulle reasoned that the US missiles would simply attract Soviet missiles to French territory. And if the Soviet Army overran Germany as everyone expected it could in 1963, France's atomic bombs aimed at a couple Soviet cities would stop the Soviets at the Rhine River. *Why would De Gaulle now substitute a derogation to the MLF when he was within striking distance of his own Polaris-type nuclear submarine?*

The answer seemed obvious. Our foreign policy had served to push both Britain and France into a path leading to independent nuclear forces, exactly the type of proliferation we were against. Twice the British had come to bat against us and they hit home runs each time. But we never even let the French into the on deck circle.

At day's end, our plane started to circle and when I looked down on Washington, all its major white marble or granite landmarks were lighted and had the shine of bright jewels of a necklace around the dark green *mall* and shadows that stretched from the Capitol to the Lincoln Memorial. From my pocket I pulled the message about who would be involved in the negotiations with the British, and I studied the names of those named to the Defense team to negotiate the "*Polaris* Sales Agreement." I recognized naval personnel on the list and saw no one from the State Department. As for the British team, we only knew the name of their head man, James MacKay, a civilian attached to the

Admiralty in London. His American counterpart was William C. Mott, Rear Admiral, USN, whom I would meet in a few days.

A lot of water had gone over the dam since I had read the secret cable describing McNamara's shouting match with Thorneycroft only a month earlier in London. December 1962 had been one month in which both non-proliferation and statesmanship each earned a black eye.

Chapter 15

The Royal Navy arrives

I doubt that anyone in January 1963 would have ever thought that the curse of proliferation might haunt mankind until the end of time, but our neat and orderly studies and policies of October 1962 which led to the MLF proposal had fallen into disarray. Actually, the Cuban Missile Crisis had interrupted our protective vigil over Europe while our astonished allies watched us sail to the nuclear brink without once seeing the need to ask their opinions before we drew a trigger-line in the ocean some 500 nautical miles from Cuba.

During January we heard and read that the Kennedy administration had given France the same *Polaris* offer as we had given the United Kingdom at Nassau. Cdr. Tom Rhees and I couldn't help wondering whether our briefing on the *Roosevelt* had been part of that mysterious grand offer to De Gaulle, or whether our nightmares were accurate and that we had been THE offer that everyone was hinting at. Privately, however, we knew that during the last three years the Royal Navy, the British Defense Ministry or even NATO had never received such a painstakingly prepared briefing as the one we had given Defense Minister Messmer and his team.

But the French team received nothing about our submarine or the nuclear warhead which the British could receive through channels other than Special Projects. As for information about the nuclear submarine, even those of us in the Navy disagreed about how much the Royal Navy had already learned through its inroads elsewhere in the Navy rather than through SP.

For purposes of clarity and insight I'll quote two key paragraphs from the joint statement by Kennedy and Macmillan at Nassau on 21 December 1962:

> Paragraph 7. Returning to POLARIS the President and the Prime Minister agreed that the purpose of their two Governments with respect to the provision of the POLARIS missiles must be the development of a multilateral NATO nuclear force in the closest consultation with other NATO allies. They will use their best endeavors to this end.
>
> Paragraph 8. Accordingly, the President and the Prime Minister agreed that the United States will make available on a continuing basis POLARIS missiles (less warheads) for British submarines. The United States will also study the feasibility of making available certain support facilities for such submarines. The United Kingdom Government will construct the submarines in which these weapons will be placed and they will also provide the nuclear warheads for the POLARIS missiles. British forces developed under this plan will be assigned and targeted in the same way as the forces described in paragraph 6.

As far as I was concerned, the key word in Paragraph 7 was "MUST." But if the UK and the US could not bring France along into the MLF, big countries would be reduced to little boys arguing over the rules of war games in a sandbox. To many people the word "must" was a contingency insofar that if the MLF proposal should fail to be adopted, the provision of the missiles to the UK could be canceled. And the key word in the next paragraph was "WEAPONS," because it implied more than the simple missile without spelling it out. Interpreting this implication correctly would erupt in our faces very soon.

Meanwhile, on 14 January De Gaulle picked his press conference as the right forum to return the "shaft" by sinking any chance Britain had to join the Common Market. He publicly applied France's veto to London's application, and then he gave a cold shoulder to the MLF without completely giving it a cold water douche.

When De Gaulle held a press conference, it was a major event—nothing as intimate and playful as many presided over by President Kennedy at the White House. In Paris, newsmen fought for the right to be part of a huge crowd in an equally huge meeting room. De Gaulle and his associates would prepare the questions that they thought pertinent, and would plant these questions with their favorite journalists whose favorable articles had earned them the right to be recognized in front of their world peers. Other reporters could ask questions and De Gaulle would collect several before starting a lengthy response incorporating what had been memorized.

By even including questions that sounded impertinent and provoked laughter, De Gaulle's press conferences were pure unadulterated and orchestrated theater of the highest order. And because his eyesight was failing, De Gaulle had to know the questions beforehand in order to memorize his replies. However, his comments were shrewdly crafted speeches with portions spoken in parables. By cleverly forming his sentences, he could cut up a political opponent with the skill of a surgeon with a scalpel. Should he misspeak or, God forbid, make a syntactical error, columnists and commentators would discuss the occurrence for a month, or as it has since turned out, for almost a half century.

By completely destroying Macmillan's efforts to join the Common Market, De Gaulle knew he was putting a long spike into the Prime Minister's political coffin, and was willing to wait before dealing with the next British prime minister however long it would take London to elect a successor. Even today, historians argue about what had actually transpired between Macmillan and De Gaulle at Rambouillet a few days before Macmillan met President Kennedy at Nassau.

When he shunted the MLF aside, De Gaulle left a little wiggle room for himself and for President Kennedy. But I still remembered Messmer's telltale shrug and found it difficult to recharge my enthusiasm for the MLF.

In Paris, US Ambassador to NATO Finletter asked that a senior American official be named to concentrate on the complex MLF issue because he couldn't cope with it, and the State Department started looking around for an experienced diplomat who could understand the technicalities as well as the cross currents of international politics. In addition to Ambassador Finletter, others felt over their heads in terms of added workload or complexity. New talent was added in SP, including Captain J.M. Barrett as Assistant Branch Head in SP-11 for international matters. And most of the Navy's management of the MLF was booted up to OPNAV-605E in the Pentagon which housed the new Navy Multilateral Force Executive.

During the same time period some of us named for the *Polaris* negotiations with the UK started voicing opinions about the Brits getting another free ride into the world of nuclear deterrence. One bold initiative was to have the British pay an overage or surcharge on any

Polaris procurements. But the UK government made public statements about paying what they had started calling the "actual end cost" of a missile, or getting it *wholesale*. Although there was no such thing as a "retail or wholesale price" of a *Polaris* missile, London's simplistic terminology raised the hair on the back of our necks. In the budgets of that period we'd put a round number like a million dollars per missile, knowing that no two missiles were exactly alike no more than were two slices of cheese—they were similar but not exactly identical.

On an SSB(N) going to sea in 1963, the individual price of each of its sixteen missiles could range from $900,000 to $1,100,000 (without the warhead) and still be the same missile. In addition, however, the cost of equipment dedicated to the missiles might cost another $20,000,000 per submarine, and the proportionate share of research and development cost for each missile could be $3,000,000! Our thoughts were, *"In no way would we let the British slip us the same shaft that they bestowed on the Air Force over Skybolt's R & D costs that the US taxpayers had to fork out completely."*

Our idea made its way up the chain of command in the Pentagon and at State, and at some point McNamara revealed the idea to the British. Macmillan was upset and called President Kennedy to complain it wasn't part of the Nassau deal. Luckily, Kennedy didn't cave in all the way. By the time our negotiations started on 20 February there were a number of points that we were prepared to raise that surprised the UK team.

Looking back on that period, I think the naive term of *paying only the end cost price of a Polaris missile* performed a useful service to us by alerting us to the crude appreciation and disparaging attitude the British politicians had about what it had cost America to produce the USN Fleet Ballistic Missile system, and the complete lack of British respect for the sacrifice in men, money and time that had been necessary to make *Polaris* the most precious feather—and the most expensive—in America's war bonnet (p. 356).

I distinctly remember the first day the two teams met to formally open the negotiations with each side making introductions and reading prepared statements for the record. Although we were the hosts, we certainly felt it was more like a shotgun wedding but still exhibited good manners and a gracious attitude toward our visitors. As it turned out the British team had quite a few members of the Royal Navy and many civilian members of the Admiralty, a fact that helped calm down some aggressive positions we had prepared as if we were going to duel with unappreciative and unprincipled political hacks.

Nonetheless over the next few sessions we prevailed in downsizing the group into smaller teams to study navigation, guidance, fire control, launching and other major subsystems. Our visitors soon learned there were no off-the-shelf wholesale prices and that our bookkeeping accurately accounted for every nickel spent on each in research and development, which sometimes surpassed several hundred million dollars for critical subsystems.

Much to our surprise they hadn't seemed prepared for our surcharge demand to help pay for the R&D that got us and them to that opening Wednesday session on the 20th. Like many such issues, one side or the other would have to put off a reply until guidance or instructions could be obtained from higher authority. If the British were going to build their own submarines, they realized that the key elements of the submarine were tailored for *Polaris*, and would take them years and billions of pounds sterling to develop or invent on their own, if ever. The Ship's Inertial Navigation System—SINS—had cost us hundreds of millions of dollars to perfect, and there would be a R&D surcharge of the delivered cost of the SINS unit for their submarine—whatever the final "unit" price. It didn't take long before the RN visitors wished no one had ever used any *cost* expression on Downing Street.

Other stiff arguments came up when we tried to define at which bulkhead in the submarine our agreement stopped. A bulkhead is a wall or partition between compartments or room units into which a submarine is divided. To pass through a bulkhead one goes through an opening or doorway with a solid metal door whose bank-vault-styled locks seal the bulkhead to make it watertight in the event of flooding or to contain a fire. For example, on an American nuclear submarine, there were several bulkheads that divided the nuclear propulsion section, just as others sealed off the missile compartment, the torpedo room, sleeping quarters and this was repeated on every deck-level of the submarine.

In the early years, the bulkhead near the propulsion unit kept Admiral Rickover out of Admiral Raborn's hair and vice versa. Our orders had been very clear, no British nose was to get past those bulkheads we had grown to honor, love and respect so well. And no one I knew wanted to get into a snarling cat fight with Rickover for the sake of the Royal Navy, particularly because Rickover, now a Vice Admiral, had the memory of an elephant and remembered when the Admiralty disdained him simply for being the father of that nasty idea: naval nuclear propulsion.

But it didn't take us long to recognize that our counterparts were reasonable human beings who negotiated a tough bargain. After all, they claimed, our commander-in-chief had signed off on the word "weapons" which implied the entire *Polaris* weapons system, and not only the missile. The missile was worthless if the submarine didn't know where it was, and that meant our SINS was part of the deal. "The British submarine must house the entire launching system, which wasn't designed for *Minuteman* and consequently the submarine must be constructed for those launch tubes to fit, right?"

Similar logic prevailed for the fire control system which married everything including the arming codes for the nuclear warhead, and soon just about everything except the tea makers and toilet paper dispensers were on their shipping list much to the joy of our industrial contractors. In the course of defining what they could buy and what they couldn't, we were soon in classified areas and we prepared two *Polaris Sales Agreements*, one official and unclassified, and the other official but secret.Nonetheless we repeatedly ran up against *those bulkheads*. In building their submarine they wanted to make sure the seawater intake valves were in the correct location or were large enough for the volume needed to cool the *hot* reactor, and other cute but reasonable requests that drove us both crazy and into a hornet's nest with Rickover's people. And when the housekeeping circuitry in fire control needed interface information for the nonexistent British warhead, then the Atomic Energy Commission became involved, giving us additional migraines and heartburn.

Being persistent was also a USN trait and we keep the surcharge in on everything that wasn't part of normal shipbuilding and sometimes when it was, because nothing had been given to us at SP. We had pushed the state of the art for years, often alone and often at a terrible price in American lives. The surcharge never replaced the lives, but at least recognized what we could quantify.

It was toward the end of the negotiations that another key word in Paragraph 8 was cited by the British team: "continuing." This meant that future versions of *Polaris* would be available to them, including models B3/C3, thus giving the British unfettered access to our deepest secrets, the actual improvements we foresaw and had planned to integrate into the FBM, and to the systems still in research and development. I don't know why Kennedy went along and didn't stick to the limitations in our options sent to Nassau.

Several of the members on the US team were upset by this when we met in private, but it did little good although some questions went to higher authority. Answers didn't always get back to us, and were left for another day. Toward the end of the sessions we had to face the issue of having a military liaison officer in SP, just as we had earlier with liaison officers from the Army and Air Force. This presented organizational problems because no foreigner was ever supposed to know what classified material was denied him.

Such objections were overruled, leaving some American negotiators shocked by the precedence. As the first liaison with us, the Royal Navy named Commander Wil Graham who was an intelligent and competent engineer and naval officer. Without stressing the fact, we all knew he was also an excellent intelligence officer. Personality-wise, the RN couldn't have found a liaison officer who could have made himself better liked or respected in the Special Projects Office.

Just as the technical negotiations drew to a close around mid-March, *Newsweek* magazine published a short news article on 18 March that a British spy by the name of Kim Philby was missing. We were told by the CIA that this stuttering fellow had been spying for the Soviet Union for over fifteen years. What haunted us was whether there were others like him hanging around the Admiralty. As time went on we learned that Philby had given the slip to the CIA and the UK secret services in Beirut, Lebanon, and had managed an escape to a safe refuge in Moscow.

While we waited to see what political changes would creep into the documents we had worked on for almost four weeks, we started to formulate how best to establish a day-to-day working relationship between SP and our counterparts in the Royal Navy. One thing we had done in the Technical Agreement was to provide for a "United States and United Kingdom Joint Steering Task Group" which would meet alternatively in London or Washington on a monthly basis. In practical terms we knew that many of these management meetings would take place in other cities like Sunnyvale, California, or Bath, England.

During this period, Kennedy had appointed a retired State Department official, Livingston Merchant, as his special envoy to meet with our European and Canadian allies in NATO with the MLF as his one specialized mission, and on the military side Kennedy appointed our

Vice Chief of Naval Operations, Vice Admiral Claude V. Ricketts as the military *salesman* to pitch the MLF to NATO's military officials.

It had become impossible for me to track both the MLF and the UK *Polaris* deal at the same time, particularly after the latter was formally signed by both countries on 6 April 1963. As permanent members to the Joint Steering Task Group were named by each side, the other side was notified. Among the first to be named to the United States team by the Defense Department were myself and Captain Barrett from SP, and eventually the twenty-member JSTG included five admirals. From the naval point of view I was a "plank owner"; that is, I was among the JSTG's "original crew."

In additional to that honor, I had the distinction of being the only one on the American side to have been on the team of the Nassau-presidential-position-paper writers and to have been named to the American negotiating team from the beginning, and now the only one of that group to have made it from the outset to the JSTG. And being a "plank owner" was a particularly sweet distinction because of its traditional connotation within the Navy. The other part of the tradition didn't apply any longer, the part about having an ownership share or percentage in a sailing ship-of-the line's cargo or plunder recovered from victories at sea.

Despite the satisfaction of having the documents signed by both countries, our satisfaction was devastatingly shattered a few days later, sending us in SP and the entire Navy into shock and into deep mourning.

Chapter 16

The saddest day and the longest lie

The saddest day I ever saw in Special Projects was the day that we routinely received a "CasRep" by twx. A CasRep meant Casualty Report and it often referred to someone being hurt as the result of a mechanical problem, and sometimes it might only refer to a technical breakdown of some kind for which the sender wanted immediate remedial advice. But the Casrep of 10 April 1963 had to do with the *SS(N) 593 Thresher* which apparently and unbelievably was feared lost at sea, and maybe with its whole crew during a normal shakedown cruise after it left Portsmouth, New Hampshire that morning.

As for the nuclear attack submarine *Thresher*, it had enjoyed a very special relationship with our office. Outside of all our own SSB(N)s, it had been the only one to get funding from us in order to incorporate special design and construction features to permit it to go faster, deeper and more quietly than anything we or any other navy had. She had been launched in 1960 and gone to sea. Returning to Portsmouth Naval Shipyard in 1962, she then completed nine months of overhaul and some retrofit. When she was reported lost that fatal Wednesday, just about every officer and old-timer in SP knew someone among her sixteen officers, 96 enlisted men and the seventeen civilians aboard her. At thirty-one I was considered an old-timer in the *Polaris* program. And among the seventeen civilians were several whose jobs and careers in large measure had been determined by our Chief Scientist, Dr. John P. Craven whose offices I shared at SP.

When I received the news, I was in Captain Clarke's office and the news went through SP-ll like a tragic firestorm that froze all listeners in their tracks. People just stared ahead like zombies whose automation battery had gone dead, unable to walk or turn or speak. When finally our tongues got in gear, first came the questions and the search for information. Was the boat lost? Was the crew lost? What did the companion ship have to say? What radio messages had the skipper transmitted? "Doesn't anyone have any reliable information?" shouted several officers in frustration who had called contacts in OPNAV and at Portsmouth. By the time everyone went home that night, we didn't have a great deal of information.

During the evening hours a dramatic nationwide television appearance by our Chief of Naval Operations, Vice Admiral George W. Anderson, riveted the public's attention as he gravely reported the saddest of all naval messages that the *Thresher*—that "the submarine had been lost with all hands."

For the next few days all our submarine officers formed their own "board of inquiry," and debated every new shred of evidence that could be gleaned from their own sources, and I'm sure this was repeated everywhere in the Navy where submariners congregated—all wanting to make a discovery to answer the questions, the riddles, the mysteries that were being raised everywhere. Despite the fact that a formal naval inquiry had already been ordered, no one wanted to wait for its findings. I hadn't seen any nuclear officers from Rickover's shop, but I could imagine the agony they were going through because the *Thresher* had been one of theirs, one from the tight nuclear submarine family, one from the latest litter of the run-deep-run-quietly attack boats. And in SP, no one was as personally devastated as John Craven by the developments. Although we all had other duties to perform, our stolen moments were concentrated on the reasons why we had lost this boat whose design characteristics had already been incorporated in our lead boat of the new *Lafayette* class of SSB(N)s, some of which would be outfitted with our *Polaris A-3*.

In fact, Mrs. Jacqueline Kennedy had christened the *Lafayette*, and we all had a stake in that beautiful war machine whose SDAPs were already on the schedule board for test launches at the Cape.

You can't live and breathe navy ships without absorbing navy tradition, and submariners have such strong feelings about some things that I wondered at what point orders might not be followed. One was a promise from a Pentagon spokesman to use all means to bring up the victims of the *Thresher* from her grave 1,400 fathoms deep, which to laymen meant she was grounded with the 129 men who died in her, off Georges Bank east of Cape Cod in about 8,400 feet of water.

As best as we could tell in the first few days after she sank, she was at the bottom of the underwater shelf comprising Georges Bank almost due east of Boston. The notion of recovering the bodies infuriated almost every submariner I knew. Maybe other naval officers, the aviators and surface ship officers, were infuriated as well, but in 1963 not many were left in SP. Common sense dictated that the bodies be left as is. Contrary to what I first thought, it wasn't tradition that dictated a grave at sea not be disturbed. Grumbling by the submariners could not have been clearer or more simple: "Let their souls *and bodies* rest in peace."

To try to understand the outrage of the submariners, I turned to Captain Shutt, the former branch head of SP-11 and a former commanding officer of the Submarine Rescue Vessel *ASR9 USS Florikan* in the Pacific and the seas of the Far East. My old boss in SP had also served most of World War II in submarines and was qualified within the unique breed of deep sea divers—the ones with a steel helmet, heavy diving suits and weighted boots, with bars across the glass face plate and air hoses and bubbles leading to a ship on the surface. On the *Florikan* Shutt commanded ten officers and a crew of 250 among whom were thirty divers whom he described as "a bunch of feisty tigers for sure." He told me, "Death in the sea is usually fast and always cruel. When submarines sink there are no clean corpses neatly laid out, waiting for any kind of recovery operation."

Relying on his personal experiences and of those submarine commanders under whom he had served and described as "real submarine war heroes." He went on to add, "One even had the Congressional Medal of Honor," and that "Rescue operations at best were only partially successful." He reflected on the circumstances of the *Thresher*'s loss and continued, "The ugly fact is that there is no way of physically handling human remains inside a hull at that depth. Add to this the problem of coping with what hungry, scavenging sea life will do to any remains which are accessible..."

Dick Shutt dismissed the spokesman's promise about bringing up the victims as a "public relations fairy tale."

True, we did recover some gloves of different colors and other artifacts from the site but for as long as I was with the Navy I never heard of a body being successfully recovered from the *Thresher* by a Navy ship or any other kind of ship.

During the following weeks, hundreds of theories were explored and rejected, but some seemed to survive all efforts to discredit them. Standard procedures established by the Bureau of Ships for bringing any nuclear submarine down to test depth were reviewed time and again. What could happen at 300 feet that wouldn't happen at 250 feet? What could happen at 350 feet that wouldn't happen at 300? And so on and on to that secret depth beyond 400. Eventually the finger of accusation pointed to new equipment retrofitted into the submarine during the nine months of her overhaul, and to *defective deep submergence welding* on her pressure hull during that period in Portsmouth. In time these causes seemed to be exonerated and other accusatorial scenarios replaced earlier ones.

But I couldn't share the technical details with my brother Normand because he was very busy secretly briefing key senators and representatives in Congress about another horrible consequence of the *Thresher*'s sinking. None of the families of the civilian victims could receive any insurance benefits because no one could prove their son, husband or father had been aboard the submarine.

As I explained several times in earlier chapters, the movements of nuclear submarines were top secret, and whenever we civilians went out to sea on one we lied whenever we countersigned our travel orders, and by so signing we swore an oath to their truthfulness. In such orders we could admit that we were authorized to travel to a pier or a nearby missile assembly building at Cape Canaveral. The fact that a submarine just happened to be nearby was never mentioned, nor that we would even board her. Had we done so we would have been liable for arrest and time in jail.

Hundreds of us in SP and the Navy had lied for years. Because the lie had been committed to protect national security we felt we were doing our duty. Never had we imagined for a moment that if something happened to us while on an official mission our government insurance benefits would have been voided, that our families would have been denied death benefits and compensation because we had signed that lie. But a white lie or a dark one under oath, even under orders to do so, was still a disenfranchising lie.

Under a shroud of secrecy, the White House and the Congress quickly realized the unfair situation that Navy civilians, and in some cases other government personnel, had been forced into. The damnable perjury was on paper for all to see while we were performing our duty, and underwater duty was always risky. In order to correct a very messy situation and without breaking security regulations while debating this mess openly in the senate and house, Congress met in a very rare private session after midnight without press, public or staff, and enacted the necessary retroactive legislation which President Kennedy immediately signed.

Over the last thirty-eight years I don't ever remember this remarkable action by the Congress ever being commented upon by the press. Nonetheless, we certainly appreciated it at the time and, thereafter, none of us ever had to swear again to a falsehood in official travel orders to board a nuclear submarine.

As it turned out the discussions on how we lost the *Thresher* continued unabated in substance and unresolved to anyone's satisfaction for the next several months. From the added information that came to us in drips and drabs we were convinced the crew had followed formal procedures to go down in cautious increments until she reached test depth. Simply stated, the submarine took on a few tons of water into her ballast tanks, enough to go down fifty feet, and then the crew would check a thousand and one valves, watertight doors, gauges, watertight hatches, dials, gimmicks and gadgets of every kind and description to make sure everything was proceeding correctly. Then the commander would order more ballast and dive to the next level, maybe fifty feet. Another thousand and one checks. Notes were taken and recorded as the submarine went down each imaginary step into the depths of the Atlantic. During a shakedown, naval procedures had to be followed to the letter, by every commander on every submarine, and regardless of the shipyard where she had been constructed..

By retracing the procedures, all the naval hydraulic, structural and mechanical engineers could recreate how the elements and water pressure could affect a submarine at every submerged level. One particularly gruesome scenario started to take form while we were building one hypothesis or another. This theory started in the nuclear reactor compartment where the scenario concerned the piping of seawater used to cool the super-hot nuclear core.

Obviously, the hotter the object to cool, the more was cold water needed. Every time the submarine went down to a lower level, the greater became the water pressure. Generally, the public is used to water pressure at fifteen pounds or so per square inch. But in a submarine the surrounding water pressure rises to thousands of pounds and tons per square inch, and the deeper it goes the greater the pressure. Unlike a rocket motor that resists blowing up, a submarine hull resists blowing in. And the nozzle of a rocket resisting the exhaust blasting out is contrary to a submarine's seawater valve controlling the amount of seawater rushing in.

According to one theory which was based on a message, complete or partial, about reaching "test depth," a small seawater cooling pipe maybe developed a hairline leak through which some water escaped, and driven by the pressure of the water next to the submarine, the powerful spray, probably as small as a thin silk thread, hit the crewman in front of the pipe and decapitated him. There was no other crewman present to warn the captain.

As soon as the commanding officer realized that a catastrophic accident was compounding itself in the reactor area, he assessed the energy remaining in his propulsion system. In order to rise he expelled ballast as quickly as he could but he never completely emptied the ballast tanks. By drawing on the stupendous reserve heat and power of his reactor system, he literally *flew* his submarine toward the surface. According to this theory, the *Thresher* actually broached the surface of the ocean, and like a whale whose powerful tail lifts its body upward over the surface for a few seconds, reached fresh air and then fell heavily into the waves.

Frantically, the officers and crew tried every means to blow out or pump out the excess ballast water in a last ditch effort to gain buoyancy. At some moment in their desperation the submarine ran out of stored energy that had earlier *blasted* the sub to the surface. That furious last-resort-move to reach the safety of the surface had drained the tremendous reserve of energy.

As the sub went downward, it became more and more difficult to expel ballast against the growing external pressure, and with its power lost or weakened, the sub headed deeper, at first faster and faster. No messages that I ever heard of were transmitted by the stricken submarine again. It reached test depth, then crush depth.

Without looking at the dials, the crew knew, I am sure, that the situation was critical because even at test depth a submarine starts to object vocally to where it is by telltale twists, bends, squeaks and squawks.

It was at this point in our discussions that a sense of guilt crept into my psyche as I instinctively hoped that their inevitable deaths were quick, too quick to hurt. I'm confident that there was no longer any light in the submarine, and that the stagnant air had become foul, given the loss of power. Other than prayers imploring their God and some metal twisting, the submarine must have been relatively quiet. Scientists convinced me that when the final compression crushed the mighty hull as easily as a bluejay breaks a sparrow's egg, the men were killed instantly, singed by fire less than a millisecond later, and then immediately enveloped by sea water.

All this occurred long before the lifeless submarine hulk bounced off the steep slope of Georges Bank and tumbled in the darkness to the ocean floor an eternity below. For this sad end to a routine shakedown cruise on 10 April 1963, every seaman in the world, regardless of political persuasion, probably bowed his head in silent tribute to all hands lost that miserable, heartrending Wednesday off the New England coast.

Chapter 17

Fitting in overseas

Within a few days following Admiral Anderson's disheartening announcement about the *Thresher*, I learned that Jim Calvert had been the naval officer who had most influenced the CNO to flatly admit the disaster straight out to the public. With the results very favorable to the Navy for having managed the affair with such solemn dignity, Jim received quite a few compliments. As a submariner already famous for his service during the historic passage under the North Pole on the *Nautilus*, he had reflected the sadness we all felt. When I spoke with him he had already received many kudos but appeared genuinely pleased by my call, and in turn, he asked for an update on the UK *Polaris* program.

(In-house, Jim was already "humorously famous" by being kidded about that North Pole voyage. Unmercifully did his fellow officers kid him about being the first officer since the sailing ships to have almost rammed Greenland. Apparently, the still experimental SINS aboard our first "nuke" had lost its grip on navigational reality.)

Although the *Thresher* lost eighteen times as many lives in 1963 than did NASA's *Challenger* in 1986, the earlier victims never received the public tributes that the seven astronauts did almost a quarter-century later. Indeed, the submarine service was a silent one, but no less a valiant one.

The last nuclear submarine I was on was the SSB(N) 616 *Lafayette*. The earlier SSB(N)'s I had been on had been nicknamed "Formica Hiltons." But I found the 616 a definite "upgrade" in her electronics and performance, and in her interior finishing and comfort for the crew. Without counting the levels or decks in her sail, she had several principal decks that ran the length of her pressure hull. By 1963, nuclear submarines had become formidable "men-of-war," and because the public only saw the part above water in photographs, the submarine didn't show off the glamour of a surface ship slicing through the waves.

Later, only after I had entered my first diesel submarine of that type used in World War II and the Korean War did the profound differences strike me. For example, I was startled by the absence of walking-around room in the diesel with its passageways barely wide enough for two men to pass each other. I'll never forget the tight and limited space on two short decks. In fact the radio room is a complete misnomer because it was an alcove smaller than the mop and broom closet in my grandmother's house built in 1905. The writing lid in front of the radio on which the operator transcribed Morse code or scratchy radio messages was barely large enough to rest one elbow.

However, on the *Lafayette*, the communications center was larger than the average bedroom in a modern townhouse, and its engine room was like a clean room of a modern electronics laboratory. In the diesel, the engine room reminded me of what you find under the hood of a huge diesel-powered highway truck, and the propeller shaft was no more complicated than a drive shaft of a dump truck.

Another noticeable difference was the whiff of the diesel sub which was almost as bad as the smell you get from the dirty exhaust of polluting trucks that envelops you when you're standing at a curb. World War II submariners knew that their shore leave didn't really start until they had taken two steaming-hot showers. Compared to those diesel submariners who looked like they used diesel oil in their shaving cream, today's nuclear submariners smell like pine trees after a spring rain— well, almost. Even the torpedo room on the diesel was smaller than the crew's exercise and work-out room on the *Lafayette*.

Comparing the two was an incongruous as trying to liken a two-seater crop duster to a jumbo jet.

Not once while aboard the *Lafayette* do I remember comparing her characteristics to those of the *Thresher*, but the memory of their secret association has since stayed with me. There but for the grace of God...

Like a movie idol pursued by fans who want a souvenir button or necktie, *Polaris* was pursued for any portion of its technology. To protect our country's advantages, the barrier to technical information was constantly ratcheted higher on key components like sensors, gyros, accelerometers, faster fire control computers, and inertial systems for both the missile and the submarine. While there were many, almost innumerable, key missile parts that no other nation yet had, those constituted the principal ones that needed protection, despite the pressure exerted by zealous business contractors who kept forgetting that the taxpayers had invested in the research to produce them.

In my few personal Navy documents from those years, one credited me for "being instrumental in recommending successful tactics in the negotiations between the State Department and Spain for certain rights in the Canary Islands affecting aspects of *Polaris* development." I can only guess at what the author meant or what I might have done, but it must have been OK. Oddly, I no longer remember that detail, but I do remember that my brother Normand had been intimately involved in the successful negotiations for a *Polaris* anchorage at Rota, Spain. The problem is not a bad memory, but the fact that almost everything we did in those days was classified secret, top secret or atomic, and as a consequence we kept no notes.

As for myself, more responsibilities were piled on. For example, I was designated the point man (the person who can accept blame if there's a SNAFU—an acronym for Situation Normal, All Screwed Up) "for the Joint Chief of Staff directives for the use of *Polaris* by NATO's Supreme Commander in Europe (SACEUR)," as well as being the Defense Department's point man "for the release of certain atomic information to NATO via SACEUR for the MLF," but I soon bucked that last assignment to the new MLF Executive (OP-605E).

Somewhat ironically, however, everything that I had been doing with the Office of Naval Intelligence for the last two years was formalized in writing for the first time (p. 290). It was a sure sign that Special Projects was being integrated into the routine machinery of the US Navy. Even a commendation for what I had done during the negotiations with the UK was sent to Admiral Mott and myself (and others) by Deputy Secretary of Defense Roswell Gilpatric on 16 May 1963 didn't arrive in my in-basket until two months later—I credit this delay to the cumbersome but routine ways of the Pentagon.

After Admiral Galantin added his own compliments on 25 July, the anti-climatic missive arrived in my office the following Monday. My oldest brother George, the World War II fighter pilot, had straightened me out about developing a swelled head after receiving commendations by telling me, "That piece of paper and a dime will buy you a cup of coffee." Today, however, these documents provide me with a time-line without which these memoirs couldn't have been written.

Nonetheless, some details just never seem to come back. My old colleague in Special Projects, our top budgeteer Tom Aiken, told me back in 1994, "I still remember when you ran into the burning operations center." The truth is that I barely remembered the fire or the smoke, but I still very clearly remember that pale Marine guard at the door pointing a Tommy gun in my direction afterward and wishing he really didn't have to shoot. Me, too. I've kept a warm spot in my heart ever since for all reasonable Marines.

It was now much too quiet after the MLF, Nassau, the French on the aircraft carrier, and the Royal Navy. As if to liven things up, a sex and spy scandal erupted in London over the antics of John Profumo, the British Minister of State for War, a person I had never heard of, but who was implicated in an affair that involved far more than sex. There was no question that the unfolding story sold lots of newspapers in London because the London press excoriated Profumo for stupidly sharing a prostitute who democratically shared her charms with the Soviet Naval Attaché in London, Eugeny Ivanov. The latter fact arrested our attention in SP.

Soon the London press learned that homosexuals and "other sexual perverts" (whatever that meant) had been involved in upper crust orgies, and the writers figuratively dismembered Profumo. Reeling under the weight of the revelations, Profumo found it difficult to "prove" he would not have revealed military secrets under the threat of blackmail. When he did crack, it was before his parliamentary peers to whom he lied. Ultimately he was forced to resign because he lied, and not for stupidity nor infidelity. If Profumo ever compromised any US Navy secrets or UK secrets, I never heard of it.

About this time, the Office of Naval Intelligence received a whiff that the UK was receiving more classified information than was authorized under the Nassau or the two *Polaris* agreements. Some internal reviews did suggest this, but the problem was almost insolvable because of the navy's structure, especially SP's. Once a person was accepted within SP, that person had a free run to the different technical offices. In these sectors, SP's engineers had been trained to solve technical problems and rarely, if ever, paid any attention to political ones. As far as most of them were concerned, the Royal Navy had the right to classified technical information, and logically needed them. One internal review suggested that the UK was mining the mother lode of

US secrets without justification. Even though a scathing SP report was prepared, I never learned its disposition before I left the Special Projects Office.

I had just received an attractive offer to fill a position in continental Europe for the International Telephone and Telegraph Corporation. Not only was ITT not a major defense contractor in the United States, it had never been directly associated with the Navy's *Polaris* program nor been any more than a supplier or a bit player which removed any conflict of interest for me in joining them.

Because we were so early into the US-UK program, the Navy asked me to stay a few extra months, and as an incentive gave me another full grade promotion, the fifth in four years. I doubt if such rapid increases in salary could have been possible anywhere else but in SP while it had the highest priority in the Defense Department, and because of the "special hunting license" given to Admiral Raborn.

The next US-UK Joint Steering Task Group was scheduled for early October at the Admiralty, and during the weekend after the meeting I flew to Brussels to check out the housing situation in Belgium. After I returned to Washington, I resigned from the Navy on 12 October 1963 when Admiral Galantin presented me with a warm letter of commendation. My formal connection with the Navy was cut that day, but I soon learned that a person just couldn't walk away from Special Projects or US national security or the Cold War for years to come.

When my family arrived in Brussels, ITT Europe, Inc. put us up at a Belgian hotel that catered to British visitors. It was called the Richmond House and was located at 40, rue de la Concorde, a very quiet residential street near the luxurious area called the Toison d'Or. This would be home until our furniture and station wagon arrived by steamship from the United States.

One of the habits I developed was to walk to a nearby book and newspaper store every evening to pick up English-language newspapers. On Friday, 22 November, I was surprised by the many people crowding the shop but managed to squeeze though to the counter. The radio was playing some sort of drama instead of music, and I paid no attention to the French commentary until it dawned on me it was a direct newscast from Texas in the United States. To be precise it was from Dallas. Only then did the French words make their impact: "Dallas, ambush, blood, hospital, Kennedy!" I stood transfixed with my mouth open until I realized everyone was watching me for a reaction. I asked the store manager, "Is this a true news report?"

"Oui," he answered.

I hurried to Richmond House to inform my wife what was going on in Dallas. Her reaction was disbelief and sadness, and when we spoke at dinner it was in whispers. We didn't know if President Kennedy was dead, and we had neither radio or television in our hotel apartment. After dinner I drove a rental car to the American embassy before which a huge crowd had quietly assembled. When I walked through them I noticed that they all spoke Flemish or French, but once I entered the embassy grounds, all I heard were Americans.

In the reception hall I froze in my steps when I saw President Kennedy's framed portrait draped in black cloth. Americans stood as one, dumbfounded and incredulous, and many were crying—both men and women. The simple black mourning cloth spoke a thousand sad words, and the embassy staff made no effort to send people home. As people interrogated one another for the facts, we spoke in whispers as if we were in a funeral parlor, afraid to disturb relatives gathered by the casket.

It was near midnight when I made my way again through the crowd outside, which had clearly doubled in size in less than an hour. I must have looked too sad to be Belgian because so many people expressed their condolences as I passed. Their anguish was like an anvil on my shoulders, crushing whatever stoicism I might have harbored, and welled up a great deal of sorrow inside me.

At Richmond House, my children were asleep. But my wife who was of Irish descent and had been an evangelical supporter of Kennedy and his large clan was devastated by the confirmation of Kennedy's assassination. We decided we'd get a short-wave radio first thing in the morning to receive Voice of America or Armed Forces Radio-Europe, as if only American-based reporting could be accurate or trusted at a time like this.

In the morning I went to the door to fetch the breakfast trays that the hotel staff regularly placed on the landing. To my astonishment I also found fruit baskets, flowers, offerings of food and candies, sympathy cards and notes from strangers, some smudged by the writer's tears, in Flemish, in French and in elegantly composed broken-English.

And on the following Monday morning, as was my habit I left early to arrive at ITTE's headquarters by 7 a.m. By the time I arrived the Belgian staff had already placed a vase of flowers on a pedestal covered in black cloth in front of the elevators of the main hall. Although we actually were very few Americans among the headquarters personnel, such acts as I've described are a fair representation of the grief expressed by the Belgians as the result of this American tragedy.

My assignment with ITT Europe was to bring its many manufacturing affiliates in thirteen European countries into the space age. In those days, the word affiliate was a politically correct word that had replaced the more accurate term, wholly-owned subsidiary. This European group of companies was ITT's money machine where most of the corporation's profits were generated. In New York, our new chairman Harold Geneen was much like Admiral Raborn and practiced management by objectives. And both were equally famous. In 1963 ITT had around 130,000 employees in Europe of whom there were less than fifty Americans.

ITT had been born during the American era when monopolies were broken up, and overseas subsidiaries of American Telephone and Telegraph had been purchased independently to create ITT. Most of ITT's manufacturing was in Europe, although we ran some telephone companies in South America and in Cuba. When I arrived, ITTE had no company in Europe with cutting-edge technology except our two laboratories, Standard Telephone Laboratories (STL) in Harlow, England, and Laboratoire Central de Télécommunications (LCT) in Paris, France. Of the two, STL was concentrating on Pulse Code Modulation which would revolutionize telephone use and expansion in the world. On the other hand, LCT was our only entity in Europe that had experience with missile technology, but had no satellite technology or experience.

But what we did have in Europe were mobile earth stations for satellite communications. These transportable vans had been fabricated at ITT's Federal Laboratories in Nutley, New Jersey, an operation headed up by Rand Araskok. No synchronous communications satellite existed then, but AT&T and NASA had put up an experimental satellite called *Telstar*, which had very little transmission power and required a monstrous antenna on the ground to work with it. The antenna was shaped like an old-fashioned ear horn, and only England, France, and the United States could afford such temporary earth installations. Another experimental communications satellite then in orbit was called *Relay*, and ITT's transportable earth stations had been designed to work with it. *Relay* was a low-level type of satellite that wove its orbits around the earth like yarn on a ball, and had an elliptically shaped orbit. As a consequence, an earth station's antenna was required to move and constantly track the satellite during its orbital pass overhead.

To illustrate its primitive design, it had no signaling capability or what the trade called an *order wire* to let the user know it could be used. We had to know exactly where and when it would be five degrees above the horizon. If it was also within sight of our earth station in Brazil, we talked to Rio. If it was in sight of New Jersey, we'd talk with the people there. When it was in the low part of an orbit, we'd talk for seven minutes, but if it was in the long part of an orbit, we'd talk for an hour. When the satellite dropped beyond the horizon, there were no signals for a *good-bye*. You were simply cut off and left to wonder what your last audible words were.

Another problem to be resolved was the echo phenomena by which you heard your own words coming back to you just when the other person was starting to answer your earlier question. This phenomena was always very irritating to one of the parties, and when we had run into it during the heyday of transatlantic cables we built echo suppressors. However, the key to space communications was the ability to put a communications satellite into a *synchronous orbit*. This is an orbit 22,300 miles above the equator, wherein a satellite travels at a speed proportionately faster than the earth's rotation so that from any given point on earth the satellite appears to be stationary. Consequently a ground antenna didn't have to track the satellite and could stay pinpointed in one direction.

Because the guidance of American rockets was so much more precise than anything the Soviets had, space communications were dominated by the United States and the Americans aggressively sought to *buy* parking spaces for these synchronous satellites from the United Nations agency, The International Telecommunications Union, in Geneva. These parking places were what we called the available slots in the precious equatorial belt 22,300 miles above the earth.

Bearing in mind that in 1964 the only practical small earth antenna had a diameter of thirty feet to be used with radio frequencies authorized for communications satellites. By the year 2000 the diameter of a useful roof antenna to receive color television from a satellite using different frequencies had been reduced by technological advances to only 18 inches!

A spoken word takes a split-second to reach a satellite, and another split-second to return—for a total trip of over 44,000 miles, which is why in 1993 you often saw a news commentator in Bosnia wait a second or two before answering a question from another news commentator in a major western city. Because you were a local viewer, you saw and *heard* the question before the commentator in Bosnia did. The problem of orientation was such that you saw the person hesitate when he stared into the camera, and you wondered why the simpleton took so long to answer a simple question. Even in 1995, the economy of scale prevented a small mobile satellite antenna in Bosnia to do the job that a large commercial antenna serving a western metropolitan area could do. But in the 1960s, these time delays in speaking drove users as crazy as echoes on the line. Still, these inconveniences were colossal improvements over the use of unreliable high frequency voice radio in 1955 to reach the four corners of the earth and ships at sea.

Space communications represented the only hole card that ITT Europe could play and I used it to get Europe's nose under the *space* tent. This immediately put ITTE on a collision course with Rand Araskok's operation that felt the world was its private marketplace. But from my personal point of view this was a simple rerun of interservice rivalry at the Pentagon.

In those years President Johnson's cabinet secretaries made $20,000 per year, so when ITT Europe allocated $100,000 in investment funds to me to jump-start space activities in Europe I felt comfortable because it represented a substantial amount of real money. By mid-1964 I had visited most R&D operations in our military and avionics lines in Europe whose product lines were managed by an American executive in Brussels named Art Williams. Their state of the art came the closest to space-age adaptability, but were a major disappointment for my purposes.

Perhaps it was my confidence and familiarity with laboratories during my *Polaris* years that led me to concentrate on our two labs. During my evaluation period I visited the Standard Telephone Laboratories in Harlow on several occasions, primarily because English was a common language and I thought the engineers there could catch up more quickly with the technical literature from the United States. But my New England accent or perceived American brashness and youth actually turned off some of the older engineers. Some of them wondered, *"How can this thirty-two-year-old twerp teach us anything."*

I'll never forget the first time I drove into the labs' parking lot in Harlow, England, and saw all the beautiful gold-plated hood ornaments on hundreds of cars. It turned out that the lab was experimenting with gold inlaid electronic mini-circuits, and I always retained a fear that my R&D nest egg might end up in $100,000 worth of hood ornaments. On such initial impressions were management decisions often made.

At our Paris lab, my initial impression was even more negative because the management found it very difficult to accept anyone who wasn't a graduate of the Polytechnique (France's MIT) which automatically qualified the speakers to call each other by the familiar *tu* instead of the more formal and polite *vous*. LCT also developed some hardware for France's military missiles and its managers were afraid that my presence might compromise their acceptance to their military customers. Just like my New England accent got me into trouble in Harlow, my rural Québec-rooted French horrified their Parisian sensitivities. They reacted as if I had arrived from the most rural part of southern France and asked themselves, *"How can this hayseed teach us anything?"*

Chapter 18

Soviets are no match for American mind game

It was toward the end of the afternoon on a typical cloudy day in Brussels when my brother Normand called from London to say he could visit me that evening, and would I pick him up at some obscure airfield I never heard of. When I did find the airfield it didn't have any runway lighting for the good reason it was nothing but a grass airstrip much like the one in Rhode Island that we used to fly out of during World War II when Norm got his pilot's license in the event he was called up. If he had to go, he wanted to go into the Army Air Corps like our older brother George.

But there were a few floodlights at each end of the field that went on just before a small twin-engine plane landed, out of which Norm descended. Apparently the plane was a military liaison flight which explained the mystery of using an airfield out in the boonies. The fact that he was the only passenger wasn't surprising because of the way that the Navy's Special Projects Office operated. We had arranged to go to dinner together before bringing him to my home for the night in the area of Brussels called Ukkel (Uccle in French).

Near the urban woods called Le Bois de la Cambre was a charming restaurant called the *le Chalet Suisse* where we went to enjoy *une fondue bourguignonne* in a quiet corner I reserved.

He explained, "Admiral Smith asked me to speak with you."

"What's going on?"

"Intelligence sources have been telling our technical people that *Polaris* components have made their way to Russia."

"How are they doing it?" I asked.

"We're not sure. Levering (Admiral Smith) wants you to give us some ideas where to look."

"What kind of components are we dealing with?"

"Gyros, accelerometers—their sensors mostly."

We interrupted our conversation when the waiter set up our metal pot in which the vegetable oil was already bubbling, so we turned the flame down before putting any meat in to cook. Soon the wooden plates with various sauces were placed before us, and the wine was poured. Whenever a waiter lurked nearby we spoke of other things, like President Johnson's efforts to implant his branding iron over Kennedy's brands. In fact, our *Polaris B-3/C-3* had been re-baptized as the *Poseidon* missile. Once we were alone we returned to the problem at hand.

"Have any of SP's contractors been authorized to manufacture key components in Europe?" I asked.

"No, we just don't have any idea how it's being done. Our big problem is that most CIA people wouldn't know a gyro if one fell into their laps."

"The types of precision machine tool and microelectronic welding machines needed to manufacture those components just don't exist in Western Europe yet," I opined. "I'd tend to look for the trail starting with export license applications for the type of manufacturing equipment needed to make them, and be on the lookout for shipments of manufacturing drawings from our contractors' plants."

Although I had left the Navy almost a year earlier, I still spoke of SP and its contractors as "our" and "us."

My brother anticipated my question about the UK *Polaris* program. He explained, "The Admiralty has no time to make their own so they'll buy straight from the US—for the moment. Everything the Royal Navy will receive will be accounted for. Right now they're concentrating on building their own submarines, and won't need missiles, let alone missile parts, for at least two more years."

Just before he left to return to London the next day, Norm reminded me, "Don't put anything in writing, just give me a call from your house. If it's not me, someone else you know will come here to meet you."

That was the last time I saw him in Europe while he was in SP, but some years later we met in Paris when he was on his way to Geneva for the "seabed-free-of-nuclear-arms" negotiations on behalf of the US Arms Control Agency.

As part of my familiarization with the technical abilities of our European companies, I flew to Stuttgart, Germany to visit some of the main plants of Standard Electrik Lorenz, the third largest electronics manufacturer in West Germany. Only SEL's competitors Siemens and A.E.G. were larger. For the first time I used the company's small private plane, a twin-engined *Gulfstream* that carried a bar and five passengers. In it were two fellows from New York headquarters whose names I no longer remember but whose personalities I'll never forget. They were, I hate to admit, smart alecks who considered World War II as a needed but failed form of urban renewal in Europe. To reinforce their architectural bias they disparaged the tile roofs so typical of most residential construction in western Europe, and ridiculed the homogeneity of the roofs around most of the airports in Europe.

Our conversation never really turned to any pleasant subject but I kept my temper under control. Finally, the subject of President Johnson came up, and one said, "Our southern boy'll be no better than the Irishman."

The other added, "Well, at least we got rid of him. Good riddance."

Never in my wildest imagination did I ever think any Americans would wallow in the murder of our president like pigs in swill, and the ensuing argument became animated and disagreeable. As we approached Stuttgart, our pilots turned back and shouted at the top of their lungs, "Seat belts! We're coming in!" and whatever else that might calm down their three passengers. Luckily SEL had sent two cars to meet us, an average one for me and an oversized one for them. We didn't bother to say good-bye.

Even before my service with the Navy I had never campaigned for Kennedy but had organized a colorful rally in the Social area of Woonsocket, Rhode Island, for US Senator Estes Kefauver of Tennessee. And I had done that at the request of J. Howard McGrath, recently the Attorney General of the United States and a former Governor of Rhode Island. That request had been prompted by former President Harry S. Truman who was angry at Adlai Stevenson about something and wanted to break the solid delegation put together by then RI Governor Dennis J. Roberts in favor of Stevenson. The 25-year-old pawn in this imbroglio was myself who somehow managed to find a half-vote in the Rhode Island delegation for the Mafia-busting, Davey-Crockett-raccoon-capped senator from Tennessee. If this political convolution doesn't confuse the reader, bear in mind that ex-Attorney General McGrath had been fired publicly by President Truman some time before McGrath's telephone call to me. Sure'nuff, politics do make strange bedfellows.

As it turned out, Stevenson won the Democratic nomination for President, and Kefauver beat out freshman Senator John F. Kennedy for the Vice Presidential slot in 1956. They lost to Eisenhower and Nixon, but Kennedy got even in 1960 and won all the marbles.

In Germany, SEL had an impressive industrial base but very little R&D capability and definitely no leading edge technology except in battlefield military radios and in some airfield navigational equipment. Their nominee to my committee was Helmut Heinz, a former Luftwaffe fighter pilot, who was well beyond the average age of the other committee members from other countries. This was typical of Germany where all my interlocutors were either too young or very old because Germany had lost all its middle-aged men during the war. Because SEL was so profitable it had no time for diversion into the future, and it took me over two years to convince SEL to hire a young Ph.D. to handle space-related projects.

ITT's $100,000 was starting to burn a hole in my pocket, so I opted to put it all in one place—at LCT in Paris to fund a four-man space research study group, one I could use to put space proposals together and to help sister-companies in Europe. The laboratory's personnel was the most gifted and competent but also the weakest in speaking English.

On the plus side was the fact that the national French market had the only real contract opportunities for space research.

On the negative side was the fact that LCT would never be awarded an important prime contract from the French because it was American-owned. In fact, LCT couldn't even get on many bidders' lists at the time. But the new European Space Research Organization established its administrative offices in Paris, and its technical and contracting offices in Delft, Netherlands, thus broadening the customer base. In time, ESRO issued an important request-for-proposal to develop a scientific satellite dubbed *ESRO I*. With so few opportunities then available I went all for broke to win this competition.

Contrary to all our competition who rallied behind aircraft manufacturers like Hawker Siddeley and Sud Aviation, much like the space industry did in the United States, I formed a consortium behind our laboratory LCT, and selected Contraves AG of Zurich, Switzerland, for the structural elements. While LCT kept the housekeeping for itself, it assigned the power supply subsystem to its sister company Bell Telephone Manufacturing in Antwerp.

This meant that I had to spend considerable time in Paris and I always stayed at a quiet boutique-type hotel called the Windsor Hotel. It was typical of most snobby hotels where no one at the front desk ever recognized a paying customer until the guest had stayed there fifty times. But in the end I used their staff almost like my own and they treated me like family even if it took two years for the management to warm up.

One evening I was eating dinner by myself in a Left Bank bistro, and the noisy men at a table next to mine were generously drinking wine and discussing business which turned out to be a competing bid for the *ESRO I* satellite. Some of their technical and financial ideas were innovative, and when I returned to my hotel I decided to call an emergency meeting in the morning with some of my key players to see if we could take advantage of this newly acquired intelligence. By making adjustments both in strengthening our own cost bid, and by introducing language changes in the technical sections to torpedo that particular competitor we spruced up LCT's bid. The hotel's staff typed up much of what we needed to get done.

On the Friday just before the last weekend when our sealed bid was due for submission I went over it in Brussels with Art Williams whose own competitive spirit caught up with the challenge. He decided to put up some contingency money to sponsor a film to accompany our proposal. After calling Contraves where our satellite mock-up was stored, they agreed to write up a script, find a cameraman, and an engineer who spoke English-English as opposed to American-English to narrate it. I flew to Zurich on Saturday morning with one of our public relations experts from the Netherlands. The poor soul almost never traveled by air and I learned why.

As we approached for the landing he turned white, squeezed the armrest until his knuckles were as well, and mopped up perspiration pouring from his forehead. Later he explained he had been shot down in Indonesia by Japanese *Zero* fighters during World War II before he had gained enough altitude to engage them, and woke up in a tree. It took a bit of trying before I understood he had been a Dutch fighter pilot flying an American-made Brewster *Buffalo*, a 1930s pursuit plane that the US Navy had replaced with the Grumman F4F *Wildcat*, and had been a prisoner of war under the Japanese for the next four years. There was no escaping World War II twenty years after it was over.

Top photo. Georges Phélizon pointing to the ESRO I satellite during a press briefing at L.C.T. in Paris on 16 June 1967. In middle background in front of the cabinet is Hervé Tanter, Managing Director of the laboratory.
LCT photo courtesy of Georges Phélizon.

Bottom photo. The ESRO I flight unit 1 being tested and mated to the *Scout* launch vehicle's fourth stage in Dallas, Texas. March 1968.
NASA photo courtesy of Georges Phélizon.

Apparently the technical evaluators of the *ESRO I* bids in Delft loved the movie and viewed it several times to accept the innovative vertical *shelves* conceived by our Swiss colleagues. This permitted the heat to dissipate more easily because the scientific experiments would generate more heat inside the satellite than the ESRO engineers had first thought. We learned that our technical proposal was number one and that the case rested on the cost proposal and politics. Once our cost proposal was compared to the others, we again came out on top. Only some major political obstacle could now scuttle our bid. Even though our French competitors tried to influence the French delegate to oppose LCT, the government felt it would be more embarrassing *not* to support LCT's French bid than any other option on the table despite LCT's parentage.

When LCT's victory became known it caused quite a sensation. As far as ITT was concerned, it was the first time any ITT entity had ever won a prime contract for a satellite anywhere. It meant that several million dollars in applied research would go to LCT without one red cent being put up by corporate headquarters—a real first for our continental lab. In April 1965 the chestnut blossoms dressed up avenue Breteuil where LCT was located in Paris, and added some natural cheer to the newly acquired spirit of its engineers and technicians who were flushed with their highly acclaimed international victory. Today, LCT's former building is the headquarters of Michelin guide books and maps.

Leaving satellite making to LCT, I concentrated on other new projects and on the completion of my survey of our other European affiliates to see what they could do in this new marketplace.

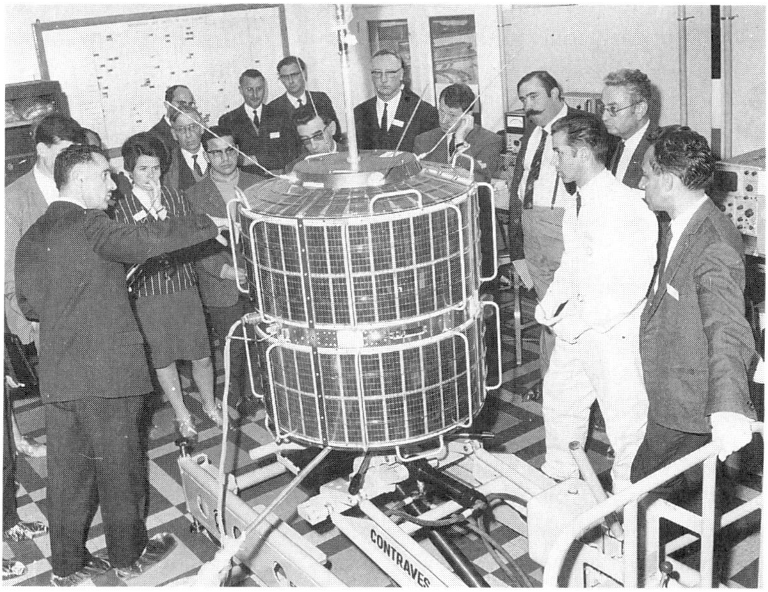
CONTRAVES

Unfortunately, the competitive victory attracted invitations from many of our European companies for me to speak at conferences, conventions and dinners in Lisbon, Madrid, Rome and elsewhere. When I had to go to Rome I made a side trip to visit the NATO missile testing range on Sardinia, and when I returned to the Italian capital I went to dinner with two top marketing men from our Italian affiliate FACE. In short order I learned the difference between an Italian gentleman from the north and one from the south because my two hosts were as different as Confederate cavalryman Jeb Stuart was from Union cavalryman George A. Custer during the American Civil War.

To me the Italian argument was insignificant but to my hosts it was the end of the world as they argued over my simple question, "Why were there two bidets in my bathroom at the swanky Excelsior Hotel on Via Veneto?"

With all the passion that only Italians can conjure, one claimed this was to accommodate a businessman traveling with his daughter, and the other pooh-poohed that contention and maintained it reflected regional prejudices. Soon they were standing and used their fingers to poke holes in the clouds. Not only did other guests start taking sides, but even the staff seemed to wade in as well. The trouble in such a circumstance is that the argument started in broken English and fractured French, but as it developed into philosophical differences it drifted into serious Italian where I was left in the wake of an obviously rich debate that earned rahs or boos according to the division of northern and southern Italians dining in the restaurant. By the time the waiters served cognac, the well-lubricated diners could barely keep their noses out of the snifters. Obviously, all had a Roman good time.

The next day they took me to Vatican Radio to sell its engineering clergy on space communications, and if they ever needed any technical or financial information on the cost effectiveness of proselytizing via satellites, all the good padres needed to do was to call on either one of my colleagues.

Although there was almost no way for me to get FACE into space activities, the potential for SEL in Germany threw different contradictions at me. Like the French market, the German one was controlled by the government and the major companies knew which portions of the market was earmarked for which company. Everyone was expected to know and keep his place, and real competition was only rarely permitted.

The main difference in Germany was the existence of the Soviet armies in East Germany and the existence of a divided Berlin. Like all major employers, SEL was required to keep some product lines in West Berlin in order to provide local jobs and income. Of course, the main occupation there was espionage and no one would manufacture anything but the simplest radios or telephone hand sets. So many threats had been heaped on the poor Berliners by the Soviets that they were very nervous and the West German government even gave them "jumpy money" as an annual cash bonus for staying in Berlin and not jumping ship.

Every company operating in West Berlin lost money because of transportation costs, excessive production costs, increased security problems and a thousand adverse influences of the Soviet embargo. Our subsidiaries there received generous tax credits and deductible expenses to compensate for our "forced" presence in West Berlin. I saw first hand how greatly did Germany suffer from the Nazi totalitarian regime under Hitler, and as I said earlier, the industrial managers I dealt with were often either twenty-seven-years old or fifty-seven. Those between were buried in shallow graves stretching from Berlin to Kiev and Stalingrad. The absence of this generation spoke loudly in German society.

One of my American friends from New England was in charge of security for our few plants in West Berlin. For reasons that will become apparent I'll only refer to him as "W.H." to protect his memory and his family. Whenever W.H. came to Brussels we'd take a break to meet for a coffee or a beer at a café at *Place Saint-Jean* in the Belgian capital.

I'll try to reconstruct one of our conversations.

"I reviewed a book called *The Berlin Wall* for *The Washington Sunday Star* a few years ago. Did you read that book?" I asked.

"Yes, but I live the problem everyday," he replied.

"What do you mean?"

"Hasn't anyone told you about the damn parking lot next to our main SEL plant?"

"The one near the wall?" I asked.

"Right. Everyone's on my tail about it."

"You've lost me..."

W.H. explained, "A tunnel under the wall comes out in my parking lot, and every night I have a dozen East German refugees using it to enter West Berlin. I use trucks and flatbeds to hide the opening. One of these days the East German guards will see what's going on."

"What's a few dozen refugees on top of the two and a half million already out of East Germany?"

"That's not what worries me."

"Well?"

"It's the others, the ones I let use the tunnel to sneak into East Germany," said W.H. Then he added, "There's a lot of pressure on me. You should come to see..."

He didn't have to spell out the pressure on ITT and SEL to let secret agents use this tunnel. With a secret asset like our parking lot, not only the CIA would want to use it, but also the British Secret Intelligence Service, often called Military Intelligence or MI6, the French SDECE, and even the West German BND. Although there was no serious commercial or consumer market in West Berlin there was a great market for intelligence-gathering electronic equipment to snoop on everything going on in East Berlin. In this area of subterfuge, ITT companies were well-placed to provide US intelligence services with American-made-to-order eavesdropping equipment and devices, often called *spook equipment*—all of which was manufactured in the US for obvious security reasons. So much of this equipment was jammed under typical tile-covered roofs in Berlin that the city earned the nickname of *spook-capital* in espionage circles.

As unique as were circumstances in the besieged city of West Berlin, so were they in West Germany. In order to build up its wartorn economy, the government in Bonn was always bringing deals to industry to prevent industrial failures and job losses. One day in Brussels, Art Williams flagged me as I passed his door. "You know anything about Focke-Wulf?"

"Only that they built one of the best fighter planes Germany had in World War II," I answered.

"Well, New York wants us to assess its facilities—to see what we might be able to do with it."

I reacted with surprise. "Do we own it?"

"SEL owned 28% of it before the war," Art replied, "Maybe we're being asked to increase the stake, or sell whatever equity is left..."

What I did know about Focke-Wulf was that one of the V-2 engineers from Peenemünde had gone to France after the war and had helped to develop the *Véronique* missile for the French. Recently he had returned to Germany and was development manager for Focke-Wulf. Since Germany couldn't produce missiles or fighter planes under prevailing international law, I couldn't imagine why Focke-Wulf had someone with that much rocket experience at its main plant in northern Germany. And that's where I went as soon as I made arrangements. I remember getting on well with the development manager, mainly because he knew some of the Peenemünde crowd that worked on *Polaris*.

For the next two days I toured the machine shops and the assembly areas where small private aircraft similar to *Piper Cubs*, *Taylor Crafts* and *Cessnas* in the United States, but a bit smaller than *De Havilland Beavers* in Canada. They seemed to have two models, a two-seater and a four-seater, and every office had framed photos of each. Because I was leaving on the third day I finally asked, "The Focke-Wulf 190 was one of the most famous fighters in the world. How is it that you have no photos of it anywhere in the plant?"

One of them answered, "Ah, zo, the vor is over."

"OK, the war's over, but nothing prevents you showing that you have a solid background in aviation..."

Following a telephone conversation between my guide and maître D of the company's executive cafeteria, I was told we'd have a farewell lunch for me there with all the people I had met over the last few days. We walked across a paved lot and entered one of the oldest buildings, apparently one that had survived bombing attacks in the war. The executive dining room was on the second level and we ascended the stairs.

As we approached the dining hall's entrance the entire wall to my right was a mural of a World War II manufacturing line of Focke-Wulf 190 fighter planes in the final phase of assembly when wings were joined to the fuselage. It was quite an impressive enlargement showing at least thirty fighters. The far end of the photo mural showed a finished fighter being pushed outside by workmen through an open hangar door.

After I returned to Brussels I reflected on my visit to Focke-Wulf. I had seen no vestige of its former self and capabilities. The situation reminded me of US procedures during the war when a fighter pilot always noted the performance of a plane in the plane's log book when he returned safely. At one time, my brother George checked out P-40 *Flying Tigers* from General Claire Chennault's squadrons in China. If any P-40 could fly, George would earmark it for lend-lease to Moscow as the Soviets battled the German armies at the gates of the city. One day George climbed into the cockpit of a P-40 and in the log book the last pilot had written, "Junk the son-of-a-bitch." George didn't bother to risk his neck testing it when an expert had already expressed his opinion.

I wrote up an unfavorable opinion on the future of light aircraft in a overly crowded and limited marketplace. "If we own it, we should unload. If not, we should walk from the deal." While I was at ITT, I never heard about Focke-Wulf again.

Meanwhile ITT Europe coined money for corporate headquarters and because of these profits Geneen and his people spent a week, almost every month in Brussels. They'd easily fill two 707s at times, and no one wanted to travel with an insomniac like Geneen who would lay spread sheets all over the aisles making it difficult to tiptoe around the boss when you were headed toward the toilet. Invariably he'd ask you questions while remaining oblivious to your body twisting in agony.

Hundreds of general managers from around Europe attended these General Managers Meetings which started early and never finished. All the product line managers in Brussels were on call and little notes circulated that indicated when Geneen wanted to meet with you at 4 p.m., 11 p.m., or even 2 a.m. During one meeting, one of our European General Managers suffered a heart attack in the late evening, and everyone thought Geneen would amend his ways and adjourn these meetings before midnight.

Well, they were partially right and Geneen did make one change. At every GMM thereafter, there was an ambulance stationed at the front entrance 24 hours a day until Geneen and his people returned to New York.

At one point Geneen was so frustrated with European GMs that he called in the American product line managers stationed in Brussels. In this private meeting, he said, "I'm going to give you a hard time tomorrow. I'll say things to you that I can't say to Europeans, and you'll probably wish you had never met me. I want to bring up all the issues you can't get them to agree on, because I want to clear the air."

After Geneen apologized in advance, we dutifully attended the meetings affecting our product lines, and whenever we brought up unresolved issues, Geneen shredded us for not forcing the issues or for wasting money through delays. He'd give us three months to wipe up loss lines, and six months to reassign personnel from an entire division. It was brutal, and the Europeans were spellbound at the sight of our loss of blood over their own procrastinations. But Geneen made his point with them, and things went a bit more easily for us thereafter.

The only exception to Geneen's well thought-out game plan was when I recited my unresolved issues with Federal Labs in New Jersey who always skinned me with excessive inter-departmental charges because they felt Europe owed them a premium on space projects. Most people in the room had never heard anyone criticize the US group on any issue in front of all the power in New York. I knew that the top research people there like Henri Busignies and Al Cookson supported me, as did Bob Kirk who was responsible worldwide for my product line. I cited chapter and verse about ITTFL's lack of cooperation while Geneen was getting madder and madder until he slammed his palm on the long table, "Well, someone's got to fix this problem!"

Everyone burst out laughing because only he could do it. Nonetheless I made my point and relations improved somewhat between ITT Europe and ITT Federal Laboratories in New Jersey.

Chapter 19

US corporate manners in Europe

Under Harold S. Geneen the company lived and died by the profits generated by product line managers, and when we were asked to provide a written report on any problem, it was expected to be one-page long. Anyone with at least half a brain was expected to rework and rewrite the problem until it fit that single typed page. Geneen didn't care if there were thirty annexes because if he was still interested after the first page he'd read more.

For the six years I was in Europe for ITT the one-page rule never changed. For Europeans who had been trained to progress logically item by item and almost never expressed a recommendation first, and oftentimes not at all, it was difficult for them even when they wrote English well. On the other hand, Americans had no trouble expressing a recommended course of action in the first sentence and justifying it in a few paragraphs.

One of ITT's most profitable activities was long distance communications which was often called "long lines" in the trade. Obviously, space communications was as *long line* as one could get. All services from cables, wireless, hard wire, microwave and space satellites fell into the same pool of activity, and ITT's worldwide communications were handled by those specialists who knew how to wholesale and retail great bulks of telecommunications traffic. Like water in a pipe, telecommunications flowed in channels and could be also compared to beams of light.

If a beam from a flashlight could be compared to a single telegraph line, then twelve beams would constitute a telephone line. Two hundred forty flashlight beams side-by-side could be compared to one television channel. Thus 2,880 telegraph channels could also be equivalent to one black-and-white television channel. Although these values could change according to the type of radio frequency involved and other technical factors, these examples provide the wide range in values that affected the sales prices of telecommunications in the marketplace. Obviously color television required more capacity in transmission.

Whenever ITT's long line people needed backup on communications satellites for customers in Africa or the Middle East they would ask for me to meet their customers who were always government representatives. One such occasion proved to be very embarrassing to me and to ITT. I was asked to meet a cabinet minister from the government of Haile Selassie, Emperor of Ethiopia.

After being introduced to him in the Swiss city of Geneva, we met again in the German city of Munich where we both stayed at the Vierjahreszeiten Hotel which was then expanding and construction activity was everywhere. My intention was to drive the minister to our satellite ground station at Raisting for a visit. It was a beautiful clear day and the valley fields were covered with yellow colza blossoms. From the station's van he'd have the chance to speak by telephone to someone several continents away.

"Ethiopia will purchase a major earth installation, a turn-key operation that will make us the first PTT (governmental Postal, Telephone and Telegraph services) in Africa with satellite connections to the entire world," he boasted.

I realized that a turn-key operation meant more to ITT than a basic earth station and antenna but also would include other hardware like microwave links and overland lines depending on the station's location.

He must have repeated six different ways how the procurement would take place, and that among the ministers it was his turn to tell the others which competitive proposal was acceptable. "We each have our turn," he explained, "and this time it's mine."

"Then the cost factors will be very important..."

He laughed, "Who cares which installation we buy, the only cost factor that'll count will be the one I think is important."

To make sure there were no tricks involved in the satellite hook-up he had a diplomat he knew in Brazil waiting at our ground station there to speak to him in Amheric which is not exactly taught by all foreign language departments in the world's universities. Because the Ethiopian sale represented a multimillion dollar opportunity for ITT, I was careful to wine and dine my ministerial guest. But I soon realized that he was no ordinary customer when he let me pay but asked for the original receipts on meals, wine, rental car receipts, hotel rooms—for everything. He intended to put all these on his own expense account for repayment even though I paid for everything. At our last dinner together he made it plain to me that the only bids that would be retained for official Ethiopian consideration were those that contained a minimum of one million dollars in cash paid to him under the table so-to-speak.

By the time I returned to Brussels what really bothered me was how to recover my own money from this outrageous experience. I had spent my advance and had no receipts to justify my expenses. Art Williams was the contact point for the communications executive involved and promised to take care of my account. But the consequences of the out-and-out bribe was another kettle of fish that involved several ITT operating companies and several area executives with jurisdiction over that area of the world.

Most foreign companies and all our competitors could write-off bribes as special expenses, putting US companies that couldn't on a very uneven playing field. It was difficult to hide a million or more dollars in an annual statement in the 1960s, and for most companies such an amount represented almost 8% of annual profits after taxes.

A closed meeting of almost a dozen ITT executives involved was convened in Brussels to discuss the Ethiopian procurement. Another problem we faced was the large volume of ongoing telecommunications business we had there, and the question of whether we'd be blackballed if we didn't make a serious effort to keep the emperor's cabinet happy. We didn't know whom in Ethiopia our *lead-minister* had in his pocket. Although other people in the room knew this minister better than I, many questions were directed at me because he had made such a direct pitch through me.

In the end it was unanimously decided that we'd pass on this opportunity for a major sale. The final decision couldn't have been clearer or more decisive. As for our existing business, we were protected by long term commitments and felt that any short term perturbations could be ridden out. We didn't even refer the question to Geneen. The problem had been dumped into our lap and we decided to walk from the deal.

Although we were sometimes accused of being ruthless and aggressive competitors, the company actually was straight-laced compared to many others in the international marketplace, especially the non-US companies.

Being that there were so few Americans in Europe within our workforce, we tended to have dinner when we ran into one another on the continent. On one occasion in Paris, I ran into several visitors from the states and we organized a dinner together. As was often the case, the visitors from the states weren't accustomed to ample wine at dinner and still had a drink or two at their hotel bar before meeting at a restaurant.

By the time the main course arrived, it wasn't unusual to have one or two ready to sink under the table. However, on this occasion one of the visitors who was on the NATO circuit—trying to sell US-manufactured equipment to NATO—was openly stating the names of NATO officials he claimed were open to bribes. I was so shocked by his bad behavior that I wanted to leave, but felt obliged to stay to lessen any damage to ITT that he might cause. When I returned to my hotel I called Art Williams in Brussels even though the hour was late. Because so many of the military products that ITT sold to NATO were under his aegis, I knew that if these products weren't his he'd know whom to speak to.

The following morning I boarded an early train bound for Brussels and went straight to ITTE's office. By the time I arrived Art Williams had already arranged for the talkative salesman to return to the US immediately. As a result of this unfortunate experience, a regulation was issued by ITT in New York that required any person visiting Europe on business from the US to get approval for that visit from the appropriate ITTE product line manager beforehand.

By any comparison, the staff in Brussels was small in light of the business it handled, and in many ways it reminded me of SP in Washington. We traveled almost 80% of the time which was difficult on families. The only advantage was that we only had to pay 20% of the annual personal income tax to Belgium. Probably the most important family problem we faced was the absence of a school with an American curriculum.

Upon arrival in 1963, I had enrolled my children in the British-run International School. Every American family had problems with the staff there to whom the most routine matters were world-shaking problems. We all found them stuffy, snobby and insufferably mean-spirited disciplinarians by American standards. Even before the first school year was over several American fathers united to establish a new school for the growing number of families being sent to Brussels by Proctor & Gamble, International Harvester, Clark Equipment, Eastman Kodak, ITT and many others.

Some of us went to England to recruit a religious order of nuns and others negotiated with the city of Brussels to acquire an unused school property. We managed to collect pledges from American companies to cover deficits and nonrecurring expenses, and pledged attendance of school-aged children (born and unborn) from non-Catholic families as well as Catholic ones to reach the needed minimum number. Even my daughter, Monique, who was born a month before the school opened, was pledged. By September 1964 we were able to open St. John's International School under the management of the Sisters of the Faithful Companions of Jesus. Its first principal was Sister Mary-John, F.C.J.

Twenty-five years later the nuns invited me as co-founder to be the school's Commencement Day speaker at its silver anniversary for the graduating class on 2 June 1990. The school had grown so big it had moved to Waterloo and had over 700 students from kindergarten to high school seniors. It had become the largest international school with American courses of study in Europe. Sister Barbara Hughes, F.C.J., the Superintendent of the school, wrote me that the graduating seniors were quite "chuffed" at the idea I would be there. I was proud, too. Their choice of adjective demonstrated that many in the graduating class had English origins. Quite a switch had come about at St. John's after twenty-five years!

ITTE purchased an elegant manor house at the Bois de la Cambre in Brussels and on opening night when the visiting firemen from headquarters were in town, they and the entire local staff and spouses were invited to the gala. Near the main kitchen in the basement the servants' dining room had been converted into a mini-casino, while the rooms on the upper levels were reserved for cocktails and dancing. A good game of table stakes Baccarat developed in which almost everything I did ended up in a nine and my pockets were soon stuffed with chips and Belgian francs. It was one of the hottest streaks I ever had and I'm sure the other players were happy to see me pass the bank and cash out.

Flush with my victory I went upstairs to have a drink and join in with the corporate chatter. Quite soon one of the visitors from New York came over to socialize and it was obvious that he had been hard at work drinking while I had been downstairs slaving away at Baccarat. As fast as anyone could say "Jack Robinson" I was once again embroiled in an argument with a New York *ace* who boasted of saving corporate headquarters an immense fortune by cutting out the annual leaves for expatriates (like me), and reducing these to once every three years. His head must have been stuffed with semiconductors instead of brain cells because the so-called savings was limited to the few of us in Brussels.

He obviously thought I was from headquarters and that I would have pinned a Distinguished Service Cross on his chest. I argued we had contracts and to pull such a fast one without advance warning constituted some kind of fraud on fellow-Americans, and that we were generating all the profits that permitted headquarters to squander these hard-earned spoils on morons like himself. Void of any sense of humor, he said that if he had things his way, he's send half of us back. At this point, I could tell I absolutely couldn't get along with this disagreeable fellow. Because I didn't want to ruin an overwise very nice evening, I drifted off and soon forgot about him.

But he didn't forget the dressing down and in the morning called Tim Dunleavy, President of ITT Europe. He and Tim mixed it up, and then Tim called around to find me. As I heard it from Art Williams, Dunleavy thought the fellow's announcement at a cocktail party had been bad enough, but the fact that he was a vice president at headquarters gave him some privilege. They must have gone a few rounds because Tim got him to hold off for a year, and go two years instead of three. As Tim put it, "We could go to the well at least one more time before the new policy kicks in."

Home leave was one of the best benefits we had because if we didn't use it we could draw the cash and go anywhere else with it. With my family of six children, this was worth more than a month's salary. Considering the alternatives, the Americans in Brussels were happy with me, but I figured that somewhere in that headquarters on Park Avenue a third New Yorker would gladly slip a shiv between my shoulder blades.

Although I really had no military lines, the fact that I had responsibility for sponsored new research usually resulted in requests that I make the first steps for new advanced products from plants in North America. At our laboratories in Fort Wayne, Indiana, a series of spectacular night vision products had been developed from sniperscopes to field glasses that saw everything at night as if it were high noon. I arranged for these to be tested in an equally spectacular underground NATO facility outside Paris.

Inside its cavernous expanse we set up our equipment and once we were ready the engineers used a rheostat device to lower the light value to that of three stars, then two stars, then to one dim star that reduced the cavern to what appeared to me as pitch-black darkness. But the slightest amount of ambient light was enough to let these lenses provide as much light as you'd expect outside on a sunny afternoon. No part of any distant target escaped resolution by the sniperscope, and I could read newspaper headlines a hundred yards away with the night-vision field glasses. I had rarely seen a demonstration that succeeded so well, and the subsequent world leadership in this domain by our Fort Wayne labs never surprised me.

Our Paris lab was a small jewel in ITT's crown and was top heavy with talent that ran down to every level. During the German occupation in World War II, German armed guards were constantly posted at LCT. In no time, every time a German soldier's radio went off-kilter he brought it to LCT to be repaired. In time, LCT engineers were constantly leaving work with an electrical apparatus under their arm that attracted no particular attention from the German guards. One day an engineer named Henri Busignies walked out with rolls of engineering drawings and some electrical gizmos that passed for radio components. He crossed Paris and made his way across France, hence to Algeria, Morocco and Portugal where a tramp steamer took him and his family to the USA via Bermuda.

A week later in January 1942, he showed the US Navy the secrets of a high frequency/direction finder to locate any radio transmitting messages. This HF/DF was called a "Huff Duff," and the US Navy told him to build four prototypes and eventually a production line to produce all he could for destroyers hunting German U-boats and U-boat wolfpacks that were sinking millions of tons of allied shipping in the Atlantic.

With this secret invention, the War of the North Atlantic switched to an American advantage after March 1943 as German submarines were being sunk with regularity because of the LCT invention. The only Huff Duff prototype left in France stayed hidden under a pile of coal near the furnace in the sub-basement of the laboratory at 46 avenue de Breteuil for the four years the Germans occupied Paris and prowled around the lab.

During the 1960s LCT developed a laser range finder, the first in Europe, that permitted a tank to fire at another accurately in a twentieth of the time it took other tanks to establish the range of an enemy by optical triangulation. The ruby laser permitted an accuracy of a about six feet which was fabulous in battlefield conditions.

When military officers wanted a demonstration and were English-speaking I'd often take them to the roof of LCT which provided a beautiful panorama of the Paris skyline, and to the east the horizon was punctuated by the two towers of Notre Dame cathedral. Due to the optical illusion from our viewing point, the towers that reached 226 feet above the island in the Seine River appeared perfectly juxtaposed three kilometers away. However, with the laser range finder the user immediately ascertained the distance of the south tower, the one made famous by the hunchback Quasimodo in Victor Hugo's novel, at around 2,814 meters and the north tower of *Notre Dame de Paris* at around 2,826 meters.

Another LCT invention that eventually caused friction between French President Charles De Gaulle and US President Lyndon B. Johnson was a Doppler radar called *RATAC*. Its amazing military application was to detect motion several miles away. The French army had used a predecessor called SDS in Algeria and could detect infiltrators trying to sneak through military lines, and an experienced operator could distinguish between a man and a woman, walking or on a bicycle or riding a donkey, and pinpoint their location within a few yards. Of course it could easily pinpoint helicopters, tanks, trucks and cars many miles away at night so long as they were moving, as well as airplanes taxiing on a runway.

Somehow the Algerians captured a SDS (*Surveillance du Sol*) during the Algerian conflict, and it ended up later being used by the Syrian army. During the lightning Six Day War, Israeli forces captured the SDS that had been with the Syrians, and it was at that time that the US Army learned the operational qualities of this equipment. Naturally, any radar that could pinpoint an infiltrator in the rugged Algerian mountains could detect a Viêt Cong infiltrator on the Hô Chi Minh jungle trail in Vietnam. The US Army wanted it for Vietnam, but De Gaulle opposed the war so openly that he refused to let the American-owned LCT export any units to the US or to any ally that might re-export it to the US.

When the French army demonstrated the *RATAC* to NATO forces in Germany in early 1969 near the East-West German border, the device gained legendary status. Using a very experienced operator, the equipment tracked a young East German couple walking in the country several miles away and even to the haystack where they *rested* for a romantic interlude. As their lovemaking reached increasingly energetic heights the Doppler interpreted their romantic progress until, as one witness joked, the *heat* blew tubes in the unit. Of course, the modern equipment had no tubes but the point was made and the legend was circulated despite the radar's secret status. The US Army wanted it for Vietnam more than ever.

ITT Cannon in Belgium had a colorful character as marketing manager who became a good friend. As a paracommando member of the active military reserves, he was constantly parachuting from airplanes during air shows around Belgium. When things in the Belgian Congo got out of hand as rebels there raped and killed Catholic nuns and other colonials, Belgium prepared several regiments of these paracommandos to pacify the most troubled areas. The airplanes to transport them were to be furnished by the United States, and when reports circulated that the raped nuns were being fed to crocodiles the paras were dispatched quickly. My friend saw considerable action, was captured and hung by his thumbs for days until he made good his own escape. When I saw him again, he had been through hell and looked it.

In those days Belgium was very pro-British if they came from areas liberated by the British forces under Marshal Bernard L. Montgomery, or pro-American if they came from the Bastogne area and the Ardennes where the Americans had resisted the German attacks at Christmas 1944 in the Battle of the Bulge. One of our Belgian engineers, Henri Gustin, was very pro-American and had volunteered to go fight shoulder-to-shoulder with the Americans who were slugging it out in the mud on Heartbreak Ridge during the Korean War.

Duty at ITT Europe was never routine. In early 1966 a mysterious caller telephoned me at our headquarters. Although his accent was American he refused to identify himself until I reacted to his cryptic explanation, "Red told me to call you." That could only mean my old boss Admiral William F. "Red" Raborn from Special Projects. President Johnson had named him a few months earlier to be the new Director of the Central Intelligence Agency.

"Now what?" I thought after I agreed to meet him for lunch the next day at a private and secluded club in the Brussels area.

Chapter 20

The long reach of intelligence techniques

The one thing that Brussels had that not even Paris and other major European cities could imitate were the many elegant and private properties nestled in luxurious green settings that the Belgian rainy weather kept thick and vibrant. By the time I met the CIA representative I had reconstructed in my mind the reasons why Admiral Raborn had wanted him to meet with me. But in that business I thought I'd wait for him to declare himself because his nickel paid for the initial telephone call.

A.B. introduced himself as the area director for the CIA, and explained as his icebreaker that his last assignment had been in Iran where he had been mixed up with the internal politics involving Shah Rizah, former Prime Minister Muhammad Mossadegh and the de-nationalization of the bits and pieces of the Anglo-Iranian Oil Company. I can't remember which side he was on during Iran's "white revolution" largely because the CIA would have had someone on all the sides. Although it was all very interesting I didn't know if the admissions were nonfiction, misinformation, disinformation or imagination.

When we got down to the basics at hand, A.B. was most interested in a recent visit I had made to the Technical Laboratories of Sud Aviation near the city of Cannes on the French Riviera. I made many trips there during a consortium build-up to bid on an ESRO satellite called *TD-1* because it would eventually be placed into orbit by an American *Thor-Delta* rocket. But one of the trips had produced a bizarre, almost contrived series of circumstances.

At the time of my visits there the facility housed Sud Aviation's *Groupe Technique de Cannes* which was responsible for the most advanced and applied research of supersonic flight, satellites and IRBM missiles for De Gaul's strategic *Force de Frappe*. The "GTC" represented the cutting edge of French technological prowess. In fact, the technical director with whom I dealt in Cannes, Roger Beteil, became the technical director for the final development of the Anglo-French *Concorde* supersonic airliner that made aviation history.

Following a meeting about bidding documents some of us were invited to visit an large assembly area in what I thought was a factory building. Our viewing point was a small elevated office with windows on three sides near the ceiling.

What I saw below me was a virtual carbon copy of the US Naval Weapons Annex in Charleston, South Carolina. That was where warheads were fitted to *Polaris* missiles. My bug-eyes must have amused my hosts because the visit and its content had been entirely unexpected by me. On the assembly floor below were what could have passed for first stages, second stages, interstages and re-entry bodies of *Polaris* missiles, in various stages of assembly. Behind two desks was what I perceived to be a milestone chart.

Quickly, my eyes sought the number of missiles that would roll out for the next few months. Because I couldn't get near enough to the assembly floor I couldn't pace off any major missile component to see whether the French IRBM was more-or-less the same size as a *Polaris*. If anything, French security was never lax and I couldn't understand why I was permitted to visit the area.

Later, nothing much was said about this visit, and I returned to study all the draft administrative and technical bidding documents that were still in French. As the day wearily bore on, other reviewers bid good-bye for the evening. When I rose to stretch and call it a day, it was already late and dark out. I looked for my escort to be led out but there was none. *"What the heck?"* I thought.

I made an effort to find a security guard or anyone alive, and the first exit door I tried was locked. Amazingly enough, when I retraced my steps I found the door to the control booth of the assembly area UNLOCKED! There were enough vigil lights for me to make my way down the spiral metal stairs to the assembly floor and while I walked toward the far exits I paced off the *Polaris* look-alikes. They certainly were alike.

The first door I tried had an interior bar release that showed it could only open toward the exterior. Only gingerly did I open it to peek out, not knowing what security might be posted outside. About fifteen feet from the door was a perimeter chain link fence, about ten feet high, with barbed wire at the top. To my right was a tall lamppost with a single floodlight and recessed into the fence in the glow of the light was a guardhouse, the same one at which I had checked in earlier in the day, and where I had left my United States passport.

Suddenly, a fast moving shadow caught my eye. It was a large unmuzzled German Shepherd guard dog very much like the one I had in Brussels. Because my children and "Buddy" liked to chase me around our property on weekends I knew how quickly that dog could overtake me. After calculating the headstart I'd need to outrun the dog to the guardhouse, I slowly closed the door.

Knowing that there weren't thirty-nine solutions to my predicament, I double-tied my shoelaces, tucked in my shirt and tightened my belt. It would do me no good to start a run unless I could see where the dog was before I committed myself, and to dash for it when the dog would be looking in the opposite direction. I knew he'd hear me almost immediately but two extra strides were better than none. A major disadvantage to my plan was the fact that I didn't know if more than one guard dog had free rein in the zone between the building and the security fence, and the door only permitted me to easily look in one direction. Unfortunately the other exit doors were similarly hinged to the same side and there were no windows.

Needless to say I was very careful when I opened the door again, and after what seemed like an eternity, conditions were as right as they were going to get and I sprinted for the guardhouse. From somewhere came a growl. At the guardhouse I flew through the door and slammed it behind me while a mouthful of hot breath and glistening white teeth fogged up the door's window. The poor guard woke up and blanched when he saw me and heard the racket raised by the dog. I smiled and pointed to my passport which was still in its pigeon hole of his desk. Very weakly did he examine the photo in the passport, and then tapped the closed document in his open palm. He and I both knew his job depended on the next few minutes. By his complexion and hair I reasoned he was from North Africa and didn't want to jeopardize a good job.

In French I told him, "If you won't tell anyone, I won't either."

He asked, "Do you have a car?"

"Yes, it's there in the parking lot."

He thought my suggestion was as reasonable as any other solution, all of which could cost him and he decided, "Here's your passport, now please *fichez le camp.*"—*Get out of here.*

While I drove back to headquarters after my lunch with A.B., I wondered by which of two routes the story had reached Raborn. I had written to my old boss Captain Dick Shutt about the incident and he was so close to Admiral Raborn that I thought the loop had been closed that way. But I had also informed my brother Normand and in turn Admiral Smith could have called Raborn. At least the system was still working.

Because the French had accomplished things of their own, there were no reasons to think that the Soviets could get something from the De Gaulle government. The only explanations I have ever fathomed from this bizarre experience was that the French wanted the United States to know how far they had gone on their own, or that the CIA had a hand in arranging all this with the firm knowledge that I was probably the only American in Europe who could appreciate what was in that assembly room. I knew that I'd never know for sure.

ITT had enjoyed a very profitable year and we had acquired AVIS Rent-a-Car during 1965, and just before New Year's we learned that American Broadcasting Company wanted to merge with ITT. Geneen wanted nothing to rock the boat during the merger process because so many US governmental agencies were potentially involved to approve or invalidate the pending deal. Only one person in Europe was authorized to deal directly with ABC's overseas department and I was selected. As far as the overseas department was concerned, its non-news market was the sports coverage of the Olympics whose coverage ABC-TV pretty well dominated.

Television link-ups by satellite were still science fiction to most people, and the best I could do was to help schedule flights to carry films to Montreal where the cross-continental distribution would originate. In preparation for future coverage, ABC wanted to have the exclusive coverage of the 1968 winter games from Grenoble, France, and of the 1968 summer games from Mexico City.

When I had a meeting at ABC in New York I'd usually stay at the new Americana across the street from their offices. On the way to one early morning meeting, I ran into Admiral Raborn in the lobby while he was still CIA director. We avoided talking about the CIA and went over old times in the *Polaris* program. Although he was pressed to attend some meeting where he was to speak, several of his aides kept a polite distance. Like him, they all wore civilian clothes. I took the chance to tell him how worried Levering Smith was about technological know-how getting into Soviet hands. Red told me, "Admiral Smith is right, of course." That was the last time I saw Raborn (p. 325).

While at ABC we discussed the bidding for the 1968 Olympics. As for the French side, the bidding was to be straight forward. Not so, however, on the Mexican side. I was told that Mexico had a three-person selection committee for the Olympic games, and that its members included people close to the president, like his chauffeur, the president's brother and the president's wife or maybe his sister. The deal had all the earmarks of an Ethiopian auction, and I was glad not to be part of it. Unfortunately the ABC-ITT merger dragged on for two years and was unfairly embroiled in national politics.

Finally Geneen decided enough was enough and walked from the deal. Also, he got rid of about five hundred television sets at ITT where our executives had watched the "Batman" TV show whenever the series was on because it had greatly improved ABC's ratings. It was one of the most repeated jokes by anyone from Europe who visited the Park Avenue headquarters during the merger period, and they marveled at the highly-paid executives who took an office *time-out* whenever Batman and Robin made their appearances on ABC-TV.

In Brussels, changes were brewing for the Americans there. Jim Lester was to replace Tim Dunleavy's as president of ITT Europe, and plans were afoot for many of us to be transferred to national companies. A Canadian scientist Joe Halina arrived as a deputy to Art Williams while Art prepared to enter the Spanish group of ITT companies. Lee Chaves would go to the German group, and I would go to the French group and so forth. Although ITT headquarters thought their integration idea was grand, the national companies were definitely not thrilled. But before I was transferred there still was a great deal of wood for me to chop.

In Montreal, representatives of our affiliate ITT Canada made two trips a year to Europe to find subcontracted work for its work force. Their marketing manager was Jack Farrell, an engaging person whom it was easy to justify helping. For reasons I never learned the New York crowd wanted to move ITT Canada from Québec to Ontario, and eventually did. But I collaborated with Jack Farrell for years anyway. Another bright engineer from that organization who often interfaced with me was Guy Julien. Both of these men stayed with ITT until the company left Québec.

Simultaneously with Art Williams' departure for Madrid was Dr. George R. Arthur's arrival in Brussels to replace him, and our new research director for ITT Europe was Dr. William H. "Bill" Foster. They proved to be my godsends when I eventually went to Paris. Arthur was the main link to Europe for Bob Kirk who was in New York, and Foster was likewise for Al Cookson and Henri Busignies there. Ironically, when I drove in Paris with my family in 1967, we passed remnants of the US troops who were going in the opposite direction toward Belgian following De Gaulle's ouster of all NATO forces from French territory. So long as the Vietnam War continued, the rate of the anti-American political crescendo never decreased during the entire duration of my French assignment for ITT. Considering how important was governmental direction in the French commercial marketplace, I felt an ominous shiver when the local US Armed Forces Radio station went off the air in the middle of a world series ballgame. There would be no more sharp cracks of bats in September, sounds that were very American and impossible to explain to foreigners.

And if there was no welcome mat in France for Americans in general, there certainly was none for me in particular when I arrived at LCT. Because I knew so many people there, and considered them more than friendly acquaintances, I was taken aback when I learned that I had been assigned no office space, no secretary, no parking space, no telephone and not even a chair to sit on. Although my transfer had been under discussion for six months, and all the French objections smoothed over, I had expected their preparations to have been completed.

Even though I learned that the others from ITTE assigned to national companies had been subjected to similar forms of gracious welcomes, I was doubly amazed because the French normally exhibited very correct manners in their comportment, and I had made measurable contributions to their acceptance in the international marketplace. It was obviously more difficult for them to accept an American inside the organization at the management level than to integrate an engineer on a temporary assignment. But I had been forewarned by ITT's American human relations experts to expect a difficult time.

In any event I didn't intend to be a wallflower and commandeered a rarely used office in the executive suite and was promptly denounced for "squatting." Tough. I stayed until I had my own. Finally, a beautiful young woman was assigned as my secretary. Whatever her talents were, they didn't include typing in English. However, she could have auditioned for the Miss Universe contest and her habitual low necklines proved it. I raised the dickens over several others in a series of wonderful young women who never measured up to the type of bilingual secretarial dynamo I was used to.

Eventually I was given a private office and a bilingual executive secretary who took shorthand in two languages. Even better was the fact that Paulette was a Corsican with the smarts and temper to match her loyalty, and had been the executive assistant at Trans World Airlines in France. Just when I thought I had started to luck out, Paulette brought to my attention that certain categories of meeting notices sent to me were always arriving a day or two after the meeting had already been held.

Usually these meetings involved requests and justifications for research subsidies from New York which first went to Brussels. Such requests required the endorsement of a product line manager, in this case George Arthur, whose activities would benefit from any breakthrough for new products or for new applications of existing products. Additionally, the director of research in Brussels also had to endorse the activity as being attainable and a worthwhile use of limited resources in money or scientific manpower.

But LCT was doing things the old way, and had forgotten why I was there. I was expected by Brussels to endorse the request and by so doing I would certify that the request was not just a bookkeeping way to cover up cost overruns in some other area or to pay for some research activity that had never been approved by either Brussels or New York.

After LCT waited for approvals that didn't arrive and I started to ask questions about the requests, LCT's managers learned that their requests were being bounced back to me by George Arthur and Bill Foster who refused to budge until I was in the circuit like I was expected to be. Miraculously the meeting notices started arriving beforehand like they should have, and Paulette was quick to pick up on this wind shift.

Before I had left Brussels, Arthur and Foster had agreed to protect me with a policy of "no signature, no funding." This was a simple extension of the American doctrine of "grab a person by his funding and his heart and mind will follow." Whatever I was learning would someday be included in a manual to be given to managers being transferred to a foreign company. In 1967, ITT had no written guidelines, and it had been one of the premier American companies with a presence overseas for nearly forty years!

Meanwhile almost all of the new markets for electronics were concentrated in communications and meteorological satellites, space research and small earth station antennae. Insofar as missiles and rockets were concerned, the die had been cast and those safely inside the rocket cocoon were the first to receive any new business in that sector. In the United States, Congress established a Communications Satellite Corporation, "COMSAT," as the monopolistic vehicle to put order into the expanding use of radio frequencies. Thereafter, COMSAT initiated an international monopolistic vehicle called INTELSAT for International Telecommunications Satellites.

When the first INTELSAT request for proposals was issued there was a worldwide scramble to form competing consortia much like the one I formed for *ESRO I*. However, with the prevailing and growing nationalistic trends it was obvious to me that we'd never win a prime contract again for many years and it was better to be under the umbrella of a "national" company and grab as many subsystems as I could for our affiliates.

In order to broaden the Space Study Group at LCT I formed a separate meteorological study group under Jean Turrière. Also I had earlier negotiated with Radiation Systems, Inc. in McLean, Virginia to send their engineering officer George Chadwick to lead a week-long debate-seminar with my French engineers and mathematicians on satellite communications and small earth antennae.

Neither Radiation nor Chadwick needed the money but a business link with an organization in Europe was worth their effort. For me it represented the chance to have an option for more economical expertise than I could get from ITT Federal Laboratories. Moreover, Radiation was one of the world's leaders in small earth antennae. What I never told anyone at LCT was that Radiation was also at the cutting edge of telecommunications technology for the American defense and intelligence agencies. The "Chadwick" seminars turned out to be a huge success for both sides and continued for several years in nonclassified areas.

Although the communications satellite market exploded like a mushroom, the number of players was not large so it was usual to fight one company today only to find yourself allied tomorrow. Among the savvy American satellite companies was TRW and their representative in Europe was Philip Newton a tough competitor or valuable ally depending on the day of the week, and a gentlemen at all times. For a while we saw a lot of each other. But, by and large, the key players were in the United States and the travel involved was tough on the wear and tear of a person's body. Often a consortium would include a US company on the east coast and another on the west coast which involved very long flights to attend meetings.

On one occasion I went to SEL in Stuttgart, and then went to catch a flight to Boston from London. On the transatlantic leg I sat next to Walt Rostow whom I had not seen in almost four years. He had moved over to the White House after Kennedy's assassination and was very much a key adviser to President Johnson on Vietnam. I happened to tell him about all the underground manufacturing facilities around Stuttgart. He said, "During the war I flew countless missions in B-17s to bomb them." With a laugh he added, "It's obvious we never got them."

When I arrived in Boston I was immediately driven to Raytheon, the company with the lead on the electronics, and I think ITTFL had the communications package with back-up from ITT Europe to build up the foreign content. (In time all satellites started to look alike.) The next day we all flew to California to meet with our structural contractor into whose satellite envelope our packages had to fit. Within a few days I was on a turnaround flight back to Europe.

Back in Paris I often visited foreign embassies and military missions for business ends even if some of them were *unfriendly* toward the United States. While in one such *unfriendly* mission I was being escorted down several flights when we passed an old-fashioned telephone junction box, the kind that was very easy to tap.

At a subsequent US embassy reception I told one of the diplomats about the situation, knowing that he's pass it on to the in-house intelligence operative. Sure enough, I was contacted for the particulars. Although nothing obliged me to do so, I felt I had a duty to my country to step up to the plate when I was the only person who could make a difference.

On another occasion LCT received a general request for proposals from the Romanian Railroad Authority which was seeking a nationwide communications network based on all its hardlines and electrical lines that followed every railroad bed and tracks from the capital Bucharest to just about every town and hamlet in Romania. Our deputy GM Henri Dasse-Hartout reviewed it and wisely bucked it to me. After reading the RFP several times to make sure my eyes weren't deceiving me, I wondered how in the world the Soviet ally had sent this to an American-owned company.

From the intelligence point-of-view the technical recitals alone were a goldmine. Romania was a key Warsaw Pact country and for it to solicit outside the Communist zone indicated how little confidence it had in the Soviet Union or its allies to offer the state of the art in vital communications.

There was more than an adequate lead-time for the CIA to buy a front—that is, a company with no political baggage that could be used to coordinate a bid to *control* access to communications in a key Balkan country. Because the possibilities were countless I made a back-up copy of the documents and sent the originals to Ken Vigue, one of ITT's key managers in Washington. If anyone had a successful relationship with the CIA it was Ken and he was constantly trading with all the intelligence agencies to gain advantages for ITT. The Romanian package was definitely worth a series of brownie points.

On another occasion the Warsaw Pact ally Hungary issued an RFP for remote meteorological stations to gather weather information. After speaking with the contact person by telephone, it was clear that they spoke English more easily than French so I made arrangements to go to Budapest from Vienna. When I landed in Vienna it was the first time I had been there since I was a student at the University of Vienna in 1951—sixteen years earlier, when the city was divided into multiple zones and one main international zone whose control changed monthly between the Soviet Union, the United States, the United Kingdom and France.

Austria regained her complete independence in 1955 and it was with a sense of freedom that I flew to Vienna so easily. The last time I traveled to Vienna, it had to be by train through Linz to enter the Soviet Zone, and the train went very slowly and was stopped every twenty minutes by Soviet soldiers armed with machine guns and accompanied by attack dogs. They examined my "gray card" and felt it to see if it were genuine, and forced me to have multiple vaccinations because they wouldn't accept the World Health Organization card saying I had all my shots. For years thereafter my memories of Soviet soldiers were enriched by the pus that oozed from both my upper arms.

Chapter 21

Porous Iron Curtain

Following the main road toward Budapest from Vienna, I headed for the same border crossing through which many of the 200,000 refugees had escaped from the Soviet troops that invaded Hungary with 2,500 tanks in 1956. The Hungarian revolt against Communist rule had lasted a brief ten days and was quickly snuffed out by the massive Soviet intervention. Footprints of history were everywhere in the countryside just as they had been described by my professor of Geopolitics at the University of Vienna, even to the pattern of fieldstones on Austrian roofs compared to the rooftops in the Tyrol or in Carinthia on the Yugoslav border. Such details had also been taught to enemy paratroopers so they would know over which part of Austria they were floating downward.

Although the Austro-Hungarian Empire had lasted only about a half-century, the two parts had many similarities in 1967. Both were predominantly Christian, although Hungary had twice the percentage of Protestants than Catholic Austria had. In the agricultural fields of eastern Austria one could still see Roman cemeteries and Caesaristic arches of triumph in the middle of recently plowed fields. These monuments still endured after 2,000 years, and marked the far reaching expansion of Rome's frontiers. But as History had shown, when an empire crumbled the erosion started in the periphery far from the core. And when the Roman empire decayed, the first pieces to fall were far from Rome.

The closer I drove to the Hungarian border the more isolated I felt because oncoming traffic was so light. Even before the border became evident I saw the tall watchtowers in the distance, and when I was near them I saw the high wire fence topped by razor-wire that seemed to extend hundreds of miles, northward toward Czechoslovakia, and southward toward Yugoslavia. Behind the fence was a swath of grubbed land several hundred yards wide and a forest beyond that cleared strip. At the armed crossing point I stopped for a passport and visa check and a thorough examination of my luggage in the trunk. As I stood next to the car, the border guards performed their search, and I could see the barrels of machine guns protruding from the closest watchtower.

The travel time to Budapest was only a few hours or so but I passed several troop concentrations of the Soviet army in the woods. Although the daylight was waning I could see them through clearings and where the forest had been thinned. In the villages many teenagers congregated near the town's central church to attend evening devotions. Church services were one of the few authorized activities for crowds to assemble under the Communist rules, and the Hungarian teenagers took full advantage of this rule to meet one another under the Soviet noses. During my time in Hungary I never saw the occupying Soviet troops on the streets, unlike Vienna during its occupation by the four powers when my schoolmates and I were always ducking away from the Soviet street patrols whenever we heard their jack-booted cadence on the stone streets.

Traffic was light in the capital city and I noticed that shop windows didn't offer any of the latest goods that could be found in Vienna. In fact, the only thing Budapest had in common with Vienna was the Danube River which cut the Hungarian capital into Buda on the right bank and Pest on the left. This would be a new experience, and I was looking forward to learning how the Communists conducted business with westerners.

The next morning I went to my first meeting in the meteorological offices where I was escorted to a room with bare furniture, wooden chairs and nothing on the walls but cracks, flaking paint and one framed picture of the Bolshevist revolutionary Vladimir I. Lenin, the father of Communism and the Soviet Union. Three women greeted me, and when the local Communist cell leader arrived they fell silent. I followed their lead by standing. Before I knew what was happening I was forced to listened to his harangue as he praised the superiority of Lenin and Communism in broken English. I couldn't believe that participants in a business meeting could be subjected to such political nonsense in memory of a demagogue. Luckily he shut up after ten minutes and stomped from the room. The women immediately escorted me to a laboratory where they outlined their equipment needs for transmitting remote collections of weather data to a central collection point.

After we agreed to meet again the next day, I asked the woman who appeared to be senior, "Where are the men?"

She appeared startled by the question. "What do you mean?" she asked.

"This is the first time I've seen only European women in managerial jobs, and I haven't seen any men except for the preacher," I said.

The *preacher* remark elicited smiles all around. She answered, "The men are working in the factories and fields where they are more efficient than we are."

That evening I went on my own for dinner as I had done the night before, and I noticed that many restaurants hung a heavy carpet as a second door as much to reduce sound toward the outside as to cut drafts. The two restaurants I visited had musicians playing a violin or zither to accompany a pianist or an accordionist. The most surprising occurrence was the popularity of a love song denounced by Moscow and prohibited from being broadcast on the radio—*Lara's Theme*, the MGM song written by Maurice Jarre for the award-winning Hollywood movie *Doctor Zhivago*.

Actually the book had been written by the Russian novelist Boris L. Pasternak and published in Italy in 1957 because no publisher in the Soviet Union could. The following year Pasternak won the Nobel Prize for Literature but couldn't receive it because of Communist interference. This was just one more sign that the Soviet Union was starting to unravel at the edges.

True, this recital is more of an anthropological insight into one Warsaw Pact society twenty-two years before Communism fell apart than it is a key to understand how they tried to do business with the west when Moscow let them get away with it. After our last meeting, I was invited to lunch with the dozen women I had been dealing with. That was a nice touch, and I looked forward to it. When we arrived at the restaurant, the preacher was there waiting and my spirits waned. However, everyone was in a relaxed mood especially after consuming a few bottles of that deep red wine commonly called "Bull's Blood." They were interested in stories about the United States, but when I told them about all the Hungarian refugees working in Montreal when I visited there, most of the women dabbed tears from their eyes. I had forgotten that many Hungarians had emigrated to Canada in 1956. I glanced at the preacher to see his reaction, but all he did was frown at their emotional display and said nothing.

Soon the women started writing the names and Canadian addresses of brothers, cousins and friends who had escaped in 1956. On the other side of these slips of paper they wrote their own addresses and other information. Not one explained why she did this or what she hoped I would do. Theirs were silent pleas. Later, when we shook hands on the sidewalk, the preacher slipped a piece of paper into my hand in such a way that none of the women would notice. When I examined it later, he had done the same.

On the way to the airport from my hotel in the late afternoon, two cars behind us collided and a police motorcyclist stopped my taxi driver. I was afraid we'd be involved and that I'd miss my flight to Vienna and Paris. After ten minutes the policeman told us we could leave. In halting German, my driver explained with some contempt that policemen in civilian clothes who had been following us had collided with a taxi who had cut off their unmarked car. I had seen them handcuff the offending taxi driver and cart him off. Actually, I hadn't noticed anyone tailing me. No other untoward incident prevented me from leaving Budapest.

When I returned to Paris I learned that ITT had a telephone operation in Chile because one of my former schoolmates from Assumption Prep in Massachusetts was a missionary there, and desperately needed a telephone. Even though people in Paris still had to wait several years for a telephone, apparently the wait was far longer in Chile. From his letter I gathered that he had been waiting for years already. I soon prepared a letter to my Chilean counterpart in which I did my best to solicit his cooperation on behalf of my former classmate. I also wrote to my old chum and asked him to write again, particularly if he didn't get his telephone for the mission.

Anxious to get a paid study for LCT's Space Study Group I investigated the rumored French satellite project and learned that the Québec government had been briefed about it when they met in Paris with General Aubinière, the head of the French space agency, and that the Québeckers were interested to see whether the *cultural French communications satellite* could exchange French television and other cultural programming with their own provincial programming since the

French overseas territories of Saint Pierre and Miquelon were so close to the province.

It would do me no good to knock on any doors at the French space agency so I decided to knock on doors in Québec instead where I'd get a fair hearing. Personal contacts in Québec learned that the man in charge was Claude Morin, Under Minister of Intergovernmental Affairs for the Province of Québec, and I arranged to meet with him "next to the counter of fresh oranges in a supermarket in Québec City." After *vetting* my veracity, Morin was satisfied and we met in government offices thereafter. Through him I soon met the man in charge of the planning on a daily basis, Jacques Gauthier, Vice President of Radio Québec, and Special Advisor to the Prime Minister of Québec Province, Daniel Johnson, Sr.

Most people failed to understand that Québeckers were nothing more than Americans who speak French. They thought, acted and did business exactly like Americans, and they usually vacationed in the United States, and I never knew one who didn't have a relative in New England or in Woonsocket, Rhode Island where I was born. When they retired they stayed in Québec or the United States. This was very different from the English-Canadians for whom *making-it-good* meant moving to England, or felt a kinship with the things-English more than things-American. I have yet to meet a French-Canadian who has retired to live in France. Anyway, I got along famously with the Québeckers and I had an advantage over all French competitors because not a one of them had a clue about what made a Québecker tick.

From the technical point of view the proposed study pushed the communications' state of the art to the limit, a perfect fit for ITT and LCT. Involved would be a satellite with several television channels, and the ability to handle and retransmit huge volumes of data, and which would be compatible with the smallest earth stations that could be envisioned for areas far from normal television access. I was surprised to see how far the Québeckers had gone to define their modern needs, especially to tap into what they called *"banques de savoir,"*—banks of knowledge in libraries and in medical research archives. Being well acquainted with the designed capability of all the communications satellites on the drawing boards, I knew that none had the exciting applications of what this Franco-Québec project promised.

As soon as I returned to Europe I informed George Arthur and Bill Foster about the wide range of applications for the future of telecommunications, and they agreed to support my efforts to acquire the study contract. Back at LCT the reaction was less enthusiastic because the project was undefined and the French government might blackball our efforts. I thought, *"Oh, how the French liked everything to be defined, just so and spoon-fed!"* From my point of view, it was a perfect opportunity to define the study outline, make it fit and get the customer to buy the ideas. I knew this is what Québec wanted and expected. Actually, LCT's initial reaction by some in top management was extremely encouraging to me because all our French competition would most likely react in the very same and predictably conservative manner, leaving the field open for us to get a headstart!

The head of the French Study Group was Georges Phélizon and he didn't want to miss this unique opportunity, and during our discussions he made the case for a pre-study in order to identify all the reasonable options and to define how to proceed. I agreed that he should go for it, and as soon as we could put it on paper, we'd present it to Claude Morin and Jacques Gauthier in Canada. While Phélizon and his engineers were working on their *pre-study* I kept other assignments away from them as best I could.

Meanwhile I was concerned about the pedagogical applications of the satellite project and the fact that LCT had top notch engineers and scientists but no senior talent in the teaching disciplines or in instructional techniques, especially Instructional Television—ITV. I hired as a consultant a former White Father missionary with thirty years experience teaching in Africa and who had two Ph.D. degrees, one of which was in audio-visual applications. At the time I wasn't thinking of anything like "Sesame Street," only because I didn't know what anyone really needed.

During one luncheon break from LCT, Phélizon and I walked over to the cafeteria at UNESCO whose headquarters were near LCT. It was the only place I knew in Paris where I could get a pint of milk with my meal without being insulted for asking for it instead of wine. In the UNESCO book shop I picked up a technical paper published by Stanford Research Institute in California that described the use of satellites for ITV and Instructional Radio, and discussed ongoing experiments in India and the Ivory Coast whose projects were funded by the Ford Foundation in New York. As soon as we returned to the laboratory I asked my missionary to learn all he could about these projects, in particular the one in the Ivory Coast where they spoke French. While I stayed in touch with Gauthier in Montreal, I encouraged my researchers to flush out their ideas, knowing that it takes time for research to bear fruit.

Another project I was pursuing for our manufacturing affiliates was a contract for radios to be distributed among Laplanders who lived north of the Arctic Circle in Sweden, Norway, Finland and the Soviet Union but with the majority of them living in Norway. ESRO had started launching sounding rockets to measure scientific information on weather and communications phenomena resulting from the aurora borealis as the northern lights were known in the scientific community. Just north of the Arctic Circle in Sweden was the city of Kiruna which I started visiting because the Kiruna Geophysical Institute was located there. The scientific experiments in *ESRO 1* and possibly for *TD-1* were being developed by the Institute.

The justification for the bulk purchase of radios for the nomadic Laplanders was to be able to warn them when a sounding rocket was on its way down somewhere on Lapp territory. These portable radios would have to be switched on remotely to be effective, otherwise the batteries would wear out. Temperatures north of the Arctic Circle could range as low as minus 60°F or even colder in the winter, much like northern Québec, when batteries run down very quickly. Consequently, I had two good reasons to visit Kiruna and our affiliate SRT in Stockholm frequently. I particularly liked Sweden, its inhabitants and its wooden architecture that reminded me of New England.

Travel was a wearying part of my position and whenever I could I would avoid it. I shunned technical conferences like the Black Plague and would send deserving engineers to deliver papers in my place. And when it came to hand deliver very confidential and important documents I would usually try to send Paulette my *bachelorette* assistant who was always ready to go. Eventually she met her future husband, and the last time I saw them they had been married over twenty years.

One mystery about Paulette remained a secret for several years. Periodically an old Jewish gentlemen would call me from London. I never knew how or why he had my name or my telephone number or the name of my secretary. After the usual exchange of politeness he's always ask, "How is Paulette?" and "Are you treating her all right?"

"Why not ask her yourself?" I'd think. But by his voice I felt he was quite old, and even if he was direct and nosy, he was never offensive in his questions. I never doubted that he liked her but I didn't know why. And I never felt I should ask Paulette directly—at least not for a few years.

The first anniversary of the *ESRO 1* contract passed quietly at the laboratory but unusual threats of strikes by students circulated in Paris. Since De Gaulle was going ahead with his plans for a state visit to Romania no one paid any serious attention to the student problems. The truly big news was that Vietnam peace talks were scheduled to start in Paris. The month of May promised to be interesting in the French capital, and everyone looked forward to the national holiday on Wednesday, 1 May 1968.

Chapter 22

French distractions and projects

As if someone had dropped a burning match on a trail of gunpowder, the famous May events of 1968 (*les événements de mai*) spread like wildfire. What started with campus protests on 2 May by university students at Nanterre, a town not far from Paris, was taken up the next day by the students at the Sorbonne in the heart of Paris. For the next ten days the students faced off with police not only in Paris but across France. From my first hand observations the only solid complaint they seemed to have was the educational straight-jacket that forced French college students to study certain majors even if not enough jobs for them existed in those sectors.

Like anti-Vietnam protests on American college campuses that spread across the country, the rebellious fever spread quickly in France. In very little time French labor unions started joining in, and the events that opened the floodgates to violent street protests have remained something that foreigners have rarely understood.

During this period of unrest almost all of ITT's thirty French factories were occupied by labor strikers. In some cases ITT's managers were locked in their offices, but there was no abuse of them and they were fed. Nevertheless, they remained prisoners. Generally the list of managers to be locked-in were prepared before the vote by strikers. On one occasion my name was listed and a labor representative at LCT suggested that I go for a walk, but the periodic votes by LCT's workers never resulted in one for occupation. Eventually, only the managers and their immediate staffs worked.

Electricity was cut off several times a day so people tended to stay out of elevators, and water was often cut off as well. In homes and apartments, people learned to store water in basins and bathtubs. For almost the entire period no international calls were permitted, and often there was no local telephone service. Not to be left out, even bank employees went on strike. Consequently, no automatic deposits and withdrawals took place and cash couldn't be withdrawn.

For example, my own salary disappeared as did my landlord's rent receipts. The French equivalent of the teamsters' union refused to deliver food to markets nor gasoline to many stations, and people pushed their cars from station to station just to get twelve quarts of gas.

At airports across France the air controllers struck and no airliners, domestic or foreign, could land safely at major airports. Most trains no longer operated, buses stayed in their terminals and the Paris metro rarely functioned when it was supposed to. Bicycles became the social rage and necessity. But sometimes things did work but no one knew when they would nor for how long.

Eventually, President De Gaulle described these events in a controversial fashion. Governmental spokesmen claim that De Gaulle said, "Reforms, OK. Disorder (*'chienlit'*), No." But what I saw and heard on television was a De Gaulle who played carefully on words when he distinctly pronounced every syllable of the word *'chienlit'* whose three syllables *chie-en-lit* clearly stated, "Crap in one's own bed, No." Maybe the politically correct journalists heard one version, but the rank and file among the Frenchmen probably heard what I did.

Almost every day I found instructions in my mail box on how to fabricate homemade Molotov cocktails, and how to perform other unsociable acts like calling the Presidential Palace when phones were working in order to jam De Gaulle's switchboard. Newspapers? Radio and TV news? Forget it. We could have been on Mars as far as reliable news coverage was concerned. Even if some newspapers were printed out of the country very few circulated inside France, and often television screens went blank.

When housewives walked two miles to find a grocery store open, the clerks insisted that the purchases be paid in cash and in the exact amount. Because small denominations and coins became difficult to obtain, people were soon *stuck* with large bank notes which meant that more groceries had to be purchased to equal the smallest denomination one might be carrying. This produced accusations of hoarding, and arguments erupted between customers. Many stores had more shelves bare than stocked. As long as cash held out at LCT, the managers could draw against unpaid salaries but the denominations were too large to be useful. How the regular employees managed I never learned, but they certainly suffered even more.

One of the first things I did was to commandeer the gas in the tanks of AVIS rental cars and all but a few gallons of that gas from every car was siphoned into as many jerricans as my missionary could buy in surplus stores, and I stored these behind the bushes in my yard in the town of La Celle-Saint-Cloud. Because there were no longer any controls on the French side of the borders, I assigned a rental car to my missionary. We placed as many jerricans as the car could carry and he went to Belgium to *fill up*. I had him do this twice during May and then I made gas from this stockpile available to the other managers at LCT.

Usually we didn't have a clue what-in-the-world was going on in the world or in the rest of France. After surveying around Paris I learned that ITT had a telex line operating at the Hilton Hotel which was and still is located near the Eiffel Tower. When I went there and identified myself, the hotel manager gave me free access to the telex machine. A telex was nothing more than a large typewriter linked to other typewriters a hundred or a thousand miles away. Whatever key you struck on your keyboard the other typewriter would print the same. Although that type of tele-typewriter has long ago gone out of style it worked much like e-mail today but was a thousand times noisier. Once you typed in the correct address, whatever you typed clanked out noisily on the correct telex at the other end.

If the message was urgent you'd hit the bell button and a bell would ring at the other end to let the operator there know that the arriving message was urgent. On the roll of paper at the other end, a drawing of a bell was printed on the paper. At the end of the message another bell warned that the message was terminated, and the operator would rip the sheet from the machine and a "gopher" would carry it to the addressee. In those days, almost every news room and business in the world used telex despite its bells, clanking and noise.

To make sure that ITT headquarters in Brussels knew that this message was different I hit the bell key and kept ringing it until the carriage returned for the next sentence. By the time my message was finished, Brussels was on the return line asking so many questions about what was going on in the ITT companies around Paris that it filled a sheet almost three feet long! Obviously, different managers in Brussels had simply added their questions to a memory tape, ready to transmit it to Paris at the first opportunity. I advised them that it would take a few days for me to get back and we set a precise time and day when they could expect me again.

On some days, the school buses transporting my children were stopped in the middle of confrontations between riot police lines and rampaging students. Wide-eyed, the horrified children watched the Molotov-cocktail-attacks by one side and the tear gas counter-attacks by the other. Soon even the school buses had no gas. From every crane at construction sites hung red flags, and sometimes black anarchist flags.

At the Renault factory a picket line was set across the road to stop vehicles entering Paris, and when they stopped me I saw an life-sized straw effigy of De Gaulle hanging by the neck. During the third week of these events I had a kidney stone attack and was transported by a neighbor, in exchange for two jerricans (ten gallons) of gas, to the American Hospital of Paris in the suburb of Neuilly.

At each of the hospital's two entrances were armed French soldiers behind protective walls of sandbags. These were the only French soldiers I ever saw deployed during the entire period of unrest in Paris. From my hospital window I could see a construction crane flying its red banner. After three days I was released into the chaos which ruled supreme over the French capital.

At boarding schools the school year was closing and my oldest son was about to come home from Fribourg, Switzerland, but there was no way for the 15-year-old to travel to Paris. President De Gaulle had returned from Romania on the 18th and somehow the government reactivated television and everyone could see the disoriented President try to explain away what was occurring. Only Prime Minister Georges Pompidou made any sense as it appeared to me. Anyway, TV soon went blank again, confrontations continued to be violent and all the shortages became more acute.

On Monday, 27 May, I succeeded in telexing ITT Europe headquarters and told them to be prepared to receive my son André from Fribourg and to send the company plane to an airfield at Villacoublay where they could pick up my family for a flight to Brussels. This was the same airport near the place where President de Gaulle had barely escaped assassination in 1962. In the event they didn't hear from me again, they were to send the plane on Sunday, June 2nd.

The next day I was in LCT. Paris was eerily quiet under a bright sun, and late May flowers bloomed everywhere. Because I avoided the elevator I used the stairs and found no one on several floors. Finally I walked to Dasse-Hartout's office and found him standing with his back to me as he looked out over Avenue Breteuil. He stood quietly with his hands clasped behind his back. Normally he had a serious bent if not a stern one, and because he didn't react to my entrance I considered leaving. But I asked, "Is everything OK?"

Without answering me he turned and I was shocked to see the forlorn expression in his eyes. I asked, "What's wrong?"

He brushed my question aside and said, "The last time I saw the city so bright and so quiet, just like it is today, was when the Germans marched in to occupy Paris in 1940."

Early that week someone had discovered that the guards at the Eiffel tower were watching television and the government investigated to learn why and how they received television while no one else could. They soon learned that the television transmitter at the top of the tower had been cut from power but that Belgian programs could be picked up within the structure. The government collected some engineers including a few from LCT to repair and boost the transmitter and it went on the air the next day to reach all of Paris and its suburbs.

This helped to call together people who were tired of the chaos and anarchy in the streets, and on Thursday, 30 May, over a million French answered the call and marched down l'avenue des Champs-Elysées to protest the strikes and to support the government. That rally broke the back of the student and labor-led revolt, and on Saturday I used the Hilton telex to cancel the need for the emergency evacuation by company plane that ITT had scheduled for the next day.

Like waking up from a nightmare and regaining composure, the French rapidly put things into order as if nothing unusual had happened. To a foreigner the events had been a bewildering experience, and whatever changes the riots and disorder influenced came about slowly, although in what I thought was a jealous fit, De Gaulle soon dismissed Pompidou as Prime Minister.

I started planning a family vacation, something calm to put Paris behind us. For a long time I had wanted to visit Israel but its borders had been closed to most visitors ever since the Israeli-Arab *Six Day War* the year before. But I was able to secure reservations at Nahr el Kalb in Lebanon and let my family plan for this while I caught up with my postponed trip to Niger south of the Sahara.

In this remote and desolate area of Africa the French Cooperative Aid program had instituted a bold network of instructional television in one language in a land-locked country where desert nomads spoke any one of a dozen languages of which not one was written. From a scientific viewpoint, this was a laboratory situation where ITV started from scratch because reading, writing and arithmetic were non-existent.

Prior to my leaving Paris, I met with Philippe Rossillon who headed an office to propagate the French language. He explained the unique importance of this language experiment in the former French colony, and the backing of the De Gaulle government for its success.

Hamani Diori, the president of Niger, was a former schoolteacher whom I met while I was there, was very proud that in Niamey an outdoor studio had been built with four or five huts to produce ITV segments. This was a clever adaptation of a teaching technique to keep the video background recognizable and friendly to young viewers, and everything had been done to have the studio-village resemble any that one might discover in the desert.

The French educators in charge of the programming kept strict accounting of every French word used and would never permit a word's second meaning to be introduced until the first meaning had been used a half-dozen times on television. Only common first names were used, the kind that any nomad child could relate to and had heard before. By the clever use of animals in motion and of a *dancing ball*, letters were formed on the screen in a simple way that children could imitate with a stick in the sand floor of the huts that were used as classrooms.

In a colossal error the president had insisted that the first classroom be constructed with cinder blocks, but when I visited that structure it was easy to understand why it remained unused because it was like an oven inside. In the grass huts I visited, the breeze entered through the walls and kept the rooms comfortable by comparison.

President Diori had expressed to me his desire to be integrated into a satellite ITV network so he could reach every remote water point in his country—places where his nomadic citizens would congregate during their wandering. In particular he wanted them to have one vehicle language, in this case French, so that they could converse with one another and with people from neighboring French-speaking countries like Mali and Chad.

But Niger had almost no communications and very little electricity. Outside Niamey there was no mail service because the villages had no names, and often they remained empty when a tribe and its goats moved on to another nameless place. Often we arrived in a village only to find that everyone was gone, leaving it neat for the next return visit. In order to visit the *school* we'd travel over the hardpan Sahel until we found a classroom and its monitor.

Normally the teachers were boys recruited to monitor the playing of the ITV tapes and to correctly turn on the television set which was powered by automobile batteries. Another reason boys were recruited was because they were stronger and could carry the equipment and also pedal the stationary bicycle whose generator recharged the storage batteries that ran the black-and-white TV set.

But the modern educators soon collided with tribal culture and tradition. Tribal chiefs objected to tribal boys spending a great deal of time in the schoolrooms when there was so much to learn about hunting and making weapons. Soon only girls learned how to count, write and read. Because older girls also attended classes, the horrified French educators were regularly confronted by pregnant girls made so by the young monitors with an insufficient number of bicycles to burn off excess energy. Although everyone in the villages seemed to write off the birthrate factor, the hormonal oversight had not been factored by the conscientious educators into the advanced pedagogical equation for desert instruction.

We'd usually head into the Sahel in the early morning when the temperature was a cool 90°F and return to our meeting place outside the city for a late lunch when the temperature reached 120°F in the shade. The *colons*, as the French foreign aid workers called themselves, didn't seem to mind having me ask so many questions. Their enthusiasm reminded me of Peace Corps workers I ran into, and at the end of each afternoon's session one or another of the colonials offered me a horse to ride.

Invariably the horses were desert-bred Arabian horses and always a stallion because no one would ever demean himself in the Sahara by publicly riding a mare. I always had a *colonial* ready to accompany me, and on one occasion I learned something concrete about desert manners and desert language.

We had headed inland after failing to ford the Niger River at nightfall, and near an oasis some wild camels attacked our horses and scattered us. By the time I had my stallion under control I was hopelessly lost, and the star-filled night did nothing to orient me because I had no idea in which direction I could find Niamey. I cantered along until a fire appeared in the distance so I headed for it. As I neared it I saw that it was a small communal fire around which several tribal families were cooking their main meal. At the limit of the fire's light I saw youngsters chasing young goats, and I knew that soon they would see a horse and rider approaching.

The first to see my white shirt in the darkness were the sharp eyes of the children, and in a language I couldn't understand, excited shouts announced the arrival of a solitary horse and rider. Naked children and older boys in loose shirts that reached their ankles raced toward us. The horse danced nervously as their shouts grew louder. Only when they noticed the color of my skin did the younger girls shout, *"Je parle Français, monsieur."*

In return I said, "I speak French, too. Can someone point out the direction of Niamey?"

For the benefit of the elders, they translated what I said. Immediately, the older men stood and pointed in the same direction. One who appeared to be the oldest came to my horse and patted its neck, and he pointed up to a star indicating which one I should use to guide me. I understood his meaning without knowing what he said, but a desert chorus of young girls eagerly translated my "thank-you's."

All the nomads applauded when I turned my horse in the right direction and they returned my wave. I gave my horse his head and the stallion loped easily for miles until I saw a weak light swaying side to side. About a half mile farther, the light became a lantern held by a stablehand who had been sent to be my beacon to the club where the colonials had already opened a bottle of not-very-chilled-champagne in celebration of I'm-not-quite-sure-what.

During the clinking of glasses one colonial told me that Air Africa had not called the capital. Consequently, he advised, he extended my hotel room another night. In 1968-Africa, the airlines sent word ahead of time to advise when the scheduled jet plane bound for Paris would stop. No-call meant no-flight. Printed schedules didn't amount to much and no one commiserated falsely about a change in plans. This meant one more sleepless night listening to quarrelsome hippos, lusting in the Niger River, who hung out below my hotel window.

Two days later I was alerted that an *Air Afrique* 707 was coming and I was driven to the airport where the jetliner landed in a whirlwind of dust that didn't clear until three of the four engines was turned off about a quarter-mile from the simple dust-covered and spider-infested terminal. It was easy to remember the huge multi-colored spider that hung by a thread over my passport while the border policeman debated whether to stamp my passport around the spider or to rid Niger of one pest by spreading the arachnid's innards across two pages of my passport. While he cogitated, the spider shot up the thread and defused the problem.

On the trip to Paris I made notes of what I learned but didn't realize then that if the new data didn't apply to Québec they'd be applicable for other projects in the Canadian Yukon, The Northwest Territories, and Alaska in the USA. Once back in Paris we learned that we would be receiving the formal contract for the Franco-Québec study which I dubbed "Project Memini." Borrowed from the name of my Assumption High School yearbook, the Latin word meant "I remember," and was a fitting name for Québec whose official motto was "*je me souviens*" which also means "I Remember." The Quebeckers liked it, adopted it as the study's name and welcomed Phélizon as the study's manager.

During the course of study I devised a bilingual survey instrument to statistically quantify the volume of communicable data needed for medical, scholastic, technological and cultural interchanges in addition to television—black-and-white as well as the new color transmission techniques.

On our distribution list was every potential user in every French-speaking country and some in non-French-speaking countries. A remarkable expression of interest came from the new National Center for Biomedical Communications (NCBC) of the National Library of Medicine at the National Institutes of Health in Bethesda, Maryland, and its director, Dr. Ruth Davis, flew to Paris to meet with me.

Her operation was amassing archival records related to diagnostic data whereby doctors anywhere could transmit key data about a patient's condition to the NCBC where a computer or a medical analyst could compare the information to other sets of similar diagnostic data, identify the illness or provide guidance on how to isolate its exact identification, and instruct the doctor on how the illness had been successfully treated elsewhere.

In particular, it was important for Dr. Davis to know how data resulting from the *Memini* project might be collected, stored and, most of all, retrieved by a potential medical user in Racine, Québec, as well as by another doctor in Fargo, Oklahoma, or how emergency data could be transmitted in useful form from an emergency room or ambulance to a diagnostic center. Without our having realized it, breakthroughs in medical communications were being pioneered by Québec's Project *Memini*.

Ironically some of the people in public relations in New York tried to get me to drop this project at LCT because they judged the French-subsidized project was *unamerican*. After an exchange of red-hot telexes between me and New York, copies of which went to Brussels, ITTE wrote off New York's objections as paranoiac. I remember thereafter that George Arthur jokingly referred to my telexes as being printed on asbestos because they smoked but didn't burn. Years later, ITT companies in the United States exploited *Memini*'s findings to establish an important industrial lead in medical communications.

Chapter 23

International spats and uncommon valor

When I visited Beirut, Lebanon in 1968 it rightfully deserved its title of "Paris of the Middle East" because of its elegant tree-lined boulevards. Grand hotels like the Phoenicia, whose unique glass-walled swimming pool formed the wall over the bar, had a worldwide reputation. The city's waterfront was a playground renown throughout the Mediterranean, and along with Syria the country had a long background with France. At that time French was widely understood in hotels and large stores.

Since then, Beirut has been bombed, shelled, invaded, burned and subjected to widespread damage inflicted during its vicious civil war. No open signs predicted the events seven years later that destroyed so much of Beirut, and many historic sites in Lebanon have since been lost forever.

It was interesting then to see the various religions interact so naturally and easily almost everywhere, but the exception was south of Tyre and Sidon, cities that soaked in the historic footsteps of the Phoenicians, Romans, Jesus Christ, Crusaders, Saracens, Jews, Turks and Arabs. Near the Lebanese border with Israel were some of the most depressing shacktowns that existed anywhere in the world.

Corrugated tin-covered shacks housed tens of thousands of Palestinian outcasts living in abject poverty, dust and misery. Whether they were Muslim or Christian meant no difference, they were cast-off refugees who had never left their own territory, people with no country, a constituency without representation, nothing but nonentities that no other countries in the Near East or the world wanted.

Lebanese soldiers or police stopped our car and made us leave the area. The idea then was that these miserable Palestinian enclaves didn't exist so long that no outside witnesses would care to remember.

Nonetheless, whether Christian or Muslim, the Lebanese proved to be hospitable and generous hosts without giving one sign or reason that they hated each other, although no people elsewhere could conceivably blow car horns more angrily or shake fists so expressively, without regard to religious preferences.

When I returned to LCT most of the personnel was on vacation which is a habitual occurrence during August in France. Georges Phélizon had left word that some decisions were needed from Québec and when I reached Jacques Gauthier in Montreal he was about to leave for a United Nation's Conference on Peaceful Uses of Outer Space in Vienna. We agreed to meet at the Intercontinental Hotel there, and I called Guy Julien in Québec who was now on LCT's payroll and asked him to join us in Vienna.

It was during one of our meetings when we heard that the Soviet Union and most of its Warsaw Pact allies had invaded Czechoslovakia. Since Bratislava, one of the principal Slovakian cities, was less than forty miles from Vienna, the news caused an uproar in Austria. The other Warsaw Pact countries in the invasion were Poland, Bulgaria, East Germany and Hungary where I had been only five months earlier. Gauthier, Julien and I decided to drive to Bratislava to see if we could help with refugees. Along the way we noticed the absence of oncoming traffic, and the only distinctive landmarks were monuments of Roman construction and well-preserved epitaphs chiseled in Latin on the tombs of Roman soldiers and colonials.

Just before we reached the abutment of the bridge across the Danube River several heavily-armed Austrian border police jumped in front of our rental car to flag us. Even from our vantage point we could see Soviet-manufactured tanks stationed before the bridge ramp on the Danube's Bratislava side, and we knew that no refugees would be leaving Czechoslovakia. The internal riots, repression and censorship that followed are now history. I had firsthand reason to recall how helpless a person can be when facing armed authority that exercises its will, with or without justification.

Two schoolmates, Frank Kiely and Robert Simmons, and I were on the Orient Express on our way to Ljubljana in Yugoslavia when

Communist troops stopped the train in a forest less than forty miles from the Austrian border in 1951, and at gunpoint forced us to leave it. Whether this was due to our American passports, without any explanation nor answer to any of our questions, they led us through the woods until we reached a small clearing where a rickety passenger car sat idle on railroad tracks of a spur line. Pointing with his rifle, the squad leader indicated the place for us to stand between a pile of dirt and the tracks. On the far side of the dirt pile was a deep hole recently dug. Whatever was the intended use of the long, narrow hole in the ground has remained a mystery etched indelibly in my mind.

Soon a coal-burning engine came around a bend in the tracks and backed to the passenger car to which the soldiers coupled it. The steam engine appeared to be vintage 1930s and spilled the blackest smoke I'd ever seen, and the soldiers pushed us aboard where they locked us into a compartment without any indication of where we were being taken. The soldiers wore snappy white uniforms and their white hats with brown leather rims had a bright red star in the front. When we were finally freed from the compartment, different soldiers led us to a guardhouse at the fence delineating the US-UK Military Zone of Trieste—now part of Italy.

However, the Italian-speaking guards refused to let us remain without proper papers and stamped our passports *Exit* a few minutes after having stamped *Entered*. But the Yugoslav guards forced us back each time. My old passport is still stamped multiple times on 11 July 1951 (p. 303), showing how capricious destiny and survival could be. Eventually we were rescued by two allied soldiers on a routine jeep patrol, one a British Tommy, the other an American GI.

Communist rule remained arbitrary and intensified boldly with time. In 1968, as we drove back to Vienna from the border area with Czechoslovakia, we were sobered by what we had seen. To change the depressing topic of conversation we talked about how satellites would revolutionize the many limitations terrestrial communications imposed on society.

Later, Guy Julien told me about a project being sponsored by the Canadian government in Ottawa to extend instructional television into the isolated communities in Canada's far north. Before we boarded our different flights, Guy promised to learn more about the new federal project as soon as he returned to Montreal.

By the time I returned to Paris, Paulette had arranged my incoming letters, telexes, letters to sign and medical insurance claims that she kept straight for my family. Paulette knew every ache, pain and cavity that my six children ever had. Separately stacked were news clippings, magazines and corporate releases. Among the latter were announcements about the acquisition of Sheraton Hotels and the Rayonier company which had an important presence in Québec. Among my messages was one from someone at headquarters whom I didn't know. He turned out to be a person assigned to the Sheraton acquisition, and he asked if I could check out a few applicants in Europe being considered by Sheraton as general managers for two hotels yet to open in the Mediterranean area. Soon his counterpart in Boston was also calling me for similar help. Other than ABC and Gilfillan, only Sheraton requested my assistance from time to time while all the other new acquisitions in the US like Hartford Insurance, Aetna Finance and General Controls never had reason to.

When Guy Julien got back to me from Montreal, he informed me that the federal government of Canada did have plans on the drawing board to improve communications in the far north, and that Gilles Bergeron was the man in charge in Ottawa. I made plans to meet with him after my next trip to Québec for a regular coordination meeting on the *Memini* study. We were never sure whether our provincial customer would want the meeting in Montreal or Québec city where all the ministers had offices.

When I finally met Bergeron I discovered a person who would normally pass for a user of telecommunications, as opposed to someone who was more interested in the potential of a satellite technique. Maybe it was because he had been recently in the provincial ministry of education in Québec that he looked at the far north as a pedagogical and cultural challenge, not only in English or French, but also in various Indian and Inuit dialects. The domain of his challenge was huge, almost half the size of the entire land area of the United States, but with less than 100,000 people spread thinly across the vast expanse. The ongoing Niger ITV project interested him greatly because many of its problems and aims fit the remote communities he'd be trying to reach in the Arctic *desert*.

During this same visit to Ottawa I saw my former ITTE colleague Joe Halina who had left Europe and was in the office of the Director General of Telecommunications for the federal Canadian government. While there I also met with Marc Lalonde, Chief of the Cabinet of Canadian Prime Minister Pierre Elliott Trudeau, and with Jean Chrétien, Canadian Minister of Indian Affairs and Northern Development.

Eventually Lalonde became Minister of Energy and later Chrétien became Prime Minister of Canada.

In the late Parisian winter I went to the casino at Enghien-les-Bains just outside Paris and had another remarkable run at the Baccarat table. But this time there was another man at the table had was also having a great run, and between the two of us not many others stayed at the table very long. He was the Ambassador of North Vietnam, and the fact that he was playing against an American attracted onlookers five or six deep around the table. We exchanged bank rôles several times during the evening, but neither of us could dominate the other but we skinned anyone who dared join in. I knew he was very much involved in the Paris peace talks to end the Vietnam War, but that's as far as it went. When he finally left the table, he didn't shake hands with anyone. I left soon thereafter and pocketed my poke for a rainy day.

Shortly after that event I received a unexpected call from President Diori of Niger who was in Paris. He asked me to meet with him for a confidential meeting at his hotel near the Arch of Triumph on the following Sunday morning. When we met he explained a political predicament he was in as chairman of an international francophone conference to be held in West Africa. All costs for this conference were subsidized by France and Canada without whose financial support the conference couldn't take place.

The pivotal point on which his dilemma rested was Québec's invitation. France insisted that Québec be invited first—before Canada, and if not, no financial subsidy would be forthcoming from Paris. De Gaulle was still smarting from Trudeau's jabs following the French President's "Vive le Québec libre" speech. On the other side of the ledger, Ottawa insisted that Canada be invited before Québec or else no Canadian subsidy would be available. Trudeau was still furious for what he perceived as French meddling in internal Canadian affairs during De Gaulle's triumphal reception by Quebeckers when the French president visited their province in 1967.

"Quite a puzzle, Monsieur le Président," I admitted.

"This is my personal Gordian knot, but I have no sword to slice through its complexity like Alexander did," he acknowledged.

"Why come to me? I've no influence with all these personalities."

"My situation is desperate, and you're the only neutral I know who isn't disliked by any of the four sides."

"Four?" I asked.

"Yes. Ottawa and Québec over there, and Paris and Niamey over here. My intermediary can't be a citizen of any of those places otherwise at least one of the others will be offended."

"Can you control the postmarks?" I asked.

"Of course."

After exchanging a few ideas, I left the president and promised to get back to him. I admitted to myself that diplomatic pettiness threatened to wreck an international conference that had a great deal of meaning to governments representing 127 million people. I was also very concerned about my rôle in a purely political embroglio in which my company had no legitimate business interest at stake. Of the four players Ottawa and Québec were the key ones. No one had to ask De Gaulle or his new prime minister Couve de Murville whether France would go along with any deal that Québec's premier was comfortable with. De Gaulle was very predictable. Although Prime Minister Daniel Johnson of Québec had been recuperating from a heart attack, I knew that the people around him were also predictably reasonable and that the premier himself felt that the reactions to De Gaulle's speech from the balcony had been blown out of proportion.

In Ottawa, Marc Lalonde, the Chief of Cabinet, had impressed me as a pragmatic politician but one with no time for pussyfooting or bickering. The only asset I had in this affair was the obvious absence of an axe to grind, consequently I resolved to keep my rôle inconspicuous and quiet while making direct contact with Claude Morin in Québec City and Marc Lalonde in Ottawa. Both men recognized President Diori's dilemma and resolved to discuss it privately to find an out for everyone concerned.

Later, when I next met with Lalonde, he said, "We met in a hotel." With a smile he joked, "We agreed not to leave the room until we had a deal." The only detail Morin gave me was, "Well, we'd meet in the Château Laurier often to resolve such disputes in those days. We actually reduced our Niger agreement to writing."

While I studied the communications project for the far north I discovered that in neighboring Alaska, Mike Gravel, my former classmate from Assumption in Worcester, Massachusetts, was running for United States Senator in 1968. Because Alaska had similar concerns and issues as those I found in the Yukon, I sent him some position papers on communications and transportation in Alaska's interior to help him in his campaign.

Little did I realize how important an issue was that of communications. In Alaska's largest city, Christmas television shows didn't arrive there for viewing until the Easter barge arrived in Anchorage from Seattle, Washington. In 99% of the state's interior no Alaskan with an emergency could get near a phone without rowing on a river and portaging for two or three days to reach a telephone or a bush plane.

After Gravel was elected US Senator, he came to Paris before being sworn into office in Washington, and while he was in France I had the opportunity to describe how easily Alaska's statewide communications problems could be solved through satellite technology that had no climatic barriers. During the spring of 1969 we stayed in touch while ITT sent me to some of the American subsidiaries to determine which one I should be transferred to from Paris. Before reaching that point, Senator Gravel, who was the strongest anti-Vietnam War lawmaker in Washington, asked me to join his staff in his office in the United States Senate.

While I was preparing to leave LCT, Dasse-Hartout asked that I not forget the study available in Ottawa, so I spoke with Gilles Bergeron who intended to award the study to Georges Phélizon's Space Study Group at LCT. Because of my timetable, he promised to come to Paris for the contract signing. But my most unexpected surprise came from Paulette who tearfully hoped to follow me to the United States, and she asked if I could help find her a job there. I knew all her qualities in French and in English but had never seen her resumé, so I asked her for a copy in English if she had one because that's what I'd show people in the US.

The next day it was on my desk, and one detail stumped me completely: "CG awarded posthumously."

"Paulette, what's this CG?"

"That's the *Croix de Guerre avec palme* awarded to my father. He was executed by the Nazis in 1944."

"What did they accuse him of?"

"They caught him in the middle of the night sabotaging German fighter planes, just before the allied armies broke out of Normandy."

I was very impressed because I had never had an association with anyone close to a genuine hero, one whose award was equal in import to the Congressional Medal of Honor in the United States or the Victoria Cross in Britain. Although she later gave me the details of his death, it is with the benefit of hindsight that I can put his deed in the context of the time it occurred on 10 August 1944—dates that meant more to me after I represented President Bill Clinton at the reception given by the city of Saint-Malo to the US veterans of the 83rd Infantry Division who liberated that city.

The event coincided with the 50th Anniversary of the Normandy Invasion on 6 June 1944, and President Clinton had more commemorations to attend that he had time for. The Saint-Malo reception for surviving members of the 83rd was scheduled on 4 June 1994 in order that the veterans could join the President for the official ceremonies at the US military cemetery near Omaha Beach in Normandy two days later.

Historians, movie producers and the general public have forgotten that the allied troops had been bottlenecked in Normandy and Brittany for over two months after the Normandy landings, and elite German armored divisions and veteran troops had pounded the younger allied soldiers trying to pierce the German lines. The only bright light during those dark days was expressed in an overstatement by General Hap Arnold of the American Army Air Forces in his report six months later to the US Secretary of War Henry L. Stimson: "The Luftwaffe was conspicuous by its absence." Even the classic movie "The Longest Day" gave the impression that Hitler sent aloft only two Messerschmitt 109 fighter planes to oppose the landings, but the landings lasted far more than one day, and the US cemeteries in Normandy and Brittany contain graves of many American airmen.

The Germans actually had plenty of planes but would pick and choose their missions because of the overwhelming numbers of allied planes. In fact, the German Luftwaffe had 150 bombers at Bourget airfield just north of Paris that escaped allied aerial reconnaissance for over two months.

When the 83rd was ordered on 3 August 1944 to remove the Nazi forces dug in at the medieval fortress inside Saint-Malo, its troop columns marching in that direction "were strafed by German fighter planes," according to the Division's official battlefield report in the National Archives. Most of the American troops trying to fight their way out of the pocket they were in remained about 145 miles from German fighter squadrons at small airfields west of Paris like the one at Toussus-le-Noble in the region southwest of Versailles.

This airfield was part of the hidden line of defense the Germans had established in an almost straight line south of Paris, a zone containing Tiger tanks, armored vehicles, fighter planes and crack troops in woods between towns like Trappes, Guyancourt, Toussus-le-Noble, Saclay and Orly. German artillery was hidden under hay stacks, tanks inside barns and warehouses and fighter planes in hangars resembling cattle barns.

On Monday, 7 August, three powerful Panzer divisions with heavy armor and the best German tanks suddenly attacked the Americans. According to US General George C. Marshall: "The enemy's crushing heavy attacks were launched in a desperate hope of driving a wedge to the sea through Avranches to cut off General Patton's forces." The three German divisions struck the allied flank at Tessy-sur-Vire a few miles south of St.-Lô.

In the drawing rooms of Nazi collaborators in Paris and in the Principality of Monaco, most still believed that the Germans would drive the allies and the upstart Americans back into the English Channel. Even a casual review of the division rosters of their dead buried in US military cemeteries in France reveal that 10 August 1944 was a particularly devastating day for American mortality.

In Saint-Malo, the 83rd Infantry Division was engaged in "bitter street fighting" as the Americans fought house-to-house and sometimes hand-to-hand in combat that was reminiscent of the bloody episodes at Stalingrad over a year earlier, or in the fields and woods at Petersburg, Virginia, exactly eighty years earlier during the Civil War. But while Americans were killed from one end of Brittany to another in Normandy, Nazi collaborators and their German occupiers had their own private agendas.

Recently the National Archives in Washington have revealed that tens of millions of francs poured through Monaco via a Nazi bank set up by a Swiss Nazi named Eugène Johannes Charles. According to secret French reports translated by the American wartime Secret Services, "At the beginning of 1943, Charles was asked by the Reichsbank to create...a secret affiliate of the Reichsbank. Charles selected Monaco because he had obtained the needed consent of Prince Louis II through the intermediary of the Vichy French Minister of State Emile Roblot."

Reichbank strongman Emil Puhl had a representative in Paris named Dr. Karl Schaeffer, who kept an eye on Germany's only operating bank in France which was tied financially to Hitler's air force chief, Field Marshal Hermann Göring. Interestingly, Göring referred to the bank as his "Aerobank." But the Charles Bank in Monaco would be different because all the other banks there were affiliates and, for a cut in the deal, Louis II permitted the creation of a German bank near the Monte Carlo casino.

To cement the side deals, Roblot met with Schaeffer and Charles on 3 August, the day Eisenhower ordered the 83rd to take Saint-Malo, which Hitler ordered for the first time that the German troops "defend to your last cartridge." The encounters in Monaco were obviously chummy because after the next meeting on 10 August, the dark day around St.-Lô and in old Saint-Malo, Charles wrote to Roblot, a letter later captured, in which he wrote, "How happy I am to learn that Louis II wants to buy participation in the bank."

Top photo. On 10 August 1944, this elderly French woman in a Saint-Malo suburb talked with young American GIs whose units of the 83rd Infantry Division had just pushed the Germans out of the neighborhood where she lived.

Bottom photo. Paris liberated, 26 August 1944. A French collaborator in central Paris with blood streaming down his face after being beaten by local Parisians being led off to safety by French police. Following the liberation, France went through a "cleansing purge," and no one knows how many thousands were accused and executed without trial. After the hair of women so accused was shaved off, the women were marked naked through the local streets and often shot. Other collaborators, usually less rich than Florence Gould, found protection.

Both photos were originally US Army Signal Corps photos. From the World War II Record Groups at the National Archives and Records Administration, College Park, Maryland.

9080-GV2

It was an easy deal for the Prince of Monaco to make because Göring's bank in Paris had already transferred 75 million francs to be laundered by the Charles Bank in Monaco. In Paris, a US-born Nazi collaborator, Florence Gould of San Francisco, was closely watched by the French underground. Their reports differed from her official biography she commissioned. Her biographer described her as "one of the world's richest women who always held a glass of champagne."

In her elegant Parisian apartment at 129 avenue Malakoff, she hosted a luncheon every Thursday for thirty guests, for over four years—guests who were later identified as Gestapo and other Nazi collaborators. One US investigator during the war reported to Washington that Florence "confessed her relations with the Germans (including the Gestapo) and notorious French collaborators during the occupation...including her lover Ludwig Vogel, an engineer with the Focke-Wulf Aircraft Company who took Florence Gould to Germany under a false name, where in Friedrichshafen she visited an aircraft factory..."

Florence Gould even gave Eugène Charles 7,700,000 francs in three cash payments between May and August 1944 (p. 327) in order to be "a silent partner" in the Nazi's Charles Bank, and when she returned to Paris she also was convinced that the German army would push the allies back into the sea. But not everyone believed that. As if all the French railroad workers realized the desperate situation around St.-Lô, they went on strike on the 10th all over France in solidarity, on what they called "a patriotic strike," to the dismay and anger of the German army that was trying to move ammunitions and supplies to the front.

From London, French General Koenig sent word to his underground resistance fighters in France to sabotage German military assets. Before leaving for work on the 10th, Fratacci heard the coded message on BBC to go into action again. "I remember," said Paulette, "that he would move thumb tacks on a map after listening to the BBC." As usual on that afternoon, Antoine Fratacci pedaled his bicycle about 20 miles from his home in Vanves to his security job at Toussus-le-Noble. He brought with him what he needed to sabotage a German fighter plane as he had done repeatedly for his underground unit called "Coutal."

Antoine Fratacci faced extreme danger as he sneaked into one of the hangars in which the Germans had secreted squadrons of Focke-Wulf 190 fighter planes since 1942. Firefighter Fratacci pulled himself up on the wings of a plane as he had done forty times in the past, and crept to the fuel tank cap to unscrew it just like a person does to fill up a car at a filling station. While he prepared to pour a half-quart of carbon tetrachloride into the tank that would cause the plane to stall in flight, German guards caught him red-handed with the fire extinguishing solvent still on his person.

There was no trial. There was no sentence. Antoine Fratacci was shot point-blank by a German warrant officer as a saboteur. Because there were no trial records, his family never received any reparations from Nazi Germany. It took five years before there was any financial assistance from France for his widow and three young children. Although there are plaques commemorating his sacrifice in France and on the island of Corsica, there is no note or memorial anywhere explaining why so few German fighter planes attacked allied forces in Brittany and Normandy in early August 1944. According to official records as recent as 1997, Antoine Fratacci had also been an underground agent since 1941 for the British and Free French forces in London, and "not one of the forty Focke-Wulf 190s he sabotaged at Toussus-le-Noble ever returned from its next flight."

During the next few years many military awards were given him posthumously including written recognition on 6 May 1946 from British Field Marshal Bernard L. Montgomery citing Fratacci "who laid down his life that Europe might be free (p. 347)."

After Paulette's tears and my last meetings with colleagues in LCT. My family and I left on the liner *France* from Le Havre for our trip home.

Afterword

A few hours following Antoine Fratacci's summary execution, Canadian troops broke through the German lines near the razed city of Caen in Normandy, and they fought fiercely to gain access to the road leading to the small town of Falaise about nineteen miles to the southeast. A few days later, General George C. Patton's troops also broke through German lines not far from St.-Lô, and the Americans rushed toward Falaise to join up with the Canadians who captured the town on the 13th. Once Patton closed the pincers on the 19th, the North American troops slammed shut the Falaise Pocket on six German Divisions. The German defeat in the Falaise action permitted the allies to break out from Normandy after being blocked for two and a half months by German defenses, thereby releasing allied troops for the race to Paris, the Rhine River and Germany beyond.

After Paris was liberated by French and American troops, the German High Command decided to return the 150 bombers at Le Bourget to Germany, but also authorized a short side-flight over Paris first. Consequently, General Desslach's Air Wing Number Three spitefully ruined the Saturday night celebration of Paris' liberation on August 26th by bombing the city's 12th arrondissement from the Gare de Lyon to the Gate of Picpus near the Château of Vincennes. This, the biggest air raid on Paris during World War II, killed 213 and injured 914 others.

Had I known of the heroism of Paulette's father, I would have understood the interest and affinity of the old Jew in London for the daughter of a man who opposed Hitler at the risk of his life, even if Antoine Fratacci had probably never known about the Holocaust.

Between 1960 and 1990, the US Navy's Fleet Ballistic Missile improved from the two-stage 30-foot *Polaris* missile to the three-stage 44-foot *Trident II*, and the cost of a single missile increased from one million dollars to almost $31,000,000. The range of the FBM has been extended from 1,200 nautical miles to over 4,000, making the Fleet Ballistic Missile the only weapons system in the world capable of hitting any target on this planet from a submerged nuclear submarine lurking beneath the waves.

Before 20 July 1969, Senator Mike Gravel (D., Alaska) was joined by Senator Ted Stevens (R., Alaska) to twist any arm capable of helping to bring live-television coverage of man's landing on the moon to Alaskans at the same time as everyone else in the world would watch it. I was their point man to get it done, and I enlisted the help of Herb Bennington, an engineering wizard with the Defense Department Research and Evaluation office at the Pentagon. With Senator Stevens available to clear the decks of any obstructions among President Nixon's Republican appointees, Bennington and I collaborated through the Michigan Air National Guard to transport classified equipment to Anchorage for elaborate research tests substituting high-speed data with wide band telecasts at the end of a runway at Anchorage's International Airport.

Meanwhile, Senator Gravel also wanted Kodiak Island to receive the live telecast, and this presented me with peculiar technical problems. In my attempts to solve them, I shuttled between Anchorage and Kodiak seeking a solution. Part of the problem related to RCA's thirty-foot antenna and earth station sitting idle on the Pacific island of Guam but with no budget to move it. However, I knew that my former Navy colleagues in the Special Projects Office had a *Polaris* re-supply ship sailing regularly between Guam and Bremerton in Puget Sound near Seattle, Washington.

Long before the NASA Apollo flight to the moon, I made a deal with the Navy to permit RCA to load the Guam earth station on the deck of the re-supply ship during its next return run. My deal with RCA was to have the company pay for the unloading from the Navy ship when it arrived in Bremerton. However, there was a strike going on and the longshoremen refused to unload the crates and, of course, Navy personnel couldn't. Luckily, the longshoremen's union owed Senator Gravel a favor. Characteristically, the strikers refused to accept payment for their labor in unloading the earth station. Not only did they unload it for free from the Navy ship but they also loaded it for free on the Seattle barge bound for Alaska.

But I was still far from home plate on this deal. RCA paid for the barge to offload the antenna and earth station at Kodiak. But other communications union workers, in sympathy for the longshoremen's strike, threatened a boycott if the equipment was offloaded and assembled despite a union picketline, but they claimed not to be against their local neighbors viewing the major worldwide event. While I tried to figure a way around this without losing union support for Senator Gravel, the local chief of police solved my problem.

Being a man of few words and no time for nonsense, the lawman told the potential strikers that he'd throw them in jail and the cell keys into the Gulf of Alaska if they didn't cooperate. Because of the lawman's action, as well as those of RCA, the Navy and the cooperation of the local union leaders, Kodiak's 5,000 residents watched Astronaut Neil Armstrong take his first steps on the moon at the same time as people in New York and Paris. So did all the Alaskans who went to Anchorage to watch the event live. Actually Neil Armstrong's words were heard several seconds later in Anchorage than in Kodiak. Because of technical limitations, the television transmissions using a secret US spy satellite were so tight that two half-pictures were electronically "glued" together to form a complete picture for distribution by local TV transmitters. But there was no extra room for NASA's voice channel.

Although few people knew how we actually got it done, the Canadians came through for us by permitting Alaska to use a spare telephone channel on a overland copper wire through the Yukon Territory. By carrying the voices of the astronauts on the moon overland from Dawson, it took more time for the sound to arrive in Anchorage. Since the astronauts had helmets on, no viewers could see the lips of astronauts moving many seconds before their words came out! So much for lip synchronization in the space age...

Following a telephone conversation between me and State Senator Mouton of Louisiana during 1969, I was contacted by former US Congressman James Domengeaux of Lafayette, Louisiana whom I met shortly thereafter. He was the principal behind an organization called The Council of the Development of French in Louisiana—CODOFIL.

I discussed this project with Philippe Rossillon, whom I had met before my trip to Niger the year before. He became the energetic architect of a program that sent many French instructors to Louisiana.

With the support of new French President Georges Pompidou, this *foreign service*" permitted young French volunteers to teach French to youngsters in a *foreign land* rather than serving out two years of compulsory French military service.

The foreign land in question consisted of the parishes in Louisiana identified by Jimmie Domengeaux as needing French language instructors! The last time I saw Jimmie and his law partner Bob Wright in Lafayette, the program had been going strong for twenty years.

I realize that military historians may have some unanswered questions related to the RATAC Doppler radar that President Lyndon B. Johnson wanted for use in Vietnam and that President Charles de Gaulle opposed its export from France. After both men left the political scene, LCT's affiliate in California, ITT Gilfillan, started to produce the equipment for the US Army.

It's important to realize how important the discovery of the Huff Duff direction finder was in winning the Battle of the Atlantic during World War II. The situation was so desperate that the only way to beat the German U-boat wolfpacks was to build *Liberty* transport ships faster than the German Navy could sink them. In 1942 alone, the Germans sank over 8,400,000 tons of allied shipping in the Atlantic sea lanes between the United States and England. Until the Huff Duff went into service around March 1943, the Germans had lost only 151 submarines from all types of hostile action between 1939 and 1943. Thereafter, the rate of sinking U-boats increased from only 24 per year to over 145 submarines per year by surface ship action alone!

One of the best kept secrets has been the battle experience of the successor to the RATAC, a new Doppler radar called RASIT which was purchased by the military in Argentina. During the Falkland Islands War, the Argentineans used RASIT to accurately locate warships of the Royal Navy. Once the warships were located, the Argentinean Air Force used the French-made *Exocet* air-to-ship missile to sink one.

During President Nixon's re-election campaign in 1972, my former company, ITT, became embroiled in a series of scandals involving the site of the Republican convention, internal affairs in Chile and its relations with the CIA in South America. Eventually all these events became part of Congressional probes, especially one by the Senate Select Committee on Intelligence chaired by Senator Frank Church. Because of my experience with the State-Defense Military Information Control Committee and ITT overseas, the senate committee was anxious to hear from me.

Before I testified behind closed doors, I learned that my old friend who supervised the tunnel under the Berlin Wall was scheduled to testify before me. W.H. and I spoke by telephone and he was as anxious to see me again as I was to see him. It had been about nine years since the last time we had coffee at Place Saint Jean in Brussels. I agreed to go to the Senate office before he was scheduled to testify so that we could catch up on old times. When he failed to show, the committee asked me to fill in, and I testified for almost five hours straight.

All the senators on the committee were reported present but I only remember Senator Muskie of Maine whom I knew pretty well, and the questions by Senators Church, Percy and Symington whom I had never met before. Standing behind them were over twenty staff members, and the staff director sat to my right and Senator Percy to my left. I should mention that Charles Percy was an old colleague and friend of ITT's chairman Harold S. Geneen from their early days when both were at the Bell & Howell Company.

When we went past noontime, Senator Church sent out for sandwiches and coffee so that we continued through the lunch hour and the hearing never skipped a beat.

As I departed at the hearing's conclusion, several staff members and senators thanked me. One staff investigator told me, "Until you testified today, I never really understood how things were done."

In the waiting room I turned to the Staff Director who was escorting me out, and asked him where W.H. was.

"He's not coming," he announced.

"Well, that's a surprise," I admitted. "He promised to come early so we could get together. He was still assigned to Berlin the last time I saw him."

He startled me when he added, "The New York Police found him dead in a local hotel room early this morning."

"Good Lord, what happened?" I asked in surprise.

"The police say it was suicide, he had a plastic bag over his head."

"You don't expect me to believe that bull—he was anxious to see me. Besides, he lived in New York—why the hotel?"

"That's all I know right now. Sorry," he said.

"Well, I'd appreciate your telling whomever you're dealing with that I object to this story about suicide..."

The Church committee's report was released on 26 April 1976. I never bothered to read it because I was sure it wouldn't contain any of my classified testimony, and I never learned more about W.H.'s death than what I've written above.

When I look back on those years, my colleagues and I chalked up many more successes than failures in our fight against godless Communism. Among our great disappointments has been the proliferation of nuclear arms.

Without any doubt in my mind, after the battle for technological supremacy, the United States has failed in the domain of nuclear proliferation. Despite the pious almost placid objections from Washington about nuclear testing by Pakistan and India, those two countries continue their regional rivalry. The revelation during 1999 about nuclear data misappropriated from Los Alamos on the design of the warhead for the Fleet Ballistic Missile raises life-and-death questions about America's cavalier security measures and sound-bite patriotism prevalent today in the United States.

Our victory in the Cold War meant keeping the Soviet Union in a memory-box, and delivering a world free of nuclear terror for the children of our children. Unfortunately no statesmen step forward to provide a compass heading on this objective. In reality, there is no political constituency for the non-proliferation of nuclear arms. It should come as no surprise then that there are no longer any serious public debates on engaging treaties and issues, while we-the-people passively vegetate like bumps on a log. In our complacency, Washington makes casual commitments that dilute the independence of the United States and weakens, as the Soviet Union never could, our hard-won security—rendering our Cold War victory hollow indeed.

The Florence Gould Foundation in New York, established after Florence's death, today supports many cultural and civic projects that benefit Americans and French citizens alike. The many millions of dollars spread around by the foundation have been buying off the consequences of Florence's unfaithful hijinks and her profitable collaboration with the Nazis in occupied France during World War II.

No IRS study was ever made to identify any part of the Gould fortune derived from Nazi collaboration.

While Gould used her money to successfully fight off criminal accusations after World War II, the family of hero Antoine Fratacci struggled to make ends meet. His wife, Suzanne, started to learn of his underground activities against the German occupiers only after the war. She told Paulette and her younger sons, Simon and Jean, that the last time their father left for work on his bicycle she told him, "Antoine, you look tired, I want you to rest quietly this weekend. Now at least he's resting..."

Appendixes

U.S.GOVERNMENT DOCUMENTS ORIGINATING IN WASHINGTON

Defense Department

Navy Department

State Department

White House

Congress

Miscellaneous

U.S. NATIONAL ARCHIVES
Safehaven/Nazi Gold files

FRENCH AND BRITISH DOCUMENTS

ASSISTANT SECRETARY OF DEFENSE
WASHINGTON 25, D.C.

INSTALLATIONS AND LOGISTICS

MAR 1 6 196[illegible]

Dear Admiral Galantin:

I want to thank you for the excellent PERT presentation you arranged at our request for General Lavaud.

While it is regrettable that General Lavaud was unable to attend, I understand that his aides were quite favorably impressed.

Please convey my personal appreciation to your staff for the excellent job, particularly to Mr. Bernard Poirier for his very able and conscientious assistance.

Sincerely,

(Signed) Thomas D. Morris

THOMAS D. M[illegible]
Assistant [illegible]
[illegible]

Rear Admiral I. J. Galantin,
Director, Special Projects
Department of the Navy

16 March 1962 from Thomas D. Morris, Assistant Secretary of Defense (I&L) Re: Gen. Lavaud.

ASSISTANT SECRETARY OF DEFENSE
WASHINGTON 25, D.C.

INTERNATIONAL SECURITY AFFAIRS

MEMORANDUM FOR THE SECRETARY OF THE NAVY 21 NOV 1962

SUBJECT: Letters of Appreciation

I enclose letters of appreciation from the Counselor of the State Department for the services of a number of Navy Department personnel in preparing the presentation of the Multilateral MRBM Force concept given the North Atlantic Council on 22 October 1962.

Largely due to their efforts, the presentation appears to have been markedly successful. Please convey my appreciation, in addition to Mr. Rostow's, to these officers and Mr. Poirier, for their notably competent and productive effort.

SIGNED

Henry S. Rowen
Deputy Assistant Secretary

7 Inclosures
1. Letter of appreciation to LCDR R. R. Jefferson
2. Letter of appreciation to CDR F. F. Clifford
3. Letter of appreciation to CDR L. L. Jackson
4. Letter of appreciation to CAPT J. E. Clarke
5. Letter of appreciation to CAPT F. H. Michaelis
6. Letter of appreciation to CAPT C. Jackson
7. Letter of appreciation to Mr. Bernard W. Poirier

21 November 1962 from Henry S. Rowen, Deputy Assistant Secretary of Defense (ISA), Re: MLF.

THE SECRETARY OF DEFENSE
WASHINGTON

MAY 16 1963

MEMORANDUM FOR REAR ADMIRAL WILLIAM C. MOTT

THRU: THE SECRETARY OF THE NAVY

SUBJECT: Negotiation of United States and United Kingdom Polaris Sales Agreement

It is my pleasure to extend congratulations and thanks for the very timely and successful negotiation of the United States and United Kingdom Polaris Sales Agreement. You may take justifiable pride in the fact that, with respect to its substantive content, essentially the same agreement which you and Mr. James Mackay of the British Admiralty drafted during the period from February 20 to March 16, 1963 has been signed by representatives of both governments and has entered into force. It is now serving to give effect to one of the important understandings reached between President Kennedy and Prime Minister Harold Macmillan at Nassau in the Bahamas on December 18 to 21, 1962.

Your activities have fully justified the designation of the Department of Defense as the responsible United States Agency for the negotiation of the Polaris Sales Agreement as well as my appointment of you as Chief Negotiator. Your accomplishment is a distinct credit to you and to each of the members of your negotiating team. I wish you would extend my appreciation to those who participated with you and under your direction in the drafting and negotiation of this historic agreement.

Well done! /s/ Roswell Gilpatric

COPY

16 May 1963 from Roswell Gillpatric, Deputy Secretary of Defense, Re: US-UK negotiations.

DOWNGRADED AT 3 YEAR INTERVALS
DECLASSIFIED AFTER 12 YEARS
DOD DIR 5200.10

~~DOD DIR 5200.10~~

DECLASSIFIED.

TOP SECRET
SECRET

CO Pers. file

2 December 1955

MEMORANDUM FOR: Rear Admiral Clark (Op-51)
Rear Admiral Raborn (Office of the Secretary of the Navy)

Subj: ICBM - IRBM

1. It is quite evident that we must move fast on this fleet ballistic missile and that our present schedules for shipboard launching are not good enough. I think that the first service that demonstrates a capability for this is very likely to continue the project and the others may very well drop out. This missile must be fired from a ship just as early as possible even though the equipment in the ships is not as desirable as can be conceived. For example, the equipment for the location of a ship need not be too accurate for the test firing. The launching could take place from the vicinity of Banana River where the ship can be located exactly.

2. In view of the fact that the President wants a report monthly I, of course, will want a report weekly and, like the President, I will want it to be a progress report.

3. If Rear Admiral Raborn runs into any difficulty with which I can help, I will want to know about it at once along with his recommended course of action for me to take. If more money is needed, we will get it. If he needs more people, those people will be ordered in. If there is anything that slows this project up beyond the capacity of the Navy Department we will immediately take it to the highest level and not work our way up through several days. In taking this type of action we must be reasonably sure we are right and at least know the possible consequences of being wrong because we will be disrupting many other programs in order to make achievement in this one if we are not careful. That is all right if we really make an achievement.

SECRET
TOP SECRET
DECLASSIFIED

Page 1 of 2 pages Copy No. 10 of 10 Copies

FILE COPY

Reproduction of this document in whole or in part is prohibited except with permission of the issuing office.

TOP SECRET
DECLASSIFIED

4. The Air Force has got a tremendous amount of enthusiasm which they demonstrate behind their project and we must have even more. The awards should be made to companies as soon as possible and our major contract awards, I think, should be made by the 15th of December.

5. The next report on this should be made by somebody who is enthusiastic, who gives evidence of his enthusiasm, and whose knowledge demonstrates that he has a thorough grasp of the problem and is pushing ahead just a little bit faster than anybody else could.

ARLEIGH BURKE

Copy to:
Op-09
All Deputies

DISTRIBUTION:

Copy #1 ADM CLARK
Copy #2 ADM RABORN
Copy #3 Op-09
Copy #4 Op-01
Copy #5 Op-02
Copy #6 Op-03
Copy #7 Op-04
Copy #8 Op-05
Copy #9 Op-06
Copy #10 - Green

RADM CLEXTON E.W.

Author's note: **President Eisenhower insisted on a monthly report, and the Banana River is really a lagoon next to Cape Canaveral. For years, the first sentence of paragraph 3 was a reporting criterion at every SP Monday morning management meeting. Raborn's criteria for reporting by exception were: (1) "I can handle the delay, Admiral, and here are my solutions" ... (2) "I'm in trouble and need your help, Admiral" ... (3) "You're in trouble, Admiral! and you need help from the CNO" ... (4) "The CNO needs the Secretary on this one, Admiral." Felt pressure and competition from the USAF and from the rest of the Navy is clear in this letter. To report a problem without offering solutions was unacceptable in the Special Projects Office.**

~~BEARDSLEY~~
EMSEY
JACKSON

DEPARTMENT OF THE NAVY
SPECIAL PROJECTS OFFICE
WASHINGTON 25, D.C.

IN REPLY REFER TO
SPLe:CNP:pfo
File No. 12,340
Ser. No. 0988-SP

~~CONFIDENTIAL~~ Downgraded to unclassified by originator. CNP 2/3/61
~~CONFIDENTIAL~~ NON-CLASSIFIED

29 APR 1960

From: Director, Special Projects

To: Comptroller, Department of the Navy

Subj: Special Assignment of Mr. Bernard W. Poirier (Code NCR-2242); appreciation for (U)

Ref: (a) SP ltr Ser. 0713-SP of 25 March 1960

1. Reference (a) requested the services of Mr. Bernard W. Poirier in connection with the preparation of a brochure, dealing with the Fleet Ballistic Missile Program, for presentation to NATO. Mr. Poirier's services were made available to this office on 31 March 1960 and on 1 April 1960.

2. Mr. Poirier was extremely helpful in the preparation of the NATO brochure. He supplied and obtained information, used in the preparation of the French version, which would have been difficult if not impossible to obtain otherwise.

3. It is with pleasure, therefore, that I express my sincere appreciation for the expert assistance of Mr. Poirier and for your cooperation in making him available.

W F Raborn

W. F. RABORN

Classification cancelled or changed to* Unclassified
by authority of originator on 3 Feb 1961
/s/ (above)
BUREAU OF NAVAL WEAPONS

~~CONFIDENTIAL~~
NON-CLASSIFIED ~~CONFIDENTIAL~~
NavCompt Cont. No C-8030
Log 3,555,525

29 April 1960 from Admiral William F. Raborn.

DEPARTMENT OF THE NAVY
SPECIAL PROJECTS OFFICE
WASHINGTON 25, D.C.

IN REPLY REFER TO

SP-11-RGS:keh
12 AUG 1961

From: Director, Special Projects

To: Mr. Bernard W. Poirier (SP-1101)

Subj: Avoiding conflict of interest during outside employment

1. During your previous employment as Budget Analyst in the Special Projects Office (SP-13215), you have undertaken on your own initiative and during off-duty hours to write articles for certain technical periodicals and news media in the field of astronautics, geopolitics and economics. Before undertaking this outside employment, you made a full disclosure of what this employment involved and took pains to avoid any work that tended to conflict with your Government employment. In the first place, you did not permit your outside efforts to interfere with the demands made upon you by your work as Budget Analyst, both during normal duty hours and during authorized overtime as required by your superiors. In the second place, you avoided writing about any matter involving the POLARIS Program, and exercised a continuing discretion, including consultation from time to time with BUWEPS Counsel (L-3), to avoid so much as the appearance of outside work that might be incompatible with your Government employment.

2. You have now been selected to fill the new billet in SP-11 entitled Staff Coordinator for Foreign Programs (SP-1101), based in part upon the experience which you have acquired and contacts gained during your outside employment described above. I am informed that you wish to continue such outside work during the time you are employed in the SP-1101 billet. Accordingly, the purpose of this letter is to acknowledge your disclosure of this intention and to authorize you to continue such work subject to certain limitations and safeguards which you should scrupulously observe, as you have in the past, in order to avoid possible conflicts of interest that may arise between such outside employment and your new official duties.

3. At the outset, it is to be noted that your new duties in the SP-1101 billet will bring you much closer to the work which you propose to continue in your off-duty hours,

---

12 August 1962 from Deputy Director, Special Projects Office, re: Avoiding Conflict of Interest.

SP-11-RGS:keh
12 AUG 1961

and to this extent you must exercise renewed care in avoiding any possible conflict of interest which may arise. First, as a member of the SP team you must continue to make yourself available for whatever regular and overtime work is required of you by your superiors without permitting your outside commitments to interfere in any way with the demands thus made upon you by the Government. Second, you must not use for private gain any official information which is not available to the public. Finally, you must not exploit your official position in any way or do anything that is incompatible with the best interest of SP or the Government, to which you owe your first allegiance. In this connection, you should keep your private work and the subject matter it involves clearly separate from your official duties, and you should refrain from using or making reference to your official position in developing contacts for your private writing. To observe the distinction which I have noted will require a continuing exercise of discretion on your part. This discretion must be brought to bear on a case-by-case basis, and if you have any doubts in a particular instance, you should immediately make such disclosure to your superiors as you feel is necessary.

4. The risk of your involvement in a conflict of interest, although somewhat enhanced by the new official duties that you are assuming, is not of such order as to require a prohibition of your outside employment. In my opinion, it is clearly in the best interest of the Government for you to continue to write for publication articles of technical interest in the field of astronautics, geopolitics and economics, so long as you observe the safeguards noted above. The benefit to the Government will result chiefly from the broadened background knowledge of your technical specialty which you can bring to bear in the performance of your official duties.

T. J. RUDDEN, JR.
Deputy Director

15-18 May 1962 program introducing the briefing team for the seminar at NATO Headquarters, Paris, France, on the Program Evaluation and Review Technique—"PERT."

POLARIS
MANAGEMENT
TEAM
NATO
SEMINAR

EQUIPE
DE DIRECTION
DU PROJET
POLARIS
SEMINAIRE
OTAN

REAR ADMIRAL IGNATIUS J. GALANTIN, USN
DIRECTOR, SPECIAL PROJECTS

Admiral Galantin has complete management control of the combined government-industry effort for the research, development, testing, production, training and support for sea-based fleet ballistic missile systems. His naval career includes recent duty as Director of the Anti-submarine/Submarine Warfare Division, Office of the Chief of Naval Operations. From November 4, 1959 to January, 1961, he was Commander Cruiser Division TWO and Commander of Task Group Gold which comprised half of the Sixth Fleet. Earlier, from September, 1957 to November, 1959, he was Deputy Chief of Staff for Logistics and Administration on the staff of the NATO Commander in Chief, Allied Forces Southern Europe.

Amiral Galantin est chargé de la direction totale de l'effort combiné gouvernement-industrie pour les recherches, développement, essais, production, entraînement et appui pour réseaux sur mer de fusées ballistiques. Sa carrière navale comprend comme service récent le poste de Directeur de la Division de Guerre Anti-sousmarine/sousmarine, Bureau du Chef des Opérations Navales. Du 4 novembre 1959 à janvier 1961 il fut Commandant, 2e Division de Croiseurs, et du "Task Group Gold" qui comprenait la moitié de la 6e Flotte. Avant cela, de septembre 1957 à novembre 1959 il fut Deputé-Chef de l'Intendance et de l'Administration, affecté à l'Etat Major du Commandant Chef OTAN, Allied Forces Southern Europe.

Page 2 NATO program on PERT

GREETINGS TO THE DELEGATES!

It is a great pleasure to participate in this seminar with such distinguished friends in an area of mutual interest — management of weapons production. It is of particular interest to me since it permits me to renew friendships and associations formed during my NATO duty from 1957 to 1959.

Those of us speaking to you during this seminar are members of the Special Projects Office of the United States Navy. This office has total management responsibility for the Polaris submarine missile program. It serves as the focal point for the combined effort of more than 11,000 contractors and Government laboratories engaged in this program.

Because of the complexity and scope of this unique program, special management devices are employed. I hope our management experience accumulated during the six years in which the Polaris system has progressed from basic development to full production will be of some help to you. I am sure we will benefit from this opportunity to spend to few days with you.

This booklet has been prepared to identify the various officials with whom you will be speaking during the seminar. This booklet highlights as well the points we will cover in detail during the daily sessions.

I. J. GALANTIN
Rear Admiral, United States Navy
Director, Special Projects

NATO Building
Paris, France
15 May 1962

COMPLIMENTS AUX DÉLÉGUÉS !

C'est pour moi un grand plaisir de participer à cette conférence avec des amis si distingués, sur un sujet d'intérêt mutuel,—l'Administration de la Production des Armes. Celà m'est d'autant plus agréable que celà me permet de renouer des amitiés et connaissances formées lors de mon service à l'OTAN, entre 1957 et 1959.

Tous ceux d'entre nous qui vont avoir l'honneur de vous parler, font partie du Bureau des Projets Spéciaux des Forces Navales des Etats-Unis. Ce Bureau a la charge complète de l'Administration du Programme Polaris, et concentre les efforts combinés de plus de 11.000 entrepreneurs et des laboratoires du Gouvernement enrollés dans ce Programme.

En raison de la complexité, et de l'étendue de ce programme unique, nous nous sommes vue obligés d'employer des moyens administratifs tout à fait spéciaux. Je veux espérer que notre expérience acquise au cours des six ans qui ont vu se développer le Projet Polaris depuis son stade initial jusqu'à sa mise au point complète, pourra vous être de quelque utilité, et je suis certain que nous pourrons bénéficier de ces quelques jours passés ensemble.

Ce pamphlet a été préparé en vue d'identifier les différentes personnalités qui auront le plaisir de discuter avec vous au cours de ce séminaire. En outre, il vous donne une idée générale des points d'intérèt qui seront discutés en plus gran détail durant les Conférences.

I. J. GALANTIN
Contre-amiral, USN
Directeur, Projets Spéciaux

Edifice OTAN
Paris, France
15 Mai 1962

Page 3 NATO program on PERT

MR. GEORGE W. BERGQUIST
DIRECTOR, PLANS AND PROGRAMS DIVISION
SPECIAL PROJECTS OFFICE

Mr. Bergquist heads the division in the Special Projects Office which develops program and logistic plans for the Polaris effort; prepares, justifies and administers the Polaris budget, coordinates continuing evaluation of program progress, explores advanced management concepts, provides Polaris training facilities, administers personnel and organizational plans, operates the Polaris management center and conducts operational research studies.

M. Bergquist, dans le Bureau des Projets Spéciaux, est à la tête de la division qui développe le programme d'intendance pour le projet Polaris, prépare, justifie, administre le budget Polaris, coordone l'évaluation continue du progrès du programme, explore les théories d'administration avancés., prévoit les facilités d'entraînement, pour le projet Polaris, dirige les plans de personnel et d'organisation, opère le Centre d'Administration Polaris, et conduit des programmes de recherches.

CAPTAIN RICHARD G. SHUTT, USN
HEAD, PLANS AND PROGRAMS BRANCH
PLANS AND PROGRAMS DIVISION
SPECIAL PROJECTS OFFICE

Chief planning officer for the Polaris Program. Develops time phased plans and schedules for the production of major elements of the Fleet Ballistic Missile System. Develops and coordinates plans for logistic support, personnel, training and foreign applications of Polaris.

Officier d'Administration du programme Polaris. Développe les plans et horaires nécessaires à la production des principaux éléments du système FBM. Développe et coordonne des plans pour l'intendance, le personnel, l'entraînement et les utilisations de Polaris à l'étranger.

MR. BERNARD W. POIRIER
COORDINATOR FOR FOREIGN PROGRAMS
PLANS AND PROGRAMS BRANCH
PLANS AND PROGRAMS DIVISION
SPECIAL PROJECTS OFFICE

Coordinates the review and the formulation of planning and policy guidelines for foreign program proposals on sea-based ballistic missile systems vis-a-vis national priorities on Polaris, resources and long range research implications arising therefrom.

Coordonne le contrôle et le développement des principes et cours d'action gouvernant les programmes à l'étranger, en relation avec les priorités nationales sur Polaris, les ressources et les recherches futures nécessaires.

COMMANDER JOHN J. S. DANIEL, USN
HEAD, PROGRAM EVALUATION BRANCH
PLANS AND PROGRAMS DIVISION
SPECIAL PROJECTS OFFICE

Responsible for continuous and independent evaluation of the status of the Polaris Program and supports all technical groups in PERT operations and related management systems.

Est responsable de l'évaluation continuelle et indépendante du Projet Polaris et soutient tous les groupes techniques des opérations PERT et des services d'administration afiliés.

Page 4 NATO program on PERT

MR. THOMAS H. ENZOR
SUPPORT PROGRAM EVALUATION SECTION HEAD
PROGRAM EVALUATION BRANCH
PLANS AND PROGRAMS DIVISION
SPECIAL PROJECTS OFFICE

Evaluates the progress and status of major segments of the FBM support program, provides guidance and consulting services for implementing management techniques such as PERT, Line Of Balance and program management plans.

S'occupe de l'évaluation du progrès et du fonctionnement des principales phases du programme de support FBM, donne conseils et directions nécessaires à la mise en usage des Techniques d'Administration tels que PERT, Line of Balance et méthodes d'administration.

COMMANDER H. D. BUTLER, USN
ASSISTANT TO THE TECHNICAL PLANS OFFICER
TECHNICAL DIVISION
SPECIAL PROJECTS OFFICE

Monitors and coordinates technical planning in the specific areas of guidance of the Polaris missile and of fire control and navigation development and production in the Fleet Ballistic Missile Program.

Surveille et coordonne les plans de développement technique dans les domaines de guidage pour la Polaris, contrôle de tir et équipements de navigation pour le programme FBM.

CAPTAIN J. L. P. McCALLUM, USN
DIRECTOR, FLEET BALLISTIC MISSILES DIVISION
OFFICE OF THE CHIEF OF NAVAL OPERATIONS

Within the Office of the Chief of Naval Operations, Captain McCallum is responsible for the coordination of research, development, evaluation, production and Fleet Support of Fleet Ballistic Missiles Systems.

Responsable pour la coordination des recherches, développement, évaluation, production, et ravitaillement par la Marine pour le système FBM.

Page 5 NATO program on PERT

Concept of the POLARIS weapon system management is unique. Total responsibility for the program is delegated to the Director, Special Projects. His responsibility includes planning, research and development, facilities, production, specialized training of personnel, and management of fiscal and other resources. Selection and training of personnel to man the weapon system and its supporting components are a part of his assignment. This total responsibility is a one-package responsibility encompassing all elements of the program; missile with its facilities; prototype launching ships and the submarines; the personnel to man the system and training facilities and command communications.

To discharge this unique concentrated authority effectively the Director, Special Projects controls all expenditures from a "Management Fund." Administration of this fund is an important part of his duties. It is believed that this affords the most accurate and complete accounting of the costs of a weapon system program to be found within the national defense organization. By effectively combining under a Navy weapon system manager, all the elements of technical direction and management, including planning, financial inspection and other resource matters, the Navy made a significant contribution to the art of administering a complex weapon system.

Administrative procedures were streamlined to the maximum. This permitted quick and coordinate action by all offices and agencies participating with Special Projects Office in the Fleet Ballistic Missile (FBM) program. The FBM program is reviewed and approved as a total package by the respective Ballistic Missile Committees of the Navy and Office of the Secretary of Defense. The Navy Ballistic Missile Committee, with the Secretary of the Navy as Chairman, establishes over-all program policy. The Chief of Naval Operations establishes the operating and performance requirements.

The Director, Special Projects, as weapons system manager, has broad discretion to specify and coordinate requirements of all necessary areas of work. He has authority and control of available funds to make the numerous quick technical decisions on alternate scientific and engineering courses of action involved in such a complex system. This authority has unquestionably expedited the program.

L'idée d'Administration de Système d'Armement Polaris est unique. La responsabilité totale du programme est déléguée au Directeur, Projets Spéciaux. Sa responsabilité comprent l'organisation, recherche et développement, installations, production, entraînement spécialisé du personnel et administration des ressources financières et autres. Il est aussi responsable de la sélection et la formation du personnel nécessaire au fonctionnement de Système d'Armement, et de ses éléments complémentaires.

Cette responsabilité totale est une responsabilité "en bloc," comprenant tous les éléments du Programme; la Fusée et ses installations, les navires prototypes destinés à son lancement, et les sous-marins; le personnel nécessaire au fonctionnement du système et aux facilités d'entraînement, et du système de communication.

Pour s'acquiter effectivement de cette autorité unique le Directeur, Projets Spéciaux contrôle toutes les dépenses d'un "Fond d'Administration"; l'administration de ce fond est une partie importante de ses devoirs. On pense que cela permet une comptabilité plus exacte et complète du coût d'un Programme d'Armement qui puisse être trouvée dans toute l'Organisation de la Défense Nationale. La Marine a grandement contribué à l'art d'Administrer un système d'armement complexe, en combinant effectivement sous un seul Directeur tous les éléments de Direction technique et d'Administration.

Les procédures administratives ont été simplifiées au maximum. Ceci permet une action rapide et coordonnée dans tous les Bureaux et Agences participants au programme FBM avec le Bureau des Projets Spéciaux. Le Programme FBM est revu et approuvé en bloc respectivement par le "Ballistic Missile Committee" de la Marine et du Bureau du Ministre de la Défense. Le "Navy Ballistic Missile Committee," sous la présidence du Secrétaire de la Marine établit une ligne de conduite générale pour le Programme. Le Chef des Opérations Navales établit les conditions requises afin de mener à bien l'exécution du projet.

Le Directeur, Projets Spéciaux, a le pouvoir de préciser et de coordonner, à sa discretion, les exigences de toutes les différentes branches du travail. L'authorité et le contrôle des fonds disponibles lui permettent de prendre rapidement de nombreuses décisions techniques nécessaires dans un système aussi complexe. Cette

Page 6 NATO program on PERT

nique), which has been widely adapted and utilized in whole or in part by other Services and private industry, for the purpose of research and development management. This statistical technique is programmed on digital computers, and is used for measuring and forecasting development progress by SP as a planning and a decision-making tool for saving time in achieving end objectives.

PERT recognizes three factors that influence achievement of program objectives: time, resources, and technical performance specifications. It employs time as the variable to reflect planned resource-applications and performance specifications. An electronic computer processes the major sequential events in the current plan with estimates of time and range of time necessary to complete each activity between successive events. The time estimates which are supplied by contractors' personnel responsible for doing the particular tasks or activities include the "most likely time," "optimistic time," and "pessimistic time" for each activity.

The computer provides expected dates for completion and probabilities for meeting objectives by the scheduled time. PERT highlights the areas requiring management decision, and reveals both criticalness and slack in the sequential plan for accomplishing the effort. PERT can also simulate the effects of alternate choices of action prior to management or technical decision.

The results of these "need-to-know" reporting systems and conference reports are used to provide a comprehensive and current record of planning effort, performance facts and program evaluation in the SP Management Center. The management planning and control system enables the Director and his staff to keep informed of progress and enables prompt decisions or, if necessary, referral to higher authority for resolution. Internal balance, integration and coordination of the entire research and development effort is assured.

In conclusion, the Special Projects Office organization, its programming and management systems, the SP Management Control Center, and forward-looking decision-making processes have been critically reviewed by government, private industry, and institutions of higher learning. Many have since adopted it for management of their own programs.

Un compte rendu hebdomadaire couvrant le travail de la semaine passée est présenté chaque lundi matin au Directeur et à son entourage. Dans certains cas, le Bureau des Projets Spéciaux demande aux principaux entrepreneurs d'-utiliser une technique d'Analyse de Production. Cette technique demande l'établissement d'un horaire pour les divers matériaux et permet de comparer le progrès avec les horaires établis pour le produit fini. Ce système assure un horaire de production regulier et un contrôle efficace de la livraison du matériel.

Au debut de 1958, le Bureau des Projets Spéciaux développa un nouveau système d'administration connu sous le nom de PERT (Program Evaluation and Review Technique), qui fut largement adapté et utilisé-soit dans son ensemblé, soit en partie, par d'autres services et par l'Industrie Privée, en vue de recherches, et du développement de la direction. Cette technique de statistiques est etabliée grace à un calculateur du cerveau électronique et est utilisée par BPS pour mésurer et prévoir le progrès de développement, en tant que moyen de faciliter les décisions qui permettent de gagner du temps pour obtenir le resultat prévu.

PERT reconnait trois facteurs qui influencent l'accomplissement de la tâche prévue: temps, ressources, et précisions sur le rendement technique. Le temps est employé comme élément variable, pour démontrer l'utilisation prévue des ressources et les spécifications du rendement. Un calculateur électronique analyse les principaux événements, par phase, dans le plan en cours, avec l'évaluation du temps et de période de temps nécessaire pour compléter chaque activité, entre des événements successifs. Les estimations de temps, fournies par le personnel des entreprises industrielles chargés d'un travail particulier, comprennent "limite de temps vraissemblable" "Prévision optimiste" et "prévision pessimiste," pour chaque activité.

Le calculateur procure les dates aux-quelles on peut espérer compléter le projet, et la probabilité d'arriver au but du programme dans les limites prévues. PERT met en valeur les services demandant une décision de la direction, et démontre la présence de danger et de retard dans ce système de décentralisation.

Les résultats de ces systèmes de rapport "besoin de savoir" et de ces rapports de conférences sont employés pour procurer un bilan com-

Page 7 NATO program on PERT

préhensif et actuel des efforts d'organisation, de la performance et de l'évaluation du Programme au Centre de Direction du BPS. Ce système de contrôle et d'administration permet au directeur et à son entourage de se tenir informé du progrés et lui permet de prendre des décisions immédiates ou, si besoin est, de faire appel à un supérieur pour une décision. L'équilibre interne, i'intégration et la coordination de l'effort total de recherche et de développement est assuré.

En conclusion, l'organisation du BPS, ses systèmes de programme et de direction, le centre de contrôle de direction du BPS et ces procédés d'avant garde ont été analysés soigneusement par le Gouvernement, l'Industrie et des Etablissement d'Education Supérieure; depuis, beaucoup d'entre eux l'ont adopté pour la direction de leurs propres programmes.

Page 8 NATO program on PERT

DEPARTMENT OF THE NAVY

POSITION OR JOB DESCRIPTION

EMPLOYEE [X] JD [ ] No. 622015

	POSITION OR JOB TITLE	SCHED. OR SERV	SERIES	GRADE/ PAY LEVEL/ FORMULA	CLASSIFIERS INITIALS	CLASSIFICATION OR RATING OFFICIAL (Signature, Title and Date)
1. THIRD ACTION						
2. SECOND ACTION						
3. FIRST ACTION	Administrative Officer	GS	301	12	DAE	ROBERT J. STIRRUP 6/28/62 Supv. Position Class. Specialist
4. RECOMMENDED	Administrative Officer	GS		12		5. NAME OF EMPLOYEE: Bernard W. Poirier

POSITION OR JOB LOCATION

6. ACTIVITY - NAME AND LOCATION: Bureau of Naval Weapons - Wash., D.C.	9. (3rd): Plans & Programs Branch (Sp11)
7. ORGANIZATIONAL SUBDIVISIONS (1st): Special Projects Office	10. (4th)
8. (2nd): Plans & Programs Division (Sp10)	11. ORGANIZATIONAL TITLE OF POSITION OR JOB (If any)

12. EMPLOYEES NOW PERFORMING DUTIES (Ungraded jobs only)

(No.:)	(Title:)	(No.:)	(Title:)

REASON FOR SUBMISSION

[X] 13. DUTIES AND RESPONSIBILITIES NOT ELSEWHERE DESCRIBED - COMPLETE DESCRIPTION ATTACHED.

	POS. OR JOB#	CLASS. OR RATING
14. ATTACHED AMENDMENT NO. ____ TO.		
15. IDENTICAL TO.		
16. ATTACHED STATEMENT OF DIFFERENCE TO.		
17. REPLACES.	61-0887	GS-1082-11
18. OTHER (Specify)		

CERTIFICATIONS:

The description of the duties and responsibilities of this position or job is complete and accurate.

	DATE
19. SIGNATURE (Employee)	
20. SIGNATURE AND TITLE (Immediate supervisor): K. G. SHUTT, CAPT, USN, Hd, Plans & Programs Branch (Position No., Classification or Rank)	6/19/62
21. SIGNATURE AND TITLE (Person authorized to establish position or job): V. C. DOMBNICK, Hd, Management & Manpower Br.	6/19/62

22. REMARKS

Not suitable for i.a. action
Suitable for vice action
Competitive level: A-M

Based on qualifications in and application of knowledges in the fields of (1) Foreign affairs GS-130-0 series; (2) International Relations GS-131-0 series, (3) Intelligence GS-132-0 series; (4) Technical Writing and Editing GS-1083-0 series; and (5) Security GS-080-0 series.

23. CLASSIFICATION OR RATING RECERTIFICATION:					

Cover sheet, June 1962 GS-12 Job Description Bureau of Naval Weapons

ADMINISTRATIVE OFFICER (Technical Information)

GRADE: GS-12

1. INTRODUCTION

The position of Administrative Officer (Technical Information is located in the Plans and Programs Branch, Special Projects Office (SP). The Incumbent is responsible to the Head, Plans and Programs Branch for:

Obtaining and analyzing foreign sea-based ballistic missile program (e.g., NATO) requirements, policies, proposals and requests in accordance with directives from higher authority. Included, for example, are foreign program proposals transmitted via the Office of the Chief of Naval Operations to the Special Projects Office on matters relating to NATO ballistic missile force concepts. In February 1962, for example, a NATO European proposal responsive to the President's multinational sea-based deterrence NATO force concept was transmitted from the Office of the Assistant Secretary of Defense (International Security Affairs) via CNO to SP for review and assistance in establishing a Navy position. The material generated by the incumbent was included in the final memoranda transmitted to high authority. The same material was hand carried by an official of OASD/ISA to NATO headquarters in Paris the same day it was transmitted from Special Projects and CNO. Another example is a recent promulgation by OSD of a new weapons system concept evaluated from the points of view of political applicability for NATO use, sea-based capability and technical feasibility. It was further evaluated from the point of view of availability of resources versus existing Navy plans for use of future resources.

Providing expert assistance to formulators of Navy and DOD policy relating to possible foreign use of POLARIS or other sea-based ballistic missile systems. This includes advising those persons who inquire into the political-military background of previous proposals in order to evaluate Navy position vis-a-vis new proposals. CNO constantly refers matters originating in individual NATO countries to SP for evaluation of foreign ballistic missile progress, compared to the FBM Program, in order to determine possible needs for changes to Navy or national policy. For example, experimental sea-based ballistic missile programs such as Italy's are referred to SP for evaluation and

Page 1 GS-12 Job Description June 1962

policy recommendations, particularly when new requests for information are received by CNO from the Department of Defense or the Department of State.

Preparing oral and/or written reports on international developments or foreign programs affecting current plans, programs and requirements of the Fleet Ballistic Missile Program. Requirements for reports of this nature have been increasing in urgency and scope as the result of increased interest in foreign program applications of POLARIS by high level U. S. and foreign officials. As proposals originating at the State Department and the Defense Department are generated with increasing frequency, the incumbent reports the pertinent highlights affecting the Special Projects Office to cognizant persons who may be called upon to comment on partial or relevant questions pertaining thereto. Without this coordination, vital in cases involving foreign participation in weapons studies or NATO nuclear forces, cognizant officials would not know beforehand the impact of each others' judgement on the total question being proposed by higher authority.

Correlating, analyzing and reporting on foreign proposals or programs, determining their importance and potentialities, and maintaining informal liaison with U. S. agencies and bureaus active in international military affairs and with international organizations (e.g., NATO) or friendly foreign governments or their representatives. Inevitable changes within the national policies of each of fifteen NATO countries constantly requires evaluation of the impact on possible foreign program applications of the FBM Weapon System. The incumbent is required to evaluate the impact of policy adjustments informally to make coordinating review on Navy policy more accurate and fruitful.

Consistent with overall U. S. national security objectives and in consonance with United States plans and official policy, analyzing reports on international political and military factors, technical publications required, training or exchange programs to be instituted, and studies of international resources and requirements as they may have an impact on the Fleet Ballistic Missile Program requirements. There has been an increased tempo of national effort by high national authority to define new policy in the above areas with NATO allies and within both defense treaty obligations as well as existing national legislation. A constant informal liaison is required to maintain essential working relationships in these areas to insure that a currency

-2-

Page 2 GS-12 Job Description June 1962

of plans and purposes in sea-based missile proposals remains consonant with FBM Weapon System capabilities and sea-based system potentialities. The continuing evaluation of new factors provides the Special Projects Office with the background necessary to evaluate formal or informal proposals under consideration by higher authority.

Preparing reports and summaries on international developments, proposals or policies as they may influence policy, plans and programs outlined by SP, CNO or other higher authorities. This requirement is essential to keep top Navy management informed of pending policy changes or factors which if implemented in the future could affect Navy policy planning or program requirements.

Conducting studies of foreign resources and foreign industrial practices as they might be utilized in foreign programs utilizing elements of the FBM weapon systems. This has been required for planning conferences involving foreign nationals as scheduled by the Office of the Assistant Secretary of Defense (International Security Affairs) and other high authorities. Increased planning in this area is evident among higher authorities in areas affecting the Fleet Ballistic Missile System; this in turn generates the need for increasing effort by the incumbent.

2. DUTIES

A. Implementing those responsibilities listed in the INTRODUCTION.

B. Analyzing U. S., OSD, Navy and foreign inquiries and preparing replies on matters relative to the Fleet Ballistic Missile Program in consonance with the foreign policy and the security objectives of the United States.

C. Keeping his superiors informed of foreign development, programs, meetings, and proposals wherein knowledge of the aforesaid is beneficial and essential to the Special Projects Office, the Navy and DOD.

D. Assisting and advising the Chief Scientist and the consulting Senior Scientists of the Special Projects Office in those areas of foreign technical research and development which may influence basic or applied research for the FBM and/or Advanced Sea-Based Deterrent; this includes preparing background papers in the above areas for utilization by the Chief Scientist, such as his contribution to "Chief Scientist's Addendum" to the 26th Systems Appraisal Committee Report to the POLARIS/SSBN Steering Task Group (STG). This report, which was delivered to the STG 17-19 January 1962, concerned a seabased Mobile Mid-Range Ballistic

3

Page 3 GS-12 Job Description June 1962

Missile system to meet strategic responses envisioned by the Secretary of Defense.

E. Acting as a direct liaison between the Chief Scientist and the Plans and Programs Branch to ensure close coordination and consistency of planning and action in areas of mutual interest and responsibility such as NATO applications of POLARIS and future sea-based missile system possibilities.

3. CONTROLS OVER THE POSITION

The Head, Plans and Programs Branch (Captain, USN) is the supervisor of this position. Within the outlines of the Branch Head's guidance, authority is delegated to and responsibility exists with the incumbent to make decisions and take action with regard to the duties and the responsibilities outlined above. The incumbent is further responsible to perform these duties within directives and the objectives as established by the Secretary of Defense, the Chief of Naval Operations, Director, Special Projects and other high U.S. authority.

The work of the incumbent is subject to review and direction by the Branch Head to assure fulfillment of total requirements, objectives and conformance to U.S., DOD, Navy and SP directives.

The guidelines that exist are extremely broad in nature, not direct, constantly changing, highly political and require more than usual interpretation and a unique judgement.

4. QUALIFICATION REQUIREMENTS OF THE WORK

The incumbent must have knowledge of the character and requirements of the Fleet Ballistic Missile System, of foreign economics, International Law and foreign business customs. He should have knowledge of foreign geographic areas and of foreign customs and practices gained through residence, study, business and commercial activities or other experience in foreign activities. His college education should include the study of International Law, Economics, and Statistics. He must have experience in international shipping and international correspondence as well as experience in writing material suitable for publication since written expression is important to the mission of this position.

The incumbent should have a speaking and reading knowledge of a foreign language spoken in one or more NATO countries and the rudimentary knowledge of a second foreign language.

-4-

Page 4 GS-12 Job Description June 1962

DEPARTMENT OF THE NAVY
SPECIAL PROJECTS OFFICE
WASHINGTON 25, D. C.

IN REPLY REFER TO
Sp144-JJF:ldh
12454
10 JAN 1963

From: Director, Special Projects
To: Mr. Bernard W. Poirier

Subj: Letter of Appreciation

Encl: (1) Copy of AstSecDef Memo to SecNav dated 21 Nov 1962
(2) Letter of Appreciation from the Counselor of the Department of State dated 5 Nov 1962

1. Enclosures (1) and (2) are delivered with congratulations.

2. Copies of enclosures (1) and (2) will be placed in your official record.

IJGalantin

Cover letter of 10 January 1963 Congratulatory message from Admiral I.J. Galantin.

Employee Copy

DEPARTMENT OF THE NAVY

POSITION OR JOB DESCRIPTION

NAVEXOS-4543

[X] PD [ ] JD NO. ______

OFFICIAL CLASSIFICATION OR RATING ACTION

POSITION OR JOB TITLE	SCHED. OR SERV.	SERIES	GRADE/ PAY LEVEL /FORMULA	CLASSIFIERS INITIALS	CLASSIFICATION OR RATING OFFICIAL (Signature, Title and Date)
1. THIRD ACTION					
2. SECOND ACTION					
3. FIRST ACTION Administrative Officer (Foreign Information)	GS	301	13	BFF	ELIZABETH S. WILLIAMSON Position Classification Specialist 8-27--63

4. RECOMMENDED Administrative Officer (Technical Information) GS 301 13

5. NAME OF EMPLOYEE Bernard W. Poirier

POSITION OR JOB LOCATION

6. ACTIVITY - NAME AND LOCATION Bureau of Naval Weapons - Wash, DC

7. ORGANIZATIONAL SUBDIVISIONS (1st) Special Projects Office

8. (2nd) Plans and Programs Division (Sp10)

9. (3rd) Plans and Programs Branch (Sp11)

10. (4th) Foreign Planning Officer (Sp1101)

11. ORGANIZATIONAL TITLE OF POSITION OR JOB (If any)

12. EMPLOYEES NOW PERFORMING DUTIES (Ungraded jobs only)

(No.:) (Title:) (No.:) (Title:)

FOR INITIATING OFFICE ACTION

REASON FOR SUBMISSION

[X] 13. DUTIES AND RESPONSIBILITIES NOT ELSEWHERE DESCRIBED - COMPLETE DESCRIPTION ATTACHED.

	POS. OR JOB#	CLASS. OR RATING
14. ATTACHED AMENDMENT NO. ______ TO.		
15. IDENTICAL TO-		
16. ATTACHED STATEMENT OF DIFFERENCE TO-		
17. REPLACES-	62-2015	GS-301-12
18. OTHER (Specify)		

CERTIFICATIONS:

The description of the duties and responsibilities of this position or job is complete and accurate.

19. SIGNATURE (Employee) — DATE 8/19/63

20. SIGNATURE AND TITLE (Immediate supervisor) — J. M. BARRETT, CAPT, USN Asst Branch Head (Position No., Classification or Rank) — DATE 8/19/63

21. SIGNATURE AND TITLE (Person authorized to establish position or job) — V. G. DOMENICK, Head, Management & Manpower Branch — DATE 8/19/63

22. REMARKS

Not suitable for i.s. action
Suitable for vice action
Competitive Level: A-W

23. CLASSIFICATION OR RATING RECERTIFICATION:

Cover sheet, August 1963 GS-13 Job Description Bureau of Naval Weapons

ADMINISTRATIVE OFFICER (TECHNICAL INFORMATION)

GS-301-13

I. INTRODUCTION

This position is that of Foreign Planning Officer (SP-1101) in the Plans and Programs Branch (SP-11), Special Projects Office (SP) and is responsible to the Assistant Head (SP-110) (U. S. Navy Captain), Plans and Programs Branch.

In the international area, the Plans and Programs Branch is responsible for (1) coordination of SP activities in training, policy planning and schedule-programming for the joint United States and United Kingdom Polaris Program, (2) coordination of requirements put on SP by higher authority regarding the NATO Multilateral Sea-based Surface Ship Force and (3) advising on or coordinating information to be released to foreign governments regarding the Polaris Fleet Ballistic Missile weapons system.

The incumbent of this position is responsible for preparing reports, summaries and other information for the Assistant Branch Head or the Branch Head. The information developed is used by the United States Project Officer, Special Projects Office or the Royal Navy as it relates to the U.S.-U.K. joint Polaris Program. The incumbent is responsible for preparation of similar material for various NATO plans, such as the Multilateral Force proposal. This material is used by the office of the Chief of Naval Operations, the Office of the Secretary of Defense or by the State Department. In addition, he is a member of the U.S.-U.K. Joint Steering Task Group and serves as a standing member of that body's Secretariat.

II. DUTIES AND RESPONSIBILITIES

A. The incumbent prepares and promulgates, upon direction, reports and summaries of policy or objectives of the Special Projects Office under the Polaris Sales Agreement signed between the United States and the United Kingdom, April 6, 1963.

Page 1 GS-13 Job Description August 1963

B. The incumbent reviews reports prepared elsewhere for consistency in policy regarding the joint U.S.-U.K. Polaris Program and reports his findings and recommendations to his supervisor who is the U.S. Executive Secretary of the U.S.-U.K. Joint Steering Task Group.

C. (1) The incumbent serves as U.S. Recording Secretary on the U.S.-U.K. Joint Steering Task Group (J.S.T.G.). The incumbent has already been performing this duty for the J.S.T.G. whose membership of approximately 20 people has included five flag officers.

(2) The incumbent is responsible for promulgating the directives issued by the J.S.T.G. and assists in monitoring the implementation of directives issued by the Project Officers sitting in the J.S.T.G.

D. As directed, the incumbent monitors U.S. efforts in areas where little or no precedence exists and in areas which are required for implementing the U.S. portion of the U.K. program. He attends those pertinent meetings to advise and to recommend suitable courses of action consistent with policy.

E. As assigned, the incumbent will serve as a standing member of U.S. negotiating temas involved in formal negotiations with the U.K. The incumbent, for example was a member of the group which prepared papers for the Nassau meeting of the President during which he made a Polaris offer to the United Kingdom and to France. Subsequently the incumbent was commended for his duty as a member of the U.S. delegation which negotiated the Polaris Sales Agreement; and was later a member of the U.S. group which executed the Polaris Technical Arrangement and its modifications.

F. As assigned, the incumbent serves as a member of groups or committees established for other foreign programs affecting the Polaris plans and programs. For example, the incumbent was commended for duty at the State Department when assigned there during 1962 by the Navy and the Defense Department for work on preparing U.S. position papers on a U.S. study regarding NATO nuclear weapons systems. The study eventually served as the basis of a U.S. proposal to its allies.

- 2 -

Page 2 GS-13 Job Description August 1963

G. The incumbent maintains close liaison with the Navy Multilateral Force Executive (OP-605E) and will advise and respond to his needs regarding Polaris plans and programs.

H. The incumbent will maintain close liaison with the Office of Naval Intelligence (OP-92) and advise or respond to his needs. For example, the incumbent served closely with that office to formulate the Navy's directive relating to disclosure of Polaris information in the joint U.S.-U.K. Polaris Program. On another occasion and upon the recommendation of OP-92B3 and OP-751 the incumbent was named as the Department of Defense channel for release of certain atomic information to NATO via SACEUR (SHAPE HQ) regarding the NATO Nuclear Multilateral Force.

I. The incumbent will maintain liaison with OP-61 regarding Polaris matters affected by State Department activities and will assist in formulating and coordinating procedures to accommodate approved foreign visits, briefings or other matters. For example, the incumbent has been named action officer by CNO and by Assistant SECDEF for briefings to the NATO Military Committee and to the NATO Councial stationed in Paris. The incumbent was also instrumental, in conjunction with OP-611, in recommending successful tactics in the negotiations between the State Department and Spain for certain rights in the Canary Islands affecting aspects of Polaris development. On another occasion, the incumbent was assigned temporarily to duty directly under the Assistant Secretary of Defense (ISA) and (I&L) for giving the first highly classified Polaris briefing to the Head of the French IRBM Development Agency.

J. All the above duties are required to assist the Assistant Branch Head and the Branch Head to discharge their broadening duties and responsibilities augmented by increased foreign and domestic demands on the Polaris Program.

K. The incumbent will prepare, develop and coordinate plans and recommendations in international areas where action will affect Polaris planning and programming.

L. Provide expert assistance to formulators of Navy and DOD policy relating to possible foreign or international use of Polaris or other sea-based ballistic missile systems. For example, the incumbent was assigned to work closely with an action officer of the Joint Chiefs of Staff regarding SACEUR's employment of Polaris. The incumbent was also responsible for preparing documentation which insured the Navy's position in a reply to DDR&E, OSD, regarding Polaris and Missile-X, would be consistent with overall national policy vis-a-vis

- 3 -

Page 3 GS-13 Job Description August 1963

nuclear arms proposals to NATO. Similarly, the incumbent was repeatedly assigned as action officer regarding the question of U.S. cooperation in Italy's independent development of a sea-based ballistic missile launching system.

M. Responsibility for the work of others.

As assigned to him, the incumbent will be responsible for the work of temporary or permanent personnel directed to participate in policy planning, procedure planning or coordination of projects regarding the Polaris Program in the foreign area of the Plans and Programs Branch.

III. CONTROLS OVER THE POSITION

The Assistant Branch Head, Plans and Programs Branch, (Captain, USN) is the supervisor of this position. Within the scope of the incumbent's position, he is expected to make appropriate decisions where responsibility rests to do so. For policy and professional judgment, the incumbent will follow the objectives and directives established by the Secretary of Defense, the Chief of Naval Operations, the U. S. Project Officer of the U.S.-U.K. Polaris Program, the Director, Special Projects and other higher authority.

The guidelines that exist are extremely broad in nature, constantly changing, political and require more than usual interpretation. The position permits considerable latitude in locating information and making personal contacts.

IV. QUALIFICATION REQUIREMENTS OF THE WORK

The incumbent maintains close and constant contacts with SP program managers, with OPNAV and DOD personnel; and when required, close contact with State Department and foreign personnel The position requires broad experience and sound judgment to recognize the areas in foreign programs where a change in policy may affect Polaris plans and programs and report such developments in a timely manner.

The incumbent must possess thorough knowledge and familiarity with technical and scientific program managment techniques and administrative procedures.

- 4 -

Page 4 GS-13 Job Description August 1963

The incumbent must possess the intelligence, leadership and ability to formulate, coordinate and execute broad plans, policies and procedures and be foresignted to judge the adaptability or promise of new ideas or proposals.

- 5 -

Page 5 GS-13 Job Description August 1963

DEPARTMENT OF THE NAVY
SPECIAL PROJECTS OFFICE
WASHINGTON 25, D. C.

IN REPLY REFER TO

25 July 1963

From: Director, Special Projects

To : Mr. B. W. Poirier

1. Admiral Mott, who was Chief U. S. Negotiator of the US/UK POLARIS Sales Agreement, has sent me the attached letter of commendation addressed to him by the Deputy Secretary of Defense. In his transmittal, Admiral Mott said, among other things, "Of course I couldn't possibly have negotiated the Polaris Sales Agreement without the cooperation and help of your people."

2. You are one of the people to whom Admiral Mott referred in that statement, and therefore I am happy to pass on to you a copy of Secretary Gilpatric's letter. I want also to add my thanks for a job well done.

I. J. GALANTIN

Attachment

25 July 1963 "Well done" from Admiral Galantin on US/UK negotiations.

UNITED STATES AND UNITED KINGDOM

JOINT STEERING TASK GROUP

SECOND MEETING LONDON

OCTOBER 1963

CLASSIFICATION UNCLASSIFIED DATE 29 August 1963

ORIGINATING CODE U.S. Exec. Sec'y PAGE 1 OF 1

To: U.S. Executive Secretary, J.S.T.G. (Via SP-50)

Subject: U.S. Delegation to Second J.S.T.G. Meeting

Ref: (a) J.S.T.G. proposed agenda, dtd 9 Aug 63(SP11,SP50,SPUK)

1. In accordance with Section 15.6 of the Technical Arrangement, as modified, the United States Project Officer has appointed, in addition to Captain Barrett, USN and Mr. B. W. Poirier, as stated in reference (a), the following persons to attend the Second J.S.T.G. meeting from 1 to 3 October, 1963, at London and Bath.

AIKEN, T. W., Mr., (SP-13)
BERGQUIST, G. W., Mr., (SP-10)
BROWN, J. A., RADM., USN, BUSHIPS (SP-002)
  or as alternate, SONENSHEIN, N., Capt., USN, BUSHIPS
CROWSON, D. L., BGEN, USAF, JRSWG (AEC/DMA)
GOODING, R. C., Capt., USN, (SP-24)
HAMILTON, A. G., Jr., Capt., USN, (SP-203)
JULIAN, A. J., Cdr., USN, JRSWG, (SP-272)
SANGER, F. M., Capt., (SP-200)
VAUGHN, J. R., Mr., (SP-1324)
ZOELLER, R. J., Capt., USN, (SP-26)

2. Rear Admiral I. J. Galantin, U.S. Project Officer, will head the U.S. Delegation.

3. Mr. Aiken and Mr. Vaughn will arrive on 25 Sept. with Detailed Two Year Budget draft for joint review prior to J.S.T.G.

Respectfully,

J. M. BARRETT, USN
U.S. Executive Secretary

U.S.-U.K. POLARIS PROGRAM ________ CLASSIFICATION UNCLASSIFIED

Enclosure (1)

29 August 1963 US/UK JSTG London Meeting Notice

DEPARTMENT OF THE NAVY
SPECIAL PROJECTS OFFICE
WASHINGTON 25, D. C.

11 October 1963

From: Director, Special Projects

To: MR. BERNARD W. POIRIER

Subj: Letter of Commendation

1. On the occasion of your departure from the Special Projects Office, I wish to commend you and to express my appreciation for the many invaluable contributions you have made to SP in the more than three years you have been a member of the organization. Your efforts in our international program were a major factor in the successful negotiation of the U.S.-U.K. Polaris Sales Agreement and in the establishment of the present good working relationship between Special Projects and the U.K. Polaris Executive Organization.

2. Particular recognition is due you for the manner in which you have so ably represented SP in international matters to the Office of the Secretary of Defense and the Department of State. I wish to add my own commendation to that already expressed by Messrs. Gilpatrick, Morris, Rowan and Rostow in their letters of appreciation for services you have rendered both to SP and on behalf of SP.

3. You have been an excellent source of accurate information to the senior members of the SP organization in matters pertaining to foreign programs. Your departure from SP is a great loss to the organization, but I am pleased that your abilities have brought you such an excellent opportunity in industry. I wish to extend my best wishes for your continued success in your future endeavors.

I. J. Galantin
I. J. GALANTIN

11 October 1963 Letter of Commendation from Admiral Galantin

DEPARTMENT OF STATE
Counselor and Chairman
Policy Planning Council
Washington

November 5, 1962.

Dear Paul:

As you know, during September and the early part of October of this year, Mr. Bernard W. Poirier, served as a member of a State/DOD team preparing a presentation of the Multilateral MRBM Force concept to the North Atlantic Treaty Organization which took place in Paris on October 22.

This work involved extensive and repeated revision of the DOD study on that subject based on a previous Navy study. The presentation had, of course, to be compatible with United States policy in the nuclear field, and in many other areas of concern in dealing with our NATO allies. The work was therefore of a most delicate and demanding nature, going beyond military and technical matters. In all these respects, Mr. Poirier performed most valuable services. I should therefore now like to thank you for making him available to us, and to express to you our appreciation for the outstanding contribution that he made. The implementation of this important policy objective of the United States rests heavily upon the contribution made by Mr. Poirier and his Navy colleagues, and I wanted you to know of my personal gratitude and of that of the Department.

Sincerely yours,

Walt

W. W. Rostow

The Honorable
Paul H. Nitze,
Assistant Secretary,
International Security Affairs,
Department of Defense,
The Pentagon.

5 November 1962 State Department letter from Walt W. Rostow

June 2, 1994

THE WHITE HOUSE

WASHINGTON

Message Commemorating the 50th Anniversary of D-Day
to the veterans of the Saint-Malo Fortress campaign
the United States III Army 1944
83rd Infantry Division
329th, 330th, 331st Inf. Regiments

Warm greetings to everyone gathered to commemorate the fiftieth anniversary of the D-Day invasion of Normandy -- and the beginning of the end of the Second World War.

Fifty years ago, much of Europe remained imprisoned behind the walls of fascist aggression, and the flame of freedom seemed on the verge of being extinguished across that beleaguered continent. On June 6, 1944, a 100,000-man American assault team, supported by air, sea, and Allied Forces, stormed the beaches of Normandy, marking the turning point of the European war. After two years of planning, the Allied Forces had executed Operation Overlord, the largest and most ambitious amphibious operation in military history. Steadily and valiantly, these American patriots marched onward to liberate Europe, helping to secure freedom's riches for countless citizens of the world.

The heroic men who fought and died during those difficult days helped to give rise to a new era of hope and progress, starting a trend toward democracy and human dignity that continues to this day. In the wake of the Cold War, the world is filled with opportunities for the success of these fundamental ideals. The peoples of nations around the world persist in throwing off the shackles of tyranny and in seeking the blessings of liberty. On this historic occasion, we, the benefactors of the freedom won by our courageous Armed Forces, rededicate ourselves to embracing these epic changes. In memory of all those who lost their lives on Normandy's shore, we reaffirm our commitment to building a safer, more peaceful world for the generations to come.

Best wishes to all for a most memorable observance.

2 June 1994 President Clinton's letter on the occasion of the 50th anniversary of the Normandy invasion. In the archives of Saint-Malo, France.

CONGRESSIONAL RECORD — APPENDIX

A875 *February 13* *1961*

Soviet's New Budget Heavy With Arms Spending

EXTENSION OF REMARKS
OF

HON. OVERTON BROOKS

OF LOUISIANA
IN THE HOUSE OF REPRESENTATIVES
Monday, February 13, 1961

Mr. BROOKS of Louisiana. Mr. Speaker, in looking ahead to the future it is essential that we remain aware, to the best of our ability, of what our chief competitor is doing. To that end, I call to the attention of the Members an article on the Soviet Union's budget which appeared recently in the periodical Missiles and Rockets.

The article follows:

[From Missiles and Rockets, Jan. 23, 1961]

SOVIETS' NEW BUDGET HEAVY WITH ARMS SPENDING—ROCKET RESEARCH INCREASED BY 18.7 PERCENT; TOTAL MILITARY EXPENDITURE APPEARS TO BE FROM 42 TO 59 BILLION RUBLES; GROSS NATIONAL PRODUCT DIFFICULT TO ESTIMATE

(By Bernard Poirier)

Russia's space age budget for 1961 maintains the high level of military spending established in 1960—with an 18.7 percent increase in rocket research and a 3.4 percent stepup in cold war spending.

It also adds 3 billion new rubles to stimulate Soviet industry.

These increases are among many contained in the 1961 spending program rubber-stamped by Soviet parliamentarians at their annual budget session. It is a record 77,589-million-ruble budget—4 billion more than in the 1960 total.

The figure is given in the new rubles which took effect on January 1. The new ruble is worth 10 old ones, and the Russians officially claim that it is worth $1.11 American. It is doubtful that this ruble is less elastic than the old model.[1]

As always, the total budget is subdivided into five categories. The national economy gets 33.9 billion, or 44 percent, of the total. Earmarked for social and culture is 27.1 billion, 35 percent. State administration gets 1.1 billion, and 8 percent—6 billion—is contained in the secrecy-wrapped unspecified funds category.

Concealed spending: The Supreme Soviet allocated 9.3 billion to the military departments. However, total military assets include several other activities which must be accounted for. A case in point is the unspecified 6 billion administered by the Committee on State Security (KGB). Most experts say the money is expended to enforce internal adherence to the Politburo line, to subsidize illicit Communist activities in foreign countries, to buy friendly officials of uncommitted or neutral countries, and to maintain all forms of intelligence activities.

Appearing before the assembled Soviet delegates, Finance Minister Vasily Garbuzov said that 3.8 billion was available for scientific research, which encompasses rocket development. Russian secrecy being what it is, this amount, impressive though it is, may not represent the true total.

The 4-year growth in rocket research and development represents a 153 percent increase since their first space budget was adopted in 1958, 2 months after Sputnik I erupted in world headlines.

Russia can be expected to increase pressure on the United States and its free allies by means of space propaganda and development of large rocket vehicles and heavy payloads.

The Russians believe that their efforts to gain world supremacy are aided by achievements beyond the frontiers of space. Their budget commits them to follow their revolutionary course with all the weapons necessary to its attainment. To accomplish this, some sacrifices have apparently been forced on Russian citizens.

Consumer pressure: Discontent at the ward level was reflected in questions from the delegates. Both Garbuzov and Power Station Construction Minister Ignat Novikov promised the Soviet deputies prior to the budget's approval that electrical capacity would be augmented in 1961 by 7,800,000 kilowatts. They also promised to increase supplies of home repair materials, footwear, wines, confectionery goods, and chemical and electrical machinery.

It was announced that investments in principal industries would be increased as follows:

	1960 (percent)	*1961 (percent)*
Iron and steel	20.0	31.0
Chemical	30.0	42.0
Petroleum	15.0	16.0
Mechanical	30.0	40.0
Agricultural	11.0	12.8
Total investments	11.0	12.6

No itemized amounts were revealed, but overall industry received 15.6 billion, agriculture, 3.3 billion; local economies, 3.1 billion, and transport-communications-commerce, 9 billion. (Industrial self-financing is estimated at an additional 24 billion.)

Military outlay: There is no procurement of weapons or other war materials; therefore, no funds are allocated for this purpose.

[1] Prior to the close of 1960, the U.S.S.R. worked on a basis of 4 rubles equals $1. Since January 1, 1961, a new ruble has been created whose gold content gives a relation of 1 ruble equals $1.11.

However, the ruble does not have any practical use in trade outside the Soviet bloc countries, and the relationship may be regarded as artificial. To some extent, Soviet authorities recognize this fact; when the official rate was 4 equals $1, foreign tourists were paid at the rate of 10 equals $1.

Congressional Record reprint of author's article published on 23 January 1961.

CONGRESSIONAL RECORD — APPENDIX A876

Russia manufactures its own tools of war and buys from itself at any price it cares to establish for bookkeeping purposes. These paper adjustments, however, are considered support costs for weapons manufacture. Various analysts, comparing these costs to armament procurement, have set the value between 20 and 35 billion.

Social and culture contains a second military-type activity, in addition to rocket research. This is the physical education portion. Funds in this innocently entitled area supposedly support preinductee military training and home guard fitness programs. But some observers state categorically that the whole amount has a military character.

A conservative estimate of the minimum military category appears to be around 22 to 24.3 billion new rubles. Weapons support costs, 20 to 35 billion, should be added to this total. For purposes of comparison, the actual military effort appears to be between 42 and 59 billion:

Military effort:	1960	1961
Direct appropriation	9.4	9.3
Physical education	4.7	5.2
Scientific research	3.2	3.8
Espionage, etc	6.2	6.0
Total	23.5	24.3

GNP engima: The Russians have never admitted any figures for their gross national product, and speculation on their gross national product leaves much to be desired. An easy comparison between their military spending and gross national product is not readily available, as it is in free countries. There is no problem in determining, for example, that U.S. defense spending is less than one-tenth the gross national product.

The Russians are on record with at least one of the factors making up a gross national product total—industrial production. Industrial production figures should be hard or fixed once they have been determined, but the Russians' extravagant treatment of hard figures would baffle anyone. It is problematical whether a better analysis can be made of their industrial production claims than their nebulous budget categories.

In 1952 the Soviets claimed that their 1928 IP had been 10.5 percent of the U.S. IP and 32.7 percent in 1937. These Russian "hard" figures became hopelessly contradictory by 1957 and they were revised to 6.7 percent for 1928 and 24.7 percent for 1937.

However, in 1958 Khrushchev pulled the rug from under his statisticians by proclaiming that Soviet industrial production was pegged at half the U.S. effort. (According to the year-old 1957 revision, the 1958 IP should have been 72.8 percent.)

Naturally, the Soviet numbers jugglers reestablished their revision of supposedly hard historical figures to support Russia's latest spurious claim.

It is generally believed that the most believable IP figures were established by the Russians themselves in 1934, when their 1928 effort was described as a shade over 10 percent of the U.S. IP effort in 1928. Also, at least four analysts of Russian economics estimate the maximum average annual growth of Russian IP over the last 30 years as between 5.47 percent and 6.5 percent, basing their calculations on Khrushchev's claim.

Others often describe Russian's gross national product as half that of the United States. Therefore, their military spending would represent a greater percentage of total gross national product than the U.S. percentage of defense spending.

From the few perceivable rays of light penetrating the Russian smokescreen over their actual budget and economy, several conclusions are inescapable:

1. Russia commits a greater portion of its national wealth to financing military and cold war utensils than does any free country.

2. Russia is augmenting its annual investment in rocket research for space achievements and military potential.

3. There is evidence that satellite bloc countries support Soviet rocket production and development to a much greater degree than any comparable cooperation exists in the West.

4. There is no evidence of Communist redundancy of effort in rocket development—such as military versus "scientific"—or one Communist bloc country funding a rocket development while another pursues the same course.

5. Western plans designed only to match Soviet programs are insufficient. Programs should be implemented to surpass the Russian effort by material investments and increased mutual cooperation in utilizing vast Western resources in the development of rocket technology.

6. The annual Russian claim that their military spending has been decreased is nothing more than a subterfuge. They have annually increased military investments, international Communist programs and usurious foreign aid programs.

7. Russia has one goal—world supremacy which denies human rights. Space propaganda is one most useful tool to this end, despite the cost.

Official Soviet budget

[All figures in billions of new rubles]

Principal categories	1957	1958	1959	1960	1961
National economy	24.5	25.7	30.9	31.0	33.9
Social and culture	18.8	21.2	23.2	24.7	27.1
Armed forces	9.7	9.6	9.6	9.4	9.3
State administration	1.2	1.2	1.2	1.1	1.1
Unspecified (espionage)	6.2	5.0	5.9	6.2	6.0
National debt				.2	.2
Total budget	60.4	62.7	70.8	72.6	77.6

Page 2 of Congressional Record reprint of 23 January 1961 article by the author.

№ 955925

OCCUPATIONAL FORCE TRAVEL PERMIT
LAISSEZ-PASSER DES FORCES D'OCCUPATION
Пропуск для оккупационных войск

BERNARD WILFRED POIRIER
(Name, nom, имя и фамилия)

US Civ
(Rank, Grade, чин)

ppt# 433860
(Army No., Numéro Matricule, и удостоверения личность)

Tourist
(Organization, Unité ou Service, организация)

is authorized to travel from
est autorisé(e) à voyager de
имеет право ездить из
Salzburg, Austria

to
à
в
Vienna, Austria
and return.
et retour.
и обратно.

Restrictions or limitations if any
Restrictions ou limitations eventuelles
Имеются ли какие нибудь ограничения
via Enns

Bernard Wilfred Poirier
(Signature of Bearer, Signature du titulaire, подпись владельца)

Following World War II, the four occupation powers in Austria issued travel permits, known as "gray cards" for travel through the Soviet occupied zone, the only one requiring such controls. Americans applied to the "United States Forces, Austria" military post in Salzburg for one which was usually valid for one month. Soviet military authorities restricted Americans' entry via the Enns rail stop, near Linz. British citizens had to enter via Graz, and French citizens could enter via either Soviet gateway.

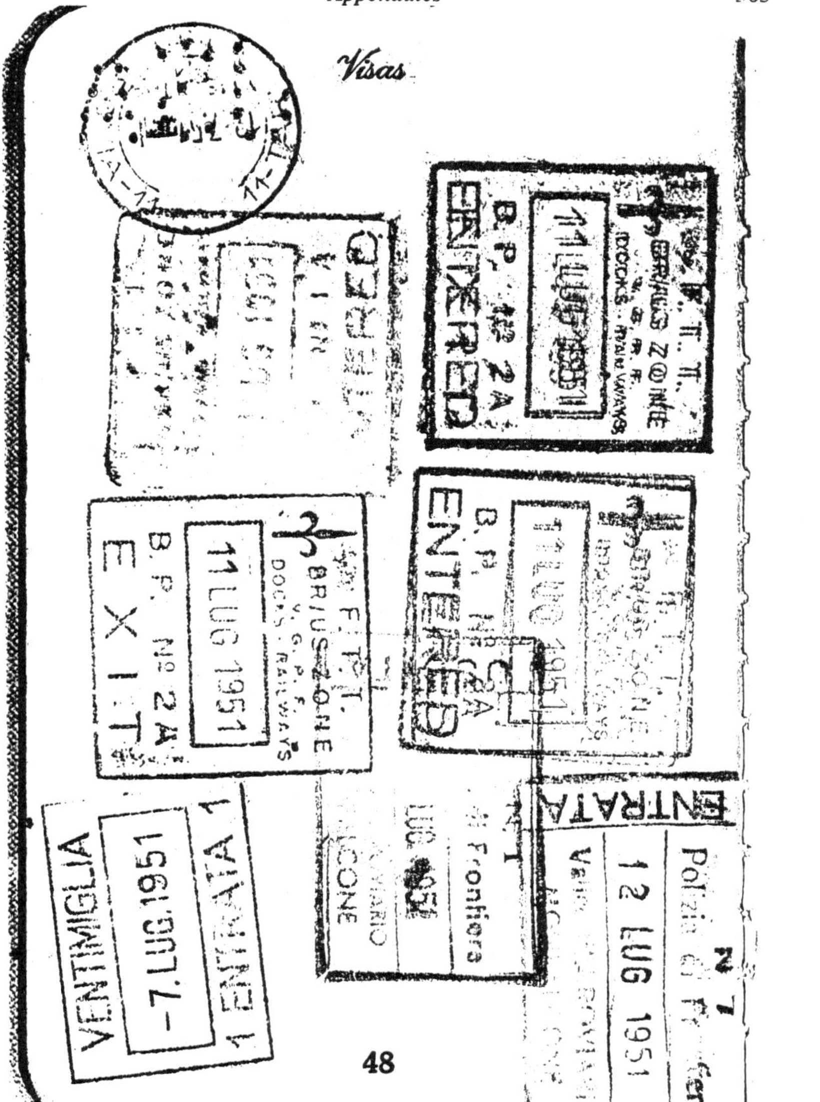

Multiple enter and exit stamps, some stamped one over another, demonstrated the stand-off between Yugoslavian soldiers and Italian guards during the Cold War. The issue was resolved by American and British soldiers (see chapter 23).

ISI THE INTERNATIONAL STATISTICAL INSTITUTE
L'INSTITUT INTERNATIONAL DE STATISTIQUE
32 SESSION 30/5-9/6 1960 TOKYO 17

MEASURING THE STATISTICAL INTERRELATIONSHIP OF ROCKET TECHNOLOGY AND CRYPTOGRAPHY

by

BERNARD W. POIRIER

Part 1. The Mean Length Formula.

Technological achievements in rocketry since 1944 have given rise to a new language field in science. This development is of critical precision and importance. It is natural, therefore, that the most difficult science of languages, that of statistical use of cryptography, is affected by this development.

Ordinarily, cryptography is considered to have one function—that of aiding military intelligence and national security. However, among other possibilities, cryptography can play a most important role in a space weather system which can pay for itself in a few years. This is a system consisting of several tele-satellites orbiting in space.

Up to the time of the launching of Sputnik I on October 4, 1957, it was generally agreed that letter frequencies corresponded to the order listed for each of the languages in Table 1 and Table 2 with the highest frequency listed first.

Table 1

DUTCH	e n i a r d t o g l s h r v m u w j c z b f p x y q
GERMAN	e n r i s t u d a h g l o c m b z f k w v p j q x y
SERBO-CROATIAN	a o i e s n j r t d u v p l k m g c z b h f q w y x
RUSSIAN	о а е н и р в т с л к д м б ы з х я у г й п ч ь ж ю ш щ э ф ц і ѣ ъ

Table 2

ENGLISH	e t o a n i r s h d l u f c m p y w g b v k x z q j
FRENCH	e a s n t i r u l o d c m p v f q g b h x j y z k w
ITALIAN	e a i o n l r t s c d p u m v g h f b q z j x k w y
SPANISH	e a o s n i r l d u c t m p b h q g v y j f z x k w
PORTUGUESE	a e o r s i n d m t u c l p q v f g h b j z k w y

May-June 1960 Scientific paper, "Measuring the statistical interrelationship of rocket technology and cryptography," for the 32nd session of the International Statistical Institute, Tokyo, Japan.

Firstly, consider that the new advances in rocket weapons are inversely affecting the importance of conventional weapons. As for the statistician's role in this science, we find that he is inseparable from the problems of decrypting regardless of the capacities of various electronic computers. Table 3 in this paper indicates that rocketry has provided new letter frequencies in most languages when the literature treats this subject. Old statistical relationships appear to be insufficient to meet the demands of these linguistic changes.

Table 3

Space Age Frequencies

ENGLISH	E 119,	T 93,	I 93,	R 87,	A 82,	S 78,	O 70,	N 59,	C 52,	L 52,
	U 33,	P 32,	D 25,	M 21,	G 19,	F 15,	H 13,	Y 12,	B 10,	K 10,
	V 6,	W 6,	J 5,	Q 3,	X 3,	Z 0-1.				
GERMAN	E 136,	R 95,	S 80,	U 69,	T 67,	N 64,	A 59,	I 53,	L 51,	F 49,
	G 46,	H 35,	O 35,	K 30,	C 28,	B 28,	D 21,	P 17,	W 16,	M 16,
	Z 9,	V 2,	J 1,	Q 1,	X 1,	Y 0-1.				
FRENCH	E 185,	I 84,	S 80,	A 80,	R 76,	T 68,	O 66,	N 60,	U 58,	L 47,
	P 34,	C 32,	D 29,	M 20,	F 19,	G 17,	B 12,	V 10,	Q 9,	H 8,
	J 3,	X 3,	Y 2,	K 1,	W 1,	Z 1.				

The frequencies in Table 3 exist in passages and descriptions pertaining to the new concepts in weapons and in rocket technology relating to space exploration.

An electronic computer cannot decide between a correct and an erroneous interpretation. Electronic computers, therefore, cannot provide the solutions required in this role as easily as a statistician who finds himself considering not only a particular language, but variations of meanings and usages within the same language and between authors. Many identical words ascribe different meanings in different nations and sometimes differences among different groups within the same nation. Words, phrases, whole concepts are borrowed, corrupted, and reused. The glossary which follows this paper lists many of the commonly used expressions as carried by magazines on rocket technology.

Short concise messages today provide an unusual frequency to certain letters when treating this subject, resulting in unrecognizable word lengths and their averages based on the unusual frequencies of several or all crypto-letters used. The main reason seems to be that technological advances in the concept of weapons systems taxed excessively the ability of scientific terminology to keep pace.

The word length formula

$$ML=\left(\frac{T}{\sum x_i}\right)^2 \frac{\sum_{i=1}^{N}(f_i)^2}{\sum_{i=1}^{N} f_{xi}}$$

based on prior samplings of *Mean Lengths* must stand careful statistical analysis and in some cases, it will be necessary to establish a correction. T equals the total *usable* letters in the originating language's alphabet, $\sum x_i$ equals the total number of crypto-symbols in the message, $\sum(f_i)^2$ equals the square of the frequency

— 2 —

Page 2 May-June 1960 Scientific paper, Tokyo.

of each crypto-letter or symbol having been totaled, Σf_{xi} equals the total of each individual instance of a different crypto-letter used in the cryptogram. The correction itself will depend on the amount of words borrowed from Russian origin or from American origin or both. We find that many key words are borrowed from one or both of these sources. The Russian influence is more pronounced in certain languages while the American (US) influence predominates in others.

Diagram 1

Average Word Length Chart to October 4, 1957

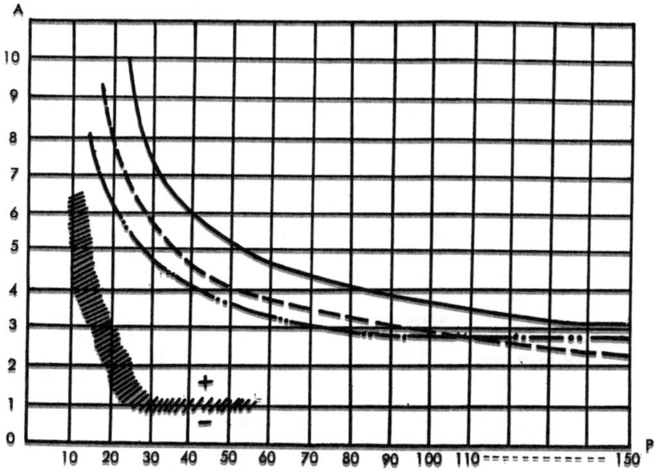

Symbol Designations for Diagram 1

P=Total crypto-letters in cryptogram

A=Average word length by languages

=Russian monoalphabet

=French monoalphabet

=English monoalphabet

=Polyalphabet

+=Russian poly....extremity

−=Others poly....extremity

Following are four examples of applicable cryptograms (possible since October 4, 1957) to the graphs in Diagram 1 (above) using the *ML* formula as explained on page 2 of this paper. Two of the cryptograms are on space age subjects using space age terminology, while the remaining two examples are on space age subjects using pre-1957 scientific terminology.

— 3 —

Page 3 May-June 1960 Scientific paper, Tokyo.

Example 1:

ZOMYY	NYFYA
OCXYY	FUHWY
YBCYL	YHUJI
AYYXY	LYWIH
HUCMM	UXWYT

$$ML=\left(\frac{T}{\Sigma x_i}\right)^2 \frac{\Sigma(f_i)^2}{\Sigma f_{xi}} \qquad ML=\left(\frac{26}{49}\right)^2 \frac{321}{16}$$

$ML=5.64+$ true $m=6.12$

Diagram 1 Graph (French)$=4.2\pm$

Key=COSMIC Type=Mono ---

Decrypted, the message reads "Fusée téléguidée lancée hier en apogée de reconnaissance".

The English translation is "Radio guided rocket launched yesterday with a reconnaissance apogee".

The word length result here through the *ML* formula exceeds the monoalphabet range for this type of message. The message itself has become possible only since October 4, 1957.

The second example uses the same type of terminology.

Example 2:

XGZBG	JGVTZ
TEWXY	LJVVK
JNTMK	VRIVR
VMBHG	ZFEZH
NXGNV	CVRZI
XYTBU	CVAOP

$$ML=\left(\frac{T}{\Sigma x_i}\right)^2 \frac{\Sigma(f_i)^2}{\Sigma f_{xi}} \qquad ML=\left(\frac{26}{57}\right)^2 \frac{231}{20}$$

$ML=2.40+$ true $m=6.33+$

Diagram 1 Graph (French)$=$ $.9\leqslant x\leqslant 1.1$

Key=WELCOME ; ASTRONAUT Type=Poly ---

Decrypted, the message reads "Engin spécial de fusée TquatreA réaction ionique nucléaire faible".

The English translation is "Small nuclear explosion series rocket engine for Tfour A (T-4A) missille".

The *ML* result 2.4 indicates an extreme range monoalphabet cryptogram originating in Serbo-Croatian (not shown in Diagram 1). The reading is a bit out of range for any polyalphabet message although it is such a message. This cryptogram would not have been feasible prior to October 4, 1957.

Example 3:

ыеюан	юаохю
iвфот	шъоюр
шоцзщ	аншкр
щяыеш	фщофш
каошф	чцкию
юхещо	шедфт

— 4 —

Page 4 May-June 1960 Scientific paper, Tokyo.

$$ML=\left(\frac{T}{\Sigma x_i}\right)^2\frac{\Sigma(f_i)^2}{\Sigma f_{xi}} \qquad ML=\left(\frac{34}{60}\right)^2\frac{248}{22}$$

$ML=3.61$ true $m=7.5$

Diagram 1 Graph (Russian)=4.8

Key=октября Type=Mono — —

The message as decrypted reads "плоскость орбнты автоматическая межпланетная станция до обьлета лунві". (Translation same as Ex. 4)

In this cryptogram, the key was applied to the order of frequency as listed in Table 1, page 1, instead of to the normal Russian alphabet. While there are 34 letters in the Russian alphabet, here we use 32 since the letter з is found only in words whose origin is foreign to the Russian language and the letter ѣ is very rare. This *ML* result is below the normal reading for a message of 60 symbols or letters as provided in Diagram 1 on page 3, but it still is within the monoalphabetic range for a message utilizing pre-war scientific terminology.

Example 4:

IETGW	XETMK
TCXVM	HBKXW
XETLM	TMBHG
BGMXK	IETGX
MTBKX	TNMHF
TMBJN	XTOTG
MJNBE	TBMTI
IKHVA	XETEN
GXABC	DEFGH

$$ML=\left(\frac{T}{\Sigma x_i}\right)^2\frac{\Sigma(f_i)^2}{\Sigma f_{xi}} \qquad ML=\left(\frac{26}{82}\right)^2\frac{616}{18}$$

$ML=3.4+$ true $m=5.5\pm$

Diagram 1 Graph (French)=3.3

Key=SPUTNIK Type=Mono — —

Decrypted, the message reads "Plan de la trajectoire de la station interplanétaire automatique (MAS) avant qu'il ait approché la lune".

The English translation for both examples 3 and 4 is "The planned trajectory of the automatic interplanetary station (Lunik III) before it approached the moon". This is a space age message with pre-war terminology.

Part 2. Quick Sampling Technique.

There is a simple quick sampling formula for testing what may appear to be new "subject frequencies".

This quick sampling formula is expressed as:

$$\left[\frac{R_1}{F_1}=S_1,\ \frac{R_2}{F_2}=S_2,\ \frac{R_3}{F_3}=S_3,\ \cdots\cdots,\ \frac{R_N}{F_N}=S_N\right]$$

$$\sum_{i=1}^{N} S_i(100) \doteqdot \sum_{i=1}^{N} \bar{D}_{Ia}+\bar{D}_{IIa}+\cdots\cdots+\bar{D}_{Na}$$

— 5 —

Page 5 May-June 1960 Scientific paper, Tokyo.

In this quick sampling formula, R equals the frequency of an individual letter in a sample paragraph, F equals the total amount of letters in the entire sample paragraph, $\bar{D}$ equals the mean frequency per thousand letters of the same letter as R_i as previously found, and a equals (the assurance that the comparison is applied to letters in the same language).

When the crypto-statistician first comes upon a subject matter which appears to offer a new structure to his recorded frequency tables, he may conduct a quick sampling technique in order to determine the probability whether a more thorough examination is warranted.

Example of Procedure :

(The Italian passages which follow appeared in *Rivista Aeronautica-Astronautica-Missilistica*, Dec., 1959)

"Un progetto di veicolo spaziale propulso ad energia atomica, studiato dai tecnici della Lockheed. L'insieme dovrebbe essere inviato nello spazio spinto da normali razzi ad energia chimica..."

This brief passage indicates abnormal frequencies for a number of letters ; such as, an abnormally high reading for "*i*" in relation to the percentage of the top five letters, and the abnormally low readings for some others, like "*c*", "*u*", "*p*" and "*g*".

A second passage in this same magazine source reads as follows:

"L'Esercito è interessato, dal punto di vista militare, a determinare il genere di atmosfera in cui opereranno i missili balistici intercontinentali e gli anti-ICBM".

Here again is an abnormally high reading for "*i*", and also for "*t*" and "*n*". Yet the usual top four frequencies in Italian are E 130, I 110, A 100, and O 80.(+ −).

In the second passage "*i*" is read 24 times and its sample frequency here is c. 18.

$$\frac{R_1}{F_1}=S_1,\quad S_1=17.7,\quad \bar{D}_{Ia}=11$$

Combining the "*i*" frequency for both passages=c. 15.

The frequency distortions would hold true whether S_n included a series of the highest five or ten or a random selection of three high frequencies and three medium frequencies, et cetera.

In French the usual frequency for "*e*" approximates 170, but in rocketry terminology since October, 1957, "*e*" approximates 185. Differences in other frequencies with the new frequency stated second are "*a*" 97–80, "*r*" 65–76, "*L*" 60–47.

The crypto-statistician will find many interesting developments in the examination of this quick sampling technique in literature treating rocket technology and new weapons systems.

Part 3. Space Weather System through Cryptographic Statistical Safeguards.

Let us consider a peaceful utilization of statistical cryptography. This would be realized by employing internationally accepted cryptographic symbols in the use of weather *tele-satellites* permanently placed in orbit. If in an equatorial orbit, they would be placed at a sufficient altitude to appear stationary over a given point on earth while traveling at the proper velocity. The tele-satellites would be positioned over the most universally recognized breeding areas of natural storms. Diagram 2 gives such an illustration for an equatorial orbit. Details of a polar orbit will be described below.

Diagram 2

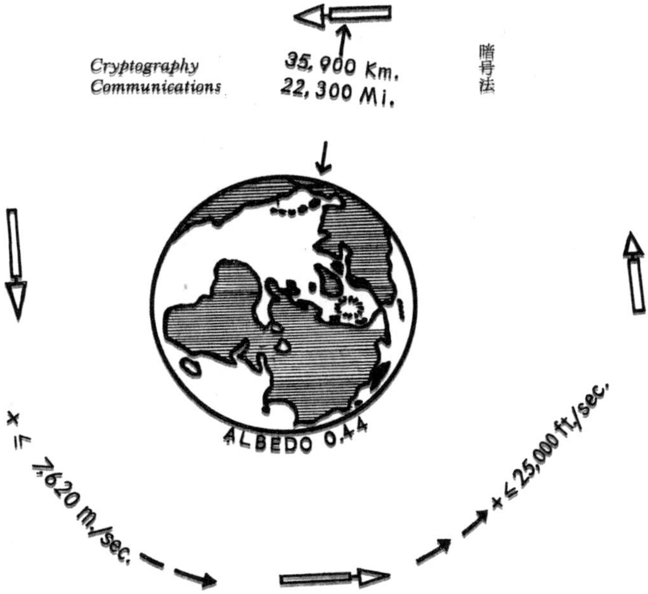

A satellite in Polar orbit would not appear to be fixed to a space location perpendicular to a given point on earth as could a satellite in a proper equatorial orbit. However, seven vehicles following each other in a polar orbit by approximately twenty-four hours at the same altitude and launched so as their initial orbit would be along a common meridian could be useful. Having an altitude similar to that proposed for an equatorial orbit but having a somewhat higher velocity would keep at least one satellite in range of a major earth weather station frequently enough to provide important data.

The satellite body would contain at least a cross sectional albedo reading electronic detector which upon a given signal would read data by cross sectional readings. These readings would correspond with the three dimensional readings made possible by telephoto apparatus installed at both ends of the satellite body. This space system, if in an equatorial orbit, could employ four satellites in orbits

Page 7 May-June 1960 Scientific paper, Tokyo.

of 35.900 km. apogees with a minimum of 1° deviation and with proper velocities adjusted for distance to increase the orbital velocity of 7.620 meters per second. The proper speed and height would make each satellite appear stationary within line of sight of a mother ground station. An illustration of such a tele-satellite for a space weather system is provided in diagram 3 of this paper.

As a permanent power supply and optical aide for tracking, the satellite would have a Venetian Silicon Screen to be released into position by a small harnessed steer-jet type capsule. The capsule would be triggered once the satellite is separated from the nose cone beyond the earth's atmophere.

Relatively little thrust would be necessary to extend and unfold the venetian-styled silicon screen to its full length behind the satellite body. The silicon strips or wafers would be exposed to sunlight regardless of the screen's horizontal position. A double tow line of course would guaranty its relationship with the satellite.

Diagram 3

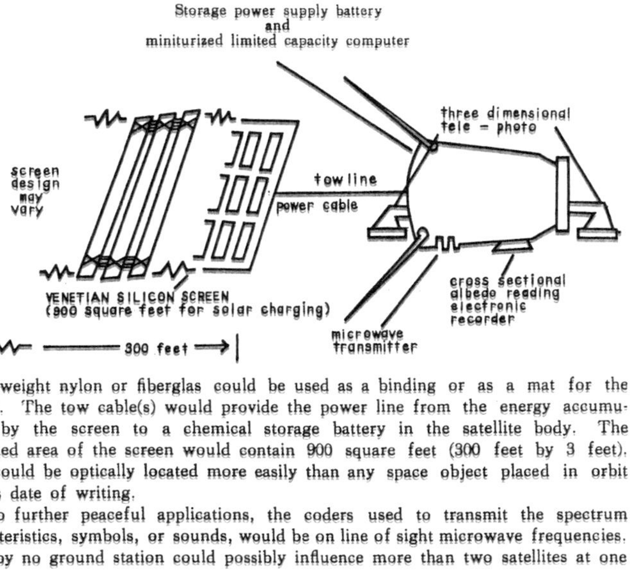

Light weight nylon or fiberglas could be used as a binding or as a mat for the screen. The tow cable(s) would provide the power line from the energy accumulated by the screen to a chemical storage battery in the satellite body. The extended area of the screen would contain 900 square feet (300 feet by 3 feet). This could be optically located more easily than any space object placed in orbit to this date of writing.

To further peaceful applications, the coders used to transmit the spectrum characteristics, symbols, or sounds, would be on line of sight microwave frequencies. Thereby no ground station could possibly influence more than two satellites at one time.

Inspection teams would monitor the manufacture of the satellite parts. No special or secret capacity could be built into the agreed upon electronic reading or transmission systems. The programming of the computing and transmitting systems would then fall within the statistical limitations of cryptography. Any nation

— 8 —

Page 8 May-June 1960 Scientific paper, Tokyo.

within the field of view of the satellite would also be in line of sight of the space vehicle. Since only microwaves would beused, any affected nation could monitor the transmissions. An illogical reply by the satellite could easily be decrypted by a statistician since the possible variations would have been limited through the monitoring during the manufacture of the satellite.

Here, complex computers could solve transmissions more rapidly than a human. But the machine's inability to make judgments assures the statistician's role in utilizing fully the peaceful applications of a space weather system.

The design of such a tele-satellite as outlined briefly in Diagram 3 does not preclude facilities for the surveillance of solar disturbances, cosmic eruptions, et cetera.

An equatorial orbit or a polar orbit could be utilized for such a system. A polar orbit initiated along the 80°W and 100°E meridians, for example, or an equatorial orbit would be desirable. For either type orbit, major ground stations might be located in Japan, United States, Australia, and Chile. An equatorial orbit might include ground stations in India and in Hawaii. More stations could be utilized for a polar orbit and most certainly might include Russia, Colombia, and Sweden. The latter orbit would be preferable if polar readings are desired while the former would be appreciably more beneficial constantly to the greatest number of people.

Protection of property, planting and harvesting of crops, air and sea transportation are among the things which would be aided by this system.

A space weather system, controlled, monitored, and with its accuracy guaranteed by means of statistics would save countless lives and millions of dollars now lost yearly to the ravages of storms.

Glossary*

Anti-aircraft weapon
Flugzeugabwehrwaffe; Arme de défense antiaérienne; Arma antaérea; Arma antiaerea (a/a), contraerea (s/s).

Air-to-air missile
Luft-luft flugkörper, luft-luft geschosse; air-air fusée; Aire-Aire proyectil; Missile aria-aria; Air-to-air missile weapon.

Air-to-surface missile
Luft-boden flugkörper, Luft-boden geschosse; Air-sol fusée, Air-surface (eau) fusée; Aire-tierra proyectil; Missile aria-superficie; Air-to-surface missile weapon.

Air-to-underwater missile
Luft-unterwasser flugkörper, luft-unterwasser geschosse; Air-sous surface fusée, air-sous mer fusée; Aire-debajo-agua proyectil; Missile aria-subacqua; Air-to-underwater missile weapon.

Anti-tank
Panzerbekämpfungs; Anti-chars; Anti-tanque; Anti-carro.

Anti-missile defense system
Flugkörper-abwehrsystem; Système de défense anti-engins; Sistema de ingenio anti-proyectil; Sistema de anti-missile; Anti-missile defence system.

* Glossary contains expressions commonly found in each language in newspapers and magazines and does not represent the best translation. American followed by German, French, Spanish, Italian, and British, when different.

— 9 —

Page 9 May-June 1960 Scientific paper, Tokyo.

Apogee
Erdferne, apogäum; Apogée; Apogee; Apogeo.
Ascent
Aufstieg; Ascension; Subida, ascensión; Ascensione.
Astrobiology *(space medecine)*
Astrobiologie (Raummedizin); Astrobiologie (medecine spatial); Astrobiólogico (medicina espacial); astrobiologia (biologia razzonautica).
Astronaut
Astronaut, Astronaut; Astronauta; Astronaute; Spaceman.
Astronaut's quarters
Pilotenkabine; Habitacle du capsule; Cabina tripulada; Navicella, abitacollo; Spaceman's quarters.
Ballistic trajectory
Flugbahn ballistisch; Trajectoire balistique; Trajectoria balística; Traiettoria balistica.
Blast off
Zündung; Décollage, riposte; Desató; Decollo, fase.
Booster rocket
Starthilfsrakete; Fusée d'accélération; Cohete-auxiliare, motore auxiliare; Razzo ausiliare.
Bumper
Schutz-schild; Blindage; Blindaje; Traboccante.
Burnout velocity
Brennsschluss-geschwindigkeit; Vitesse au moment d'arrêt de combustion; Velocidad cerrando; Velocità scarica.
Brake Rocket (retro-rocket)
Bremsrakete; Rétro-fusée, fusée-frein; Retrocohete; Retrorazzo.
Ceiling
Giphelhohe; Plafond; Techo; Plafond; , —, Height attainable.
Cluster
Bundel; Grappe; Grupos; Gruppo, groppo; , —, bundle.
Development
Weiterentwicklung; Développement; Desarrollo; Sviluppo.
Escape velocity
Kreisbahngeschwindigkeit; Vitesse dite de libération; Velocidad de escape; Velocità di scampo; , —, (orbital velocity).
Experimental rocket
Versuchsflugkörper; Fusée expérimentale; engin expérimentale; Cohete experimental; Razzo sperimentale.
Firing
Abwurf; Tir; Tiro; Tiro.
First stage
Erste stufe; Première étage; Primera etapa; Primo stadio.
Flight
Fluge; Vol; Vuelo; Volo.
Flight duration
Flugdauer; Temps du trajet; Duración de vuelo; Durata di volo; , —, flight life.
Guidance
Lenkung, Zieldarstellung; Guidage; Gobierno; Guida.
Infrared surveillance
Infrarot-erkundung; Surveillance infrarouge; Reconocimiento infrarrojo; Ricognizione infrarossi.
Initial thrust
Startgewichtschub; Poussée brute; Empuje inicial; Spinta iniziale.

— 10 —

Page 10 May-June Glossary in scientific paper, Tokyo.

Intercontinental Ballistic Missile
Ballistischer langstrecken-flugkörper; Engin balistique intercontinental; Proyectile balístico intercontinental; Missile balistico intercontinentale.

Launching tower
Startgestell; Tour de lancement; Torre de lanzamiento; Torre di lancio.

Liquid Hydrogen
Flüssiger Wasserstoff; Hydrogène liquide; Hídrogeno líquido; Idrogeno liquido.

Liquid Oxygen
Flüssiger Sauerstoff; Oxygène liquide; Oxígeno líquido; Ossigeno liquido.

Liquid propellent
Flüssigtriebwerke; Propergol liquide; Propulsado líquido; Propellenti liquidi.

Manned
Bemannter; Habité; Tripulado; Umana (...all'Uomo).

Mental Reaction
Geistige reaktion; Réaction mental; Reaccion anímico; Reazione mentale.

Missile
Flugkörper, geschosse, (Swiss: lenkwaffe); Fusée, Engin; Proyectil; Missile;, —, missile weapon.

Missile range
Versuchsgelände; Champs de tir; Campo de lanzamiento; de proyectil, (polígono de proyectiles); Campo missilistico;, —, Long Range Weapons Testing Range.

Nickname
Deckname; Sobriquet; Se denominó; Denominato.

Nuclear propulsion
Atomarem antrieb; Propulsion atomique; Propulsión nuclear; Propulsori nucleari (propulsione atomica).

Orbit
Umlaufbahn; Orbite; Órbita; Orbita.

Payload rocket
Trägerrakete; Fusée Porteuse; Proyectile portador; Razzo vettore di lancio.

Physical reaction
Körperliche reaktion; Réaction physique; Reacción físico; Reazione fisico.

Race into Space
Kampf um den Weltraum, (Eroberung des Raumes einen Wettlauf); Course à l'espace; Carrera espacial; Curso in spazio.

Radiation
Ausstrahlung; Radiation; Radiación Radiazione.

Range
Reichweite; Portée, rayon d'action; Alcance; Gittata, portata, raggio d'azione.

Reconnaissance satellite
Satellit aufklärungs; Satellite de reconnaissance; Satélite de reconocimiento; Satellite per ricognizione;, —, Reconnaissance artificial earth-satellite.

Recovery
Erde zurückkehren; Récupération; Recuperación; Ricupero.

Ship-to-ship missile
Schiff-schiff flugkörper, Schiff-schiff geschosse; Navire-navire fusée; Proyectil navió-navió; Missile nave-nave; Ship-to-ship missile weapon.

Small nuclear explosion series rocket
Kleinatomistisch-explosion Reiherakete; Engin special à réaction ionique nucléaire faible; Motor-cohete de iónico pequeño nuclear; Razzo a ioni di minuti propulsori nucleari;, —, (nuclear ion rocket).

Solid propellent
Feststoff; Propergol solide; Propulsante sólido; Carburanti solidi, propellenti solidi.

—11—

Page 11 May-June Glossary in scientific paper, Tokyo.

Space capsule
Raumkapsel; Satellite-capsule; Cápsula espacial; Capsula spaziale.
Space probe
Flugerprobung; Exploration de l'espace; Mision extraterrestre; Velvivolo spaziale; , —, escape mission.
Space research plans
Raumforshungsplanes; Programmes de recherches spatiales; Proyectos de desarrollo espacial; Progetti di ricercatori spazoali.
Space ship (Space vehicle)
Raumfahrzeuge; Véhicule spatial, véhicule de l'espace; Espacionave, astronave, vehiculo astronáutico; Nave spaziale, veicolo spaziale; , —, spaceship.
Spent
Ausbrennen; d'arrêt de combustion; Consumiando; Acarico.
Stage separation
Stufentrennung; Séparation d'étages; Desprendendo; Separazione degli stadi.
Static ground test
Raketenprüf-statischer; Essais statique; Ensayo estático; Prova statica al suolo.
Steering jet rocket
Steuerrakete; Gouverne de jet; Cohete-gobierno, (volante líquido); Razzo di correzione.
Surface-to-air missile
Boden-luft flugkörper, boden-luft geschosse; Sol (terre)-air fusée, surface (eau)-air fusée; Proyectil superficie-aire; Missile superficie-aria; Surface-to-air missile weapon.
Symbol designation
Schlüssel-bezeichnungen; Sigle correspondant; de designación; Sigle usate.
Thrust
Schub; Poussée; Empuje; Spinta.
Unmanned
Unbemannter; Inhabité; No tripulado; Disabitato.

The Mean Length Chart in Diagram 1 of this paper was adapted from information contained in General Luigi Sacco's "Manuale de Crittografia".

The terminology contained in pages 9 to 12 was selected from a more complete glossary originally prepared by the paper's author for the weekly American magazine of World Astronautics "Missiles and Rockets", published by American Aviation Publications, Inc., Washington, D.C.

RÉSUMÉ

Ce Papier présente l'interrélation statistique entre la technologie des fusées/engins et la cryptographie.

Ici, on considère la cryptographie comme la science historique des messages militaires au moyen d'abréviations convenues entre deux personnes et deuxièmement comme une nouvelle science statistique pour garantir l'usage ou l'emploi des signaux permettants de transmettre de l'espace les renseignements metéorologiques à une station terrestre.

— 12 —

Page 12 May-June End of Glossary in scientific paper, Tokyo.

La technologie évoluée par le progrès des fusées/engins dans l'armement des pays et dans la course en l'espace a donné une nouvelle importance aux armes non-conventionnelles. En conséquence, les cryptogrammes de forme historique ne suivent plus les formules traditionnelles quand elles se forment de mots ignorés avant le lancement de Spoutnik en Octobre, 1957. Ce Papier contient, par exemple, trois cryptogrammes d'origine française et une d'origine russe. Leurs frequences (de cryptolettres) peuvent être comparer à la table de Gén. Luigi Sacco empruntée de son "Manuale de Crittografia" par la formule

$$ML=\left(\frac{T}{\Sigma x_i}\right)^2 \frac{\Sigma(f_i)^2}{\Sigma f_{xi}}.$$

La troisième partie du Papier explique la manière d'employer une système pacifique de cryptographie dans les "satellites d'observations metéorologiques". Il y a autant de pays qui trouveront un grand secours des observations des phénomènes atmosphériques qu'il y a de pays qui se douteront des intentions pacifiques de telles satellites sans une garantie absolue contre leur emploi comme "espion espacial".

Comme remède ylang-ylangeux pour ces administrateurs soupçonneux, on offre ici les garanties nécessaires...une par la fabrication contrôlée des éléments qui formeront les systèmes principales de chaque satellite sous un plan international, l'autre par les garanties statistiques pour remettre les signaux cryptographiques de commande aux satellites et de leurs reponses.

Les illustrations qui proposent les "abat-solaire-Vénitiens" comme sources d'énergie électrique et la forme générale des satellites sont originales de l'auteur.

Une glossaire termine le Papier. Il contient des mots et des termes du sujet des fusées et de l'espace comme on en sert dans les journaux et revues en Américain, Allemand, Français, Espagñol, Italien, et Anglais.

Errata:

Table 1, Page 1: (Russian). Strike out the second to last letter: b
Table 3, Page 2: (French). U 53
(German). C 23, B 23

Glossary, Page 9: (Anti-aircraft weapon)

contraerea (s/a)

Author's professional address:

Navy Comptroller's Office
Navy Department
Pentagon
Washington 25, D. C.

Page 13 May-June Errata of scientific paper, Tokyo.

NATO's FIFTEEN NATIONS

VOLUME 7
NUMBER 3

JUNE - JULY, 1962

LIGHTNING ROD IN THE SEA

by

BERNARD W. POIRIER

Reprinted for Special Projects Office with permission of NATO'S FIFTEEN NATIONS

(Original article appeared in the June-July issue of that magazine)

U.S. Navy Reprint Cover. June-July 1962 "Lightning Rod in the Sea" in *NATO's Fifteen Nations*, Volume 7, Number 3, Amsterdam, Netherlands. Published with the permission of Mönch Publishing Group, Bonn, Germany.

Lead page of author's article in "NATO's Fifteen Nations," June-July 1962.

◁ *One of the most dramatic photos among the hundreds that have been taken of Polaris and up to this moment the only one of this kind that has been made available for publication: a 2,500 kilometer range Polaris A2 is launched from the missile test ship "Observation Island", EAG 154. This surface ship has two launching tubes and was the first ocean going vessel to fire Polaris missiles. It operates out of Cape Canaveral, Florida. The next generation Polaris (A3) will have a 4,000 kilometer range*

The opinions or assertions in the article are the personal views of the author and are not te be construed as the views of the United States Navy or the United States Defense Department.

Political accord among several sovereign States is sometimes difficult to crystallize, even with the best of intentions among all participants or even when they have historic bonds of intimate association. An international agreement requiring a knowledgeable interpretation of military posture, scientific state of art, and weapons design hardly benefits from easily derived solutions.

One paramount political-military issue faced by NATO concerns a multinational nuclear force to strengthen the military defenses of NATO Eurasia and for additional nuclear stability in the more critical areas of the spectrum of conflict where an aggressor may miscalculate the sincerity of the United States' pledge to defend its allies.

NATO Secretary-General Dirk U. Stikker recently admonished those who recoil from considering ramifications of nuclear war because the subject was "nightmarish".

BERNARD W. POIRIER

Coordinator for Foreign Programs, Special Projects Office, Dept. of the Navy, Washington, D.C.

IN THE SEA

In some circles, however, the measure of acceptability of nuclear attack by any nation has been continually debated – seemingly moreso after the subject was demorphiated by Herman Kahn. But for a political resolution in NATO which would assume a new and wider scope of military preparedness, all factors of warfare affecting national destinies must be considered, and it is upon a foundation of several military and scientific factors that a political solution can be built.

One such factor is that a nuclear bomb publicly described as having a yield of between 13 kilotons and 20 kilotons killed about 100,000 people outright and destroyed 63,000 out of 90,000 buildings in the urban area of Hiroshima. Of the total population of perhaps more than 300,000, another 30 % was seriously injured. Russia has only about thirty cities of equal or more population than pre-war Hiroshima. Major retaliation, or even limited residue retaliation, is hardly acceptable to the Soviets as the price for unstabilizing NATO Eurasia.

A case of empirical building blocks does not appear necessary here to substantiate the axiom that an aggressor planning a surprise attack will select a plan which would best neutralize or eradicate the enemy's capacity to defend or to counter-attack. A defender with the means to do so, and with a national policy of non-aggression, has the obligation therefore to credibly exhibit a capacity to survive maximum aggression and to accurately deliver an unacceptable blow in retaliation. The same obligation is attributable perhaps to an Alliance of nations in which each member is equally subjected to outside threats against valued unregimented freedoms.

Stability over the area forming the bulwark of Western

Page 1 of author's article in "NATO's Fifteen Nations," from July 1962.

U.S. NAVY PHOTO

Ready for countdown. Polaris crewmen monitor panels in missile compartment (second level) as they await signal to commence "count" for launching Polaris missiles

(Author's note: Early in the Polaris Program this area of the weapon system became known as "Sherwood Forest". Not everyone agrees on the origin: whether it was because the 16 tubes were the closest thing to vegetation to be seen for several months at a time or, more analytically, because for the crew, like Robin Hood, it is safe to be hidden in Sherwood Forest.)

civilization is a necessary goal if extension of personal freedoms and effective constructive programs are to radiate from the North Atlantic core. In this time period, one major tool in a program of stability is the deterrent. The political significance of the deterrent is that it will or should impede an unstabilizing event such as armed aggression whether in the form of unlimited war or a single nibbling "fait accompli" type of aggression. This impediment becomes a hindrance to an aggressor. If the impediment does not in effect deter him, the aggressor may still elect to react by planning military aggression if his political or paramilitary actions have failed.

A QUESTION OF CHOICE

Confronting the Western policy maker, then, are several shapes to the tools he might choose. Military factors as well as political and economic ones will help determine the mold from which the tool or deterrent will emerge. Deterrents with known locations are prime targets to any potential aggressor, and assuming his attack would include missiles at one stage or another of the conflict and the target is a missile site, the harder the target (reinforced concrete silos, etc.), the more missiles or larger warheads the aggressor may be called upon to use. If the target has restricted inland mobility, the aggressor may select to use as many missiles as required to saturate areas of the weapon's movement based on latest intelligence reports.

Thus, from a defending missile site is born a nuclear lightning rod along which the weight of an attack will be funneled. Hardened sites will capitalize on factors of invulnerability so long as the aggressor remains ignorant of the locations or has no capability or desire to increase his accuracy or the yield of his warheads. In any event, the hardened site whose location is accurately known will only increase an aggressor's investment in either the number of missiles or the size of warheads. Such a disadvantage exists for any deterrent where the means exist to detect it and where blunting fire will be attracted.

This cycle can continue: greater hardening of sites with known locations followed by greater yield. Concealment increases the value of hardened sites by at least several orders of magnitude, and the number of missiles required to destroy it then theoretically approaches infinity. Concealment here is the great advantage; it must be scrupulously adhered to. Immunity from enemy intelligence is essential. Examples of two other alternatives are limited (restricted) mobility and indiscernible (random) mobility — modes which compound the difficulty of an aggressor in terms of investment, technology, intelligence and operations.

Mobility becomes harnessed or constrained when restricted to movements which reflect a decipherable pattern. A perfectly adequate weapons design from a military point of view may be completely unacceptable, however, to the policy maker. Systems designed to support theatre commanders for

Page 2 of author's article in "NATO's Fifteen Nations," from July 1962.

continued

Missile canister is lowered into place over the hull of the USS "George Washington", SSBN-598, Fleet Ballistic Missile Submarine, at a Navy Pier in Charleston, South Carolina

U.S. NAVY PHOTO

field operations are clearly desirable, but certain strategic concepts could suffer from inherent and restricted operations since one can presume weaponized units would be isolated from densely populated areas where collateral damage from blunting fire is undesirable or where intelligence agents might record movements more easily. Moreover, a land system is confined to avenues of traffic which can accommodate weaponized units by reason of weight limitations, physical measurements or even local politics.

If, for example, mobile systems were introduced into Western Europe, unrestricted mobility is unlikely and, when compared with sea-based mobility, the security and logistics problems could present difficult problems in system survival. This becomes particularly significant in matters of security, accidental interference and rolling logistics support. Gambling on reasonable statistical probability that sufficient targets will be destroyed, an aggressor could adopt a plan calling for calculated saturation of areas within known patterns of landlocked operations.

The defenders would most probably retain a residue of surviving units to assure some retaliation, but survivability much beyond the period of early response is questionable. Limited response, nonetheless, may be unacceptable to the aggressor and, for the defender, a saturation strike would probably envelop some populated centers even if the first strike was relatively limited.

THE PROBLEM OF SECRECY

Concealment of hardened sites espouses the advantages of sparsely settled areas where exact locations can remain unknown and where construction might remain undetected from observation aircraft or unreported to an enemy by a member of the local labor force. Such secrecy is truly difficult, if not impossible, to achieve in highly populated areas. Once known, such deterrents could be eradicated with sufficient ballistic accuracy and adequate warhead yields. Where incoming ballistic flight time and warning time is short, particularly over Europe, the efficient recourse for a mobile strategic land based deterrent is to "go", to launch the missiles before absorbing the attack. Any system requiring almost instant readiness requires quick and positive detection, perfect identification and snap political judgment. The whole system demands certification of an armed attack and a communicated declaration of nuclear war within ten minutes. Although such readiness might be supported by the technical state-of-art, the command concept is both unacceptable and unrealistic in societies which insist on deliberate judgment as criteria of political leadership.

If a ballistic missile attack was initiated from Western Russia against hardened or mobile sites in Western Europe, a 1,500 mile range missile armed with a large yield warhead would need only moderate accuracy to be effective. Accurately delivered strikes (based on short intelligence-cycled

Page 3 of author's article in "NATO's Fifteen Nations," from July 1962.

enemy intelligence) would be adequate to destroy or incapacitate mobile units. Larger yields would be required against hardened sites.

In this connection a graphic analysis by Pierre Gallois in "*L'Avenir de l'Alliance Atlantique*" analogized recent papers which attempt to determine the identity of optimum system concepts and the selection of best conditions to force the greatest investment upon a potential war planner. Through an omission in the analysis, however, restricted mobility appears equated to true random mobility. On the other hand, an understatement of ballistic accuracy tends to augment the number of missiles required in the aggressor's inventory.

Gallois' important contribution, that of a study of invulnerability and of investment, is a step in determining that a deterrent should not have its survivability left to the discretion of an enemy who "might" elect to accept retaliation by refusing an adequate investment where the end values are reasonably known.

It has been suggested that five properly placed one-megaton warheads can destroy a city the size of Moscow as completely as (if not more thoroughly than) a single twenty-megaton-bomb.

So should NATO's lightning rod be designed to absorb high yield warheads or scattered saturation of smaller yield warheads?

DOES THE DETERRENT STILL DETER?

History has shown how the United States nuclear deterrent has shielded Europe. The question of this deterrent maintaining this role has been more debated than doubted. The preoccupation of NATO allies on this subject appears often concerned in the press with what the Soviets may believe rather than what they themselves believe.

Let us assume that stability is threatened if the United States deterrent capability is not credible in certain exchanges, and that a NATO deterrent is desirable at least to prevent miscalculation on the part of the Soviets. That is to say, if both the United States deterrent and a separate NATO deterrent are pledged to the defense of NATO Eurasia, it would be clear to potential aggressors that most likely both, but at least one, would retaliate. If this concept better buttresses stability, then the United States investment

At sea aboard the USS "Theodore Roosevelt" Lieut. R. E. Arrison and Chief Torpedoman Perry, monitor communications in missile compartment

NAVY PHOTO

Page 4 of author's article in "NATO's Fifteen Nations," June-July 1962. Original page numbers are correct and represent reprint-omissions of two pages of display advertising.

continued

Polaris Test Vehicle carrying instrumentation package in nose cone (March 1, 1962, Cape Canaveral)

U.S. AIR FORCE PHOTO

is well worth the investment of sharing in a NATO nuclear force. The United States commitment to collective NATO defense would be no greater and no less than today's pledge, and the question of trading Chicago for Copenhagen would become just more empty.

Both the Eisenhower and Kennedy Administrations have offered nuclear force possibilities to the Alliance. The most recent affirmation was by McGeorge Bundy of the President's White House staff in a December speech citing POLARIS submarines and a multinational sea-based missile force. (Confirmed again at the Athens NATO meeting in May-Ed.).

A basic issue before NATO is whether each member is willing, on nuclear matters, to share a degree of national destiny with one another in a workable manner, and by so doing, create a NATO nuclear force which clearly no combination of European investment can independently produce in the same time period. Once political agreements are effected, operational frameworks can then be incorporated under multinational command.

The political-military question of command and control is a related basic issue. It was called without solution in early reports, but solution and intention are not the same and if NATO intends as a group to acquire this capability then a solution within workable parameters could become more apparent and would encompass at least this premise: that the weapons system design shall have the military ability to respond to multinational political authority.

Member States might have several legal problems to resolve: the character and scope of a "North Atlantic Treaty Nuclear Structure", independent facilities and so forth. In any event, agreement of criteria would probably include that the system be politically wieldable and militarily flexible (this includes command and control): that in a statistical sense it be invulnerable, a subject discussed earlier, and that in numbers and capability it be adequate but not oversized.

SAFETY MEASURES

A multinational system, to be politically wieldable, must first maintain established safeguards against unauthorized use; and to be successful, have representation throughout the system: planning, command and operations, all of which assume obligations of investment and resources.

In situations of war, delays in decision-making processes

NATO'S FIFTEEN NATIONS. June-July 1962 73

Page 5 of author's article in "NATO's Fifteen Nations," from July 1962.

demand system survivability. Retaliatory capability must be inherent in the weapons system design allowing it to wait out the decision process. Yet there are great psychological advantages for some preplanned reaction to obvious situations; such as, if a nuclear attack was levied simultaneously on London, Oslo and Paris, the military command could automatically initiate preapproved Plan X. If reaction to obvious situations garnered approval beforehand, there could be operational implementation without delay, causing an aggressor to pause and/or to stop.

To support all eventualities, the system should offer instant readiness – the ability to launch accurately any number of armed missiles within a few minutes of command. Additional weapons system flexibility enhances the proposed force's capacity to militarily enforce its programs. This flexibility is gained from a system which can react almost instantly to command and verification of Plan X and which can implement any target designation without delay. So long as the technical state-of-art developed for weapons systems is available, it is left to political authority to agree on a structure without imposing burdensome constraints complicating functional response on command. The system's capability would not be restricted to predetermination of assignment, since versatility and flexibility have been already demonstrated in over 100,000 man/days on-station experience by the United States; considerably more latitude in controlled response that can be surmised from an analysis offered recently on Judgment and Control in Modern Warfare. *

A multinational force presumably would contain many new regulatory procedures, among them a single authoritative command control center. Also, where men of different nationalities may be called upon to serve together for extended periods of time, one code of discipline and of military justice is required or should be permitted. Deviation from a one-code procedure would create unbearable problems for normal military discipline.

Representatives in the North Atlantic Council may prefer to delegate such considerations, but it would appear certain that answers to such questions require close political and military ties since judgments will be required on the many facets of command and control. The "golden key" may be the glamorous question in literature and in fact, but agreement would be essential on initial assignments, promotion standards, reassignments – questions which require legal bond.

New organizational concepts for NATO were recently advanced by Alastair Buchan of the Institute for Strategic Studies in London. ** It is reasonable to assume that the creation of a NATO nuclear force would necessitate creation of a new and perhaps independent structure within NATO. It might house several planning divisions, all obviously internationally staffed with major political-military links concentrated in relationships of the North Atlantic Council, the NATO Nuclear Strike Command (if it can be called that) and SACEUR. Actual implementation of Council resolutions would be executed and refined within the military framework where multinational planning, targeting, communications and logistics would be molded into workable form.

The size of a NATO force should be adequate and not oversized – adequate to cover targets without becoming so large as to become a counterforce, since this does not appear to be what is required, nor so large as to be excessively expensive. A size enabling the force to cover ten times the targets normally designated as essential for the defense of NATO Eurasia might serve as the widest parameter for determining oversize. The benefits arising from a number well below such a figure may more closely reflect the Alliance's objectives. So long as NATO is a defensive community, the nuclear force would be a timely extension of its mission if the members agree on the requirement. To overbuild this capability could appear as an over-investment reverting the inertia of Alliance growth to a pendulous swing into the past of outdated military and political philosophy under the guise of achievement.

The paramount consideration will remain political – that the system will not be used without authority, rather than it will fail to respond upon proper command. The first constraint implies an equal veto for each member; the second, sound military and scientific planning. Both appear to have solutions. The concept of a NATO nuclear system involves a circular philosophy in which the system design demands critical components – men of NATO. No single individual assigned to the force could ignite a series of events resulting in nuclear detonation some 1,500 to 2,500 miles away. There are normally enough keymen in systems such as those suggested for each man to individually perform his duties within a design fabric that meshes perfectly. One broken human thread in working the weapons system's machinery halts any effort to apply the weapon without authority. Whether these men are of the same nationality or not, the system constraints are the same, yet a firm command loosens a finely integrated power against which there is no known defense or countermeasure.

The vital link is between man and authority. Whether the lightning rod is in the sea or not, there can be no mechanical or electrical overrides to man's judgment and performance, and each man's performance is an indispensible cog in a weapons system function. This, coupled to his physical command over equipment area, negates the possibility of substitution without concurrence. If a shield over NATO Eurasia is to be held aloft from the expanse of the sea, it is probably upon the anvil of such system mainstays that NATO's nuclear Excalibur will be tempered.

---

* *S. Zuckerman, Foreign Affairs, January, 1962.*

** *Survival, January - February issue, 1962, Foreign Affairs, January, 1962.*

Page 6 of author's article in "NATO's Fifteen Nations," from July 1962.

The Washington Post

THURSDAY, APRIL 5, 1990

LETTERS TO THE EDITOR

Adm. Raborn's Triumph

The Post's obituary [March 13] of Adm. William Raborn, a former CIA chief, triggered the memory of those of us who had been "kidnapped" by him to develop the world's first submarine-launched nuclear missile, the Polaris. Adm. Raborn had a "hunting license" giving him the right to have any Navy civilian or officer for a small team in SP. SP meant the Special Projects Office, a cover-up name to hide the office's secret mission. It was hidden in temporary wooden buildings on Constitution Avenue across from the Federal Reserve building. One notable neighbor in these wooden buildings was Adm. Hyman Rickover, developer of the first atomic-powered submarine.

There was tremendous pressure on the United States at the time. Only the Soviet Union had intercontinental missile capability, and President Eisenhower chafed under Nikita Khrushchev's threats to take out eastern U.S. cities. The White House needed people like Adm. Raborn to succeed.

Adm. Raborn was always around—weekends and holidays. Everyone worked compulsory overtime. There were no vacations. The admiral's presence was a morale-booster. This pressure lasted several years.

I was under 30 then, and I can recall him hailing me as I ran down a corridor. He was pleased to see me running. Later, one of his regular morale-boosting comments at meetings was his ability to identify his team members because we ran everywhere. The in-house joke was that to succeed with Adm. Rickover you had to speed-read and with Adm. Raborn you had to run a three-minute mile.

Launching missiles in the early years was a combination Fourth of July and Bastille Day: lots of fireworks when missiles broke in two or twirled like a majorette's baton.

Whenever we went to sea to test-fire missiles, each of us harbored private thoughts of seagoing disaster. If something happened, no one would know we were missing. Everything was secret. We could tell no one that we were going to sea in a nuclear submarine. It was not until we lost the USS Thresher with all hands that we were able to have real travel orders, covered by insurance.

The pressure eased on Adm. Raborn and SP as Polaris-equipped submarines went operational and returned safely from long and silent patrols.

Adm. Raborn stayed faithful to all his SP team members, never failing to recognize one or to take a moment to share old memories, even after his unhappy CIA tenure. Nuclear deterrence was his life's great triumph.

BERNARD W. POIRIER
Paris

5 April 1990 *Washington Post* letter to the editor regarding the *Post*'s obituary of former CIA director, Admiral William F. Raborn.

Herald INTERNATIONAL Tribune

THURSDAY, APRIL 5, 1990

LETTERS TO THE EDITOR

Dedicated to Deterrence

Your obituary *(March 15)* for Admiral William F. Raborn Jr., the ex-CIA chief, triggered memories of how he "kidnapped" me and others to develop the world's first submarine-launched nuclear missile, the Polaris. At the time, only the Soviet Union had intercontinental missiles, and President Eisenhower chafed under Nikita Khrushchev's threats.

During work on the project, Admiral Raborn was always around. Weekends, holidays. Everyone worked compulsory overtime. No vacations. The admiral's presence was a morale booster. The pressure lasted several years.

Whenever we went to sea to test-fire missiles, each of us harbored private thoughts of seagoing disaster. If something happened, no one would know we were missing. Everything was so secret we could tell no one that we were going to sea in a nuclear submarine.

There were a few foreign and ex-Peenemünde scientists on our team. At one classified briefing, a NATO Luftwaffe pilot noted my partner's heavy accent and asked him if he had been a Messerschmitt pilot. "No," my colleague answered, "I flew Spitfires." He had been a Free Polish volunteer in the RAF and had come to the United States in 1945.

The pressure eased on Admiral Raborn as Polaris-equipped submarines went operational and returned safely from long and silent patrols. The admiral stayed faithful to his former team members, never failing to recognize one or take a moment to share old memories, even after his unhappy CIA tenure.

Nuclear deterrence had been his life's great triumph.

BERNARD W. POIRIER.
Paris.

5 April 1990 *International Herald Tribune* similar but differently edited letter to the editor regarding the obituary of Admiral Raborn.

J. E. CHARLES & Co
BANQUIERS
SOCIÉTÉ EN COMMANDITE MONÉGASQUE
MONACO

REPRÉSENTATION
BARCELONA

TÉLÉPHONE 017-61 & 62
ADRESSE TÉLÉGRAPHIQUE
CHARLEBANK - MONACO

Monaco, le 7 Aout 1944

Madame FRANK JAY GOULD
129, avenue Malakoff
PARIS

Chère Madame,

Nous avons l'honneur de vous informer que, conformément à vos instructions, nous avons crédité le compte de Madame Isabelle LACAZE chez nous, d'un montant de 200.000 Frs.

- Deux Cent Mille Frs. - Valeur 27 Juillet 1944

Après cette opération, votre compte se solde chez nous par un montant de DEUX MILLIONS de Frs. (2.000.000) à votre crédit .

Veuillez agréer, Chère Madame, l'expression de nos meilleurs sentiments .

J.E. CHARLES & Co :
J. Charles

7 August 1944 Credit notice to Florence Gould from Charles Bank, Monaco, confirming the 2,000,000 French francs she had deposited to date in the Nazi bank. U.S. forces and their allies were still bottled in by the German army in western France.

CONFIDENTIAL

HEADQUARTERS XVIII CORPS (AIRBORNE)
218th C.I.C. Detachment

APO 109, US Army
20 February 1945

SUMMARY OF INFORMATION

SUBJECT: FRANK J. GOULD.

TO : Assistant Chief of Staff, G-2, ETOUSA, APO 887, US Army

THRU : Assistant Chief of Staff, G-2, Hq. FAAA, APO 740, US Army

Reference attached clipping from Stars & Stripes, dated 18 Feb 1945, quoting Mrs. Frank Jay Gould as saying that she had invested in the Monte Carlo bank to keep the enemy "from carrying off her husband...67 years old and a sick man..."

The undersigned officer talked on two occasions with Frank Gould last December at "La Colombe d'Or", St. Paul, A.M., where Gould was living with a young woman. In answer to a casual question why the Germans had allowed him to go unmolested during the occupation, his reply was because "I have not crossed a frontier in 14 years". He then produced his American passport to establish the present fact of his American citizenship. When asked what he had done in the last war for the Allied cause, Gould said he had gone to Paris to see what he could do, was there told the war would be over in four months, so he returned to the Riviera to wait and has been there ever since!

Sources believed reliable at Nice reported that Gould was not deported because of his wife's close friendship with ranking German officers. Whatever the facts of this may be, it can be unequivocably stated that Gould was far from being an ailing, sick man as recently as three months ago.

The undersigned's chance meetings with Gould resulted from the fact of the undersigned's former regiment, the 517th Parachute Infantry, was engaged near Nice at that time. Other officers were present on these occasions and can supply any depositions which may be desired.

Request information be forwarded to Treasury Department or to appropriate French Agency conducting this investigation.

ALBIN P. DEARING,
Capt., Prcht.Inf.,
C.O., CIC Detachment

1 Incl:
Clipping fr Stars & Stripes,
dtd 18 Feb 1945.

cc to AC of S, G-2, Hq. XVIII Corps (AB)

CONFIDENTIAL

20 February 1945 Counter intelligence letter from Headquarters, XVIII Corps (Airborne).

AIRGRAM

DIV. OF FOREIGN ACTIVITY CORRELATION APR 7 1945 DEPARTMENT OF STATE

APR 18 1945 DEPARTMENT OF STATE

SECRET

FROM: Paris

DATE: March 9, 1945, 5 p.m.

REC'D: March 23, 1945 3 P.M.

DIVISION OF WORLD TRADE INTELLIGENCE MAR 29 1945 DEPARTMENT OF STATE

SECSTATE, WASHINGTON

No. A-300, March 9, 1945, 5 p.m.

SANTHAVEN.

Secret intelligence made available by United States Government sources to the Embassy with regard to Florence Gould (reference Embassy's secret airgrams No. A-259, February 28 and No. A-295, March 6, 1945) indicates:

1. That her participation in the Banque Charles was an outgrowth of the many close and confessed relations she had with the Germans (including the Gestapo) and notorious French collaborators during the occupation;

2. That her recent explanation of her participation in the bank (as given in her written statement summarized in Embassy's airgram No. A-259) does not correspond with the explanation she gave to the OSS, Paris, on October 18, 1944.

3. That after the liberation of France, she has clandestinely corresponded with Ludwig Vogel, engineer of the Focke-Wulf Aircraft Company, who is held as a German prisoner in Paris; that she has received for safekeeping from Vogel, who is alleged to be her lover, at least 75,000 francs sent by him from his prison.

4. That although it has not yet been determined whether Florence Gould knowingly served as an informer to the Gestapo, there is evidence that the Germans regarded her as an informer.

During

800.515/3-945 CS/EG

APR 19 1945 Confidential File

LIAISON OFFICE MAR 24 1945 DEPARTMENT OF STATE

DCR - ECA Dir.

Dist.

9 March 1945 OSS/Paris embassy letter to the State Department regarding Florence Gould. Documents recovered by the National Archives and Records Administration, Washington, D.C., and College Park, Maryland.

A-300
Paris

- 2 -

During the occupation, Florence Gould had social relations with the following principal Germans and French collaborators:

Werner Klingeberg, Director of Deutsches Nachrichten Buro, Paris
Willy Gretsch, of the Abwehr
Walter Stefens, of the Abwehr
Colonel Patrick (Garther) of the Abwehr
De Lestandi, of Le Pilori, one of the most Fascist of French newspapers
Marcel Peter, Director of Le Petit Parisien
Odenwald, of the Gestapo
General Medicus
Knochen, of the German Secret Service
Countess de Chambrun, daughter of Laval
Carbuccia, of the collaborationist newspaper Gringoire

At the request of Gretsch of the Abwehr, Florence Gould employed as her secretary Gretsch's mistress, Mademoiselle Gaillard who, with Gretsch, has now been implicated in the establishment of a clandestine radio station reporting to Germany on Allied activities in the Paris Region. According to Mrs. Gould's maid, artistic luncheons were held at her house during 1943 each Thursday, the guests at these luncheons being French and German writers.

It is clear from the evidence available that Florence Gould knew of the official connections of the Germans whom she met and entertained.

According to one reliable report, Ludwig Vogel took Florence Gould on one or two trips to Germany under a false name and without itentification papers. One of these trips was to Friedrichshafen, where Florence Gould was permitted to visit an aircraft factory.

On October 18, 1944, Mrs. Gould was questioned about her participation in the Banque Charles by the OSS in Paris. She stated that in March 1944 she was in Monaco with Ludwig Vogel. In the course of their stay, she spoke of several attempts by various groups to get permission from the Prince of Monaco to establish an international bank there. Vogel then mentioned the fact that Baron Charles (J. E. Charles) had in November 1943 obtained permission to establish such

a bank.

Page 2 of OSS/Paris embassy letter of 9 March 1945 to the State Department regarding Florence Gould.

- 3 -

a bank. In May 1944, Warcinski, German Commissar for the Gould interests, introduced Charles to Mrs. Gould who outlined his plan, which included the participation of Gaussbeck and Le Cesne. Charles refused to give details on how permission was obtained from the Prince. Mrs. Gould stated that the attractive part of the proposition for her was the permission itself. She admitted to the OSS investigator that she expected the bank would be impounded when the Americans landed in the south of France. However, she believed that when the situation had cleared she would be in a position to render services to the United States, which would benefit from a bank in a protected zone. She intended to render these services by turning over her limited interest of 5,000,000 francs. Since Mrs. Gould stated that her only interest was to create a refuge for American money during time of war, and did not emphasize the motive she now claims she had, namely to save Mr. Gould from deportation, some doubt is cast on her later story.

Mrs. Gould also claims to have been in touch with a Frenchman who was secretly working for one of the United States intelligence services in France during the occupation. It has been confirmed that she did have some relations with this person, but there is as yet no evidence that she ever gave any important information or that she disclosed to him her relations with the Germans. Mrs. Gould also stated that the reason she had social relations with so many Germans was that she sought their protection because she feared she would be suspected by them and sent to a concentration camp because of her services for the Allied intelligence. However, according to her own admission, she was not in contact with the Allied intelligence services until December 1943, whereas most of her relations with the Germans began before that date.

With regard to Vogel, Mrs. Gould is attempting to show that he is really an anti-Nazi. She has admitted that in addition to the 75,000 francs which he sent her in a letter from Prison, he also left with her 500,000 francs for safekeeping.

CAFFERY

LEF/gp

2 copies to American Embassy, London.

Page 3 of OSS/Paris embassy letter of 9 March 1945 to the State Department regarding Florence Gould.

Secret

RECEIVED JUN 1 1945 DOCUMENT SECURITY FEA

Paris, May 12, 1945.

No. 1936

SECRET

SUBJECT: Safehaven Report No. 6 : Further Information on the Banque Charles Case.

The Honorable
The Secretary of State,
Washington.

Sir:

With reference to the Embassy's previous communications on the Banque Charles case, (Secret despatch No. 1430, March 26, 1945, and Airgrams A-295, March 8, and A-300, March 9), I have the honor to transmit as an enclosure to this despatch:

1 - a translation of a memorandum dictated by Baron Johannes Charles on April 24, 1945;
2 - a statement of additional information on the case obtained from French sources;
3 - notes on a conversation with Charles; and
4 - translation of a letter from the Reichsbank to the German Consulate in Monaco, dated October 17, 1943.

This information was obtained through the OSS, Paris.

On the basis of this information the following significant facts in the case appear to be confirmed:

1 - The Banque Charles was a secret affiliate of the German Reichsbank.

2 - It is Mr. Frank J. Gould and not Mrs. Gould who appears to have been the principal American collaborator in the Bank. This would seem to indicate that Mrs. Gould's statements represent an effort on her part to shield her husband.

3 - Some of the funds placed at the disposal of the Bank appear to belong to Herr Berghaus, a German industrialist.

4 - Charles appears to be hopeful that the Bank can be saved and expanded with the approval of the French authorities and, the financial help of the Worms Bank or the Neuflize Bank, and the Princess Sixte de Bourbon.

5) Charles ...

FEA SECRET ECONOMIC INTELLIGENCE DIV. DOCUMENT SECURITY SEC. 65766

12 May 1945 Paris embassy report to the Secretary of State about Florence Gould. Three classified attachments.

\- 2 -

5 - Charles is said to possess a personal fortune of about 10 million francs deposited in the Société de Banque Suisse, Zurich, and in the Banque de Sarragosse, Madrid.

Respectfully yours,

For the Ambassador:

Hugh S. Fullerton
Counselor of Embassy

Enclosures:

1) Translation of a Memorandum
2) Statement of additional information on the case
3) Notes on a conversation with Charles
4) Translation of a letter.

File No: 711.3

MAF/gp

Copy and Hectograph
to the Department.

2 copies to American Embassy, London

Page 2 of 12 May 1945 report to the State Department about Florence Gould.

Enclosure No. 1 to Despatch No. 1936.

Statement Dictated By Baron Johannes Charles on April, 24, 1945
(Translation)

I was born in Switzerland. As result of economic studies which I made I was led to the conclusion that the capitalist system, as we knew it before the war, could actually no longer exist.

Through fear of the victory of the communist idea and the communist system, I was led to interest myself in national socialism.

Wishing to harmonize my action with my thought, I left Switzerland and volunteered in the German Army at the time of the German-Russian war.

I performed some months of military service, but through my relations I was able to avoid going to the front and was transferred to the Reichsbank.

During the time I was in Germany where I had many contacts, I had the opportunity to speak with friends and to come to the conclusion that behind the façade of the regime (Translator's note: presumably the German) such as it had been presented in Switzerland, things were so abominable that I could not associate myself with it.

I therefore looked for a plausible pretext for separation while maintaining my position if possible.

In agreement with Dr. Karl Schaeffer, I prepared a plan for an international enterprise in Monaco, and with his support I was able to make some progress on it.

In the meantime, I sent my wife and my children to Switzerland pretending they were ill and told them to remain there.

Thus, free in my movements without fear of eventual reprisals, I remained in Monaco, awaiting either the creation of a democratic German Committee or German Government or, at least, of an American movement uniting all Germans who wished to liberate their country. In order to understand my position which is truly like that of numerous young Europeans, one must recall the inextricable economic situation in which we existed before the war, and remember that we were not sufficiently well informed of the real policy of the United States which appeared to us to be a defender of an outmoded and egotistical capitalist system which brought about the 1939 catastrophe.

The United States appeared to want to maintain its isolationist policy, and we had no sufficient indication that the problem of technological overproduction and unemployment was receiving the attention of the American leaders.

Since the United States intervened only very late in the conflict, we had no reason to be certain that the problem was understood in America.

That is why there was a lack of confidence shown to the Americans.

At the moment when, on the contrary, it appeared that the United States intended to resolve the problem as a whole, I tried to support their policy by establishing this bank in Monaco in which my associates and myself had no other purpose than to place ourselves between America the Lender and Europe the Borrower.

Since, when ...

Page 3 of 12 May 1945 report to the State Department about Florence Gould.

- 2 -

Since, when the war is ended, all, or almost all, of Europe will have to be reconstructed and the United States alone will have the means of doing so, I interested Mr. Frank J. Gould in the matter by pointing out to him that as an American knowing the European mentality very well, he should put his authority and his fortune at the disposition of a Bank uniting international forces towards the realization of an economic end: the reconstruction of the devastated countries.

As for the future I hope to follow exactly the same line of conduct and wish, through my relations in France, Germany and Austria, to devote myself to the establishment of an economic system which will permit the establishment of an era of prolonged prosperity.

As a father, I want to avoid having my children live through the wars that I have known.

I am actually in a position to obtain the collaboration of Herr Berghaus, German light industry magnate, Baron von Maltitz, of the Wood industry, Herr Otto Roehm, of the Darmstadt Plexiglass interests, besides Dr. Karl Schaeffer, financier with an international reputation. (Translator's note: Baron von Maltitz during the occupation of France achieved some prominence as a "purchaser" of "non-aryan" business enterprises).

I maintain excellent relations with Madame Krupp von Bohlenbach, wife of the famous Essen industrialist, with the two vice-presidents of the Reichsbank, Drs. Puhlo and Lange, and with other important officials of this institution.

Insofar as France is concerned, as soon as I am free from the cloud that hangs over me in this country because of my nationality, I shall be able easily to find among French bankers intelligent men who look at the future in the same way as I do and who are ready to put their resources at the service of economic reorganization. In this connection, I have made concrete propositions to the French Government and through the intermediary of certain lawyers, I have suggested to the Government that it increase the size of my Bank. Until now I have met with the opposition of M. Floven, Minister of Finance, who appears to be antagonistic to the Bank of France.

However I have been assured that a change in the Government is imminent and that my plan will be adopted.

With regard to my contacts, I think I can obtain the financial collaboration in this project of either the Worms Bank or the Neuflize Bank.

I also have good relations with the Princess Sixte de Bourbon, the aunt of Archduke Otto of Hapsbourg, pretender to the Austrian throne. It is not necessary to make more precise the advantage that the Bank could have from an active participation by the Princess.

I also succeeded in interesting the Prince of Monaco in my plan and he has assured me that he would officially participate in the Bank when circumstances permitted.

Finally, I should like to add that I have joined a Committee for a Democratic Germany with offices in New York, and whose leaders are Dr. Tillich and the writer, Thomas Mann.

I asked ...

Page 4 of 12 May 1945 report to the State Department about Florence Gould.

\- 3 -

I asked my associate, Herr Gausebeck to offer his services and mine to this Committee if he had not already done so.

The Bank advanced a sum of 1 million francs to Prince Léon Radziwill with the thought that the Radziwill family would remain clients of the Bank in the future and also to obtain, if necessary, the intervention of the Prince on my behalf through one of his sons who is in the British Army.

I knew Mr. Katchourine in Monaco where he was presented to me by Dr. Schaeffer. He put me in touch with the Director of the Comptoir National d'Escompte in Monaco and was to have introduced me to Mr. Raffahac, charged with an official mission for the French Government in Monaco.

Concerning the question of the use of Monaco as a means for the exportation of funds, I have not set up my Bank for this purpose and never was asked to do so.

If one examines the chronological record, it appears that I obtained permission for the Bank in my own name in October 1943, but that I carefully avoided creating the Bank immediately in order not to be obliged to conduct operations for Germany or for the Vichy Government which would have injured me (Translator's note: which would have burnt my fingers). I waited in Paris using different pretexts, preferring to do nothing until the moment was judged favorable by Dr. Schaeffer and me.

It was on July 21, 1944, that Mr. Gould, Dr. Schaeffer, Mr. Lesesne, Herr Gausebeck and I officially created the Bank which began its activity only on August 1, 1944, that is, at a time when it was impossible to require me to perform operations which would not have been agreeable to me.

Page 5 of 12 May 1945 report to the State Department about Florence Gould.

Enclosure No. 2 to Despatch No. 1936.

Notes on a Conversation with Baron Johannes Charles, April 24, 1945

Throughout the conversation the Baron's attitude was characterized by a complete confidence that "no one had anything on him" and that the Americans were about to "be reasonable and make a deal". The following are notes on the Baron's ideas.

The Baron and Schaeffer developed the idea to provide an escape for funds. They were aware of the approaching outcome of the war and wished to collaborate with the Americans. The Baron said that he formed the bank as late as possible and had held the license for some time.

Schaeffer is an anti-Nazi suspected by many Nazis, not even a party member, and was accepted for the job only because he was a great financier.

The original idea was to form a branch of a German bank, either in Tangiers or Andorra. Later the idea developed into an international bank with American participation. Now the game seems to be to get the French to back it and to recognize its international, or, at least, European value. The Baron seemed surprised that Gould did not grab the chance to get in on the bank. He says that he also tried the British in a small way, that Worms is an anglophile, and is working on the British now. But the French ministerial shake-up is slowing down negotiations and will probably continue to slow them down. The Baron says he is "just waiting".

Roblot never had much to do with the Bank Charles, although he tried to cut himself in. The Baron said he might help Roblot later to get the job of local minister of finance. The Baron says, however, that to date Roblot has dealt directly with the Prince. The Baron expects that his Barcelona bank is still working. Whole system is a series of points d'appui for whoever will back him. He is obviously a first class opportunist. The Baron talks of strong anti-communist line, appears not to trust the French, claims to have no contacts whatever with Americans.

Gausebeck was brought into the bank for practical reasons; Losane also, of whom the Baron saw little. The American (Gould) angle was a temporary one, used as a "stepping-stone", which the Baron hoped might lead into a wide field of American backing. When it was suggested that the Germans might be using him for the same purpose, he claimed that the Germans neither could nor would.

The Baron claims that there is as much French money invested in Monaco as there is German.

Page 6 of 12 May 1945 report to the State Department about Florence Gould.

Enclosure No. 3 to Despatch No. 1936.

<u>Information from French Secret Sources on Bank Charles Case</u>

Eugène Johannes Charles was born on November 7, 1913, in Geneva, son of Alfred Charles and Alice Golay. He is of German nationality through naturalization; his religion is Protestant. He is married to Zoe Zollikofer, born on March 31, 1909, in St. Petersburg, Russia. They have two children, seven years and one year of age. Madame Charles and the children are of Swiss nationality.

Charles studied in Switzerland and in Heidelberg, Germany. As a result of disagreement with his father who disliked Germany, Charles went to Stuttgart where he was drawn by what he believed to be "noble and beautiful" in the National Socialist regime. Upon the advice of Mr. Puhle, vice-president of the Reichsbank, he volunteered in the German Army to serve for the duration of the war. In September 1942, he was given a special mission in the Economics Ministry, Reichsbank Section. Shortly afterwards he was sent to Spain and Portugal where he conducted financial operations for German account.

At the beginning of 1943, he was asked by the Reichsbank to investigate the possibility of creating in Western Europe a Bank which could serve the commercial "expansion" of Germany, and which in reality would be a "secret affiliate" of the Reichsbank.

After several investigations in Spain and in Monaco, he chose the latter place because he had obtained the consent of the Prince through the intermediary of Minister of State Roblot.

Charles was in close touch with Karl Schaeffer, German Commissar of the Bank of France, who held full powers from the Reichsbank.

When the Prince of Monaco went back on his decision and did not wish the creation of an official Bank, it was agreed between Schaeffer and Charles that the Bank to be created in Monaco would take the form of a private subscription bank under the name of J.E. Charles & Co. An "associate" named August Gausebeck, German, formerly banker in New York, was imposed on Charles.

Gausebeck in turn brought the French banker Guillaume Lessens to the Bank. Charles himself brought Mr. Gould into the Bank.

The Bank was "financed" by the Reichsbank which through the intermediary of Schaeffer paid in 50 million francs. Apparently Charles denies that Mrs. Gould paid her 5 million francs subscription. (Mrs. Gould, on the other hand, claims that she paid a subscription and also an additional 2 million francs deposit in the Bank).

Questioned as to the use of the 50 millions which he claims was the bank's only resource, Charles stated that 22,850,000 francs were spent in making different purchases, 3,147,000 francs were paid to different persons for special purposes and the remainder of 24,150,000 francs were placed by Charles in different Monte Carlo Banks as follows: 5 million in the Banque Nationale pour le Commerce et l'Industrie, 5 million in the Comptoir National d'Escompte de Paris, 9,150,000 francs in the Crédit Lyonnais.

Charles also stated that the Bank expected the sum of 18,000,000 francs to be paid by Schaeffer into the Crédit Marseillais, at Marseille. This money came from capital belonging to a certain Bernhard Berghaus, Berlin industrialist for whom Schaeffer was keeping certain funds.

Charles is ...

Page 7 of 12 May 1945 report to the State Department about Florence Gould. This enclosure cites French intelligence sources.

- 2 -

Charles is said to possess a personal fortune of about 10,000,000 francs deposited in the Société de Banque Suisse at Zurich and in the Banque de Sarragosse in Madrid. When Charles was arrested he was hiding with one Roger Olivie, a harbor pilot in Monaco. He gave to Olivie 500,000 francs which were to be deposited for the account of Charles and Co., in some bank in Monaco, the sum of 1,000,000 francs to be used for the creation of a Monegasque Corporation, "Crédit Commercial Moderne", a sum of 600,000 francs for the creation of a partnership in Monaco for the exploitation of the "Bar Restaurant de la Marine", and a sum of 120,000 francs for the purchase of an automobile.

According to Charles, Jean Wagner was presented to him by Lessene and brought with him a proposal to double the French and American shares in the Bank, bringing the total capital up to 150,000,000 francs.

Jean Wagner is alleged to be a French Jew, 39 years old, who pretended to be an industrialist of Aix-en-Provence, representing a group of Jews who are allegedly anxious to participate in the renovation of the Bank.

Wagner also pretends to be very close to Mendes-France, Minister of National Economy and is reported to have made efforts through the latter to obtain the approval of the French Government to the transformation of the Bank. Charles gave Wagner a letter authorizing him to operate the Bank in the absence of the official director and another letter authorizing Wagner to take from the Bank Charles account at the Crédit Commercial of Marseille, the sum of 12 million francs out of the 18 million coming from the Bank's capital which was to be paid in by Schaeffer/

According to Charles, Wagner profited by the absence of all the directors of the Bank to open the safe and remove its contents, i.e. the sum of 236,334 francs. Finally he is reported to have disappeared together with Madame Luraschi, Charles' secretary and mistress. Charles was acquainted with Herr Kagenec, former chief of the Gestapo at Monte Carlo, but claims he never had any relations with him or with other members of the Gestapo.

Page 8 and last page of the 12 May 1945 report to the State Department regarding Florence Gould and the Nazi E.J. Charles.

IN REPLY REFER TO
FILE NO. 711.3-HJ:of

GOULD, FRANK J.

THE FOREIGN SERVICE
OF THE
UNITED STATES OF AMERICA

DEPARTMENT OF STATE

AMERICAN CONSULATE

Nice, France, September 13, 1945.

CONFIDENTIAL

Dear Mr. Fullerton:

As of possible interest, Mr. Frank J. Gould's daughter, Madame Maret, who resides in Switzerland, is at present visiting him here. She called at this office a few days ago and in the course of conversation stated that she could not understand why her step-mother, Mrs. Frank J. Gould, Paris, had not been apprehended, tried and convicted of flagrantly collaborating with the Germans during their occupation of France. Madame Maret enhanced her statement by saying that when the Germans were in France Mrs. Gould even came to Nice with a German major with whom she was openly collaborating and living, and put up at Mr. Gould's home much to his embarrassment. She added that this same German major is now employed by the Americans in Stuttgart. I could not obtain the name of the German above referred to.

Mrs. Maret stated that while Mrs. Gould's pro-German activities and sentiments were well-known, she is at the present time enjoying the continuous company of many high ranking United States Army officials.

Sincerely yours,

Hartwell Johnson
American Consul

Hugh S. Fullerton, Esquire,
American Consul General,
Paris.

13 September 1945 Letter from American Consul, Nice, France, regarding revelations by Florence Gould's step-daughter.

Questionnaire:

I) Nombre d'appareil sur le terrain ;

2° Différents types d'appareil qu'on y rencontre.

3° Nombre d'appareils par types?

4) Que fait-on sur l'aérodrome (ecole de chasse, ecole de bombardie entrainement de pilotes deja confirmés, essais d'appareils nouveaux , récéption d'appareils, construction et mise au poin dans les ateliers;

5° Nom des formation qui occcupent le terrain (troupes volentes, trou a terre , service, escadre N° ? , groupe de chasse un tel?

6° Nom des chefs (officiers supérieurs, commandant du Camp, commandan de la commandantur du camp)

Prière retourner le questionnaire avec les reponses.
Ne pas oublier quand matière de renseignement les chases les plus simples et même celles qui peuvent vous sembler les plus bêtes peuvent avoir une très grosse valeur

En conséquence fouiller done le plus possible le renseignement.

Page 1 of the 1943/44 Secret instructions from an underground superior code-named Roux to Fratacci regarding Lufftwaffe warplanes that he should recognize and intelligence needed about airfields. Discovered by Fratacci's widow about three years after his execution.

Je vous envoie un plan au I/5.000° des aérodromes de BUC et Toussus le Noble , voudriez vous en collaboration avec notre ami:

I° Tracer sur ce plan au crayon les limites des divers terrains;

2° Hachurer dans ces limites la partie non utilisable a l'attérissage qui est généralement labourée ou transformée enterrains decultures.

3° Tracer sur le terrain les pistes d'envol ainsi que lesdivers chemin s qui peuvent conduire aux hangars nouvellement construits.

4° M'indiquer les nouveaux hangars s'ils y en a (cela à leur place la plus exacte posible et a l'echelle)-sur ce plan au I/5.000° Im/m représente 5metres.

5° Me barrer d'un trait de crayon les hangars ,chemins ou constructions dessinés sur le plan et ayant disparus.

6° Me numeroter les divers batiments d'une manière quelconque à moins qu'il n' existe surles divers batiments un numérotage officiel auquel il vaut mieux se réferer.

7° M'établir un état sur lequel sera porté tout les batiments avec leur numéro et l'activité qui se déroule à l'intérieur, ~~atelier de~~ montage, hangar de garage pour appareils, etc... ....

8° Me faire un répertoire de tout lesappareils setrouvant actuellement sur le terrain ,sousla forme 6 ME I09 , 7 Ju 52, 2 Ju 88 etc... ..

9° Me relevertoutes lesinscriptionsquel'ontrouve sur les carlingues,queues,les bandes dediverses couleurs,les totems etc....

Garder ce questionnaire car les memes questions se poseront pour la mise a jour du plan du terrain de Villacoublay que je vous enverrai bientôt.

Meilleurs souvenirs et bonnes amitiés.

ROUX

Page 2 of the 1943/44 Secret instructions from an underground superior code-named Roux to Fratacci regarding Lufftwaffe warplanes that he should recognize and intelligence needed about airfields. Discovered by Fratacci's widow about three years after his execution. Roux describes what Fratacci should trace on the plans of airfields given to him, into which Fratucci should penetrate.

Moyens de reconnaître les divers types d'avions

Monomoteur (un seul moteur)

Me 109: Ailes carrées dans le bout , roue de queue non escamotable (c'est le type le plus courant des avions de chasse)

Me 109 F: Ailes pointues dans le bout,avant a forme d'extrêmité d'un cigare.

Fw 190: Le noyau de l'hélice fait nettement sailli devant le moteur,et n'est pas dans le prolongement xxxxxxx des lignes de celui-ci, la partie arrière des ailes seraccorde avec la carlingue suivant une courbe.

Bi-moteurs (2 moteurs)

Me 110 ; Bouts d'ailes carrées 2 gouvernail de direction avant de la cabin non vitré.

Do 17 (Do 215) bouts d'aile ronds, 2 gouvernails de direction

Do 217: le fuselage est nettement plus long que les gouvernails de direct et de profondeur.

Ju 88: bouts d'ailes légérement arrondis, cabine avant vitrée en 2 p en 2 parties , un seul gouvernail de direction.

He 111 : cabine avant vitée entièrement et en une seule partie , bou d'aile nettement arrondis , gouvernail de profondeur allant jusqu'au bout du fuselage.

Fw 189: appareil a 2 carlingue.

Trimoteurs

Un seul type le Ju 52 (unmoteur en bout de carlingue ,un sur chaqu aile)

Quadrimoteurs (4 moteurs)

Fw 200: on dirait qu'il existe sous la carlingue une petite nacel comme une de ballon dirigeable.

Monomoteur (bombardiers en piqués)

Ju 87: train d'atterissage caréné, les ailes semblent cassées

Avions de reconnaissance

He 126: I moteur ressemble au Morane parasol français.

Fi 156 Train d'attérissage très haut un vo etxxxxxxx devant les ailes on l'appele aussi (le mouchard , ou la cigogne)

Page 3 of the 1943/44 Roux instructions to Fratacci, citing particularities to identify different enemy warplanes.

Travail sur Plan

1° Verifier que les constructions portées sur le plan existe bien.
si elles n'existent plus les rayées d'une croix.

2° Indiquer pour les constructions existantes si elles sont en bo état, demolies et en reconstruction,
bon état: ne pas toucher au plan
en reconstruction: les hachurer.

3° Indiquer les constructions nouvelles (constructions de toutes sortes, en béton , en briques , en bois , en planches , etc...)

4° Indiquer en regard de chaque construction xx ce qui se passe à l'interieu en se référant au numérotage (Ex. construction I42 atelier de réparation de moteurs.... I47 casernement de troupe 40 hommes)
Pour ces indications il y a lieu de discerner:
les casernements (contenance)
les maisons a usage de mess d'officiers et de sous-officiers
les postes de gardes
les soutes a munitions ou a essence
les postes de radio
les hangars et ~~[struck out]~~
etc;;;.....

5° Porter sur le plan les emplacements de canons anti-aériens sous forme d'un rond rouge d'un demi centimètre de diamètre.
Porter les emplacements de mitrailleuses lourdes anti-aériennes un petit cercle noir et une flèche.

6° Tracer les abris et tranchées abris.

Nota Apporter un soin tout particulier a la mise en place exacte des nouveaux batiments et postes de D.C.A.
Fournir le maximun de détails sur l'occupation des batiments EX/ Construction 507 poste de garde effectif I sous-officier IO hommes armement individuel pour chaque une mitraillette et plus.

Pour les constructions nouvelles les numéroter en commençant au numéro I mais cercler le numéro, ③

xx ou sur une feuille de papier à part

x Porter sur plan tout les constructions les numéroter

Page 4 of the 1943/44 Roux instructions to Antoine Fratacci, asking him to correct and update air fields used by the Luftwaffe.

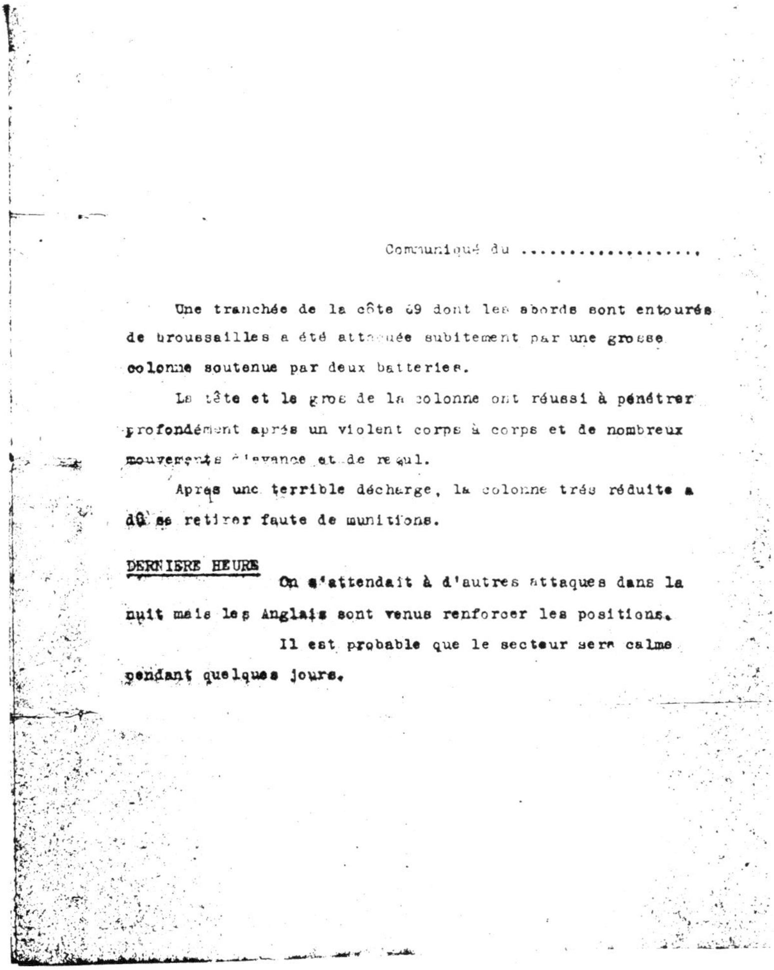

Communiqué du ....

Une tranchée de la côte 69 dont les abords sont entourés de broussailles a été attaquée subitement par une grosse colonne soutenue par deux batteries.

La tête et le gros de la colonne ont réussi à pénétrer profondément aprés un violent corps à corps et de nombreux mouvements d'avance et de recul.

Apres une terrible décharge, la colonne trés réduite a dû se retirer faute de munitions.

DERNIERE HEURE

On s'attendait à d'autres attaques dans la nuit mais les Anglais sont venus renforcer les positions.

Il est probable que le secteur sera calme pendant quelques jours.

A separate underground message probably written in July 1944, citing violent hand-to-hand fighting between British and German soldiers.

4 Septembre I944

Monsieur FRATACCI Antoine, 8, rue Gabrielle d'Estrées à VANVES a été tué à l'ennemi dans les circonstances suivantes :

Sous-Officier des sapeurs pompiers depuis 2 ans appartenait au groupement de résistance Coutal, d'ISSY les MOULINEAUX et en même temps à l'équipe de renseignements du B.M.R.A. du même Coutal.

Agent dévoué à l'extrême, toujours prêt pour toutes les missio: Sous le n° R.U.A. 34 a rendu de grands services.

En outre, s'était spécialisé dans l'introduction de tétrachlorure de cabone dans les réservoirs d'essence des chasseurs F W K I En 2 ans, a réussi à introduire ainsi 20 litres, à la dose de ½ lit. par appareil soit 40 fois. Chaque fois l'appareil a été porté manqu. dès sa Ière sortie. Surpris le II Août sur le terrain (hangard) de TOUSSIES-le-NOBLE, alors qu'il profitait d'un bombardement allié pour récidiver a été abattu sur place par un sous-officier Allemand

Ai déja demandé citation élogieuse, décoration et élévation au grade supérieur de s/officier pour ce héros de l'armée souterraine.

Laisse une veuve et trois enfants.

Jean COUTAL

Réseau BEARN

Dossier F.F.C. I5.595

CERTIFIÉ CONFORME à l'ORIGINAL
QUI NOUS A ÉTÉ PRÉSENTÉ
Vanves, le 15 SEPT 1953
Le Maire Adjoint,

VU et CERTIFIE EXACT
par le Colonel Commandant
les F.F.I. Subdivision Ouest
P.O. l'Officier Adjoint

MAIRIE DE VANVES
SEINE

4 September 1944 Underground report of Fratacci's death and heroism, crediting him with 40 aircraft that never returned to base. Underground unit known by code name "Bearn." Assumption here is that he was killed after midnight, night of 10/11 August 1944.

By this
Certificate of Service
I record my appreciation of the aid rendered by
Fratacci Antoine
who, as a volunteer of the United Nations,
laid down his life that Europe might be free.

B. L. Montgomery
Field Marshal
Commander-in-Chief, 21st Army Group

Date 6 Mai 1946
Serial No F/3614

6 May 1946 Certificate from British Field Marshal Bernard L. Montgomery regarding Antoine Fratacci's sacrifice.

EXTRAIT

du DÉCRET en date du 12 Octobre 1946

publié au J. O. du 3 Novembre 1946

portant concession de la Médaille Militaire

ARTICLE 1er – Sont décorés de la Médaille Militaire, les militaires dont les noms suivent :

A TITRE POSTHUME

. . . .

F R A T A C C I Antoine – Sergent des Forces Françaises de l'Intérieur –

"Membre du groupe de résistance d'ISSY LES MOULINEAUX et de l'équipe de renseignements du B.M.R.A.; agent dévoué a rendu de grands services en se spécialisant dans l'introduction du tétrachlorure de carbone dans les réservoirs d'essence des chasseurs F.W.K. 190; en deux ans a réussi à employer vingt litres de tétrachlorure à la dose de un demi litre par appareil; quarante appareils ont été portés manquants dès leur première sortie. Le 11 août 1944 dans un hangar de Toussus-le-Noble, alors qu'il profitait d'un bombardement allié pour accomplir sa mission, a été tué sur place par un sous-officier allemand.

Cette concession annule et remplace la citation à l'ordre de l'Armée n° 1224 accordée le 1er octobre 1943.

. . . .

CES CONCESSIONS COMPORTENT L'ATTRIBUTION DE LA CROIX DE GUERRE 1939-1945 AVEC PALME.

Fait à PARIS, le 12 Octobre 1946

Par le Président du Gouvernement Provisoire de la République
Ministre des Affaires Etrangères

signé : BIDAULT

LE MINISTRE DES ARMEES

signé : MICHELET

POUR AMPLIATION
L'Administrateur Civil
Hors Classe BERT
Chef du Bureau des Décorations
P.O. le Commandant MARCHAL

12 October 1946 Decree published in the official journal announcing the military award of "*La Croix de Guerre*" with Palm leaf to Fratacci. Signed by Georges Bidault, President of the postwar provisional government of France.

RÉPUBLIQUE FRANÇAISE

MINISTÈRE DE LA DÉFENSE NATIONALE

LIQUIDATION
DU
RÉSEAU "BÉARN"
(F. F. C.)

1, RUE VOLNEY
PARIS-2e
TÉL.: OPÉRA 76-14

Paris, le 3 juin 1954 ~~194~~

Le Commandant ULVER, Chef du Réseau "Béarn"

certifie ~~xxx~~ que FRATACCI Antoine est entré au Réseau "BÉARN" le 1er décembre 1943 et qu'il a été immatriculé sous le pseudonyme MARTIN et l'indicatif RUA/034, en qualité de Chargé de Mission de 3ème classe.

Cet Agent participa tout d'abord à de nombreuses attaques de camions ennemis; il réussit, ensuite, à pénétrer sur les terrains d'aviation de BUC, TOUSSUS et VILLACOUBLAY, pour introduire du tétachlorure dans les réservoirs des chasseurs allemands en instance de chasse. Vingt appareils furent détruits; pris sur le fait au 21ème sabotage il fut arrêté le 11 août 1944 et immédiatement fusillé.

J'atteste sur l'honneur que l'arrestation et l'exécution de Fratacci furent bien, ainsi, la conséquence de son activité de Patriote au sein du Réseau.

Ulver

3 June 1954 Statement by the commander of the "Béarn" cell of the former French Underground organization, attesting to Fratacci's execution in the course of his official underground activities under the code name "Martin" and secret membership number RUA/034. Crediting Fratacci with 20 German fighters destroyed and attacking German trucks on several occasions.

UNITED STATES

United States No. 2 (1963)

Polaris Sales Agreement

between the Government of the
United Kingdom of Great Britain and Northern Ireland
and the Government of the United States of America

Washington, April 6, 1963

[The Agreement entered into force on signature]

Presented to Parliament by the Secretary of State for Foreign Affairs
by Command of Her Majesty
April 1963

LONDON
HER MAJESTY'S STATIONERY OFFICE
ONE SHILLING NET

Cmnd. 1995

POLARIS SALES AGREEMENT BETWEEN THE GOVERNMENT OF THE UNITED KINGDOM OF GREAT BRITAIN AND NORTHERN IRELAND AND THE GOVERNMENT OF THE UNITED STATES OF AMERICA

The Government of the United States of America and the Government of the United Kingdom of Great Britain and Northern Ireland, recalling and affirming the "Statement on Nuclear Defence Systems" (¹) included in the joint communiqué issued on December 21, 1962, by the President of the United States of America and the Prime Minister of Her Majesty's Government in the United Kingdom of Great Britain and Northern Ireland, have agreed as follows :—

ARTICLE I

1. The Government of the United States shall provide and the Government of the United Kingdom shall purchase from the Government of the United States Polaris missiles (less warheads), equipment, and supporting services in accordance with the terms and conditions of this Agreement.

2. This Agreement shall be subject to the understandings concerning British submarines equipped with Polaris missiles (referred to in paragraphs 8 and 9 of the Nassau "Statement on Nuclear Defence Systems" agreed by the President of the United States and the Prime Minister at their meeting held in the Bahamas between December 18 and 21, 1962.

ARTICLE II

1. In recognition of the complexity of the effort provided for in this Agreement and the need for close coordination between the contracting Governments in giving effect to its terms, the two Governments shall promptly establish the organizational machinery provided for in the following paragraphs of this Article.

2. The Department of Defense, acting through the Department of the Navy, and the Admiralty or such other agency as the Government of the United Kingdom shall designate will be the Executive Agencies of their respective Governments in carrying out the terms of this Agreement. Appropriate representatives of the Executive Agencies are authorized to enter into such technical arrangements, consistent with this Agreement, as may be necessary.

3. A Project Officer will be designated by each Government's Executive Agency with direct responsibility and authority for the management of the activities of that Government under this Agreement. Each Project Officer will designate liaison representatives, in such numbers as may be agreed, who will be authorized to act on his behalf in capacities specified in technical arrangements and who will be attached to the Office of the other Project Officer.

(¹) Cmnd. 1915

c. A Joint Steering Task Group will be established by the Project Officers to advise them, *inter alia*, concerning the development of new or modified equipment to meet specific requirements of the Government of the United Kingdom, and concerning interfaces between the equipment provided by the two Governments respectively. The Joint Steering Task Group will comprise the Project Officers (or their representatives), and principal liaison representatives, and may include selected leaders from among the scientists, industrialists and government executives of the United Kingdom and of the United States. The Joint Steering Task Group will meet approximately every three months alternately in the United Kingdom and in the United States under the chairmanship of the resident Project Officer.

ARTICLE III

1. The Government of the United States (acting through its Executive Agency) shall provide, pursuant to Article I of this Agreement, Polaris missiles (less warheads), equipment, and supporting services of such types and marks and in such quantities as the Government of the United Kingdom may from time to time require, and in configurations and in accordance with delivery programmes or time tables to be agreed between the Project Officers. In the first instance the missiles, equipment, and supporting services provided by the Government of the United States shall be sufficient to meet the requirements of a programme drawn up by the Government of the United Kingdom and communicated to the Government of the United States prior to the entry into force of this Agreement.

2. The missiles, equipment, and supporting services referred to in paragraph 1 of this article are the following:

a. Polaris missiles (less warheads but including guidance capsules);

b. missile launching and handling systems;

c. missile fire control systems;

d. ships navigation systems;

e. additional associated, support, test, and training equipment and services including, but not limited to:

(i) test and check-out equipment, specialized power supplies, power distribution systems and support equipment associated with the items enumerated in subparagraphs a, b, c, and d. of this paragraph and adequate in type and quantity to meet the requirements of installations both aboard ship and ashore;

(ii) specialized equipment including the types specified in subparagraphs a, b, c, d, and e.(i) of this paragraph for use in such support and training facilities as may be provided by the Government of the United Kingdom;

(iii) construction spares and spare parts adequate in scope and quantity to ensure the continued maintenance of the equipment specified in subparagraph a, b, c, d, e.(i), and e.(ii) of this paragraph;

(iv) (a) latest available United States technical documentation including specifications, blueprints, and manuals covering the missiles and equipment listed in subparagraphs a, b, c, d, e (i), e (ii) and e (iii) of this paragraph in sufficient scope and quantity to cover safety requirements and permit successful transport, installation, operation, and maintenance by the Government of the United Kingdom of all equipment purchased under the terms of this Agreement ;

(b) latest available United States technical documentation, as may be necessary from time to time in individual cases, to permit manufacture by the Government of the United Kingdom to the extent necessary for the maintenance, repair, and modification of the items listed in subparagraphs a, b, c, d, e.(i), e.(ii) and e.(iii) of this paragraph ;

(v) services, including:

(a) use, as appropriate, of existing support and missile range facilities in the United States ;

(b) assistance in programme management techniques and, in addition, those engineering and lead shipyard services required to ensure proper system integration, installation, and check-out in the United Kingdom ; to the extent required and available appropriate modification, maintenance, and overhaul of the equipment listed in subparagraph a, b, c, d, e.(i), e.(ii), e.(iii) of this paragraph ;

(c) research, design, development, production, test, or other engineering services as may be required to meet specific United Kingdom requirements ;

(d) training of naval and civil personnel in the service of the Government of the United Kingdom and United Kingdom contractors to the extent to which they are involved in the inspection, installation, operation, maintenance, repair, and modification of the equipment listed in subparagraphs a, b, c, d, e.(i) e.(ii), e.(iii) of this paragraph.

ARTICLE IV

Future developments relating to the Polaris Weapon System, including all modifications made thereto, by the Government of the United States or the Government of the United Kingdom shall, in the areas enumerated in Article III, be made reciprocally available through their Executive Agencies in accordance with the terms of this Agreement, reciprocally applied.

ARTICLE V

The Government of the United Kingdom will provide the submarines in which will be installed the missiles and equipment to be provided under this Agreement, and will provide the warheads for these missiles. Close coordination between the Executive Agencies of the contracting Governments will be maintained in order to assure compatibility of equipment. Information concerning the hull, auxiliary machinery, and equipment of United States submarines transmitted under the authority of this Agreement will be such as is necessary to obtain a satisfactory interface between the equipment provided by the two Governments respectively. This Agreement does not, however, authorize the sale of, or transmittal of information concerning, the nuclear propulsion plants of United States submarines.

ARTICLE VI

1. In carrying out this Agreement, the Government of the United States will use, to the extent practicable, established Department of Defense contracting procedures and existing Polaris contracts. In any event contracts for production or work for the Government of the United Kingdom will be incorporated in or placed on the same terms as those for the Government of the United States. When appropriate the United States Project Officer will direct that amendments be sought to existing contracts and that terms be incorporated in new contracts to safeguard any special requirements of the Government of the United Kingdom in the contract subject matter which may arise in connection with this Agreement, for example, to provide for any alterations or any reduction of quantities which may be necessary.

2. The missiles and equipment provided by the Government of the United States under this Agreement shall be fabricated to the same documentation and quality standards as are the counterparts for the United States Polaris Program.

3. The missiles and equipment provided by the Government of the United States under this Agreement will be integrated with the scheduled United States Polaris Program and will be fabricated on a schedule which will make the most efficient and economical use of existing United States production lines. Deliveries will be made upon a schedule to be defined by the Government of the United Kingdom, but which is consonant with the above fabrication schedule.

ARTICLE VII

1. The Government of the United States shall ensure that all supplies (which term throughout this Article includes, but without limitation, raw materials, components, intermediate assemblies and end items) which it will provide under this Agreement are inspected to the same extent and in the same manner (including the granting of waivers and deviations) as are the counterparts for the United States Polaris Program. The United Kingdom Project Officer or his designated representative may observe the inspection process and offer his advice to the United States Government Inspector regarding the inspection, without delay to, or impairment of the finality of, the inspection by the Government of the United States.

2. The United States Project Officer through appropriate procedures will notify the United Kingdom Project Officer when final inspection of each end item will take place, and will furnish a certificate or certificates upon completion of each such inspection stating that this inspection has been made and that such end item has been accepted as having met all requirements of the relevant acceptance documentation (subject to any appropriate waivers

and deviations). Copies of acceptance documentation and quality standards, together with reports required thereby, will be furnished to the United Kingdom Project Officer or his designated representative.

3. The Government of the United Kingdom will take delivery of the supplies as agreed pursuant to Article X following inspection, acceptance and certification by the Government of the United States. Delivery to the Government of the United Kingdom shall not relieve the Government of the United States from continuing responsibility for using its best endeavors thereafter to secure the correction or replacement of any items found not to have been manufactured in strict accordance with the documentation and quality standards referred to in Article VI or to be otherwise defective. Such corrections or replacements will be at the expense of the Government of the United Kingdom to the extent they are not covered by warranty or guaranty or otherwise recoverable by the Government of the United States.

4. The Government of the United States will use its best endeavours to obtain for or extend to the Government of the United Kingdom the benefit of any guarantees or warranties negotiated with United States contractors or subcontractors.

Article VIII

The Government of the United Kingdom shall indemnify and hold harmless the Government of the United States against any liability or loss resulting from unusually hazardous risks attributable to Polaris missiles or equipment identifiable, respectively, as missiles or equipment supplied or to be supplied to the Government of the United Kingdom under this Agreement. Unusually hazardous risks, for the purposes of this Agreement, are those defined by applicable statutes of the United States, or by any appropriate administrative act under the authority of such statutes, or held to exist by a court of competent jurisdiction. The Government of the United States shall give the Government of the United Kingdom immediate notice of any suit or action filed or of any claim made to which the provisions of this Article may be relevant. Representatives of the United Kingdom may be associated with the defence, before a court of competent jurisdiction, of any claim which may be borne in whole or in part by the Government of the United Kingdom. In procurement contracts for supplies and services made pursuant to this Agreement the Government of the United States is authorized to include unusually hazardous risk indemnification provisions substantially similar to those included in its own corresponding contracts.

Article IX

1. The Government of the United States will follow its normal procurement practices in securing all rights it considers to be essential to enable it to provide the missiles and equipment to be supplied to the Government of the United Kingdom under this Agreement. In addition, the Government of the United States shall notify the Government of the United Kingdom of any claim asserted hereafter for compensation for unlicensed use of patent rights alleged to be involved in the supply of such missiles and equipment to the Government of the United Kingdom, and the two Governments will consult as to the appropriate disposition of such claim.

2. The Government of the United Kingdom shall reimburse the Government of the United States for any payments made by the Government of the United States in settlement of liability, including cost and expenses, for unlicensed use of any patent rights in the manufacture or sale of the missiles and equipment supplied or to be supplied to the Government of the United Kingdom under this Agreement.

ARTICLE X

1. Delivery of equipment other than missiles to be provided under this Agreement for installation in submarines or supporting facilities to be provided by the Government of the United Kingdom shall be the responsibility of the Government of the United States and shall be made to those locations within the United Kingdom where the equipment is required. In addition to delivery of such equipment, the Government of the United States shall, subject to reimbursement for costs incurred, be responsible for providing such technical installation and testing services as are required by the Government of the United Kingdom for the satisfactory installation, check-out and testing of that equipment in submarines and supporting facilities of the United Kingdom.

2. Delivery of all missiles shall be made to appropriate carriers of the United Kingdom or, if it is agreed, of the United States, at such United States supply points as are agreed by the Executive Agencies of both Governments. The Government of the United States shall be responsible for the initial check-out of all missiles provided under this Agreement.

ARTICLE XI

1. The charges to the Government of the United Kingdom for missiles, equipment, and services provided by the Government of the United States will be:

   a. The normal cost of missiles and equipment provided under the joint United States-United Kingdom production programme integrated in accordance with Article VI. This will be based on common contract prices together with charges for work done in United States Government establishments and appropriate allowance for use of capital facilities and for overhead costs.

   b. An addition of 5% to the common contract prices under subparagraph 1.a. of this Article for Polaris missiles and equipment provided to the United Kingdom, as a participation in the expenditures incurred by the Government of the United States after January 1, 1963, for research and development; and a contribution to Trident II research and development equivalent to $116 million in fiscal year 1982 dollars, subject to actual payments of that contribution being adjusted in accordance with an agreed inflation index.

Amendment dated 14 Oct 1982

   c. Replacement cost of items provided from United States Government stock or, with respect to items not currently being procured, the most recent procurement cost.

   d. The actual cost of any research, design, development, production, test or other engineering effort, or other services required in the execution of this Agreement to meet specific United Kingdom requirements.

   e. The cost of packing, crating, handling and transportation.

7

f. The actual costs of any other services, not specified above, which the Project Officers agree are properly attributable to this Agreement.

2. Payments by the Government of the United Kingdom in accordance with paragraph 1. of this Article shall be made in United States dollars. Payments to United States agencies and contractors shall be made, as they become due, from a trust fund which will be administered by the United States Project Officer. All payments out of the Trust Fund shall be certified to be in accordance with the terms of the Agreement. The Trust Fund will consist initially of a sum to be paid as soon as possible after entry into force of this agreement and to be equivalent to the payments estimated to fall due during the first calendar quarter of programme operations. Before the end of that quarter and of each succeeding quarter deposits shall be made by the Government of the United Kingdom with the object of having sufficient money in the Fund to meet all the calls which will be made upon it in the succeeding three months.

3. If at any time, the unexpended balance in the Trust Fund established pursuant to paragraph 2. of this Article falls short of the sums that will be needed in a particular quarter by the Government of the United States to cover:

a. payment for the value of items to be furnished from the stocks of, or services to be rendered by, the Government of the United States;

b. payment by the Government of the United States to its suppliers for items and services to be procured for the Government of the United Kingdom; and

c. estimated liability or costs that may fall to be met by the Government of the United States as a result of termination of such procurement contracts at the behest of the Government of the United Kingdom;

the Government of the United Kingdom will pay at such time to the Government of the United States such additional sums as will be due. Should the total payments received from the Government of the United Kingdom prove to be in excess of the final total costs to the Government of the United States, appropriate refund will be made to the Government of the United Kingdom at the earliest opportunity with final adjustment being made within thirty days after determination of said final costs.

4. The United States Project Officer will maintain a record of expenditures under this Agreement in accordance with established Navy Special Projects Office Accounting procedures which record will be available for audit annually by representatives of the Government of the United Kingdom.

Article XII

1. The provisions of this Article concerning proprietary rights shall apply to the work referred to in subparagraph 1.d. of Article XI of this Agreement (hereinafter called in this Article "the work").

2. The Government of the United States shall ensure that the Government of the United Kingdom will receive a royalty-free, non-exclusive, irrevocable license for its governmental purposes:

a. to practice or cause to be practiced throughout the world, all inventions conceived or first actually reduced to practice in the performance of the work ; and

b. to use or cause to be used throughout the world, all technical information first produced in the performance of the work.

3. In addition, the Government of the United States shall take the following steps to ensure the right of the Government of the United Kingdom to reproduce, by manufacturers of its own choice, items developed in the performance of the work. In respect of those elements of this right not included in subparagraphs 2.a. and 2.b. of this Article, the Government of the United States shall:

a. to the extent that it owns or controls such elements, accord free user rights to the Government of the United Kingdom ;

b. obtain the agreement of contractors and subcontractors performing the work to make available to the Government of the United Kingdom, on fair and reasonable terms and conditions, those elements which the contractor or subcontractor owns or controls at the commencement of the work or acquires during the performance of the work ;

c. use its best endeavors to obtain for the Government of the United Kingdom or to assist the Government of the United Kingdom to obtain directly or through its own manufacturers, on fair and reasonable terms and conditions, elements of this right not covered by subparagraphs 2.a. and 2.b. of this Article.

4. The Government of the United States shall also ensure that the Government of the United Kingdom will receive the same rights as those referred to in paragraphs 2. and 3. of this Article in respect of any material now or hereafter covered by copyright produced or delivered in the performance of the work.

5. The Government of the United States shall furnish to the Government of the United Kingdom, in such quantities as may be agreed:

a. all documentation obtained by the Government of the United States under contracts placed for the performance of the work ;

b. all documentation, owned or controlled by the Government of the United States, necessary for reproduction, by or on behalf of the Government of the United Kingdom, of items developed during the performance of the work.

6. It is understood that the Government of the United States will obtain for itself such of the rights referred to in subparagraphs 2.a., 2.b., and 3. of this Article as it may require for its governmental purposes.

7. The term "owned or controlled" as used in this Article means the right to grant a licence without incurring liability to any private owner of a proprietary or other legal interest.

9

8. The Government of the United States will use its best endeavours to ensure that there will be made available by United States manufacturers to the Government of the United Kingdom, on fair and reasonable terms and conditions, such technical assistance—for example, loan of engineers, or training—as the Government of the United Kingdom desires in order to permit the production by manufacturers of its own choice of the items developed in the performance of the work.

9. The Government of the United States will insert suitable provisions in all prime contracts for the work to ensure the availability to the Government of the United Kingdom of the rights, set forth in this Article, including a requirement that similar provisions be placed in subcontracts.

ARTICLE XIII

1. The Government of the United States, to the extent that it can do so without incurring liability to any private owner of a proprietary or other legal interest shall grant to the Government of the United Kingdom: (i) the right to reproduce and use, royalty-free, the technical documentation referred to in subparagraph 2.e.(iv) of Article III for the purposes stated in that subparagraph ; and (ii) a non-exclusive, royalty-free licence to practice or cause to be practiced any invention for these purposes.

2. In respect of any part of the technical documentation referred in paragraph 1 of this Article which the Government of the United States cannot furnish to the Government of the United Kingdom without incurring a liability to a private owner of a proprietary or other legal interest, the Government of the United States will use its best endeavours to assist the Government of the United Kingdom in securing for the Government of the United Kingdom on fair and reasonable terms and conditions the right to use such documentation for the purposes stated in subparagraph 2.e.(iv) of Article III.

ARTICLE XIV

1. The Government of the United Kingdom shall not, without the prior express consent of the Government of the United States, transfer, or permit access to, or use of, the missiles, equipment, services, or documents or information relating thereto which are provided by the Government of the United States under this Agreement, except to a United Kingdom officer, employee, national or firm engaged in the implementation of this Agreement.

2. The Government of the United Kingdom shall undertake such security measures as are necessary to afford classified articles, services, documents or information substantially the same degree of protection afforded by the Government of the United States in order to prevent unauthorized disclosure or compromise.

ARTICLE XV

Annually, on or before the first of July, the Project Officers will prepare a formal joint report to the contracting Governments of action taken and progress made under this Agreement and a forecast of schedules and costs for completion. In addition, other more frequent joint reports will be submitted, as agreed upon by the Project Officers, to the heads of the Executive Agencies.

ARTICLE XVI

This Agreement shall enter into force on the date of signature.

IN WITNESS WHEREOF the undersigned, being duly authorized thereto by their respective Governments, have signed this Agreement.

DONE in duplicate at Washington this sixth day of April, 1963.

For the Government of the United States of America:
(Sd.) DEAN RUSK

For the Government of the United Kingdom of Great Britain and Northern Ireland:
(Sd.) D. ORMSBY GORE

11

Author's note: The British government finally accepted the American 5% surcharge on prices (Article XI, 1.b.) for research and development costs of Polaris A-1, A-2, A-3, B3/C3. Note the strong budgetary language throughout. The B3/C3s were later named Poseidon by President Johnson. However, the Trident FBM system was never part of the Nassau Agreement nor of this agreement, and to acquire the Trident the British benefited from a "contract amendment" about twenty years later.

Index

E

F

H

K

L

N

O

P

Q

R

T

U

V

W

Y

Z

Author Biographical Sketch

Bernard W. Poirier is originally from Woonsocket, Rhode Island, where he attended public schools until he attended Assumption Prep in Worcester, Massachusetts. He studied at Georgetown University after transferring from Providence College. Later, he served two terms on the Woonsocket City Council, and in 1959 the Navy Department hired him as a civilian employee in Washington, D.C.

In late 1963 he went to ITT Europe headquarters in Brussels, Belgium, for four years and was reassigned to ITT's laboratory in Paris, France, for two years. He returned to the USA in 1969 to serve as an assistant to US Senator Mike Gravel (Dem., Alaska). In 1971, Mr. Poirier started his own environmental research company and was in business for himself in the US and in France for the next twenty-five years.

He now lives in France where he writes and occasionally lectures on the World Bank and on international finance to MBA and doctoral candidates at the International School of Management in Paris. His five children and their families live in the USA.

Facing page. The author, left, holding President Clinton's message to the US veterans of the 83rd Infantry Division and to the citizens of St.-Malo which was liberated by the American Army after the Normandy invasion in 1944. Wearing his sash of office is René Couanau, mayor of St.-Malo and delegate to the French national assembly. St.-Malo, 4 June 1994.

Photo courtesy of Charlie and Evelyn McAuliff of Troy, Michigan, members of the 83rd Infantry Division Association and of the Veterans of Foreign Wars.